CIVIC LABORS

Civic Labors

*Scholar Activism
and Working-Class Studies*

Edited by
**DENNIS DESLIPPE,
ERIC FURE-SLOCUM,
AND JOHN W. MCKERLEY**

With associate editors
KRISTEN ANDERSON,
MATTHEW M. METTLER,
AND JOHN WILLIAMS-SEARLE

**UNIVERSITY OF
ILLINOIS PRESS**
Urbana, Chicago, and Springfield

Publication supported by a grant from Franklin & Marshall College.

Library of Congress Cataloging-in-Publication Data
Names: Deslippe, Dennis, editor. | McKerley, John W., editor. | Fure-
    Slocum, Eric Jon, editor.
Title: Civic labors : scholar activism and working-class studies / edited
    by Dennis Deslippe, Eric Fure-Slocum, and John W. McKerley with
    associate editors Kristen Anderson, Matthew M. Mettler, and John
    Williams-Searle.
Description: Urbana : University of Illinois Press, 2016. | Series:
    Working class in American history | Includes bibliographical
    references and index.
Identifiers: LCCN 2016015343 (print) | LCCN 2016038411 (ebook) |
    ISBN 9780252040498 (hbk) | ISBN 9780252081965 (pbk) | ISBN
    9780252098932 (E-book)
Subjects: LCSH: Working class—History—Study and teaching—
    United States. | Working class—Research—United States. | Political
    activists—United States. | BISAC: POLITICAL SCIENCE / Labor
    & Industrial Relations. | BUSINESS & ECONOMICS / Labor. |
    EDUCATION / Organizations & Institutions.
Classification: LCC HD4824.5.U5 C58 2016 (print) | LCC HD4824.5.U5
    (ebook) | DDC 305.5/620973—dc23
LC record available at https://lccn.loc.gov/2016015343

To David Montgomery (1927–2011), Paul Young (1946–2012),

and Jake Hall (1974–2014), who embodied the ideals

of engaged scholarship and continue to inspire

CONTENTS

ACKNOWLEDGMENTS

Shel Stromquist made this book possible. He brought us together and continues to do so. Shel's tireless activism, his scholarly integrity, and his generosity are legendary. Ann Stromquist's ongoing support and the presence of Shel and Ann's family at the "Working-Class Worlds" conference made this an especially memorable gathering.

We are grateful to Laurie Matheson for taking an early interest in this collection and shepherding it into the University of Illinois Press's series, the Working Class in American History. Leon Fink, as well as Jennifer Luff and a second anonymous reader for the press, offered perceptive comments and suggestions that strengthened this book. Michael K. Honey and Erik Gellman demonstrated the qualities of solidarity and collegiality in their kind assistance during the copyediting phase. Thanks to Marika Christofides and Jennifer Clark at the press and to Deborah Oliver, this book's skilled copyeditor. We also appreciate support from David Montgomery's family—the late Martel Montgomery, Edward Montgomery, and Claude Montgomery—to include the epilogue to this volume. The Office of College Grants at Franklin & Marshall College stepped in to help fund this book's publication; St. Olaf College and the University of Iowa History Department also provided much needed funding.

The editors, associate editors, and many of the contributors to this volume first joined together at the "Working-Class Worlds: Local and Global Perspectives on Labor History" conference, held in Iowa City during the summer of 2011 in honor of Shel Stromquist. Other conference participants who we thank include Bradley Bowen, Cecelia Bucki, Robert Cherny, John Enyeart, Leon Fink, Lionel Kimble, Greg Patmore, David Roediger, Steve Rosswurm, Kerry Taylor, Roberta Till-Retz, and Sharon E. Wood. Linda K. Kerber deserves a special note of gratitude for her well-chosen words at the conference and for her encouragement throughout this process. Colin Gordon and Pat Goodwin in the University of Iowa History Department provided key logistical assistance. A host of sponsors and supporters were crucial in bringing the event to fruition: the University of Iowa History Department, the Center for Recent United States History, the University of Iowa Labor Center, the Obermann Center for Advanced Studies, the State Historical Society of Iowa, the Herbert Hoover Presidential Library and Museum, both the associate dean of humanities and the History Department at St. Olaf College, and Prairie Lights Books.

For support and patience throughout the years of conference organizing and editing, Eric is thankful especially to Carolyn, Anna, and Jacob. At the conference, Anna also helped with photography and Jacob produced podcasts of the sessions. For Dennis, Alison Kibler, Therese Deslippe, and John Deslippe were sympathetic listeners to countless descriptions of "engaged scholarship." John would like to thank his wife, Heather, and daughters, Charlotte and Eleanor. Working on this project has made him more aware than ever of the struggles and contradictions of pursuing scholarship or activism aimed at broad-based social justice while striving to do justice to the people closest to home.

CIVIC LABORS

Challenges of Engaged Scholarship and Teaching

Dennis Deslippe, Eric Fure-Slocum, and John W. McKerley

In a February 2014 column in the *New York Times*, writer Nicholas Kristof re-vived a decades-old plea for the rise of a new generation of academics engaged in public life.[1] While noting that American "anti-intellectualism" often made it difficult for academics to engage in public debates, Kristof argued that most of the problem lay in academic culture and institutions, especially tenure and pro-motion guidelines, which encouraged publications directed at academic rather than public audiences. Even if "the public" could find and access such publica-tions, readers would encounter little more than "turgid prose" intelligible only to other specialists. Resistance to these academic norms all too frequently resulted in "rebels" being "crushed or driven away." Moreover, he argued, left-leaning disciplines like sociology were so resistant to "political diversity" that they were "instinctively dismissed by the right," thereby limiting their potential audience. Overall, he found that most academics secluded themselves within the university "like medieval monks" rather than participating in the nation's "great debates." He called on them to reject their isolation.[2]

A diverse group of academics quickly responded. More often than not, they rejected Kristof's premise that scholars had retreated behind the walls of ivory towers. Instead, they replied with a bevy of contemporary examples of scholarly engagement and challenged Kristof's implication that our current moment re-flected a retreat from a golden age of public intellectuals. Moreover, while several academics pointed out that Kristof's implied definition of public intellectual re-ferred to an exclusive and top-down model, many others directed readers to the large number of people with academic backgrounds writing for popular publica-tions as well as blogging under their own names or pseudonyms. Several more pointed beyond writing to teaching as scholars' most common act of engagement, and a few suggested that acts outside the scope of scholarly labor—for example, walking on a picket line—constituted important forms of engagement as well. As for the roots of resistance to engagement, Kristof's critics tended to focus more on the *decline* of tenure and the *rise* of contingent faculty than tenure's pressures and inaccessible prose.[3]

Although much of Kristof's column arguably reflected a rather limited understanding of the lives of modern academics, scholars' reactions to it revealed a degree of defensiveness that suggested he had struck a little too close to home. At the very least, Kristof and his critics revealed both a widespread interest in some form of engaged activity as well as a sense that academic engagement or activism—while an important motivating force in many scholars' lives—remained a source of tension for people both within and outside academe. Indeed, over the past several decades, scholar-activists from a variety of traditions have written articles and books, including several collections of essays, wrestling with the relationship between scholarship and activism. The authors of these works, not surprisingly, have tended to be drawn largely from the ranks of anthropology, sociology, and critical race and gender studies, whose practitioners have often taken up these issues out of methodological or disciplinary necessity as well as the demands of activism (including, at times, personal experiences as marginalized people). In particular, these studies have been important for moving beyond the seeming contradictions of combining activism with an academic career to highlight examples of activist teaching and scholarship, and, importantly, turning a critical eye to the power relationships that exist in the academic workplace.[4]

The Labor Tradition of Scholar Activism

Perhaps the most conspicuous absence in this recent work has been that of scholars studying labor and the working class (broadly defined), who trace their lineage to some of the first modern scholar-activists during the Progressive Era and to more recent figures, including Edward P. Thompson, David Montgomery, Staughton Lynd, Alice Kessler-Harris, and Robin D. G. Kelley. To be sure, individual labor scholars of a variety of stripes have written about the relationship between academia and activism, but the last book-length study to bring together a large grouping of such scholars to reflect critically on the theory and practice of engaged writing and teaching was *Visions of History*, a collection of interviews with "left-wing historians" assembled over a generation ago by the Mid-Atlantic Radical Historians' Organization (MARHO).[5]

This volume, *Civic Labors*, seeks to address that absence by asking seventeen scholars and teachers of labor and working-class studies—from diverse backgrounds, professional positions, and stages in their careers—to perform just such a reflection, albeit in the form of essays and not interviews. Its genesis was a conference to honor labor historian Shelton Stromquist held in Iowa City in 2011.[6] Many of the discussions at panels, roundtables, and informal events at the conference turned to current struggles over immigrant rights, globalization, antiunionism, living-wage campaigns, the fight for universal health care, and deepening inequality. These and other struggles have guided conference participants' own work organizing on campuses and in communities both within and outside the United States, including public history initiatives and their teaching and mentoring of students. In turn, they have helped labor scholars construct their identities as public intellectuals, even as the meaning and significance of such identities continues to be challenged. As we began to consider a volume of essays building on the conference, we realized that directing contributors to focus on these discussions and struggles might yield important insights about scholar activism. Rather than a conventional collection of essays on the state of the field, or autobiographical accounts of veteran scholars and activists, this book sheds light on how practitioners understand the possibilities and limits of engagement in a wide range of settings.

The results of these contributors' labors are revealing. The volume supports the claims of many of Kristof's critics that engaged scholarship and teaching is and should be pursued by more than a rarified and well-connected elite—even beyond the remarkable list of scholar-activists interviewed by MARHO. In addition to emeritus and distinguished full professors, contributors to this volume include early and mid-career academics and contingent faculty, as well as labor educators and public historians, one from outside the United States. Although many engaged scholars whose work is collected here pursue the history of recent events, others conduct work embracing questions and themes drawn from earlier centuries, suggesting that, to be an engaged writer or teacher, one need not be a scholar *of* the present so much as a scholar *in* the present, immersed in the concerns of one's contemporaries.

At least two unifying factors are worthy of note. First, many of the contributors came to academia from activism or backgrounds that suggested the needs to work collectively rather than in isolation and to engage in struggles well beyond those of tenure and promotion. Next, the volume draws heavily on scholars and activists connected to Stromquist, the University of Iowa, and the Midwest more generally. While such personal, institutional, and regional ties often go unnoted (or are even suppressed in the name of neutrality or the search for professional acceptance), they are important in this context because they reveal the centrality of networks in the production not only of scholarship, teaching, and activism, but also their many combinations. In this spirit, we have sought to highlight the collective potential of academic work—yet another facet of engaged scholarship slighted by Kristof—by drawing editors and associate editors from the organizers and presenters of the 2011 conference in Iowa City without regard to rank and by stressing collaboration among editors and contributors. Moreover, in focusing attention on the Midwest, the essays complement other recent studies of Los Angeles and New York as well as reassert midwesterners' continuing importance to the study of labor and the working class.[7] Essays addressing other regional or institutional contexts help to place this emphasis on midwestern scholar-activism into a broader, comparative perspective.

The resulting volume is an experiment in democratic practice within an academic endeavor. We see it also as a demonstration of the vitality and importance of what might be referred to as "mid-level" engagement—credentialed professionals striving to connect academic and activist concerns in meaningful ways, even if at times well beyond the halls of formal power and professional associations. Most contributors are writers who hope to use their work to inspire popular movements for change or influence policymakers (often by elevating the words and ideas of the disempowered), focusing more often than not on local or statewide struggles. At the same time, they reveal ways in which engagement shapes and is shaped by teaching—whether of undergraduates, graduate students, or various groups outside the university—public commemoration and memorialization, and institution building, both within and beyond academia.

Throughout, contributors emphasize the need to go beyond consulting or mediation—roles that define academics as experts, standing outside the main arenas of conflict—to committed action.[8] By recognizing class and conflict, the frictions of daily life, as central to engaged teaching and scholarship, these labor scholars also challenge the consensus-building assumptions that tend to define many university-community collaborative efforts (and the rhetoric of the lone public intellectual) and suggest the need to continue rethinking relationships between scholars, the university, and the wider world. Moreover, as several contributors remind us, despite the potential of intellectual work to shape public discourse in important ways, the best argument (however defined) does not always win. The contributors to this volume demonstrate the many ways that scholars and teachers can be effective advocates when acting *outside* traditional definitions of their academic work, even if still within their academic workplaces and surrounding communities, by knocking on doors, standing on picket lines, writing for a broader audience, organizing college-community theater productions, and otherwise doing the hard and often anonymous labor involved in supporting the struggles of their coworkers and neighbors. These two points—the centrality of friction and an acknowledgment that academic and intellectual labor complement but never replace collective action and movement building—reflect perhaps the most important contributions that scholars and teachers of labor and working-class studies make to the scholar-activist debate.

Such activism, of course, can come at a price. Contributors recognize the ways in which conventions of professional discourse can constrain public engagement by discouraging attention to nonacademic audiences or threatening hiring, tenure, and promotion decisions. They also emphasize the particular risks of activism that challenge the managerial prerogatives of university administrators or others in power. Scholars, encouraged under normal circumstances to promote their professional writing or work with academic associations, can find their careers in jeopardy when they defy professional norms or powerful institutional stakeholders by writing or acting in collaboration with social justice causes. In such cases, they are forced to accept the hazards, endure marginalization (thus foregoing professional rewards), or reconsider their options for engagement. Alternatively, scholars find that the access necessary for influence within a social movement requires attention to organizational interests and conflicts; these range from weighty policy debates to leadership squabbles. Likewise, tight budgets, the urgency of political issues, and expectations of loyalty put pressure on scholar-activists who must seek the resources, time, and relative autonomy needed to maintain high standards of analytical rigor. Further, both the theory and practice of "social justice" present complications. The aims of social justice are neither fixed in time nor universal. Diverse historical experiences, varied perspectives, and distinct organizational interests produce many different, and sometimes competing, social justice agendas. Such challenges are indeed real and pressing concerns for engaged scholars, as they are for many activists more generally.

But contributors to this volume concur that these hurdles, even if insurmountable, are worth confronting. This volume illustrates the value that engaged scholarship holds for scholars, teachers, students, academic institutions, partner organizations, and nonacademic communities more generally. For many contributors, their engaged scholarship is driven by political or social justice commitments that overlap with scholarly interests in labor studies and the history of social movements. For many, the willingness to connect academic and activist pursuits follows also from an intellectual challenge to the goal of unalloyed "objectivity," accepting instead the role of scholars' subjectivity and recognizing that ideals of scholarly neutrality and detachment themselves are not impartial.[9] Commitments to justice and academic rigor can coexist. This does not mean that in the heat of the moment—whether on a picket line or deep within the archives—a scholar-activist will be free of any hard decisions or potential conflicts between the two. And just as scholars learn much from committed engagement, their deep-seated allegiance to rigorous standards of investigation, a determination to "get it right," benefits organizational partners who also need to keep questioning and rethinking received understandings or positions. Contributors recognize the messiness of both academic life and of social change work, and they often find genuine benefit in grappling with this friction.

The contributors to *Civic Labors*, while certainly swimming against contemporary cultural cynicism and irony, do not harbor a blind optimism that their efforts or those of their partners in activism will produce only success. A number of the stories or conflicts recounted here end in stalemate or even defeat. This does not pretend to be a book filled with narratives of unmitigated progress. And, as labor scholars, the contributors to this volume are all too aware that union density continues to decline in the United States; that the labor movement continues to struggle with internal battles over race, gender, and democracy; and that neoliberalism rules globally, even if not unchallenged. Yet, a strong current of hope, whether rooted in particular faith traditions or secular existential concerns, propels the contributors' work. As the historian and cultural critic Christopher Lasch noted, "Hope does not demand a belief in progress. It demands a belief in justice. . . . Hope implies a deep-seated trust in life that appears absurd to those who lack it."[10] So, while recognizing the flaws and partial nature of such work, this volume encourages a sober-yet-hopeful approach to engagement.

Engaged Scholars and Teachers—Past, Present, and Future

Civic Labors addresses long-standing themes in labor and working-class studies and focuses on contemporary struggles over the relationship between engagement, teaching, and scholarship. Following this introductory essay, the volume contin- ues with Shelton Stromquist's history of the early paths of engagement blazed by progressive labor economists who, at some professional risk, gave birth to labor history as a serious field of investigation and by the subsequent pioneering work of E. P. Thompson and David Montgomery, preeminent labor historians and activists who not only reshaped the academic field but influenced subsequent generations of engaged scholars. Of particular importance were Thompson's and Montgom- ery's experiences outside of academia, notably in labor and left political circles. Stromquist points out that the generation of labor historians following Thomp- son and Montgomery shared their attention to class, their affinity for grassroots activism, and their advocacy for participatory democracy. At the same time, the succeeding generations of scholars, responding to changed political and intellec- tual contexts, have pursued new forms of engaged scholarship. In Montgomery's powerful address to the 2011 Iowa City conference—made just a few months before his death and included in this volume as an epilogue—he reinforced this point: "So we've got to take these old subjects and think about them in brand-new ways, because the categories that worked for thinking about the old industrial core of the world back in the 1960s and 1970s will probably not work today."[11]

The three main sections of this book explore developments in engaged schol- arship that build on the legacies of Thompson, Montgomery, and their contem- poraries. The contributors to part 1, "Encountering Conflict, Power, and Hope: On the Front Line," discuss the opportunities and challenges posed by political and civic involvement that take place both outside and inside of academia, often during particular moments of stress or crisis. When blending roles as activists and scholars, these engaged academics encountered diverse responses from com- munity partners, university peers, administrators, and the media, ranging from acceptance to skepticism to hostility. The contributors consider also how best to bring their training and resources as academics to bear on social problems or causes of social justice. No simple set of conclusions can be drawn from these cases, but these essays raise sobering questions about the possibilities and problems raised by engagement.

Contributors to part 2, "Connecting Classrooms and Communities: Education, Outreach, and Engagement," focus on teaching in distinct contexts, including popular education, public history, undergraduate classes, and graduate training. They illustrate how immersion in community struggles and social movements creates new ways of thinking, fosters new knowledge, and leads frequently to innovative pedagogical approaches. But the institutional rewards for engaged teaching are often meager. These essays remind us also about the intimate connection between engaged education and social change that affects the teacher, the students, and the surrounding community, whether the setting is that of formal or informal schooling.[12] Part 3, "Bridging Scholarship and Activism: Paths of Engagement," examines the many ways that public engagement influences scholarly careers and work. For each of these contributors, their engagement beyond a single scholarly field or the well-worn tracks of academic publishing and into the wider world has prompted fresh insights, reshaped research agendas, created institutions, and rejuvenated scholars' commitments. These encounters throw into question and help to redefine what it means to be a scholar.

The contributors' efforts are animated by an understanding of the ways in which power and inequality shape society and people's daily lives, as well as by a yearning for social justice. But the essays are not blueprints for engaged scholarship and teaching. Neither the editors nor the contributors propose that labor historians or other labor studies scholars should follow a single path to become engaged teachers and academics. This book aims instead to highlight that location, circumstances, and timing are crucial in determining specific strategies of active scholarship and teaching. Just as place, contingency, and timing are critical analytical dimensions in labor scholars' research and writing, so they apply as well to how we might think most productively about engaged scholarship and teaching—when academics shift from simply studying agency to embracing a role as agents of change.

Civic Labors, then, is intended to prompt further discussion about engaged scholarship and teaching. The essays will help readers to think further about the theories and practices of engagement and scholar-activism, asking what publics ought to be addressed and how best to shape this engagement. The contributors drive home the point that, regardless of the scale or type of involvement, power and engagement are entwined. These stories provide hope and an impetus for scholars and teachers to engage creatively in ongoing struggles that Shelton Stromquist sees as connected, at once local and transnational: "How do we build and sustain a vital movement for social justice and equality capable of contesting for power and remodeling our workplaces, our communities and indeed our countries into the humane and just world to which we aspire?"[13] Or as David Montgomery urges, "Carry it on!"[14]

Notes

1. This plea was articulated in its modern form by Russell Jacoby in *The Last Intellectuals: American Culture in the Age of Academe* (New York: Basic Books, 1987). Regarding that work and other calls for a new generation of public intellectuals, see also Leon Fink, *Progressive Intellectuals and the Dilemmas of Democratic Commitment* (Cambridge, Mass.: Harvard University Press, 1997), 1–2, 289n1.

2. Nicholas Kristof, "Professors, We Need You!," *New York Times*, Feb. 15, 2014, www.nytimes.com, accessed Jan. 6, 2016.

3. For examples of academics' initial responses to Kristof's February 15, 2014, column, see Corey Robin, "Look Who Nick Kristof's Saving Now," Feb. 16, 2014, http://coreyrobin.com, accessed Jan. 6, 2016; Laura Tanenbaum, "A Response to Nicholas Kristof," *Jacobin*, Feb. 17, 2014, www.jacobinmag.com, accessed Jan. 6, 2016; Claire Potter, "Dear Mr. Kristof: A Letter from a Public Intellectual," Tenured Radical: The 3.0 Edition, *Chronicle of Higher Education*, Feb. 18, 2014, http://chronicle.com, accessed Jan. 6, 2016; Patricia Limerick, "From the OAH President: 'Professors—I Need Your Help!," *OAH Outlook: A Membership Newsletter of the Organization of American Historians* 3.4 (May 2014): 1, 4; and James Grossman and Jason Steinhauer, "Historians and Public Culture: Widening the Circle of Advocacy," November 2014, *Perspectives on History: The Newsmagazine of the American Historical Association*, http://historians.org, accessed Jan. 6, 2016.

4. For examples of the link between scholarship and activism from the social sciences, see Douglas Bevington and Chris Dixon, "Movement-Relevant Theory: Rethinking Social Movement Scholarship and Activism," *Social Movement Studies* 4.3 (December 2005): 185–208; David Croteau, William Hoynes, and Charlotte Ryan, eds., *Rhyming Hope and History: Activists, Academics, and Social Movement Scholarship* (Minneapolis: University of Minnesota Press, 2005); Charles R. Hale, ed., *Engaging Contradictions: Theory, Politics, and Methods of Activist Scholarship* (Berkeley: University of California Press, 2008); and Kathleen Odell Korgen, Jonathan M. White, and Shelley K. White, *Sociologists in Action: Sociology, Social Change, and Social Justice* (Thousand Oaks, Calif.: Pine Forge Press, 2011). On the particularly important roles played by critical race and feminist scholars, see also Paul A. Cimbala and Robert F. Himmelberg, eds., *Historians and Race: Autobiography and the Writing of History* (Bloomington: Indiana University Press, 1997); Julie Des Jardin, *Women and the Historical Enterprise in America: Gender, Race, and the Politics of Memory* (Chapel Hill: University of North Carolina Press, 2003); Alice Kessler-Harris, "'History Is Public or Nothing': Learning How to Keep Illusions in Our Future," in *Gendering Labor History* (Urbana: University of Illinois Press, 2007), 286–300; and Julia Sudbury and Margo Okazawa-Rey, eds., *Activist Scholarship: Anti-Racism, Feminism, and Social Change* (Boulder, Colo.: Paradigm Publishers, 2009).

5. MARHO, *Visions of History* (New York: Pantheon Books, 1983). For other examples of labor and working-class historians reflecting on the relationship between scholarship, teaching, and activism, see James Green, *Taking History to Heart: The Power of the Past in Building Social Movements* (Amherst: University of Massachusetts Press, 2000); Nelson Lichtenstein, *A Contest of Ideas: Capital, Politics, and Labor* (Urbana: University of Illinois Press, 2013), esp. 38–44 and 254–61; and Staughton Lynd, *Accompanying: Pathways to Social Change* (Oakland, Calif.: PM Press, 2013). See also Steven Fraser and Joshua B. Freeman, eds., *Audacious Democracy: Labor, Intellectuals, and the Social Reconstruction of America* (Boston: Houghton Mifflin, 1997); Daniel Katz and Richard A. Greenwald,

eds., *Labor Rising: The Past and Future of Working People in America* (New York: New Press, 2012); and Beth Robinson, Joe Walzer, Jacob Glicklich, John Terry, and Dawson Barrett, "'Opportunities of Defiance': Embracing Guerilla History and Moving Beyond Scott Walker's Wisconsin," *LaborOnline*, Aug. 16, 2013, http://lawcha.org, accessed Jan. 6, 2016.

6. In addition to many of the contributors and the editors in this book, presenters, facilitators, and speakers at the Iowa City conference included Cecelia Bucki, Robert Cherny, John Enyeart, Leon Fink, Linda K. Kerber, Lionel Kimble, David Roediger, Steve Rosswurm, Roberta Till-Retz, and Sharon E. Wood; joining us from overseas were Bradley Bowen (Australia), Greg Patmore (Australia), and Kerry Taylor (New Zealand). Podcasts of the conference sessions are housed at the University of Iowa Libraries, Department of Special Collection.

7. Regarding Los Angeles, see Ruth Milkman, Joshua Bloom, and Victor Narro, eds., *Working for Justice: The L.A. Model of Organizing and Advocacy* (Ithaca, N.Y.: ILR Press, 2010). Regarding New York, see Milkman and Ed Ott, eds., *New Labor in New York: Precarious Workers and the Future of the Labor Movement* (Ithaca, N.Y.: ILR Press, 2014).

8. Regarding mediation as a form of engagement, see Grossman and Steinhauer, "Historians and Public Culture."

9. On objectivity, see Peter Novick, *That Noble Dream: The "Objectivity" Question and the American Historical Profession* (New York: Cambridge University Press, 1988).

10. Christopher Lasch, *The True and Only Heaven: Progress and Its Critics* (New York: W. W. Norton, 1991), 80–81. On Lasch's midwestern roots, including a stint in the University of Iowa's History Department in the 1960s, see Eric Miller, *Hope in a Scattering Time: A Life of Christopher Lasch* (Grand Rapids, Mich.: Eerdmans Publishing, 2010).

11. David Montgomery, "Creative Research and Social Action," epilogue in this volume.

12. Myles Horton and Paulo Friere, *We Make the Road by Walking: Conversations on Education and Social Change* (Philadelphia: Temple University Press, 1990). See also Harry C. Boyte, ed., *Democracy's Education: Public Work, Citizenship, and the Future of Colleges and Universities* (Nashville, Tenn.: Vanderbilt University Press, 2014); and David Scobey, "Putting the Academy in Its Place," *Places* 14.3 (2002): 50–55.

13. Shelton Stromquist, "Reflections on Labor History and the Current Crisis: Revisiting Class and Community as Trans-Local Spaces," paper presented at "Working-Class Worlds: Local and Global Perspectives on Labor History" conference, Iowa City, Iowa, July 9, 2011.

14. Montgomery, "Creative Research and Social Action."

CHAPTER 1

Labor Historians and Traditions of Engaged Scholarship

Progressives, Insurgents, and the Making of a New Labor History

Shelton Stromquist

Labor historians have engaged the worlds of labor from the earliest days of the field to the present. From the beginning they wove civic engagement into the very fabric of their scholarship and historical perspective into their public advocacy. Their engagement grew organically from the history they wrote and from their efforts to make that history accessible to a wider public. But engagement brought challenges and ambiguities in both the public sphere and academic environments. They tested the limits of academic freedom, challenged the definition of what constituted "objective" scholarship, navigated the terrain between advocacy and disinterested investigation, and sought to balance the demands of academic life with those of participation in social movements.

A central objective for many labor historians has been facilitating workers' consumption of the very history they produced. E. P. Thompson, for instance, argued that his *Making of the English Working Class* (*MEWC*) was not "a book written for an academic audience," but rather for the trade unionists, teachers, and working people who attended his night classes in the industrial north of England. "I was thinking of that kind of reader when I wrote the book."[1] For David Montgomery, connecting his work to "the daily lives of working people" was critical. "It's got to be shared with them. And we've got to have their responses, criticisms, and contributions coming back." He viewed it as a "personal commitment" and "crucial to any organized form of activity." We cannot "*simply* let our historical work be professional—in the purest sense—for other historians" (original emphasis). But like Thompson, Montgomery was also quick to assert that "precisely because our historical work is politically important, it must strive for the highest standards of accuracy and rigor."[2] The search for those connections between scholarship and engagement goes back to the formative years of what would come to be called labor and working-class history but so, inevitably, do the conflicting demands of an academic culture and the political imperatives embedded in its professionalization.

The "Progressives"

When the young political economist, Richard T. Ely, stepped off the boat in New York harbor in the summer of 1880, following several years studying the "new" political economy in Berlin, he found himself swept up in a maelstrom of class conflict and new organizing by workers belonging to the Knights of Labor. He later told Joseph Labadie, "I took a vow to write in behalf of the laboring classes."[3] When he looked back more than half a century later, Ely recalled that moment in somewhat different terms. "The city was dirty and ill kept, the pavements poor, and there were evidences of graft and corruption on every hand. Is this my America? I asked myself . . . I vowed to do whatever was in my power to bring about better conditions."[4] Ely's notebooks from the mid-1880s reveal a naive enthusiasm and certain innocence about the working-class movements whose undertakings and characteristics he found himself recording. In 1887, he could write enthusiastically, "Keep off the track! The train of progress is coming! Prepare the way! . . . It rests with us so to direct inevitable changes that we may be brought nearer that kingdom of righteousness for which all good Christians long and pray."[5]

If the profound labor upheavals of the late nineteenth century proved a seedbed for both popular and scholarly interest in the "labor problem," direct engagement by these young economists with a robust producers' movement that seemed for a time to shake the very foundations of capitalism and to promise the dawning of a new cooperative era, gave their work purpose and direction. Such engagement took a variety of forms. Beyond Ely's early advocacy on behalf of the labor movement, the meteoric rise (and fall) of Edward Bemis may have been the most noteworthy example of early labor intellectuals' engagement and its consequences.

Bemis had been a student of Ely's at Johns Hopkins and a member of the group that founded the American Economic Association (AEA). He had made himself an expert in utilities regulation and public ownership. He entered into a fight to municipalize gas works in Nashville; he embraced the effort of Chicago reformers to regulate street railways and to municipalize gas works; and in the midst of the Pullman strike of 1894, he came to the defense of the strikers and advocated "public control" of the railroads. Bemis faced growing and intractable opposition from University of Chicago president William Rainey Harper, who sought his dismissal. Disappointed over the lukewarm support from fellow social scientists, like Albion Small, and even his mentor, Ely, Bemis eventually accepted forced resignation. Although he would return to an academic position in the populist-controlled Kansas State Agricultural College and eventually run Cleveland's municipal waterworks under reform mayor Tom Johnson, his career served as a powerful object lesson for his generation of intellectuals engaged with labor and reform.[6]

Part of the challenge that Ely and other political economists like John Bates Clark, Henry C. Adams, and their students faced grew out of their aspiration to claim positions of respect within an expanding academy and its professoriate. They sought to earn status and legitimacy for their investigations and in turn to shape the standards for the new university-based discipline of "political economy."[7]

But a discipline born in advocacy for labor faced new pressures and powerful challenges in the class-contested climate of the 1880s and 1890s. One after another, these young academics found their scholarship called into question, their professionalism and their very appointments challenged because of the political implications of their work and the nature of their public engagement.[8]

As Ely and another of his prized students, John R. Commons, navigated the new, more perilous political terrain after the collapse of the Knights of Labor and what had seemed a robust producers' movement, they sought to define for themselves and their fellow political economists safer paths for engagement within the shifting world of labor and social reform. As scholars possessed of new "expertise," they enlisted their talents on behalf of a labor movement that emerged with new and surprising strength after the great depression of the 1890s. In the American Federation of Labor (AFL) and its craft union affiliates, they found new partners and sought to lend legitimacy to a labor movement of scaled down aspirations.

Commons wandered in the academic wilderness after being quietly let go from Indiana University and then Syracuse, where the chancellor warned that key donors refused to contribute as long as Commons remained. Commons later noted, "So I learned the virtue of silence. It makes eulogists instead of avengers. You keep their secrets . . . I saw the same virtue of silence often thereafter."[9] Commons, with a subsidy from a benevolent investor, founded what he called a Bureau of Economic Research and enlisted Bemis, among others, to undertake contract research. When he was called to testify as an expert witness before the U.S. Industrial Commission in November 1900, he described himself as "a student and writer on economics and sociology, and have been teaching hitherto, but am not at present." When asked by a commission member to describe his Bureau of Economic Research, he responded cautiously: "That is largely a hope, a prospect. Four or five persons like myself have joined together with the idea of taking up any line of economic or political research for which there seemed to be a demand in New York City, giving information, and making it of a scientific character as nearly as we could, something reliable." Asked whether he had studied subjects such as industrial councils, unemployment, day labor, immigration and compulsory arbitration, he indicated that he had done so "as a student." But beyond that, "I have had some practical experience, having been at one time for 3 years a member of a printers' trade union and holding a case, working at night on a daily paper in Cleveland, Ohio, which has given me some insight into the matter of labor and labor organization."[10]

In working with industrial commissions, crafting new legislation that set minimum standards for workplace safety, and pursuing industrial arbitration, Commons and his students hoped to enable organized workers to improve their status
and strengthen their position within the capitalist labor market. If not arguing
for outright guarantees to collective bargaining, their work did at least delineate
a sphere of influence and public recognition for labor, limited though it might be.

But alignment with the AFL and its affiliates also meant a shared skepticism
about the potential for broader forms of organization and, with the rise of new
mass production industries in steel, meatpacking, garments, and automobiles,
a new wariness about the capacity of rising numbers of women wage earners
and new immigrant unskilled workers for self-organization. Commons joined a
chorus of reformers who worried about whether new immigrants and black migrants could be assimilated into a working class capable of self-organization and
defending reasonable labor standards. Commons described what he had learned
through his own "enthusiasm and disappointment" over "the immense problem of the federation in organizing, on the traditional American self-governing
basis, those who are too stupid to stand by each other and by leaders who try
to get for them bread and butter *now* instead of a future millennium" (original
emphasis).[11] Like many progressive reformers, Commons worried that the influx
of "other races and peoples, accustomed to despotism and even savagery, and
wholly unused to self-government, have been thrust into the delicate fabric" of
U.S. democracy.[12] They were, in his view, both unprepared for citizenship and
incapable of organizing to better their condition as workers.

Commons and his students engaged the legislative tasks of codifying labor
standards and guaranteeing a modicum of organizational security through health
and safety legislation, workers' compensation, and arbitration in a political environment of reform that tolerated only limited state intervention in the mar-
ketplace.[13] They sought to implement through expert commissions the tools for
adjusting the relations of labor and capital in ways that would reduce the intensity
of class conflict and reconcile the legitimate interests of labor and capital.[14] In
addition to testifying before the U.S. Industrial Commission, Commons authored
or contributed to a number of the commission's volumes, including the reports on
immigration and the trusts. This model of utilizing what he termed "the original
brain trust" of "trained economists" to shape public policy would be one to which
he returned over the course of his career.[15] He played a singularly important role
in crafting a model industrial commission in Wisconsin that a number of other
states mimicked.[16]

But, perhaps most prominently, in 1913, President Woodrow Wilson appointed
Commons as a public member of the U.S. Commission on Industrial Relations,
which was charged with investigating the "causes of industrial unrest," and Commons oversaw the hiring of many of his students as commission staff.[17] In that
undertaking, he ran headlong into the chair of the commission, Frank Walsh,
who sought to steer its work away from the "expert investigation" advocated by

Commons and toward a more explicit alignment with labor through the taking of often-dramatic public testimony. Walsh argued for a commitment to collective bargaining in the commission's recommendations and for shifting the balance of power from capital to labor in ways that disturbed Commons. In the deeply divided commission, Commons allied himself with a coalition of social reformers, including Paul Kellogg and Jane Addams, who shared his desire to ameliorate the relations of labor and capital.[18]

By the years of the Great War and after, Commons's view of the relationship between labor scholars and the movement they studied had moved a long distance from its inception in the tumultuous days of the nineteenth-century producerist movement. During the war, the labor movement widened its ranks to a degree and broadened its appeal. But once peacetime returned and the wave of postwar strikes collapsed, its wartime growth evaporated. Nevertheless, what came to be known as the Commons School could claim two major achievements in these postwar years: producing a "theory" of the labor movement and completing one phase of documenting the early history of labor.

The first achievement, undertaken by one of Commons's most brilliant students, whom he called "my beloved Selig Perlman," was the consequence, in Commons's words, of Perlman's turn "from Marxism to Gompers' Americanized unionism."[19] That view provided the intellectual rationale for what Perlman claimed to be the "exceptionalist" path of U.S. labor, a byproduct of the "scarcity consciousness" of skilled workers and their exclusive craft unions. By the 1920s, this principle seemed the necessary and inevitable backbone of the U.S. labor movement. Ironically, despite Perlman's own marginal status as an immigrant Jewish intellectual and former socialist who stood outside Commons's inner circle and the orbits of "practical trade unionists," he affirmed an orthodox "pure and simple" trade unionism and critique of reformism.[20]

The second achievement, however, solidified the most enduring link to labor history's future, which lay beyond the rise of industrial unionism and the statist guarantees to labor's right to collective bargaining in the 1930s and 1940s. Through their massive collecting of labor records that reached back to the nineteenth century and through their multivolume history and published documentary collections, Ely, Commons, and their students lay the foundation for subsequent studies in labor history that ironically would come to challenge the intellectual framework they had built and the boundaries to "civic engagement" they had come to accept and rationalize.[21]

Insurgents: E. P. Thompson and David Montgomery

By different routes, Edward Thompson and David Montgomery spearheaded the intellectual challenge to the progressives' early conceptualization of labor's history and their institutional engagement with ameliorative reform. Thompson and Montgomery crossed paths first in their work together at the University of War-

wick, where they contributed directly to the vitality of an academic program that
for a time functioned as the primary center for labor history studies in Britain. The
Centre for the Study of Social History at Warwick drew a talented cadre of English
and U.S. graduate students to work on master's degrees, some of whom later went
on to pursue doctorates at Pittsburgh with Montgomery, at Rochester with Herbert
Gutman, or at other British universities.[22] Neither Thompson nor Montgomery,
however, was entirely at home in traditional academic settings, where their intellectual and political commitments frequently clashed with those of colleagues more
devoted to strictly academic pursuits.

The reorientation of labor history after World War II was intimately bound
to the devolution and contested legacy of the Communist Party, the imprint of
the Cold War, and the rise of a new Left that broadened the scope of labor historians' political engagement. That reorientation is inseparable from the work
of E. P. Thompson and colleagues Eric Hobsbawm, Christopher Hill, and John
Saville, among others, on one side of the Atlantic, and David Montgomery and
his colleagues, Herbert Gutman, David Brody, and Melvyn Dubofsky, on the
other. Their work and their politics have striking parallels but also instructive
divergences. The intimate connection between scholarship and public engagement
in both Thompson's and Montgomery's work created a legacy that continues to
powerfully influence newer work in the field.[23]

Edward Thompson

E. P. Thompson's long career as a politically engaged left intellectual began, in
one sense, with the transformative experience of volunteer work in Yugosla-
via immediately after World War II, following his brother Frank, who had died
working with Bulgarian partisans during the war and who "broke open the way"
in his family with membership in the Communist Party. From 1948 until 1965,
Edward and his wife, Dorothy, who would also become an activist intellectual
and historian, worked as adult education "tutors" in the industrial towns and
villages of West Yorkshire under the auspices of Leeds University's Extra-mural
Studies Department. By his own account, he split his time between activism in
the Yorkshire branch of the Communist Party, in the peace movement, and his
teaching of history and English literature with working-class adults.[24]

Thompson's students warmly remembered him from those years in West Yorkshire working under the auspices of the Workers Education Association. He and
Dorothy lived and worked out of Halifax. As one former student remembered,
"People got to know him, admired and trusted him and that is quite an achievement. People in the West Riding do not normally open up to a middle-class
academic from the South, I'm afraid." Another, Dorothy Greenald of Cleckhea-
ton, a miner's daughter and former child worker in a woolen mill, recalled that
Thompson "brought it out that your background wasn't anything to be ashamed
of . . . that changed me really. . . . The warmth and affection past students still have

for him is not because of what he has become, but for what he was as a friend and tutor, happy, friendly and helpful, who treated all students as equals." But in his voluminous reports, detailing literally every class he taught, Thompson remembered how much he had learned from his students. Regarding a class in Morley, he wrote that "the work has been in the late 18th and early 19th centuries, and discussion has elicited a surprising and gruesome fund of memory among the older students. . . . It is difficult to believe that the industrial revolution has yet occurred in Morley, and next year's syllabus (in the later 19th century) will seem like a tour through the space age."[25]

Thompson would put his students' tutoring to good use as he began work on what he initially envisioned as an adult education survey text—"because I was hard up"—on the British labor movement from 1790 to 1945. The book's "first chapter" eventually grew into an eight-hundred-page, profoundly original work of scholarship, *The Making of the English Working Class* (*MEWC*), which would transform the historical debate on the nature and meaning of the industrial revolution for working people whose self-activity had been largely absent in the most influential historical writing on the subject. As with other work, he recalled, "the material took command of me." And, alluding to the lessons for other historians, he asserted, "the material itself has got to speak to him. If he listens, then the material itself will begin to speak through him. And I think this happens."[26]

Thompson came to this masterwork after a significant sojourn writing a massive biography of nineteenth-century socialist artist and writer William Morris. "Morris seized me," he recalled years later. "I took no decision. Morris took the decision that I would have to present him."[27] The alchemy of Morris's (and the poet William Blake's) romanticism, with Thompson's own version of communism, kindled a sensibility that would profoundly shape *MEWC*. As Bryan Palmer, a Canadian labor historian and close friend of Thompson's, has put it, "Morris's revolutionary Romanticism was driven by *anger*; but it was an anger—again like Blake's—which was cut with satire, polemic, mockery, hyperbole, abuse, provocation, framing a personality that was 'humorous, brusque, shy meditative, vehement by turns.' This did not just *claim* Edward Thompson; it *was* Edward" (original emphasis).[28]

Edward and Dorothy Thompson moved to Warwick in 1965, according to Palmer, "in part because his own work had now entered into the professional discourse and was subjected to sometimes searing critique." He also wanted to have a hand in shaping the training of young historians to avoid the pitfalls of those who never ventured into the archives, or who, in his words, "'never untied a bundle' of manuscripts."[29] The move came just two years after he published *MEWC* and was riding a wave of critical enthusiasm for the book, which David Erdman cited as a work of "profundity, breadth and quality." R. K. Webb not only believed that the book would shape the next generation of scholarship, but he asserted that such scholarship would inevitably "take the form of a commentary on it."

Richard Tilly called it "a scientific *magnum opus* happily disguised as a work of art," and some years later Joan Scott called it simply "the book that revolutionized social and labor history."[30]

Over the next five years, Thompson and his colleagues practiced a lively, "notably inclusive" style of teaching in the graduate program at Warwick that stirred new and creative thinking at the intersection of social and labor history and provided a hothouse environment in which new empirical and theoretical work took root. Thompson's brilliance was not suffocating. John Rule and Robert Malcolmson recalled that there was "no party line . . . but a common set of historical concerns, sensibilities, and questions concerning social relationships to be explored . . . sufficiently tolerant and generous to allow plenty of scope for diverse, even divergent, styles and approaches and political engagements." As they remembered, "the writing of history was for him a serious and demanding vocation, not to be confused with the limiting notion of a career." They observed also that Thompson believed deeply in rigorous training, scrupulous craftsmanship, and close attention to sources. But above all, "good social history—probing history, attentive history, and scrupulously researched history—was vital to the health of society."[31]

But Thompson's intellectual and political restlessness ultimately drew him away from a conventional academic appointment and some of the kinds of commitments and distractions it required. Students occupying the vice chancellor's office at Warwick during protests in 1970 later told him that one "bulky" file "attracted a good deal of sardonic interest" and was, as he later put it, "full of my own fatuous and longwinded attempts at resignation."[32] No small factor in his decision to leave—besides his commitment to writing, and the self-deprecatingly described "egotistical" need "to complete some of my own work"—was the running political struggle with a corporatized and bureaucratized university administration, one dimension of which the much-celebrated Montgomery Affair revealed.[33]

Then a relatively junior member of the faculty at the University of Pittsburgh, David Montgomery had been invited to hold a visiting appointment at Warwick in 1967, which he extended for a second year. Thompson described Montgomery as "a distinguished historian, the author of *Beyond Equality* (1967)," who had worked previous to his academic career for some years "as a machinist on the shop floor in the engineering industry." It had been this "unusual blend of academic excellence and practical experience" that had made him especially attractive. As it turned out, in addition to his formal teaching during his two years at Warwick, Montgomery advised a group of striking Pakistani workers and addressed meetings of "trade unionists, Labour Party members and shop stewards" on the topic of "automation and the problems of measured day-work as experienced by workers in American industry."[34]

During Montgomery's time in Warwick, students had been engaged in an ongoing campaign against the university administration over a set of grievances that deprived students (and faculty) of a direct voice in how university decisions were made, especially those that impinged on the quality of student life and opportunities for engagement with the wider community. They had a distinct sense that powerful corporate interests represented on the university's governing board ran the show. When rebuffed by the university's "building committee," students decided virtually spontaneously on February 11, 1970, to occupy administrative offices in order to press their demands and moved quickly to do so. During the first evening of the occupation, out of a mixture of boredom and curiosity, students began thumbing through files adjacent to the vice chancellor's office, and in a file marked confidential "University-Student Relations" they turned up a surprising report from an employee of Rootes Motors, a Chrysler subsidiary, who had a perfect Dickensian name. Mr. Catchpole had been delegated by the university administration to spy on a Coventry Labour Party meeting at which Montgomery had spoken. (By the time of the student occupation, Montgomery had already returned to the United States.) Thompson was immediately called, and he appeared at the meeting of two hundred occupying students. He asked to photocopy the documents and pledged to distribute copies to all university staff (faculty) the next morning. The university community was particularly outraged when the documents were publicized because of administrators' repeated assurances that they kept no files on the political activities of staff or students.[35]

The report on Montgomery's talk to a Labour Party meeting had found its way into university files by way of a managing director of Rootes Motors, who also sat on the university council and chaired its building committee. The covert investigation of Montgomery had apparently been prompted by an interest in determining whether he could be found to have violated the 1919 Aliens Restriction Act and therefore prosecutable as an "alien" for having promoted "industrial unrest" . . . "punishable by three months imprisonment."[36] The actual report eventually declared that Montgomery's talk did not appear to have violated any laws. Mr. Catchpole noted that eight people were in attendance at the March 3, 1969, meeting. "The guest speaker, Dr. D. Montgomery, spoke for about half an hour. . . . [His] speech was I felt poor in content. He warned the meeting of the danger of accepting measured day-work, which he said would remove the negotiating powers of the local shop stewards and particularly when associated with automation was entirely contrary to the best interests of the workers. He did not however give any specific examples to justify this allegation but merely referred to the general experience in American industry." When some members of the audience argued for bringing down the Harold Wilson, Labour government, organizing sympathy strikes with striking U.K. Ford workers and "that ultimately the only answer was for the workers to seize the factories," Catchpole reported, "Dr. Montgomery was, I felt, particularly careful not to associate himself with any of these suggestions." He thought that Montgomery evidenced a "definite bias against employers in general" but that his remarks did not raise "any questions of a prosecution under the Aliens Restriction Act."[37]

The report and the incident became a central issue in the ongoing campaign against the university administration, the outcome of which was less than clear-cut. In his epilogue to a short book on that struggle, Thompson wrote, "we have raised at Warwick, not only a new flag or two, but some very ancient and tattered flags, even older than those of rotten liberalism." The outcome, still indeterminate, would dictate whether the university would become an "intellectually alert, self-governing community" or "simply 'the Business University,'" and likewise the result would be "an index of the vitality of democratic process—and of the shape of the next British future."[38]

For his own intellectual and political reasons, Thompson would shortly exit the world of academia and a formal faculty appointment. He would speak of being part of an informal "collective" of historians that included "comrades" like Saville and Hobsbawm. But, implicitly drawing on his experience at Warwick, he also gave voice to a warning and a promise:

> What socialists must never do is allow themselves to become wholly dependent upon established institutions—publishing houses, commercial media, universities, and foundations. I don't mean that these institutions are all repressive—certainly, much that is affirmative can be done within them. But socialist intellectuals must occupy some territory that is, without qualification their own: their own journals, their own theoretical and practical centers—places where no one works for grades or for tenure but for the transformation of society; places where criticism and self-criticism are fierce, but also mutual help and the exchange of theoretical and practical knowledge; places that prefigure in some ways the society of the future.[39]

Thompson's own engagement along these lines brought him back to the eighteenth century as a subject of study,[40] led to occasional visiting university appointments,[41] and renewed a political engagement that encompassed both theoretical writing[42] and activism in the British and European anti–nuclear war movements.

At the end of the 1970s, Thompson professed boredom over debates within Marxism, though he certainly never divorced himself from that tradition. He wrote of his deep pessimism in "The State of the Nation," overtaken by a stifling and coercive "consensus" in which a "peculiarly British form of authoritarianism, working behind the back of the democratic process, is now bringing national life within its general closure." But, not wishing to "nourish pessimism," he summoned his own latent utopianism, reached out to elements of the New Left alternative culture, of which he had at times been critical, and looked to the future that beckoned him back to activism with a sense of urgency. Believing that his "pessimistic scenario" might be "overdrawn," he wrote that "one can even glimpse the possibility of a quite new phase of democratic and socialist insurgency somewhere ahead—a resurgent movement with new priorities, which would turn its back on the old statist norms and bureaucratic forms to be found in the orthodox traditions of both communism and social democracy, and which would address the critical problem of the restructuring of our institutions (national, industrial, judicial, local, and in communications and education) with a quite new democratic inventiveness. That may be more than we can hope for, but it would be worth working for, together."[43]

With that, Thompson leaped, no holds barred, into the Europe-wide campaign for nuclear disarmament, with which he had been connected, albeit at a lower level of activity, since the 1950s. He moved other unrelated writing and historical scholarship to the back burner, where it stayed. He became in short order a public face and voice for the anti–nuclear arms movement. Its work would consume much of his energy for nearly a decade. The NATO proposal to deploy nuclear-armed cruise missiles in Britain led Thompson to call for massive protests "in the name of human survival," and he moved into the core leadership of the new, European nuclear disarmament (END) movement. As Bryan Palmer has described it, by 1981, "he stood before rallies of 250,000; he spoke to the world." That activism would carry him through much of the 1980s. He would subsequently return, exhausted, "to his garden, both metaphorical and real" for the last years of his life.[44]

David Montgomery

Having returned to his academic appointment at the University of Pittsburgh in the fall of 1969, David Montgomery had already become a major force in launching a U.S. branch, so to speak, of the new labor history, colored now by his experience at the University of Warwick but also with deeper roots in his own activist past in the labor movement. Among other things, this would involve confronting the densely woven historiography of the progressives and their engagement with labor, which had been incorporated into the dominant "consensus" reading of the U.S. past in which working-class community, class conflict, and a socialist tradition had little purchase. In this older literature—"the standard fare of labor history before 1945," one "would never," for example, "guess that any American workers were blacks."[45]

Montgomery's practice of "the trade" of labor history was inseparable from his politics, in particular his membership in and separation from the Communist Party of the United States (CPUSA) and his experience over nearly ten years on the shop floor as a craftsman, trade union militant, and organizer in New York and Minnesota. Like Thompson, his experience with the party had a formative influence on his work as a scholar and teacher. That he and Thompson both left the party after 1956 is also significant. He nevertheless remembered the important role that the CPUSA had "as the main Marxist organization in the country," providing a crucial link between "Marxist analysis" and "effective daily action." He observed that "this connection to the everyday struggles of Americans and to an international movement for socialism guided us toward styles of social analysis that were rooted in the hard and complex realities of experience and away from phrase-mongering and dogmatic abstractions."[46]

He understood from experience the value of the party's work in the black community and the basis it provided "for united action between black and white workers." But from the perspective of a rank-and-file member of the party, who went to work every day, party leaders and activists moved in a different cultural world. They used theory to explain official texts or provide "*ex post facto* justifications of actions taken." He explained: "At my level of activity we continued from day to day doing our thing. If anything, the frequent disappearance of leadership reinforced a sense of self-reliance in the shop sections."[47]

Montgomery's work as a machinist and rank-and-file activist set apart his political experience from that of Thompson. Where Thompson worked as a "tutor," however immersed in the working-class lives of his students, and found space to write an eight-hundred-page biography of William Morris, engage with former party intellectuals in active theoretical debates, and lay the groundwork for his magisterial *MEWC*, Montgomery and other rank-and-file activists, by his account, had a very different experience. Those leaving the party in England, he noted, "stayed together as a group: published journals, had a movement of their own, had a theoretical voice," while in the United States, "people were dropping out one by one[,] and this was especially true of rank-and-file industrial workers." Montgomery continued to focus his energies on shop floor struggles but also found in Minnesota "enough of a labor flavor and enough activity around peace and civil rights . . . that there was another place where I felt at home and could act without breaking stride."[48]

With his activist career cut short—"driven out of the factory" by the blacklist in 1960—Montgomery chose an academic career as a historian, which, as he recalled, was "*not* my first choice."[49] But within a remarkably short time, he had completed a doctorate at the University of Minnesota, taken a first teaching job at Hamline University in St. Paul, and moved toward publication of *Beyond Equality*. That work did more than catapult Montgomery to the front rank of an emerging, if somewhat inchoate, group of younger historians, whose backgrounds and interests led them to study workers in new ways.[50] It also represented the most unequivocal opening salvo against a field of labor studies grown complacent and self-satisfied in its support for an imagined history of labor institutions in which the shock troops of industrialization—the less-skilled, immigrant, and increasingly female and African American—were largely absent or at least not agents of their own history.

In *Beyond Equality*, Montgomery took on a calcified Civil War–era historiography, still dominated by the conception of Reconstruction as a conspiracy of Northern entrepreneurs and reasserted the centrality of Republican initiatives to reunify the nation and guarantee the fundamental rights of emancipated African Americans. But he also challenged Commons's and Perlman's "bifurcation of types of labor leaders into wage-conscious trade unionists and antimonopoly reformers" that had become old labor history orthodoxy. They had failed, he argued, to acknowledge the fundamental proposition that "class conflict did in fact exist." Radical Republicans may have erected a new legal apparatus of equality before the law, but as Montgomery noted, "beyond equality lay the insistence of labor's spokesmen that as the propertyless, as factors of production, wage earners were effectively denied meaningful participation in the Republic. No one grasped the significance of this challenge more profoundly than Ira Steward. When labor reformers sought a remedy in legal reduction of the hours of labor, the Radicals found there was no common ground between the disputants, no common good to be sought, and the workers found their statutory victories totally impotent in the face of employer defiance."[51] Like Thompson, Montgomery wrote with a passion that captured the imagination of younger scholars and opened doors to a history that was anything but a quiescent consensus. Not surprisingly, his time at Warwick, soon after publication of *Beyond Equality*, would establish a firm foundation of friendship with Thompson and an Anglo-U.S. nexus of new approaches to labor history, grounded in a shared sense of its relevance to the world of politics and class struggle in the present.

Montgomery's approach may at first appear to have been less expressive of the moral revulsion and romantic critique of industrial capitalism that characterized Thompson's life-long fascination with William Blake, William Morris, or, for that matter, Tom Paine and William Cobbett. In his own right—although always more grounded in the gritty world of the shop floor and the working-class neighborhood as he had known them—Montgomery found in class-conscious U.S. labor activists Ira Steward, William Sylvis, John F. Bray, and in later years Samuel Lavit and Fred Merrick, critics of capitalism, whose utopian inclinations echoed his own aspirations.[52] As he noted in 1980, "when working people replace capitalism with their own society, they will create not a world without rules, but one based on rules they have made themselves for their own welfare. This is precisely why workers' own ethical codes hold so much interest for me."[53]

Thompson and Montgomery developed their own unique approaches to labor history. Their sense of working-class agency and consciousness came from sustained contact with workers—in Thompson's adult education classes over many years in the industrial towns of the North and in Montgomery's work as a machinist and labor militant alongside rank-and-file workers inside and outside the Communist Party. The results of their work converged in important ways and provided models for engaged scholarship to subsequent generations of scholar-activists.

Thompson's intellectual and political engagement reflected both his personal history—antifascist activism during and after World War II—and his efforts to craft a new understanding of class freed from the shackles of the party's authoritarian tendencies. But his scholarship also existed in tension with a Cold War political climate that for him elevated the campaign against nuclear weapons to an overriding imperative.[54]

Montgomery's engagement always had a more direct connection to the worlds of leftwing trade unionism through which he had come, and specifically to the world of skilled metal tradesmen, with whom he had such a strong identification.[55] His loyalty to his former union, the United Electrical Workers (UE), and its radical tradition and his speaking on behalf of striking miners and other tradespeople were emblematic of this continuing commitment.[56] Even as the holder of a named chair at Yale University, he could be found actively supporting striking clerical, technical, and dining hall workers and their fight for collective bargaining. He helped organize faculty and student strike support. He appeared on the picket line, on the "soapbox," and even impersonated an employer in a piece of guerrilla theater.[57]

Montgomery was a profoundly inspirational lecturer—a mix of stump speaker, storyteller, and erudite analyst—but also a very hands-on mentor to scores of graduate students, his own and others, and a whole younger generation of even "newer" labor historians, whose work he encouraged.[58]

In Pittsburgh during the 1970s, a cadre of graduate students came to work with David Montgomery, much in the manner that a young contingent of scholars joined E. P. Thompson's program at Warwick in the late 1960s. This group followed Montgomery's example and carried their academic work into the community through strike support activity, oral histories, union organizing, and community living. They examined the social conflicts and solidarities of the shop floor, the structures of power and cross-class alliances that working-class community bred, the forms of collective action that workingmen and -women devised, and the new kinds of politics they practiced. Montgomery's students saw that history brought to life in their own work and that of others through reconstructing the fabric of workers' daily lives historically. It was a given that the labor history they excavated had a direct connection to the working-class communities and struggles of the present with which they identified. That unique community of scholars would have been difficult to imagine without the mentorship and inspiration that Montgomery gave to it.[59]

Both Thompson and Montgomery, in their own ways, expressed some reservations about the thrust of the newest New Left. Montgomery was not "of" the New Left; his perspective on its development was a legacy of his own complicated relationship to the Communist Party. Thompson had been deeply immersed in the birthing of the earlier New Lefts in Britain, but he had deep criticisms of certain tendencies in the second New Left. While Montgomery observed that "any criticism of the New Left has to start with the recognition that 'thank God it was here,'" he also thought that some of its criticism of labor sounded more like "an echo of contemporary consumerist capitalism than an attack on it." He believed that "a revolutionary movement" must "address working people with understanding and respect," that it should "break down the wall[s] between it and the rest of the working people, rather than just build them up."[60] Thompson's criticisms were more pointed. Speaking in 1976, he asserted that "this New Left had elements within it that could be seen at once by a historian as the revolting bourgeoisie doing its own revolting thing—that is, the expressive and irrationalist, self-exalting gestures of style that do not belong to a serious and deeply-rooted, rational revolutionary tradition."[61] But just a few years later, on the cusp of his own return to activism, he wrote more positively, if still critically, of "an alternative culture" needing to find "ways of influencing again, in active ways, the national political life." He noted that "the notion has got about that one's gender or colour or preferences must always, in every situation, be the primary existential facts and that these differences must be nearly-insurmountable barriers inhibiting common political action. This may start from valid premises. But when the notion is pressed too far . . . this is dangerously divisive." He acknowledged that women "got hushed or annexed in mass movements of the past" and that their demands deserved "a new kind of attention." But he was reluctant to "throw away the possibility of a general movement" capable of opposing the oppressive "face of power."[62] Despite reservations about the younger generation's politics, both Montgomery and Thompson enthusiastically nurtured the new scholarship that grew from their students' political engagement.

A new labor history is hard to imagine without the profound influence of E. P. Thompson and David Montgomery. What shape did this new approach take and what specifically did they contribute? First, they provided a rich sense of the ebb and flow of working-class self-activity within the constraints imposed by evolving capitalist social relations and power. Second, both positioned artisans and skilled industrial workers at the center of these struggles. Even though both documented defeat, they also stressed the underlying and sometimes covert continuities that would sustain working-class resistance over a longer period (into Chartism on the one hand and the Congress of Industrial Organizations on the other). Third, Thompson may have been more attuned to the literary and cultural dimensions of these movements with an eye for the obscure and forgotten characters that populated or gave inspiration to their resistance. His early interest in Blake and Morris were particularly important here. But Montgomery, too, resurrected a multilayered, regionally diverse, ethnically infused working-class-in-the-making in the context of a more mature, powerful, and concentrated monopoly capitalism.[63] Within the interstices of capitalism, workers created spaces for organization and political mobilization that signaled a consciousness of class that at times could exercise significant power, while also suffering periodic erosion. As he wrote memorably in *The Fall of the House of Labor*, "the history of American workers has not been a story of progressive ascent from oppression to securely established rights. . . .

Their movement has grown only sporadically and through fierce struggles, been interrupted time and again just when it seemed to reach flood tide, overwhelmed its foes only to see them revive in new and more formidable shapes, and been forced to reassess what it thought it had already accomplished and begin again."[64]

New Labor Historians' Scholarship and Engagement

Many of the first generation of scholars inspired by the work of Thompson and Montgomery gravitated to the challenge of recovering a "lost" history of popular struggle that was neither synonymous with the trade unions and institution building of the older Commons tradition, nor with an old left tradition of Marxist scholarship associated in the U.S. context with the work of Philip Foner, among others. For many, this made reinterpreting the Knights of Labor and the broader unionism of the late nineteenth century a central project that included a focus on nascent industrial unions, an alternative working-people's culture, independent labor politics, and reintegrating ethnicity, race and gender in the portrait of a more diverse working class.[65] A veritable cottage industry of Knights of Labor studies by such scholars as Leon Fink, Susan Levine, Bryan Palmer, Greg Kealey, David Brundage, Jonathan Garlock, Robert Weir, and others recast the "making" of the nineteenth-century U.S. working class in fundamental ways. Class conflict was reintroduced as a central feature of U.S. life and a fundamental challenge to consensus historiography. Capitalism came to be seen as contingent, not preordained, and working-class republicanism became a source of inspiration for an alternative, more humane "cooperative commonwealth."[66]

Much of that new work focused on the local and a vision of class in which social relations had some structure and system but also unexpected convergences and frictions.[67] Many of these historians drew on their own social movement experience in the 1960s and 1970s and the revolt against established authority and structures of power. They called into question the established traditions and political hegemony of a corporate "liberalism" that had accommodated the persistence of racial segregation, inequality, poverty, sexism, and imperialism. That liberalism had a congenital aversion to thinking about the United States as a class society and a conviction that reform must come from above and through established political channels.[68]

This generation of labor historians had to varying degrees been participants in social movements built around popular mobilization and grassroots activism. Through these movements, they had challenged racial segregation in the South and North; engaged in direct action to oppose the Vietnam War and American imperialism; embraced local organizing around welfare rights and government antipoverty initiatives; supported farm workers through boycotts; and, through their own labor organizing in auto plants, machine shops, hospitals, post offices, and universities, furthered new democratic rank-and-file movements, and found encouragement in the strikes of the late 1960s and early 1970s—in electrical, mining, auto, postal, and health care industries.

These "engagements" provided a deep motivation to better grasp the history of popular struggles, to conceive a "useable" past, and to challenge the intellectual hegemony that consensus and organizational historians held. In university contexts, this led to new unionizing efforts among graduate students and faculty, challenges to traditional curricula and requirements, and the aspiration to create "new universities" in which the boundaries between academic work and political engagement dissolved. For many, campus struggles themselves—in Madison, Cambridge, New Haven, Columbia (Missouri), Berkeley, and Iowa City—provided the catalyst for these changes. The emergence of Black Studies and a vigorous campus-community-based feminist movement represented the leading edge of such changes. And those influences in turn reshaped the course of the new labor history.

Recent decades have seen a whole new set of insights into working-class life inspired by the effects of the political engagement of African Americans, Latinos, Latinas, and feminists. These insights have complicated and enriched understandings of class that may have been foreshadowed in the work of Thompson and Montgomery but remained underdeveloped. Historians like David Roediger, James Barrett, and Noel Ignatiev focused attention on the "white" racial consciousness of immigrant and native-born workers. In so doing, they complicated the portrait of a working class in which interracial collective action was represented as the norm. Similarly, Ira Berlin, Julie Saville, Leslie Schwalm, and others gave new interpretive emphasis to slavery as a labor system. Alice Kessler-Harris, Ava Baron, Patricia Cooper, Tom Dublin, and a host of historians of women have made gender a central category of *class* analysis and have suggested, in Kessler-Harris's provocative phrase, that we "treat the male as other." Even "newer" generations of labor historians have continued to pursue these themes with profoundly original and politically salient results. Seth Rockman has reconstructed the complex intermingling of labor systems, free and dependent, in the postcolonial city; Eric Fure-Slocum has charted the shifting terrain of class and race in post–World War II cities, and Dennis Deslippe has located the roots of new feminism in the struggles of working-class women for equity in the workplace. A number of labor historians have taken up anew the transnational and global challenge that was foreshadowed in some of Montgomery's later work. Leon Fink has looked at the transnational world of merchant seamen and Mayan immigrants; Julie Greene examined the global labor system that was essential to the building of the Panama Canal; and I have examined the transnational and comparative development of municipal socialism as a seedbed for a new labor politics in the late nineteenth and early twentieth centuries.[69]

Labor history, almost more than any other academic subfield in social history that flourished after 1960, reflected an intermingling of intellectual work and political engagement. Thompson and Montgomery, more than any others of their generation of labor historians, embodied this creative commitment to the highest standards of academic study *and* political engagement, not as separate and distinct activities but as mutually reinforcing commitments that fed off each other, enriching the scholarship on the one hand and deepening the engagement on the other. That linkage between scholarship and engagement remains one of their most important and lasting legacies and traces its roots to the very origins of the field.

Notes

1. Mark Naison and Paul Buhle, "Interview with E. P. Thompson," *Visions of History* (New York: Pantheon, 1983), 7.

2. Mark Naison and Paul Buhle, "Interview with David Montgomery," *Visions of History*, 180. In the same interview, Montgomery noted that his first published article, on the 1894 Pullman strike in Minneapolis, appeared under the pseudonym "Amos Flaherty" in a volume edited by St. Paul radical activist and writer Meridel Le Sueur: "There was never the slightest feeling that we were writing something *for* the working people. We *were* the working people of Minneapolis writing about ourselves" (176). See Meridel Le Sueur et al., eds., *The People Together: One Hundred Years of Minnesota, 1858–1958* (Minneapolis, Minn.: People's Centennial Book Committee, 1958).

3. Ely to Joseph Labadie, letter August 14, 1885, in "Ely-Labadie Letters," edited by Sidney Fine, *Michigan History* 36 (March 1952): 17, quoted in Dorothy Ross, *The Origins of American Social Science* (New York: Cambridge University Press, 1991), 105.

4. Richard T. Ely, *Ground under Our Feet: An Autobiography* (New York: Macmillan, 1938), 65.

5. Ely's notebooks from 1885 formed part of the material on which he drew for the pathbreaking volume that established his reputation as an important and innovative political economist, *The Labor Movement in America* (New York: T. Y. Crowell, 1886). They contain seemingly random jottings of a detailed sort about the labor and socialist movements, for example this one: "Mr. Strasser tells me that George McNeill . . . is one of the best-posted men in the U.S. about labor movement. Mr. Strasser says Ira Steward is one of the most intellectual men in U.S. or labor movement." He constructed lists including "Labor and Socialist Periodicals in the U.S., 1885," and, regarding the Knights of Labor, reported that "Farnam said members estimated at 800,000 in fall of 1878." Richard T. Ely Papers, Teaching and Research Files, box 29, Wisconsin Historical Society, Madison. Leon Fink provides an excellent account of Ely and other young economists' relationship to the labor movement of the 1880s and their chastening experiences within their own universities in "'Intellectuals' versus 'Workers': Academic Requirements and the Creation of Labor History," *American Historical Review* 96.2 (April 1991): 395–431.

6. Mary Furner, *Advocacy and Objectivity: A Crisis in the Professionalization of American Social Science, 1865–1905* (Lexington: University Press of Kentucky, 1975) offers the most comprehensive account of the Bemis affair. She draws significantly on Harold E. Bergquist Jr., "Edward W. Bemis Controversy at the University of Chicago," *AAUP Bulletin* 58 (December 1972): 384–93. See also Shelton Stromquist, *Reinventing "the People": The Progressive Movement, the Class Problem, and the Origins of Modern Liberalism* (Urbana: University of Illinois Press, 2006), 29–31.

7. Ross, *Origins of American Social Science*, 98–140, and Furner, *Advocacy and Objectivity*, 143–228, treat the professionalizing pressures on civically engaged social scientists of this era in considerable detail. For the emerging subfield of labor economists and historians, see Fink, "'Intellectuals' versus 'Workers.'"

8. See Stromquist, *Reinventing "the People,"* 22–32; also Fink, "'Intellectuals' versus 'Workers,'" and John R. Commons, *Myself* (New York: Macmillan, 1934), 50–62.

9. Commons, *Myself*, 61, also quoted in part in Furner, *Advocacy and Objectivity*, 203.

10. On his work with the Bureau of Economic Research, see Commons, *Myself*, 63–68; quotations are from United States. Industrial Commission, *Report of the United States Industrial Commission on the Relations and Conditions of Capital and Labor*, vol. 14 (Washington, D.C.: Government Printing Office, 1901), 32.

11. John R. Commons, "Introduction to v. III and IV," in John R. Commons, Don D. Lescohier, Elizabeth Brandeis, *History of Labor in the United States, 1896–1932* (New York: Macmillan, 1935), 3:x.

12. John R. Commons, *Races and Immigrants in America* (New York: Macmillan, 1908), 5.

13. On the limits of the Progressive Era state, see Theda Skocpol, *Protecting Soldiers and Mothers: The Political Origins of Social Policy in the United States* (Cambridge, Mass.: Harvard University Press, 1992); James Weinstein, *The Corporate Ideal of the Liberal State* (Boston: Beacon Press, 1968); and Martin J. Sklar, *The Corporate Reconstruction of American Capitalism, 1890–1916: The Market, the Law, and Politics* (New York: Cambridge University Press, 1988); but also Stephen Skowronek, *Building a New American State: The Expansion of National Administrative Capacities, 1877–1920* (New York: Cambridge University Press, 1982); Julie Greene, *Pure and Simple Politics: The American Federation of Labor and Political Activism, 1881–1917* (New York: Cambridge University Press, 1998); and David Montgomery, *Citizen Worker: The Experience of Workers in the United States with Democracy and the Free Market during the Nineteenth Century* (New York: Cambridge University Press, 1993).

14. See John R. Commons, "Is Class Conflict in America Growing and Is It Inevitable?," *American Journal of Sociology* 13.6 (1906): 756–66. To the first question he answers "yes" and to the second "no."

15. See United States Industrial Commission, *Reports of the Industrial Commission on Immigration and on Education*, vol. 15 (Washington, D.C.: Government Printing Office, 1901); and United States Industrial Commission, *Preliminary Report on Trusts and Industrial Combinations*, vol. 1 (Washington, D.C.: Government Printing Office, 1900). Also Commons, *Myself*, 73–79 (quotation on 76.)

16. Commons, *Myself*, 159–60; John R. Commons, *Labor and Administration* (New York: Augustus Kelley, 1964 [1913]), 382–424.

17. See Stromquist, *Reinventing "the People,"* 164–90, and Shelton Stromquist, "Class Wars: Frank Walsh, the Reformers and the Crisis of Progressivism," in *Labor Histories: Class, Politics, and Working-Class Experience*, edited by Eric Arnesen, Julie Greene, and Bruce Laurie (Urbana: University of Illinois Press, 1998), 97–124; also Leon Fink, "The People's Expert: Charles McCarthy and the Perils of Public Service," in *Progressive Intellectuals and the Dilemmas of Democratic Reform* (Cambridge, Mass.: Harvard University Press, 1997), 80–113; and Joseph A. McCartin, *Labor's Great War: the Struggle for Industrial Democracy and the Origins of Modern American Labor Relations* (Chapel Hill: University of North Carolina Press, 1997). Participating students of Commons included John A. Fitch, William Leiserson, and Selig Perlman.

18. Stromquist, *Reinventing "the People,"* 166, 186.

19. Commons, *Myself,* 81.

20. In many ways, the most important text of the "Old Labor History" was Perlman's *A Theory of the Labor Movement* (New York: A. M. Kelley, 1949 [1928]). See also Mark Perlman, *Labor Union Theories in America: Background and Development* (Evanston, Ill.: Row, Peterson, 1958); and on the ambiguities of Perlman's position and his complex relationship with Commons, see Fink, "'Intellectuals' versus 'Workers.'" See also Selig Perlman, "History of Socialism in Milwaukee (1893–1910)" (B.A. thesis, University of Wisconsin, 1910).

21. Richard T. Ely, *Labor Movement in America* (New York: T. Y. Crowell, 1886); John R. Commons, David Saposs, Helen L. Sumner, E. B. Mittelman, H. E. Hoagland, John B. Andrews, Selg Perlman, Don D. Leschoier, Elizabeth Brandeis, and Philip Taft, *History of Labour in the United States* (New York: Macmillan, 1921–35), 4 vols.; and John R. Commons, Ulrich B. Phillips, Eugene A. Gilmore, Helen L. Sumner, and John B. Andrews, eds., *A Documentary History of American Industrial Society* (Cleveland: A. H. Clark, 1910–11), 11 vols. For generations of labor historians, the very rich Ely and Commons collections of manuscripts, periodicals, and published works deposited with the Wisconsin Historical Society have been the foundation for studies that ranged far beyond the "old" labor history's institutional interests.

22. Notable among those Warwick students were Neville Kirk, who eventually followed Montgomery back to Pittsburgh, as did, somewhat later, James Barrett; Leon Fink pursued the PhD at Rochester with Gutman; other U.S. graduate students included Peter Linebaugh, Calvin Winslow, and Barbara Winslow.

23. The analyses of Thompson's work and influence are numerous, but should begin with Bryan D. Palmer, *E. P. Thompson: Objections and Oppositions* (New York: Verso, 1994); Harvey J. Kaye and Keith McClelland, eds., *E. P. Thompson: Critical Perspectives* (Philadelphia: Temple University Press, 1990); and Harvey J. Kaye, *British Marxist Historians: An Introductory Analysis* (New York: Polity Press, 1984). For Montgomery, see James R. Barrett, "Remembering David Montgomery (1926–2011) and His Impact on Working-Class History," *Labour/Le Travail* 70 (fall 2012): 203–23; Shelton Stromquist, "David Montgomery: A Labor Historian's Legacies," *Journal of the Gilded Age and Progressive Era* 13.2 (April 2014): 256–76; and a forum on Montgomery, Eric Arnesen, et al., "David Montgomery and the Shaping of the New Labor History," *Labor: Studies of Working-Class History of the Americas* 10.1 (spring 2013): 47–80.

24. Naison and Buhle, "Interview with E. P. Thompson," 11–12, 13. On Thompson's years as an adult educator, see Peter Searby et al., "Edward Thompson as a Teacher: Yorkshire and Warwick," in *Protest and Survival: The Historical Experience: Essays for E. P. Thompson,* edited by John Rule and Robert Malcolmson (London: Merlin Press, 1993), 1–23. Thompson finished his degree in English literature and history at Cambridge before turning to adult education in West Yorkshire in 1948.

25. Searby et al., "Edward Thompson as a Teacher," 1, 17, 9.

26. Thompson quoted in Naison and Buhle, "Interview with E. P. Thompson," 14. Thompson's gendered language and failure to take account of working-class women's experience has been much commented upon by Joan W. Scott and Anna Clark, among others.

27. Thompson quoted in Naison and Buhle, "Interview with E. P. Thompson," 13.

28. Palmer, *E. P. Thompson,* 60. See also Palmer's insightful analysis of Thompson's decision to resign from the Communist Party of Great Britain (CPGB)in 1956, 62–63, 72–77.

29. Palmer, *E. P. Thompson*, 100; Staughton Lynd, "In Memoriam: E. P. Thompson," *Georgetown Law Journal* 82.6 (July 1994): 2013.

30. The quotations from reviews of *MEWC* quoted in this chapter (Scott, 1991; Erdman, 1964; R. K. Webb, 1964–65; and Tilly, 1968) are found in Eric Arnesen, "E. P. Thompson's *The Making of the English Working Class*: Assessments after a Half Century," and in Lara Kriegel, "How It Feels to Be Fifty: E. P. Thompson and Cultural History, Past, Present, and Future," both in *Labor: Studies in Working-Class History of the Americas* 10.3 (fall 2013): 27–28 and 31–32.

31. Quoted in Searby et al., "Edward Thompson as a Teacher," 19, 22, 19, 19–20.

32. E. P. Thompson, "Highly Confidential: A Personal Comment by the Editor," in *Warwick University Ltd.: Industry, Management and the Universities*, edited by E. P. Thompson (Hammondsworth, U.K.: Penguin, 1970), 157, also quoted in Palmer, *E. P. Thompson*, 109.

33. Thompson quoted in Naison and Buhle, "Interview with E. P. Thompson," 14.

34. Thompson, *Warwick University Ltd.*, 86.

35. The details of this episode are recounted in ibid., 46–59. See also Palmer, *E. P. Thompson*, 109–12.

36. Thompson, *Warwick University Ltd.*, 86, 106–7.

37. "Report of N. P. Catchpole, Legal Adviser of the Rootes Organization, of the meeting of the Coventry Labour Party on 3 March 1969," reproduced in Thompson, *Warwick University Ltd.*, 107–8. Foreigners could be prosecuted under the 1914 Alien Restriction Act, as amended in 1919, for "sedition" or for attempting "to promote industrial unrest in any industry," under pain of fine or imprisonment. "Alien Restriction Act (Amended) 1919, Section 3, Incitement to Sedition, etc.," www.legislation.gov.uk, accessed October 5, 2014.

38. Thompson, "Highly Confidential," 164.

39. Thompson quoted in Naison and Buhle, "Interview with E. P. Thompson," 22.

40. Thompson spoke of his reasons for "looking backward" to the eighteenth century and his distrust of his critically engaging, as a historian, more recent history (post-1945) "because I am too much in there myself" (ibid., 14–16). Especially noteworthy works on the eighteenth century that Thompson published in the 1970s were "The Moral Economy of the Crowd in the 18th Century," *Past and Present*, 50 (1971); "Patrician Society, Plebeian Culture," *Journal of Social History* 7.4 (summer 1974); *Whigs and Hunters* (New York: Pantheon, 1974); and "Eighteenth-Century English Society: Class Struggle without Class?" *Social History* 3.2 (May 1978). Also see a collection of his essays on the eighteenth century, *Customs in Common: Studies in Traditional Popular Culture* (New York: New Press, 1991).

41. A partial list of visiting appointments is the University of Pittsburgh (1975) and Rutgers University (1976), and visiting lectures at the University of Toronto (1978) and Brown University (1980). Palmer, *E. P. Thompson*, 121. Thompson's Pittsburgh visit produced a memorable opportunity for a critical encounter with zealous proponents of modernization theory, which had been a longstanding target of his and Montgomery's criticism, implicit and at times explicit in their own efforts to recover working-class resistance to capitalism. One encounter, ironically, occurred after Thompson's departure. Julius Rubin, a U.S. economic historian, much enamored with modernization theory, circulated a paper after Thompson left criticizing at some length Thompson's "The Moral Economy of the Crowd in the 18th Century." After learning belatedly of the paper, Thompson furiously asked why Rubin had not had the courtesy and intellectual courage to offer his critique while he was in residence and could have replied. He was left only the option of pouring his anger into a biting, classic Thompsonian seventy-page rejoinder, which he titled "Don't Tread on Me" (copy in the author's possession). For a brief mention of this episode (though the details are

not altogether accurate) and how the paper never came to be published, see Scott Hamilton, *The Crisis of Theory: E. P. Thompson, the New Left and Postwar British Politics* (Manchester, U.K.: Manchester University Press, 2011), 221–23.

42. Thompson's return to serious theoretical debate within Marxism was signaled by his publication of "An Open Letter to Leszek Kolakowski," *Socialist Register 1973*, edited by Ralph Miliband and John Saville (London: Merlin Press, 1974), 1–100, and his challenge to the structuralism of Althusser and his followers, *The Poverty of Theory and Other Essays* (New York: Monthly Review Press, 1978). For useful discussions of these debates, see Thompson quoted in Naison and Buhle, "Interview with E. P. Thompson," 10, 16–18; and Palmer, *E. P. Thompson*, 115–25.

43. E. P. Thompson, introduction, in *Writing by Candlelight* (London: Merlin Press, 1980), x–xiv. See also "The State of the Nation" (first published in 1979 in *New Society*) in that volume, 191–256. On his professed boredom with discussions about the current state of Marxism, see his letter to Bryan Palmer, November 1980, cited in Palmer, *E. P. Thompson*, 125.

44. Palmer, *E. P. Thompson*, 126, 128–29, 142. Among Thompson's voluminous writings on the peace movement during these years, his most widely distributed and influential may have been "A Letter to America," in *Protest and Survive*, edited by E. P. Thompson and Dan Smith (London: Monthly Review Press, 1981), 3–52.

45. David Montgomery, "The Conventional Wisdom," *Labor History* 13.1 (winter 1972): 108–36 (quotations on 110, 135) is a detailed, largely critical review of the reissue of sixty books of the mostly institutional "old labor history." Gerald Grob's *Workers and Utopia: A Study of Ideological Conflict in the American Labor Movement, 1865–1900* (Evanston, Ill.: Northwestern University Press, 1961) had provided an updated rendering of the Commons School's interpretation of the National Labor Union and the Knights of Labor as ephemeral and marginal to the development of trade unionism and the AFL. Philip Taft provided the most direct link to the Commons tradition, having authored (with Selig Perlman) the last volume in Commons's coauthored *History of Labor in the United States* and his own two definitive volumes on the history of the AFL, *The A.F. of L in the Time of Gompers* (New York: Octagon Books, 1957) and *The A.F. of L. from the Death of Gompers to the Merger* (New York: Harper, 1959).

46. Naison and Buhle, "Interview with David Montgomery," 170.

47. Ibid.

48. Ibid., 173.

49. Ibid., 170–71, 173, 175.

50. Those historians earned their doctorates as follows: Herbert Gutman at the University of Wisconsin in 1959; David Brody at Harvard University in 1958; and Melvyn Dubofsky at the University of Rochester in 1960.

51. David Montgomery, *Beyond Equality: Labor and the Radical Republicans, 1862–1872* (New York: Alfred A. Knopf, 1967), vii, x, 446–47.

52. In addition to Ira Steward and William Sylvis, the transatlantic labor reformer and utopian John F. Bray, author of *Labour's Wrongs and Labour's Remedies or the Age of Might and the Age of Right* (Leeds, U.K.: David Green, 1839), always held a special place in Montgomery's heart (and his seminars and lectures), as did World War I militants Samuel Lavit (Bridgeport) and Fred Merrick (East Pittsburgh) and a host of other rank-and-file leaders and self-taught labor intellectuals.

53. Naison and Buhle, "Interview with David Montgomery," 179.

54. Palmer, *E. P. Thompson*, 49–51, 82–83, 88–99, 128–38; and Searby et al., "Edward Thompson as a Teacher," 3–4. See also Sheila Rowbotham, "'Our Party Is the People': Edward Carpenter and Radicalism in Sheffield," and Robert Malcolmson, "Fear and Hope in the Nuclear Age," both in Rule and Malcolmson, *Protest and Survival*, 257–58 and 394–416; and Bryan D. Palmer, *The Making of E. P. Thompson: Marxism, Humanism, and History* (Toronto: New Hogtown Press, 1981), 32–37, 45–51.

55. David Montgomery spoke of a "new syndicalism" with attributes "never before seen in the American labor movement," in *What's Happening to the American Worker?*, Radical America pamphlet, Madison, Wisc., 1970, 24.

56. Longtime president of the UE, Albert Fitzgerald, spoke of the enthusiasm with which members at the annual convention greeted his talks. He suggested that David should be "an annual fixture" because he "brought them more things that they can work on than anyone else that speaks before our conventions." LAWCHA, the Labor and Working-Class History Association, http://lawcha.org, accessed January 17, 2016.

57. See remembrances of Al Hart, UE editor, and John Wilhelm, UNITE HERE past president. Wilhelm recalled Montgomery's outspoken support for the Yale workers right to organize and his criticism of the university's antiunion campaign. LAWCHA, http://lawcha.org, accessed January 17, 2016. See also Toni Gilpin et al., *On Strike for Respect: The Clerical and Technical Workers' Strike at Yale University, 1984–85* (Chicago: Charles H. Kerr, 1988).

58. One among many reminiscences of Pittsburgh and Yale students is by Richard Bradley, a former Yale undergraduate, who wrote in a blog: "I could never think of David Montgomery as shy; I never saw him away from the lecture hall, where he was so enamored of his material, so completely convinced of its import and, I think you could say, its beauty, that he lost himself in it entirely; he became a man transformed. I had never had a professor so passionate about a subject so foreign to me (I was 17 at the time)." Shots in the Dark, www.richardbradley.net, accessed January 17, 2016. Or my own remembrance: "He was, of course, one of the great lecturers of his generation of scholars. Equal parts stump speaker, scholar, and public intellectual extraordinaire, he lectured seamlessly, weaving together the telling anecdote, the voice of the worker him or herself, and his brilliant insights into the broader patterns of social and historical change. But ALWAYS at the center of the story were the workers as the agents of change, the central actors in their own times, and as the reason we should care about the past (and the present)." LAWCHA, http://lawcha.org, accessed January 17, 2016.

59. We at Pittsburgh were also deeply enriched by the unique intellectual and political comradeship our colleague, scientist-mathematician-turned-historian, Steve Sapolsky practiced so generously. Always the sympathetic critic and reader of our work, even at the expense of his own, Steve inspired a special quality of community among us. We lost him much too early.

60. Montgomery quoted in Naison and Buhle, "Interview with David Montgomery," 179.

61. Thompson quoted in Naison and Buhle, "Interview with E. P. Thompson," 10.

62. Thompson, introduction, in *Writing by Candlelight*, xii–xiii.

63. Labor poets and troubadours were hardly outliers in Montgomery's lectures. He is fondly remembered for breaking into song during his lectures or re-creating, with the aid of his teaching assistants, a rendition of Paul Robson's performance of the "Ballad for Americans."

64. David Montgomery, *The Fall of the House of Labor: The Workplace, the State, and American Labor Activism, 1865–1925* (New York: Cambridge University Press, 1987), 7–8.

65. Much of the new work on the Knights of Labor was showcased at a 1979 Newberry Library conference, at which Montgomery and Herbert Gutman presided, on the 100th anniversary of the official founding of the Knights of Labor.

66. A sampler of some of the key works that contributed to this reinterpretation of the nineteenth-century working class includes Sean Wilentz, "Against Exceptionalism: Class Consciousness and the American Labor Movement, 1790–1920," *International Labor and Working-Class History* 26 (fall 1984): 1–24; Leon Fink, "The New Labor History and the Powers of Historical Pessimism: Consensus, Hegemony and the Case of the Knights of Labor," *Journal of American History* 75 (June 1988): 115–36; and of course Montgomery's own "Labor and the Republic in Industrial America, 1860–1920," *Le Mouvement Social* 111 (1980), 201–15. See also Sean Wilentz, *Chants Democratic: New York City and the Rise of the American Working Class, 1788–1850* (New York: Oxford University Press, 1984); Paul G. Faler, *Mechanics and Manufacturers in the Early Industrial Revolution: Lynn, Massachusetts, 1780–1860* (Albany: State University of New York Press, 1981); and Alan Dawley. *Class and Community: The Industrial Revolution in Lynn* (Cambridge, Mass.: Harvard University Press, 1976).

67. Such local studies included works by James Barrett, Peter Rachleff, Bruce Laurie, Cecelia Bucki, Shelton Stromquist, Peter Gottlieb, and John Bennett in the Pittsburgh context; at other centers were Alan Dawley, Leon Fink, Susan Levine, Jon Garlock, Bryan Palmer, Greg Kealey, among many others.

68. Influential work recasting the history of liberalism included James Weinstein, *The Corporate Ideal in the Liberal State, 1900–1918* (Boston: Beacon Press, 1968); Martin Sklar, *The Corporate Reconstruction of American Capitalism, 1890–1916: The Market, the Law, and Politics* (New York: Cambridge University Press, 1988); and Richard Schneirov, *Labor and Urban Politics: Class Conflict and the Origins of Modern Liberalism in Chicago, 1864–97* (Urbana: University of Illinois Press, 1998). For an account of the "Progressive Era" roots of this liberalism, see Stromquist, *Reinventing "the People."*

69. These themes are highlighted in a number of recent anthologies, including Donna Haverty-Stacke and Daniel Walkowitz, eds., *Rethinking U.S. Labor History: Essays on the Working-Class Experience, 1756–2009* (New York: Continuum Press, 2010); Richard Greenwald and Daniel Katz, eds., *Labor Rising: the Past and Future of Working People in America* (New York: New Press, 2012); and with a focus on global and transnational working-class history, Leon Fink et al., *Workers across the Americas: The Transnational Turn in Labor History* (New York: Oxford University Press, 2011). A collection of newer work by David Montgomery's students, across the generations, is Eric Arnesen, Julie Greene, and Bruce Laurie, eds., *Labor Histories: Class, Politics, and the Working-Class Experience* (Urbana: University of Illinois Press, 1998).

PART I

Encountering Conflict, Power, and Hope
On the Front Line

Encountering Conflict, Power, and Hope

On the Front Line

John Williams-Searle

As Shelton Stromquist reminds us, the connection between research, education, and activism was present at the birth of labor history. Throughout the twentieth century, historians and labor scholars believed that they could and should shape society. Especially in the latter half of the century, men and women of diverse backgrounds used their historical training to pose new and urgent questions, influencing and being influenced by important social justice movements. Progressive academics also got out of the classroom, participating in picket lines, sit-ins, teach-ins, protest marches, and union drives.

In this section, authors Ralph Scharnau, Daniel E. Atkinson, Stephen Meyer, Michael Innis-Jiménez, and Sam Davies argue that history can inspire activism, lay the groundwork for social justice struggles, and link different movements united by common concerns or strategies. Moreover, they emphasize the ways in which particular moments of conflict—historical, as well as personal and scholarly—shape these processes. Although the working class and social justice allies remain a heterogeneous group, recognizing elements of a shared history allows us to imagine a broader, more hopeful, and vibrant movement well positioned to counter injustice collectively. Alliances created by teachers, students, the public, and progressive institutions have been the targets of a sustained assault, especially by conservative political elites. The ferocity of that assault, the millions of dollars spent to attack, discredit, and disempower these alliances indicate that collective action among progressives—even in the absence of clear victories—poses a threat to the power of various elites. Hope for change might be difficult to sustain in the face of such assaults. The chapters in this section tell stories of struggle and even defeat. But they also point to successes and offer hope, including the value and power of connections between scholarly research, teaching, and activism.

Ralph Scharnau's account of the establishment and eventual dissolution of the faculty union at the University of Dubuque (UD) illustrates a moment of backlash and opportunity. As Scharnau demonstrates in "Beyond *Yeshiva*: The

Struggle for Faculty Power at the University of Dubuque," UD served as an early model for the corporatization of the university. A working-class kid who grew up to become part of the professoriate in the midst of the social movements of the late 1960s, Scharnau was critical to the early and successful establishment at UD of an NEA-affiliated faculty union, which was formed against the backdrop of student protests against the lack of racial diversity on campus. As collective bargaining began to transform the living and working conditions of the university's faculty, administrators seized on the opportunity created by the 1980 Supreme Court decision, *NLRB v. Yeshiva University* (ruling that faculty members in private institutions could not unionize since they served as managers) to decertify the UD faculty union. Despite the ruling and decertification, however, a core group of faculty activists, including Scharnau, resisted the reassertion of administrative dominance, using a combination of organizing and the administration's own faculty handbook to exercise a measure of control for almost two more decades. Although the administration would eventually put a stop to such resistance—in large part by claiming economic necessity to dissolve departments with key activists—the long struggle at UD demonstrated not only the power of administrators but also the potential influence that could be wielded by even a small group of committed and imaginative activists.

The opportunities attendant to linking education and progressive activism are also apparent in the reaction of prison authorities to Daniel Atkinson's research at the Louisiana State Penitentiary at Angola. In "'Feets Don't Fail Me Now': Navigating an Unpaved, Rocky Road to, through, and from the Last Slave Plantation," Atkinson describes his dissertation research and reactions to its ramifications at the penitentiary. Prison officials resisted Atkinson when he tried to examine black vernacular responses to white supremacy through oral interviews and recording inmate music. Atkinson's efforts to combine scholarship and activism struck a nerve when his ethnographic efforts became "something resembling a twenty-first-century slave narrative."

Atkinson's work went beyond mere ethnographic recovery to ask a fundamental question about why Louisiana expended such large sums on incarcerating nonviolent men for decades while preventing them from becoming productive, tax-paying citizens. When Atkinson's work threatened to reveal the humanity of inmates by questioning the entire plantation prison system, officials recognized the threat that Atkinson's work posed to the state's apparatus of racial control and even terror. Although the combination of research and activism in the pursuit of engaged protest limited Atkinson's employment opportunities, the cultural truth of his scholarship was apparent in the institutional resistance it engendered.

"Wandering through the Wisconsin Uprising," Stephen Meyer's personal account of the 2011 protests, acknowledges the role that a progressive historical tradition—when combined with activist educators and working-class allies—can have on sustained public protest. In response to Governor Scott Walker's issuing of Act 10, which attempted to eviscerate public-sector unionism in Wisconsin, the public drew on the state's long association with twentieth-century progressivism and descended on Madison in force to protest Walker's claims that "Wisconsin [was] open for business." Decades of studying and living labor history allowed Meyer and academic allies both to contextualize the actions of the protesters and to make connections with a tradition of activism in Wisconsin. This history inspired people's fight for their rights and fostered their belief that public protest could help address injustice.

Although Wisconsin's progressive past fueled the protest that demanded political change through a recall election to remove Scott Walker and his cronies, the recall failed and Walker remained in power. Meyer found that "a million signatures and the creativity, innovation, and energy of protesters were all trumped by money and duplicity." It is true that the Koch brothers, operating through groups such as the Wisconsin Club for Growth and Americans for Prosperity, were able to suppress progressivism in the state. It is also true, however, that the bottom-up movement frightened political elites into spending exorbitant amounts of money to counter the power of this broad coalition engaged in public activism.

As Michael Innis-Jiménez demonstrates, such potential for public activism and engaged academics also existed in Alabama in the aftermath of two disasters, "one natural and one manmade." In the spring of 2011, tornadoes had devastated communities across Alabama, including several Latino immigrant neighborhoods. Simultaneously, the state's Republican politicians, who (like their Wisconsin counterparts) found themselves in control of both legislative houses and the governor's office, launched HB 56, the Beason-Hammon Alabama Taxpayer and Citizen Protection Act. This manmade disaster of a bill was cynically designed to make life so inhospitable for Alabama's immigrant and Hispanic population that they would leave the state. Already suffering in communities devastated by tornadoes, the state's Latinos and Latinas now also feared attending public schools and could not easily do any business that required a contract. Innis-Jiménez's essay, "Immigrants in a Disaster Zone: Teaching, Learning, and Advocating Alabama's New Civil Rights Movement," recounts how the students in his service learning class studied the historical context of Alabama's antagonistic attitude toward recent immigrants, conducted oral interviews with immigrant residents, and began to understand the interrelated dynamics of activism, empathy, and humanity.

The ways that history provides context, as well as inspiration, in the pursuit of social justice was made clear to Innis-Jiménez's students when they attended a protest rally against HB 56. A multiethnic, multiracial group of over four thousand people gathered on November 21, 2011, at a symbolic site for an earlier civil rights movement: Birmingham's Sixteenth Street Baptist Church, the hallowed ground where four African American girls were murdered in a 1963 Ku Klux Klan bombing. Despite Governor Robert Bentley's efforts to distance contemporary demands for immigrant rights from the legacy of the 1960s, the prominent participation of civil rights campaigners from that era made the connection explicit. Labor, religious, and social justice organizations drew up an intertwined history of racial activism and rights protest in Alabama, reestablishing historic alliances and reaffirming their commitment to civil rights. During the course, Innis-Jiménez's students began to understand how history could influence activism. While the ultimate legislative results were mixed (HB 56 was only partially invalidated), it is clear that service learning contributed to students' new interest in civic engagement and activism.

The final essay in this section, Sam Davies's "Remembering the 1911 General Transport Strike in Liverpool," allows us to recognize that U.S. progressives do not hold a monopoly on using the past to educate and inspire activism. Davies's account of academic historians' and labor activists' plans to celebrate the centenary of the 1911 Liverpool strike reveals that using history to inform the contemporary labor movement can help to revitalize labor activism. Although the public had heard about the Liverpool strike because of the infamous Bloody Sunday shootings, there were assumptions—especially concerning the religious backgrounds of the shooting victims—that made the public's understanding of the strike rather hazy. As Davies demonstrates, new research undertaken to celebrate the centenary revitalized alliances between academics, trade unionists, and the public and galvanized the present-day labor movement. Like the U.S. scholars in this section, Davies recognizes that contemporary events often serve to foreshorten the distance between the past and present.

The chapters in part 1 reveal that academics and activists can form a potent partnership, sometimes bringing together disparate groups and inspiring them to tackle social, economic, and political injustices. The broad-based protests launched against Act 10 in Wisconsin and HB 56 in Alabama, for example, were fueled and inspired by a recognition of a shared history. Furthermore, by connecting academic research and activism, we see that knowledge can, indeed, plant seeds of hope, underpin progressive social movements, and ultimately reorient power for a more just society.

CHAPTER 2

Beyond *Yeshiva*

The Struggle for Faculty Power at the University of Dubuque

Ralph Scharnau

Labor scholars too often overlook their own workplaces. Even today, faculty unionization at colleges and universities remains a remarkably unexplored field. According to higher education professor Gary Rhoades, "One can read much higher education literature and not discover faculty unions exist. One can read many of the most widely read books on higher education and not learn that faculty unions exist. One can get a master's or doctoral degree in many Higher Education programs, and gain no knowledge of faculty unions."[1]

This essay relates my experiences with faculty unionism at the University of Dubuque (UD), a private liberal arts college and seminary in Dubuque, Iowa. As a member of the National Education Association (NEA), I helped organize our local; negotiated our first contract; held several local, state, and national leadership positions; filed grievances; went out on strike with my coworkers; and generally fought management initiatives to contain and control faculty unrest. The NEA local union offices I held included president, vice president, grievance committee member, and chief contract negotiator.

On the whole, this essay provides a firsthand account by a labor historian of the achievement and subsequent loss of collective bargaining among faculty in higher education. At least until the recent attacks on the rights of public-sector faculty, as Stephen Meyer shows in chapter 4, opportunities for such accounts were relatively rare. In the public sector, some faculty bargained in accordance with stable (if not always generous or widespread) enabling legislation on a state-by-state basis, and, in the private sector, such bargaining, initiated on a few campuses during the 1970s, had largely come to an end following the U.S. Supreme Court's 1980 ruling in *NLRB v. Yeshiva University* (NLRB stands for National Labor Relations Board), in which the court decertified the Yeshiva faculty union on the basis that its members had supervisory powers, functioned as managers, and hence were not eligible for bargaining status.

Our struggle at UD paralleled that at Yeshiva, a private, Jewish institution in New York, and was shaped decisively by that landmark case. This essay, however, seeks to go beyond established narratives about *Yeshiva* and its legacy in two ways. First, in shifting the center of the story from New York to Iowa, it reveals the extent to which the struggle for faculty power at private colleges and universities during the 1970s extended well beyond the Northeast.[2] Created in 1972, the UD local was not only the first group of professors at a four-year college or university in Iowa to bargain collectively but the first such organization formed at a private liberal arts college west of the Mississippi River (a claim also made by faculty at Loretto Heights College in Denver, Colorado).[3] Next, while *Yeshiva* is often seen as an endpoint in narratives of collective bargaining among faculty at private institutions (even if only to set off more recent organizing attempts in the post-*Yeshiva* era), the UD example demonstrates ways in which faculty adapted to the new legal terrain and carried on their struggle for power and justice for almost two decades after the decision.[4] The UD story, therefore, suggests both the challenges and opportunities to academics as union activists in the long battle against the corporatization of the U.S. university. Or, as I learned, when top UD administrators used the phrase, "we are all family here," they meant sacrificing faculty rights on the altar of administrative control.

*   *   *

My personal journey to faculty union activism relates to my class background. I grew up in a household with a father who worked as a laborer in nonunion factories, one of which was an auto parts plant where repeated unionization attempts met employer hostility and ended in failure. My mother ran a small neighborhood grocery store. Participation in protests during the turbulent 1960s provided the impetus for my emergence as a peace and justice activist. After earning an undergraduate degree in sociology, I focused on history during graduate studies at the University of Illinois and Northern Illinois University. The long quest for a dissertation topic ultimately led me to write a profile of Thomas J. Morgan, a Chicago machinist, labor leader, and socialist.[5]

Having completed the coursework for the PhD at Northern Illinois University but lacking the financial resources to continue, I accepted a full-time faculty appointment at a Methodist-affiliated, private liberal arts school, McKendree College, in Lebanon, Illinois, where I taught from 1965 to 1970. These years witnessed a nationwide surge in unionization among higher education employees, led by the professoriate. My first experience with a faculty association occurred at McKendree when I joined the local chapter of the American Association of University Professors (AAUP). A professional organization founded in 1915, the AAUP held aloft the principles of academic freedom and academic tenure and set the standards for faculty rights, due-process procedures, and working conditions. But it was not until 1972 that the organization endorsed collective bargaining, and then only after the advent of bargaining on more and more campuses and some local chapters seeking such recognition. The McKendree chapter was not one of these pioneers, however. Our local chapter sponsored speakers and social gatherings, but no significant governance, curricular, or compensation issues roiled the academic waters during my time there.[6]

My first experience with bargaining came at UD, where, after completing my doctorate (and competing against a glut of freshly minted PhDs), I accepted a job in 1970. Affiliated with the Presbyterian Church, the school had both a private liberal arts college and a seminary with a single governing board. Unlike the seminary, the college received minimal financial and other support from the church. At the time, UD, along with the city's two Roman Catholic liberal arts colleges, Loras and Clarke, formed a tri-college consortium. My position at UD involved teaching U.S. history classes and serving as head of the social studies division. In my first year there, I designed and began teaching a new one semester survey course titled American Labor History. I also began paying dues to the local AAUP chapter.[7] Based on my experience at McKendree, I fully expected to find UD to be a traditional college where a "community of scholars" engaged in teaching and research, played a central role in decision making, and enjoyed the protection of tenure. Instead, the years from 1970 to 1999 coincided with an unrelenting struggle between the faculty and the administration fueled by chronic financial hardships.

While the beginnings of these struggles arose out of particular incidents that were themselves part of the political legacy of the 1960s, their later manifestations reflected a pattern of conflict that became commonplace in U.S. higher education institutions. Despite their disciplinary differences, faculty members tend to see their roles of teaching, research, and service as the central features of higher education. Administrators, on the other hand, look on their own activities as the essence of college life.[8] When campuses erupt with faculty or student activism, administrators and board members usually stand firmly opposed to any concessions. At UD, one such eruption created the conditions that spurred unionization. The university had only one black professor, a Kenyan, who voluntarily left for another position at the end of the 1970–71 academic year. During my first two years on campus, three white faculty members were unilaterally fired for unexplained financial reasons. Protest erupted among faculty and students about the dismissed faculty. Besides protesting the faculty cuts, black students condemned campus racial bias and called for the hiring of black instructors in every department, adding a black studies major, and adopting an open admission policy for black students. Some black and white students went on strike and briefly occupied three campus buildings in March 1972. Direct appeals to the university president to reinstate the terminated faculty went unheeded, as did the black students' demands.[9]

The local association contacted the state AAUP, explaining that the arbitrary faculty discharges occurred without faculty consultation. The state AAUP contacted the president, but he was unwilling to respond to complaints about personnel matters. He argued to the UD community, instead, that financial exigency, an

AAUP-recognized ground for terminating appointments, dictated the dismissal decisions. He rejected AAUP's position that UD should follow due-process procedures of faculty-administration cooperation on termination criteria and hearing rights. Like many small colleges with little history of shared governance, the UD administration operated by managerial fiat.[10]

If the administration could summarily terminate faculty and cut programs while defying the AAUP, faculty concluded they needed to organize to protect their rights and interests. With about 75 percent of the UD faculty supporting union representation, we called a special faculty meeting and invited representatives from the AAUP, NEA, and the American Federation of Teachers (AFT) to discuss the advantages of forming a union in the spring of 1972. At this meeting, the group voted to affiliate with the NEA primarily because a cadre of NEA members already existed in the college's Education Department. Furthermore, the NEA had a well-organized network for support and advocacy that was in the process of advancing the bargaining power of public-sector teachers across the state.[11]

One of the first points of contention with the administration came over the definition of the bargaining unit. At the unit determination hearings conducted by the National Labor Relations Board office in Peoria, Illinois, the lawyer for the administration argued that department and division heads should not be eligible for bargaining status since they were supervisors. A Des Moines attorney, on retainer with the Teamsters and hired by the NEA, served as our legal counsel during the hearings. He pointed out that using the university's formula would result in one supervisor for every one-and-a-half faculty members. Although the hearing officer sided with us, the university refused to accept his determination and appealed the decision.[12] After months of stalemate, our counsel advised us that the NLRB stipulated that management could create a line of supervisors and that designating the five division heads as supervisors would likely resolve the dispute and move the process toward union recognition. The administration agreed to make division heads supervisors and hence not part of the bargaining unit. Recognizing the faculty's continuing solid support for a union, the administration gave our NEA group consent recognition. I immediately resigned my position as division head so I could become part of the bargaining unit.[13]

The first collectively bargained contract between UD's Faculty Association in the College of Liberal Arts and the University Board of Directors was signed in 1974. It took fourteen months to reach the agreement. During negotiations, the union periodically surveyed the faculty for their reactions to contractual wording. Like other higher education contracts, the management rights clauses gave the administration the traditional power to terminate faculty because of financial distress or modification or discontinuance of a program or department. Union negotiators, however, firmly rejected the administration's attempt to impose work rules. The new contract included faculty participation in evaluation, teaching load, retention, promotion, tenure, and grievance procedures as well as curriculum and salaries. It also included a strongly worded statement on academic freedom and appended the AAUP statement on student rights and freedoms.[14]

During the late 1970s, the organized faculty association successfully raised salaries, improved benefits, ensured equal treatment for women, and protected academic freedom. The union also filed unfair labor practices charges with the NLRB as a device to counter perceived administrative abuses of the contract. Meanwhile, the administration continued its efforts to strengthen management power and curb faculty power in a campaign designed to discredit and ultimately destroy the union. These efforts included the board's attempt to eliminate tenure or introduce tenure quotas, which met strong opposition from union negotiators. The university then hired a prominent union-busting law firm. The university also hired consultants as a means to move academic matters toward full administrative control, a strategy that repeatedly failed.[15]

With each contract, tensions increased. In the summer of 1981, negotiations reached an impasse over a salary and curriculum dispute. The faculty union set up an informational picket line. Despite bringing in a federal mediator, the stalemate continued. A clear majority of the union membership then voted to strike. The union pickets carried signs, shouted pro-union slogans, sang traditional union songs, and devoted one day to dressing in our formal academic garb. The administration responded by listing jobs of striking faculty in the help-wanted sections of the *Chicago Tribune*, the *Des Moines Register*, and the *Dubuque Telegraph Herald*. The union built solidarity with a telephone tree and social gatherings. Rallies of support were held on the quad but included only a smattering of students because classes were not yet in session. The NEA provided solid backing for the strikers. A few faculty members, mostly in business and economics, distanced themselves from us and crossed our picket lines. Local union officials from the United Auto Workers, Teamsters, the American Federation of State, County, and Municipal Employees, and the Dubuque Federation of Labor, as well as state NEA officers and union leaders from the NEA local at Kirkwood Community College, made their presence known on campus. These fellow unionists occasionally marched with us and contributed money. The weekly local labor paper, the *Dubuque Leader*, carried accounts of the walkout. The eleven-day strike ended when an agreement was reached with the help of the mediator on the first day of classes. The faculty won a nearly 25 percent salary increase over three years.[16]

Shortly after the strike ended, the university mounted a new and far more effective strategy to end collective bargaining. In the fall of 1983, taking advantage of the opening created by the *Yeshiva* decision, UD filed a decertification petition with the NLRB, claiming that college faculty unionization at its institution was illegal as well. While awaiting the response to its filing, the administration tried to make faculty members appear as supervisors by putting them on certain planning committees. The committees, however, had power to make only recommendations to the administration; the real decisions were still made by the board.[17]

Overtures by the faculty union to discuss differences with the president and dean were rebuffed. The student newspaper and the student government association adopted a resolution calling on the administration to reconsider its action as detrimental to the school, students, faculty, and faculty-administration relations. All faculty and student appeals for reversal of the decision to seek decertification failed. Finally, in 1988, the NLRB followed the same arguments used in *Yeshiva* and ruled two to one that the UD faculty were "managerial employees" and hence not eligible for union status.[18] The ruling ended fifteen years of collective bargaining among college faculty at UD.[19]

Following the dramatic and sudden blow of decertification, the task of rebuilding faculty solidarity proved daunting. The NEA staff and lawyers told us that appealing the NLRB ruling to the federal court would be a long and very expensive process with little likelihood of success. Overturning the NLRB decision, then, was not an option. Meetings were called to consider faculty action. But these gatherings soon became little more than short-lived, faculty-led "therapy sessions," with most faculty members accepting the union loss as a fait accompli and returning to their regular professional routines. Several faculty, however, continued their affiliations with the AAUP and the NEA in the hope that a solution could be found. In 1990, unconvinced that the associations could accomplish much, I finally decided to take action on my own. Seeking a more diverse union environment and with friends in the Dubuque labor movement affiliated with the AFL-CIO, I embarked on a personal campaign to sign up AFT members on campus. Fifteen faculty members opted for the associate membership category, while only three of us chose full membership.[20] But neither the AAUP, nor the NEA, nor the AFT could offer the organizing, financial, and legal support necessary to mount a campaign that stood a real chance of regaining collective bargaining status.

Only one avenue offered a potential way to secure at least a modicum of faculty power. The faculty handbook had traditionally functioned as a brief guide to generally accepted professional standards and expectations. Rather than simply impose a new handbook, the UD Board of Directors, in their largess, decided that they would work with the faculty to create a new, post-bargaining era governance document. In a December 1988 memorandum, the chairman of the board called for collegial board-faculty discussions to develop a new legally binding and mutually approved handbook. A group of faculty met regularly with the board's representatives to draft the new handbook. Completion of the year-long drafting process was accompanied by a generous across-the-board salary increase of 8 percent, which many faculty saw as a sop for the loss of collective bargaining. Aside from placing final decision making squarely in the hands of the board, the handbook language was largely extracted from the old contract.[21]

The new handbook stated that changes required mutual agreement between the faculty and the board and that the terms of the handbook would be legally enforceable. The "mutually agreed" and "legally enforceable" wording gave the faculty a degree of power, making the handbook akin to a contract. In accepting the handbook, it seems the board wanted to act quickly to curb any lingering militancy and to open a new era of rapprochement with the faculty. At the same time, the administration thought the faculty would understand and accept that ultimate decision-making power rested firmly and unequivocally with the board. The handbook provided for an Amendment and Revision Committee, composed of elected faculty, which would consider proposals to modify the handbook. Any modifications required majority approval of the faculty and acceptance by the board. Concerned about the administration's ongoing effort to co-opt the faculty, and unwilling to yield faculty rights, the committee adopted the "mutually agreed to" clause as a mechanism for blocking administrative proposals that faculty found repugnant.[22]

Over time, however, the administration and the board became increasingly frustrated with faculty rejection of management revision proposals. By 1996, the administration had begun characterizing the faculty as led by dissenters with no interest in teamwork, and the situation moved toward a crisis. Following the university president's unexpected resignation that same year, the board selected an interim president who also happened to serve as chairman of the board of directors. Thus the head of the university held nearly unchecked power. He staged a series of campus meetings with faculty and students, calling for a new era of unity. Finally, he cautioned that, if the faculty failed to accept handbook altera- tions, he possessed full authority to impose a new handbook. Tensions between the faculty and the administration reached a breaking point in January 1997, when the faculty voted to accept my motion to hire a lawyer and start a legal defense fund.[23]

The simmering conflict entered a final phase when the administration suddenly decided to launch twin assaults by taking aggressive actions to assert its power. In March 1998, the university took an unprecedented step by suing the faculty. In a *Chronicle of Higher Education* article, reporter Robin Wilson wrote, "No one who studies higher-education governance recalls another case of trustees taking professors to court."[24] The administration argued that the handbook was simply a policy, not a contractual obligation. Therefore, the board had the exclusive right to impose a new handbook at any time and in any way it deemed appropriate. Imposing a new handbook, moreover, required no consultation with the faculty since the board's policy-making powers were ultimate and unilateral.[25]

The other part of the board's assault surfaced in the guise of a so-called Plan for Transformation, which provided for sweeping program changes and terminating significant numbers of faculty. These changes, developed without faculty consulta- tion, generated faculty and student protest. On March 19, 1999, the new university president (who had replaced the interim president in 1998) called meetings of the students, faculty, and staff to explain the plan and push for its implementation during the 1999–2000 academic year. The president claimed that the changes were necessitated by a fiscal emergency, evidence of which was not shared with the faculty. Two faculty bodies cast doubt on the administration's depiction of the school as facing dire financial difficulties, noted the lack of measures to increase revenues, and insisted that undertaking such massive curricular changes and faculty terminations required a joint faculty-administration deliberative process of one academic year's duration. When the administration and board refused to consider rescinding its plan or to meet with faculty members, faculty, meeting on May 14, 1999, approved a resolution of no confidence in the university's management.[26]

Eager to complete the transformation task free of faculty meddling, the board announced the elimination of majors in twenty-three programs, giving the affected departments one month to respond to the downsizing. The department responses were meaningless since the board had already concluded that there would now be only fourteen majors. Ending majors in such liberal arts disciplines as history, political science, international studies, and music as well as earth science, mathematics, and chemistry was not coincidental, as these were also areas that management denigrated as dominated by the "core group of dissidents." The Plan for Transformation truly transformed the curriculum by gutting nine liberal arts and sciences majors. Using "financial exigency" as his justification for the program cuts, the president stated that faculty in the affected departments, probationary and tenured, would be guaranteed a terminal year with little if any chance of keeping their jobs beyond that.[27]

Opposition to the plan and support for the faculty came from students, alumni, unionists, and the publiz. Some students met with the president and strategized with departments. They also rallied on the quad, circulated petitions, and displayed pro-faculty messages on signs and T-shirts. Donations came in from the Iowa Federation of Teachers, the Dubuque Federation of Labor, and the AFT local at the University of Northern Iowa as well as from individuals. Alumni expressed their disapproval with letters and phone calls. The *Dubuque Telegraph Herald* published a series of letters to the editor, most of which castigated the plan and praised the faculty. These protests, however, failed to stop the administration's all-out campaign to subdue faculty unrest.[28]

The plan to dismantle a number of liberal arts and sciences majors revealed an astonishing and tragic misunderstanding of both academic and moral principles. The plan cut majors and eliminated fourteen of thirty-nine faculty positions. Management at UD relied on their power to modify or discontinue programs based on fiscal distress and market considerations. Their actions violated AAUP standards by displaying scorn for faculty rights and due process. Some of the downsized faculty stayed into the next academic year and continued to look for jobs; a few others found positions at the University of Wisconsin–Platteville (UW-P) or at Clarke or Loras. Those faculty members who lost their jobs often had many years of experience at UD and held tenured positions. Most had logged between seventeen and thirty years.[29]

As one of the downsized faculty with twenty-nine years of experience, I refused to sign a letter offering me a terminal teaching appointment for the 1999–2000 academic year. Instead, I accepted the university's buyout, which included paying my salary, pension, and health care for one year. To me, the university had become a liberal arts mausoleum, where the faculty experienced a litany of authoritarian mismanagement, fiscal irresponsibility, and corporate bureaucratization. The administration was likely grateful to rid itself of an activist faculty dissident. I was fortunate to find a one-year, full-time teaching job at UW-P and later secured a position at Northeast Iowa Community College (NICC), where there was an NEA local.[30] These opportunities allowed me to walk away from the toxic environment at UD and symbolically thumb my nose at my former employer's board and top administrators.

The cathartic experiences of teaching at UW-P and NICC stand in sharp contrasts to the final scenario at UD. The trial to determine the legality of the Plan for Transformation occurred in the summer of 1999. After hearing from witnesses for the faculty and the administration, the presiding judge ruled that the board could make the changes envisioned in the plan, but that the modifications had to go through the Amendment and Revision Committee. When the committee met in the fall of 1999, the composition had already changed dramatically. Some downsized faculty had left for other positions, some refused to serve when nominated, and others were not elected. The result was an elected faculty committee much more amenable to administrative entreaties. The committee proceeded to approve the transformation plan and amend the handbook with implementation to occur during the 1999–2000 academic year. Those liberal arts and sciences departments without majors were now mostly populated by adjuncts as the university's list of classes declined by almost one-half.[31] The twofold assaults of the suit and the curricular revisions crushed faculty resistance, turned professors into at-will employees, opened the way for loyalty oaths, and gave the president complete power to reassign faculty.[32]

* * *

In the years since our defeat at UD, examples of corporatism in college and university workplaces have only continued to mount. As the corporate model becomes more and more common in the academic world, the power of faculty employees dwindles.[33] For at least the past forty years, so-called market forces and bureaucratic structures have invaded the thinking of college trustees and administrators. This constricts faculty's traditional roles in curriculum, governance, promotion and tenure, graduation requirements, and even a say in the budget. As professorial power declines, the old period of faculty-administrative collegiality (if it ever existed) goes dormant. In its place we witness what Cary

Nelson, University of Illinois English professor and former president of the AAUP, writes about as "the proliferation of a managerial class of career administrators peopled by folks who have either never spent time in a classroom or have long forgotten the experience. . . . These people are trained to resist unionization and then, if they fail, to help insure you become a business union, rather than a broadly progressive social force."[34]

At increasing numbers of colleges and universities, then, trustees and those in upper administrative ranks treat the campus as a business enterprise, faculty as resources, learning as a commodity, and students as consumers. According to sociologist Gaye Tuchman, "Universities are no longer to lead the minds of students to grasp truth; to grapple with intellectual possibilities; to appreciate the best in art, music, and other forms of culture; and to work toward both enlightened politics and public service. Rather they are now to prepare students for jobs. They are not to educate, but to train."[35] The governing boards of our institutions of higher learning seem to want personnel policies, work rules, and centralized decision making that professors find offensive or oppressive. Rather than an environment for inquiry and criticism, the campus had become an arena for courting donors and erecting new buildings. This corporate model has become ubiquitous in higher education today.[36]

My own college teaching career parallels these changes. At UD, the board hired "managerial class" people as consultants. At first they tried to convince the faculty of the evils of collective bargaining. After we secured union status, they held numerous campus meetings designed to create a faux air of collegial relations where our interests would be protected by the administration. After we lost collective bargaining, the consultants returned with documents designed to create governance structures that reduced faculty power to polite pleading before the temple of administration. In each instance, the faculty rejected the administrative overtures as little more than surrendering faculty voice to management.[37] From management's perspective, collective bargaining had been an unwelcome addition to governance. Contractual negotiations infringed on administrative prerogatives. Yet, even after our union was decertified, the handbook caused the board and administration grief because of the "mutually agreed to" and "legally enforceable" clauses. The coordinated suit and transformation plan solved this problem by making it possible for the board and administration to exercise uncontested power. Using arguments about an innovative curricular design and the need for fiscal efficiencies, the board embarked on a strategy to remove antagonistic faculty and consolidate management's unilateral decision-making power.

But, despite such local and national trends, there are reasons for hope and perhaps even cautious optimism. According to the AFL-CIO Department of Professional Employees, as of 2015, approximately 17 percent of postsecondary teachers were union members. Although this rate of union density was far lower than secondary, primary, and special education teachers (roughly 50 percent), it was higher than the overall national average (11 percent).[38] Over the last several decades, much of the energy surrounding organizing campaigns in the sector has focused on graduate employees and (most recently) adjuncts. Despite the continued difficulties in winning certification elections, the very same concentrations of power within the administrations of colleges and universities that contributed to the decline of faculty power over the last several decades have begun to erode the foundations of the court's logic in *Yeshiva*. In late 2014 and 2015, the NLRB began to signal that it recognized the shift away from shared governance in a series of rulings, perhaps paving the way for a friendlier legal environment in the future.[39] Regardless of whether or not these opportunities materialize, however, for me, the sign in my front yard still says it all: "Proud to be Union."

Notes

1. Gary Rhoades, *Managed Professionals: Unionized Faculty and Restructuring Academic Labor* (Albany: State University of New York Press, 1998), 10. See also Stanley Aronowitz, "Are Unions Good for Professors?," *Academe* 84.6 (November–December 1998): 14–15.

2. Other institutions that saw faculty organizing efforts during this period include Fordham, New York University, the University of New Haven, and Villanova University. Manfred Weidhorn, "The Yeshiva Faculty Union: Tales Told out of School," *Academe* 84.6 (November–December 1998): 24.

3. In 1970, the NLRB initiated the first collective bargaining election at a private college or university in the United States; see Thomas J. Flygare, "Yeshiva University: Implications for the Future of College Collective Bargaining," *Phi Delta Kappan* 61.9 (May 1980): 639. UD seminary faculty, who organized an NEA local in early 1973, were the first organized seminary faculty in U.S. history as well as the first group of graduate faculty to organize in the Trans-Mississippi West. Regarding the Iowa locals, see *Iowa Higher Education Association Communique*, July 1972, 4, and September 1974, 10; *National Education Association Advocate*, October 1979, 2.

4. There are remarkably few historical studies of *NLRB v. Yeshiva*. Regarding the ruling in historical context, see Weidhorn, "Yeshiva Faculty Union," 24–26; Herman M. Levy, "The Yeshiva Case Revisited," *Academe* 73.5 (September–October 1987): 34–37; and Donna R. Euben, "Legal Watch: Academic Labor Unions the Legal Landscape," *Academe* 87.1 (January–February 2001): 85.

5. Ralph Scharnau, interview by Shel Stromquist, June 12, 2002, State Historical Society of Iowa, Iowa City, Iowa (hereafter SHSI), part 1, 1–2, 16–20, part 2, 1.

6. Ibid., part 2, 1–5; Ernst Benjamin and Michael Maurer, eds., *Academic Collective Bargaining* (Washington, D.C.: American Association of University Professors and the Modern Language Association of America, 2006), 10–11; Gary Nelson, *No University Is an Island: Saving Academic Freedom* (New York: New York University Press, 2010), 129; Aronowitz, "Are Unions Good for Professors?," 15.

7. Scharnau interview, part 2, 6–9; Ralph Scharnau Papers, Iowa Labor Collection, SHSI, box 2.

8. Gaye Tuchman, *Wannabe U: Inside the Corporate University* (Chicago: University of Chicago Press, 2009), 5–6.

9. Scharnau Papers, boxes 2, 7, 11, and 12; *Des Moines Register*, March 7, 9, and 17, 1972; *Dubuque Telegraph Herald*, March 6–8, March 15–16, April 25, May 7, and May 16, 1972.

10. Scharnau Papers, box 7; William J. Woodward, Eileen Burchell, Donald R. Wagner, and Jonathan Knight, "Financial Exigency, Academic Governance, and Related Matters," *Academe* 90.2 (March–April 2004): 104–12; Nelson, *No University Is an Island*, 54.

11. Scharnau Papers, box 11; Scharnau interview, part 2, 10–12. Regarding the NEA's statewide advocacy during this period, see Gerald Ott, interview with John W. McKerley, April 22, 2015, Iowa Labor History Oral Project (ILHOP), SHSI, and James H. Sutton, interview with McKerley, February 10, 2015, ILHOP, SHSI.

12. Scharnau interview, part 2, 12–13; *Iowa Higher Education Association Communique*, Sept. 1972, 1–2.

13. Scharnau interview, part 2, 13; Scharnau Papers, boxes 2, 7, 8, 10, and 12.

14. Scharnau Papers, boxes 7 and 8; *Iowa Higher Education Association Communique*, March 1974, 13, and September 1974, 16; Scharnau interview, part 2, 13–15.

15. Scharnau Papers, boxes 7 and 8; *Iowa Higher Education Association Communique*, March 1974, 13, and September 1974, 16.

16. Scharnau Papers, boxes 6 and 8; *Dubuque Telegraph Herald*, August 14, 16–21, 23–24, and 26, 1981; *Des Moines Register*, August 16, 20, 23, 25, and 27, 1981; *Iowa State Education Association Communique*, January 18, 1982, 12; *National Education Association Reporter*, October 1981, 9; Scharnau interview, part 2, 20–21, part 3, 1.

17. Scharnau interview, part 3, 2–4; *Dubuque Telegraph Herald*, November 9 and 11, 1983; December 15, 1983; *Des Moines Register*, November 11, 1983; *Dubuque Leader*, December 2, 1983; *Iowa State Education Association Communique*, March/April 1984, 11; Weidhorn, "Yeshiva Faculty Union," 24–26; Deborah C. Malamud, "Collective Bargaining and the Professoriate: What the Law Says," *Academe* 84.6 (November–December 1998): 18–22.

18. Scharnau Papers, box 8, copy of court decision in box 10; Judith Wagner DeCew, *Unionization in the Academy: Visions and Realities* (Lanham, Md.: Rowan and Littlefield, 2003), 45–56.

19. By contrast, the seminary faculty voted in 1985 to accept a handbook as the new governing instrument between the faculty and the university and thereby ended its twelve-year collective bargaining status.

20. Scharnau interview, part 3, 11–12; Scharnau Papers, box 10.

21. Scharnau interview, part 3, 7–8; copy of *UD Faculty Handbook*, May 1989, in Scharnau Papers, box 2.

22. Scharnau interview, part 3, 9, 12–13.

23. Ibid., part 3, 14; Scharnau Papers, boxes 3 and 13; *Dubuque Telegraph Herald*, August 20 and 21, 1996.

24. Robin Wilson, "U. of Dubuque Board Takes Faculty to Court," *Chronicle of Higher Education*, June 19, 1998, A12.

25. Scharnau Papers, box 14; *Dubuque Telegraph Herald*, March 17 and 19, April 4, 10, and 17, 1998, February 10, April 21 and 22, 1999; *Des Moines Register*, May 17, 1998, and February 11, 1999.

26. Scharnau Papers, boxes 9, 13, and 14; Donald J. Reeb, M. Elizabeth Derrick, and Robert K. Moore, "Academic Freedom and Tenure: University of Dubuque," *Academe* 87.5 (September–October 2001): 63–64, 67; *Dubuque Telegraph Herald*, March 20 and 21, and May 14, 1999; Julia K. McDonald, "Crisis at the University of Dubuque," *Iowa Academe* (spring 1999): 1, 4.

27. Scharnau Papers, boxes 4, 9, and 14; *Dubuque Telegraph Herald*, March 20, 1999; Benjamin Ginsberg, *Fall of the Faculty: The Rise of the All-Administrative University and Why It Matters* (New York: Oxford University Press, 2011), 9, 196; Reeb, Derrick, and Moore, "Academic Freedom and Tenure," 69; Woodward, Burchell, Wagner, and Knight, "Financial Exigency, Academic Governance, and Related Matters," 104–12.

28. Scharnau Papers, box 3; Scharnau interview, part 4, 1–2; *Dubuque Telegraph Herald*, April 14, May 14–16 and 23, June 2, 8, and 23, September 8, 1999, August 21 and September 30, 2001.

29. *Dubuque Telegraph Herald*, May 1, 14, and 15, September 10, 1999; Reeb, Derrick, and Moore, "Academic Freedom and Tenure," 67–68.

30. Scharnau interview, part 4, 6–7; Scharnau Papers, boxes 4 and 6. Following my year at UW-P, I explored community college teaching. Hired as a part-time instructor at Northeast Iowa Community College (NICC), my new teaching stint there started in the fall of 2000. Knowing that the NEA had been organizing instructors at Iowa's community colleges since the mid-1970s, I joined the NICC local and maintained my AFT membership as well. Early in my first semester, I was among the employees receiving a startling email from NICC President Rob Denson. It included the following words: "I am writing to ask everyone eligible to consider union membership. We have two excellent bargaining units [one for faculty and one for support staff, both affiliated with the NEA] and I am in regular communication with their leadership. In order to have a 'seat at the table' where decisions are made, you should consider membership and participation." In subsequent communications with Denson, I learned that he valued the collectively bargained contract as an important tool to negotiate salaries and other terms and condition of employment. Robert Denson to Ralph Scharnau, email September 7, 2000, and Ralph Scharnau to Denson, email May 9, 2001, both in Scharnau Papers, box 6.

31. Scharnau interview, parts 3, 17–19, and 4, 3. Copy of court ruling in Scharnau Papers, box 14.

32. Scharnau interview, part 4, 3; Scharnau Papers, box 14; Reeb, Derrick, and Moore, "Academic Freedom and Tenure," 71–72; Jim Lindsay, "No Rosy Picture Can Revive UD's Identity," *Dubuque Telegraph Herald*, July 19, 2001, 4A.

33. Cary Nelson, "The War against the Faculty," *Chronicle of Higher Education*, April 16, 1999, B4–B5.

34. Nelson, *No University Is an Island*, 140.

35. Tuchman, *Wannabe U*, 41.

36. See Ginsberg, *Fall of the Faculty*.

37. Scharnau interview, part 3, 7, 12–13.

38. "Teachers: Preschool through Postsecondary," updated February 2015, Department for Professional Employees, AFL-CIO, http://dpeaflcio.org, accessed August 16, 2015.

39. Scott Jaschik, "Big Union Win," *Inside Higher Ed*, January 2, 2015, www.insidehighered.com, accessed August 16, 2015; Scott Jaschik, "Point Park Recognizes Faculty Union, in Possible Sign NLRB Has Weakened 'Yeshiva' Decision, *Inside Higher Ed*, July 21, 2015, www.insidehighered.com, accessed August 16, 2015.

CHAPTER 3

"Feets Don't Fail Me Now"

Navigating an Unpaved, Rocky Road to, through, and from the Last Slave Plantation

Daniel E. Atkinson

Working-class studies scholars are increasingly coming to recognize the carceral state as an appropriate subject for their discipline. In 2011, the premier labor history journal in the United States, *Labor: Studies in Working-Class History of the Americas*, devoted an entire issue to the subject. Alex Lichtenstein, in his overview of the state of the literature, observes that, while some scholars of labor and working-class history have examined prisons and imprisoned workers, they have done so overwhelmingly within the context of the Jim Crow South before World War II. To improve their analysis, he recommends expanding their chronological and geographic scope and exploring such topics as the diverse forms of prison labor and the relationship between imprisoned people and society more generally.[1]

In this chapter, I take up this challenge but with a twist. Although my subject—the Louisiana State Penitentiary at Angola—is southern, I use my training as an ethnomusicologist and insight as an Afro-American to examine the very real cultural work and broader social significance of imprisoned black musicians laboring in antebellum-like conditions on a former plantation in the first decade of the twenty-first century. At the same time, I consider the ways in which my own cultural work as a scholar—while certainly not subject to the same brutalizing environment as the prisoners—was shaped by many of the same racialized power structures both within and outside its gates.[2]

In 2005, I began a series of research trips to the Louisiana State Penitentiary at Angola, often referred to by the inmates as the Last Slave Plantation, to record inmate music and oral histories for my doctoral fieldwork. Through these trips, I came to know one of the most notorious prisons in the United States, the site of nearly two centuries of the kind of casual brutality and suffering that the nation does not tolerate abroad but regularly makes excuses for on its own soil to police working-class people, especially those of color. Using inmate oral histories and music, coupled with the history of the prison and the state, I hoped to create works of art and scholarship that would reveal the prison as a palimpsest. As a former slave plantation, Angola is a place in which one can peer into an environment where black people eloquently express the human condition in the most horrific of circumstances. The prison, then, has become a nexus of Afro-American vernacular expression where prohibition of black liberty and sovereignty is more blatant than on the outside and akin to the explicit methods used during the time of institutionalized segregation.

Through my work, I hoped to foster empathy among citizens and elected officials to improve decisions regarding how we treat some of our most institutionally vulnerable people. In the process, my research revealed many of the obstacles inherent in engaged scholarship as well as those faced by Afro-American scholars in particular. Indeed, my work at the prison ended abruptly in 2009, when a published interview with a journalist resulted in me being banned from conducting research or otherwise working with inmates. Although I finished my dissertation, the experience left me to struggle to find meaningful academic work in a hostile political environment in which hiring committees regularly questioned whether I was more activist than academic.

Louisiana State Penitentiary at Angola is situated at the end of a twenty-two-mile, dead-end road on eighteen thousand acres of some of the richest farmland in the United States. Surrounded by the Mississippi River on three sides and the Tunica Hills on the other, it is roughly the size of the island of Manhattan. It is also a former slave plantation, converted to a prison shortly after the ratification of the Thirteenth Amendment in 1865. This conversion was designed to serve two purposes. The first was to pacify Louisiana elites, allowing them to preserve at least some of their status by continuing to profit from very low-cost labor.[3] The second was to find something to do with the large number of formerly enslaved people to whom almost no one from the previous power structure wanted to extend any of the most basic rights of postwar citizenship. The situation was further exacerbated by the return of Democratic control to the state (and throughout the region) by the late 1870s. This new political climate removed many of the gains made during the immediate postbellum years and, at a local level, facilitated a complete inversion of the inmate population from white to black. The new prisoners, mostly black men, were subjected to forced labor and routinely leased out to plantation owners and public-works contractors in a way that revealed the easily exploitable limits of the Thirteenth Amendment's prohibition of involuntary servitude. Thus, while Angola was fundamentally a Louisiana state penitentiary—and grew out of Louisiana roots—it also represented a much larger reality taking place across the region (and, arguably, the nation), a reality that affected millions more than those people who crossed through its gates.[4]

For these reasons, I chose Angola to begin my fieldwork because it appeared to be an ideal place to produce scholarship that might contribute to a broad, public discussion of communal responses to institutional oppression and historical power structures in the United States. In particular, I sought to understand the connections between the lives and labor of Angola's imprisoned musicians, the prison's history, and current debates around race and social justice. My plan was to use the unique perspective of the inmate musicians as a platform from which to compare inmates with the current free population, to prompt readers to think critically about the stunted legacy of the Thirteenth Amendment, and, ultimately, to contribute to a critical mass of scholarship that questioned the merit of assimilation disguised as integration. I wanted to find the answer to one fundamental question: why did a very poor, fiscally conservative state like Louisiana incarcerate healthy, nonviolent men for decades at the cost of over $17,000 each year, compelling them to pick cotton in the name of rehabilitation, while preventing them from raising their children, paying taxes, or otherwise contributing to the greater good beyond public-works projects on chain gangs?[5]

To implement my project, I recorded more than thirty hours of music and oral histories at the prison. In doing so, I was able to preserve and interpret coded information via music and testimony that suggested the ways in which inmates subverted administrative control and attempted to reassert their collective cultural experiences. Although I was not able to realize my intention of recording hip-hop as expressed by younger inmates, what I did gather was equally, if not more, valuable. It was fascinating to witness the ability of some of the inmates to employ tried-and-true methods of utilizing authorities' underestimation of them as a means to "get over," learning, in the words of inmate Albert Patterson, "It's all right to be all right." Over time, the work began to evolve from strict ethnography into something resembling a twenty-first century slave narrative.[6] Moreover, I found myself having to apply my own forms of subversion in order to continue conducting work in an environment in which administrators regarded me with growing suspicion and (ultimately) hostility.[7]

Having been in protracted communication with prison authorities for six months, my struggles began on August 1, 2005. That was the day I first entered the penitentiary, coming face-to-face with prison officials. Prior to any of the prison administration actually seeing me, for all they knew, I was white. This act of "passing" was not intended, but my last name is unusual for a black person outside of Georgia and Ohio and provided the necessary cover to gain entry. Further, I spoke "standard" English over the telephone and in previous communications had given no obvious indicators of my racial-cultural status: an educated black man with an unacceptably complex narrative and therefore, a threat to order in a place like Angola. Having dealt with this scenario at job interviews and other situations where one builds a rapport with another person before actually meeting, I was not surprised to encounter it yet again. I had expected as much from the prison administration's incredulous reaction to my initial research proposal of exploring the influx of younger inmates into the prison population and their use of hip-hop—instead of or in conjunction with gospel—as a preferred vernacular expression. Over the phone I was told "That doesn't really exist here, but we do have some amazing gospel singers!" To me, that response was a clear indicator that they did not know who I was, that they were most likely not attuned to the inmate population, and that the old adage, told to me by Louisiana-born saxophonist Jules Broussard, was still in play: "Nothin' makes Southern white folks happier than to see Niggers singin' about Jesus. [Be]cause that means they got us under control!"[8]

My suspicions were seemingly confirmed when, upon my arrival, I received what I can describe only as "the look." Not at all unique for a person of color who aspires beyond the unwritten dogma of race, class, and culture, the look, in this case, was of complete surprise and shock, revealing that I was not who was expected. Rather, I was an educated, code switching, black man who had come to conduct what most assuredly was unwelcome and potentially disruptive business. For a moment, the warden assigned to me looked as though she did not know what to do about this unexpected situation, but she quickly recovered and treated me accordingly, as an interloper. Though the prison honored our agreement— and I was granted access to the prison and its inmates—it was seemingly under protest. From my perspective, I was treated with suspicion during each of my six daily visits, during which I recorded oral histories and gospel music as inmates prepared to perform in the prison's newly renovated rodeo arena on August 6, 2005, in a revival-style gathering ironically named "The Power of Freedom."

I was allowed access only to a select group of inmates known as Trustys. This highly prized status is coveted by most inmates and, on average, takes about ten years to earn. The process can be accelerated, provided the inmate in question has a particular skill or talent that suits the needs of the administration, as in the case of most of the musicians with whom I worked. Some Trustys (class A) are allowed unmonitored access to the entire prison grounds. In special cases, under escort, they may make short trips outside of the prison for work-related events, speaking engagements, musical performances, and even family funerals. Trustys also have greater access to higher-paying, more prestigious prison jobs, but they still earn less than $0.25 per hour. The lowest-paid inmates usually work in the fields or on the farm proper as general laborers while many Trustys work indoors as cooks, inmate council, and clerical or administrative assistants in air-conditioned buildings alongside free folk. Most of the Trustys I spoke to were middle-aged to elderly and were well aware of their privileged status. They also conveyed their awareness that at any time, for any reason, their privileges could be revoked, erasing a decade or more of sustained effort.

These many layers of power made the double entendre and coded messages contained in the music and the worldviews of the musicians all the more important for the work I was trying to do.[9] In particular, inmates mixed the traditions of spirituals with those of gospel, using analogy to express present injustice while placing in God's hands any hope for redemption.[10] This mixture of forms was particularly clear in inmates' use of the word "life," as in "life, but God has a better plan for me," or "life, according to man." An inmate named Christopher

Jerome Williams expounded on this theme in his discussion of a revelation that compelled him to redefine his place in this world and the next: "'Life sentence,' it says. God has a better plan. . . . It says I have a life sentence. And I found myself asking the question, 'how could the system as we would say, give me a life sentence and God can give me life?' I posed the question to myself, I asked the Lord, 'how could man give me what You can give me? If man can give me life, then you can give me life.'"[11]

My first opportunities to showcase some of these findings came in the form of two soul-chamber recordings produced in collaboration with saxophonist and composer Howard Wiley. These recordings were designed to span the history of Afro-American music from field hollers to hip-hop. The first recording, *The Angola Project* (2005), featured tenor saxophonist David Murray, vocalist Faye Carol, and bassist Marcus Shelby, along with a thirteen-member ensemble, and, in keeping with tradition, came out of a personal need to share my experience so that it did not completely consume me. Wiley shared my love for pre-integration black vernacular expression and also openly expressed his desire to combat what he saw as a kind of "soul sickness" in the United States. The first recording resulted from my description of my experience at the prison and Wiley's arrangements of my field recordings, along with those of pioneering folklorists Harry Oster and Alan Lomax, who had worked at Angola during the first half and middle of the twentieth century. We began giving concerts and lectures in the San Francisco Bay Area in the hopes of igniting a critical discourse among people, mainly young men of color.

In October 2006, I began the process of regaining access to the prison to continue my research in August 2007. I hoped to narrow my focus specifically to inmate a cappella ensembles and to record as many of them as possible. Now that the prison administration knew who I was, they found numerous reasons to deny or challenge even the simplest requests: "We don't understand what you need"; "the music hasn't changed since your last visit"; "we haven't seen any of your writing from the first visit," and the like. My application to return was "lost" several times, but eventually Assistant Warden Angie Norwood emailed me, denying my request to return on the basis that my research would offer "minimum benefit to the prison" with its "limited resources."[12] This response contrasted starkly with that received by another ethnomusicology graduate student doing similar research at the same time: he had far fewer problems gaining repeated access to the prison. From what I could tell, the only differences between the two of us were that he had greater access to funding and was white.

For ten months, further access to the prison and inmates eluded me, even after I proposed to compensate the prison for the cost of providing me a classification officer during my visit and offered to use my rental car instead of a motor pool vehicle to traverse the prison's eighteen thousand acres. Every reason the prison administration gave for my denial of access, I found a way to alleviate, but they found new reasons to say no. In the end, Daniel Sheehy, then director of Smithsonian Folkways Recordings, saved my effort with a letter of endorsement, saying that the work I was doing was important to the Smithsonian Institution and that my recordings and photographs would become part of their collections. Whatever the reason for the administration's stalling, the letter proved to be my saving grace and my ticket back into Angola in early August 2007 for three days.

During that trip, Wiley and I worked with some of the same inmates with whom I had collaborated in 2005, as well as new ones who had been recruited by a few inmates who knew what I was trying to do with my scholarship. In some cases, I had missed inmates because the prison officials did not know of their musical abilities or because the inmates had chosen not to participate during the first round because of previous negative encounters with researchers.[13] Once it was understood that "the weird black guy from Seattle" was returning, however, a select group of inmates took great risks in curating what I acknowledge as a gift for which I could never reciprocate. One insightful inmate named Emanuel Lee introduced me to "Big" John Taylor, a master of the gospel quartet tradition who had been incarcerated at Angola since 1970.[14] The result was a second CD titled *The Angola Project: Twelve Gates to the City* (2008).[15] Howard and I attempted to channel the inspiration we received from both the inmates and our knowledge of traditional black vernacular expression into something that could both enlighten and inspire without compromising its critical edge. Toward this goal, we also were lucky enough to feature a bit of spoken word from Robert Hillary King, then the only free member of the Angola 3, a group of inmates who had been wrongfully convicted of murdering an officer at the prison in 1972.[16]

On the heels of that success, I began making preparations for a third research trip to the prison to take place in the summer of 2010. On November 18, 2009, however, after months of veiled rejections, I was notified that I had been banned from conducting further research. This was the result of the prison administration's predictable reaction to "Back to Angola," an article published in an August 2007 issue of the *Stranger*, an alternative Seattle weekly for which I had been interviewed by journalist Sam Machkovech. I was informed of my unwelcome status in a handwritten letter from Assistant Warden Cathy Fontenot, after I inquired about the identity of three inmates in a gospel quartet I photographed during my second visit.[17] Until that point, I had worked diligently to avoid this exact scenario and guarded my data fiercely. In hindsight, however, my banning came as no surprise.

Machkovech, a white man and a recent transplant to Seattle from Texas, was just getting started as a freelance journalist, and he had been sitting in on a course on Afro-American music that I was teaching that summer at the University of Washington. After hearing several lectures on black vernacular responses to white supremacy, particularly those of inmates at Angola, he requested an interview with me. I initially refused, but he was persistent and claimed to share my views on Afro-American subversion and the morally questionable research methods of Alan Lomax, for whom he had worked in Texas. I eventually relented and granted him an interview as a favor. However, I stressed adamantly that, if he were to write the article, he not mention any subversion of prison authorities on my or the inmates' part. My research was far from complete, and, given my experience with Angola authorities in 2007, I knew that the prison was looking for a reason to ban me. Furthermore, I wanted to take all reasonable precautions to avoid facilitating harm to any of the men who took great risks in speaking to me.

I told Machkovech that, if I were to be able to continue my work, the article could only talk about history, the beauty of the music, and my fondness for the men with whom I worked (all true); he would have to avoid writing of subversion or the continuation of the institution of white supremacy. He agreed, I gave the interview, and then he wrote the story as if we had never spoken of the importance of careful presentation of my work in a public forum. The article opens by referring to a line I used in the classroom and not in the interview in which I used the word "pimp" to describe myself, referring to rapper Too $hort's notion that "a pimp is someone who's paid to talk." Of far more consequence, however, were Machkovech's exposure of my criticisms of prison administrators. For example, he quotes me as saying "I wasn't there to write about the continuation of the slavery plantation system, but they kinda forced me, the administration. They had their standard Christian dog-and-pony show, saying, 'We've got these darkies in check.' I have every reason to believe that they did not think that I was black until they actually saw me. They had planned this whole thing, and it totally backfired on them."[18]

I was not allowed to vet the article before publication, but after reading it, I knew my research was over. If I were to read this article about another scholar, I would have thought the ethnographer arrogant, ungrateful for the opportunity, and ignorant of the stakes. Understandably, the prison administration treated me as it had *New York Times* journalist Daniel Bergner, who it banned after his 1998 book, *God of the Rodeo*, cast the administration in an embarrassing light. From the perspective of prison administrators, Machkovech's article cast me as yet another meddling northern muckraker.[19] His article made no mention of the work I was trying to do with the legacies of Reconstruction; of the admiration I had for the men and their music on the inside; or of the economic drain caused by prisons in the United States. Although I can only speculate as to Machkovech's goals in writing the article, I suspect that the piece was designed to gain the favor of the editing staff for future freelance work.

Ultimately, however, regardless of intent, neither Machkovech nor the *Stranger* felt they bore any responsibility for the utter collapse of my research. In an attempt to show some solidarity and empathy, although it would have no impact whatsoever, Bethany Jean Clement, the magazine's managing editor, offered to redact my name from the article. But I refused. Much like the negotiations over my initial access to the prison, I knew the first chance I had to make the magazine's staff understand my situation would most likely be the only one that mattered. This reality made the situation all the more vexing because I could not persuade them to understand the importance of my situation as it related to years of carefully planned work, now incomplete and permanently deferred. This was especially frustrating because this project was my best effort to date at making my own transition from a frustrated musician into academia, where I felt that I could affect hearts and minds toward real social change.[20]

After this initial exchange, the magazine stopped returning my phone calls and emails. I was left alone, holding the bag in circumstances not entirely of my making. Overall, the experience verified for me the continued need to *Signify* in post-integration America and to "be shore you knows 'bout all you tells, but don't tell all you knows," when there is any kind of power or access disparity. Had I been more careful with what I told him, demanded a *signed* nondisclosure agreement, or simply refused to speak with him, perhaps the situation could have been avoided entirely and my research would have had a chance of continuing.[21]

This experience with popular presentation and discussion of my work—even if we imagine it was well-intentioned on Machkovech's part—reflected one of the fundamental tensions inherent to engaged or activist scholarship. The act of publicizing such scholarship can compromise the work and the professional and activist aspirations of its creators—and, in some contexts, even jeopardize the lives of collaborators and informants. Despite my adamantly expressed reasons for tempered disclosure, Machkovech exposed my critical perspective on prison administrators, who in turn used their power over my informants to stop any further research that might prove embarrassing to the prison. Yes, I did say what I am quoted as saying in the article. It was not anything I had not said in the classroom or written in my dissertation two years later. However, I said nothing of the sort where I did not have some measure of control over the situation. I did not think it was too much to ask, given the social justice implications of the project I was trying to accomplish, that he adhere to my request. After all, peoples' lives were potentially at stake. That fact was as important for Machkovech to understand as it would be for the reader of the dissertation. Whether or not I thought my research was finished, Sam Machkovech finished it for me.

Other encounters with the press, while less dramatic, were just as revealing with regard to the limits of converting scholarly or activist insights into popular discourse. The recordings I made with Howard Wiley were reviewed in popular jazz publications and on National Public Radio, but an infuriatingly common, though expected, thread permeated the critics' discourse. While they frequently discussed the quality of production and musicianship in the recordings, they largely ignored both the content within the context of popular culture and the existence of a massive prison/plantation, where, in the name of rehabilitation, black men were being worked in conditions reminiscent of slavery, let alone the way both Wiley and I do and do not fit into the dwindling contribution of Afro-Americans to jazz music as a genre.[22] It should be noted that, unlike the prison administration, these popularizers of my work saw themselves as (at least) neutral or even as allies, revealing the potential tensions between the press and scholar-activists in general and between Afro-American scholars and white-dominated institutions (even, or perhaps especially, when professedly liberal) in particular. Or, as Maya Angelou wrote, "This rocky road's not paved for us, so I'll believe in liberal's aid for us, when I see a white man load a Black man's gun."[23]

I was able to visit the prison's annual rodeo in October 2009 and again in 2015 (because it is open to the public), but only as a spectator. I made the best of my situation in 2009, salvaging what I could of my rather incomplete research during what I expected to be my final trip for the foreseeable future.[24] Unable to maintain the cost of a thirteen-member ensemble, the Angola Project also fizzled away after two recordings and a handful of concerts. Still, despite its incompleteness, the recordings and dissertation are some of my most impressive work to date and yielded important conclusions both about the nature of the modern carceral state and about the role of engaged scholars (especially scholars of color) in studying it. In considering the labor of imprisoned people, we must embrace not only its diverse forms but especially its cultural expressions and its connections to broader patterns that transcend the prison walls. In regard to black people in particular, working-class vernacular culture—whether as a form of surviving the brutality of penal work or as a form of penal work itself—is no less significant today than it was in the time of Oster and Lomax.

As a person and scholar of color, however, it is impossible for me to escape the palpable injustice of a penal system that, between 1960 and 2005, shifted from 60 percent white to 70 percent nonwhite and that today ensnares as many as one-third of black men sometime during their lifetime.[25] On this point, Yale historian David Blight helped me bring things full circle when I stumbled across a 2008 lecture in which he quoted William Faulkner's *The Hamlet*: "Only thank God men have done learned how to forget quick what they ain't brave enough to try to cure."[26] Like many of the boys I grew up with in Southern California and other young men of color in the United States, I knew all too well that I was just one bad decision or (in the case of John Taylor) accusation away from a lifetime of virtual enslavement or even death in our prison system. Moreover, I am reminded daily that no amount of education or material wealth can erase the stigma of being a black man in the United States, and I must straddle the fine line between vigilance and paranoia if I am to succeed beyond the rather narrow confines of what the U.S. social order expects of me and people who happen to look like me. At the same time, however, I remain steadfast in my desire to combat what Nigerian writer and activist Chinua Achebe aptly calls the "malignant fiction" of social norms that benefit some people while negating others.[27] Knowing that the work I did in the past will inform what I do today and tomorrow, I would not change a thing if I had the chance. Indeed, in some ways, the story of doing the work turned out to be more compelling than the work itself; I cannot tell one story without telling the other, much as the meaning of U.S. history is shaped by the inclusion of Afro-American history in the story.

Notes

1. Alex Lichtenstein, "A 'Labor History' of Mass Incarceration," *Labor: Studies in Working-Class History of the Americas* 8.3 (2011): 5–11. See also the other essays in that volume. On the turn toward the carceral state more generally, see the articles in the *Journal of American History* 102.1 (June 2015).

2. I prefer the term "Afro-American" to "African American" because I, like most of the people I worked with at Angola, are not from Africa, but rather, are of African descent. Further, I hyphenate the two words "Afro" and "American" to honor the historic opposition to people of African descent as Americans and to draw attention to the fact that we are still quasi citizens with very few postcolonial ties to Africa, hence the reworking of the acronym for Louisiana State Penitentiary (LSP) to Last Slave Plantation by inmates (and in the title of this chapter).

3. Michelle Alexander, *The New Jim Crow: Mass Incarceration in the Age of Colorblindness* (New York: New Press, 2010), 290; Douglas A. Blackmon, *Slavery by Another Name: The Re-enslavement of Black Americans from the Civil War to World War II* (New York: Doubleday, 2008), 468; and Elizabeth Wisner, *Public Welfare Administration in Louisiana* (Chicago: University of Chicago Press, 1930), 132, 154.

4. Mark T. Carleton, *Politics and Punishment: The History of the Louisiana State Penal System* (Baton Rouge: Louisiana State University Press, 1971), 14; Reva Siegal, "Why Equal Protection No Longer Protects: The Evolving Forms of Status-Enforcing Action," *Stanford Law Review* 49.5 (May 1997): 1111–48. See also Edward W. Staggs and John Lear, "Inside America's Worst Prison," *Collier's: The National Weekly* 130.21 (1952): 13–16, and Michael H. Tonry, *Malign Neglect—Race, Crime, and Punishment in America* (New York: Oxford University Press, 1995).

5. Vera Institute of Justice, *The Cost of Prisons: What Incarceration Costs Tax Payers* (New York: Vera Institute of Justice, 2012), 28.

6. What Patterson was getting at was the classic idea that one cannot always choose a situation, but one can choose how one reacts to it. That bit of divination can take a person a long way in a place like Angola or anywhere in the United States in the context of white supremacy. This basic philosophy is common in nineteenth-century slave narratives.

7. For example, the administrators assigned to monitor me during my first visit regularly seized and read my field notes, prompting me to code switch and record my thoughts in Japanese to protect both the inmates and the integrity of my work.

8. At the time, more than half of the 5,163 inmates were thirty-three years old or younger, which meant they were raised with hip-hop as the dominant form of Afro-American popular music. For that to go unrecognized by the administration was revealing, but not surprising.

9. As a result of the politicized environment, I acknowledge that inmate responses to my questions may have been tainted or staged, especially since Trusty inmates are something like goodwill ambassadors to visitors from the outside world due to their ability to travel and perform for influential members of the public.

10. Regarding the tensions between spiritual and gospel traditions, see Melva Wilson Costen, *In Spirit and in Truth: The Music of African American Worship* (Louisville, Ky.: Westminster John Knox Press, 2004), 239; Lawrence Levine, *Black Culture and Black Consciousness: Afro-American Folk Thought from Slavery to Freedom* (Oxford: Oxford University Press, 1977), 174–89; and Howard Thurman, *Jesus and the Disinherited* (Boston: Beacon Press 1949), 112.

11. Interview, August 4, 2005.

12. Angie Norwood to author, email May 15, 2007.

13. It was an unexpected boon that the classification officer assigned to me for this trip liked the music and encouraged inmates to find other singers who even she did not know about.

14. Taylor's story is unique in that it was an open secret that he was wrongfully convicted. He was afforded respect that most inmates did not receive. His story is both compelling and one of many examples for the need of fundamental criminal justice and prison reform. His talent made him an early candidate for special treatment, but the political conditions were not to his liking, so he all but stopped singing for several years before singing for me in 2007. He died in the prison in 2014, still waiting for his conviction to be overturned.

15. Howard Wiley and the Angola Project/H.N.I.C. Music, *The Angola Project: Twelve Gates to the City* (2008). The subtitle of this second recording was inspired by the hymn of the same title, performed by the Pure Heart Messengers, which I recorded in 2005. It was reinterpreted on the first Angola Project recording, and we decided to continue the theme for the second recording.

16. The Angola 3—Robert Hillary King, Herman Wallace, and Albert Woodfox—were wrongfully convicted of the murder of officer Brent Miller at Angola in 1972 and held in solitary confinement from that point forward. King was released in 2001, after his conviction was overturned. Wallace was released from the prison in October 2013, just days before succumbing to liver failure. Woodfox was released from Wade Correctional Center in Homer, Louisiana, on February 19, 2016.

17. Assistant Warden Cathy Fontenot's handwritten letter reads as follows: "Dear Mr. Atkinson, We've received your letter requesting more information regarding your research, however, we consider our work with you completed. I find it quite disturbing that you put one face forward while here and another when you describe your visit here in 'The Stranger.' Our inmates and staff do a great deal of work to welcome and inform the public, media and researchers of all that has changed at Angola. I'm sorry you did not understand what you experienced here and would advise you to look for another prison for access in the future. For the record, you had access to inmates who were willing and wanted to talk to you, we didn't choose them beforehand. Sincerely, Cathy Fontenot" (November 18, 2009). Fontenot's last sentence is inaccurate. I never had access to inmates who were not Trustys other than the few who were in ensembles with Trustys. These inmates, therefore, were allowed to interact with outsiders in only a limited capacity. See also Sam Machkovech, "Back to Angola: A UW Professor Revisits Ethnomusicology's Birthplace," *Stranger*, August 9, 2007, www.thestranger.com, accessed Jan. 13, 2016.

18. Machkovech, "Back to Angola," 59.

19. Daniel Bergner published *God of the Rodeo: The Search for Hope, Faith and a Six-Second Ride in Louisiana's Angola Prison* (New York: Ballantine, 1998) after being granted unprecedented access to do research for more than a year. Though the book is ostensibly about the prison's annual rodeo, much of it is about his personal shock about and inability

to deal with or respect southern discourse as it relates to institutional racism in the South. A scandal arose from an alleged extortion attempt in which Warden Cain demanded $50,000 from Bergner to secure further access and continue the research for his book. Bergner refused and was banned from the prison. He eventually regained access though the court system, but this left an understandable culture of suspicion of outsiders at the prison.

20. Redacting my name from the article without working to solve the problem it created was an offensive suggestion because the act could only assuage the situation in a way that served the magazine administration's sense of guilt without admitting any responsibility.

21. Thomas W. Tally, *Negro Folk Rhymes (Wise and Otherwise)* (New York: Macmillan, 1922), 214. Signifyin' is a war using language as the weapon. According the linguist Geneva Smitherman, "Signifyin is the verbal art of ceremonial combativeness in which one person puts down, talks about, 'signifies on' someone or something someone has said. This rhetorical modality is characterized by indirection, humor, exploitation of the unexpected, and quick verbal repartee" (*Talkin' That Talk: Language, Culture, and Education in African America* [New York: Routledge, 2000], 255). Often, the Trickster figure from Afro-American cultural tradition is combined with Signifyin' to make a powerful rhetorical tool. In the case of my research, I often used institutional underestimation of my abilities to my advantage in order to turn setbacks into opportunities.

22. For examples of popular reviews of the musical projects, see Troy Collins, review of *Howard Wiley: The Angola Project*, in *All About Jazz* (October 27, 2007), www.allaboutjazz.com, accessed Jan. 13, 2016; and Patrick Jarenwattananon, "Angola, Spare Standards and a Zooid: New Jazz Albums," NPR Music, October 8, 2010, www.npr.org, accessed Jan. 13, 2016.

23. Maya Angelou, "On Working White Liberals," *Black Pearls: The Poetry of Maya Angelou*, 1969; CD reissue, Rhino Word Beat, 1998.

24. The 2015 trip was mainly to reconnect with the only man I worked with previously who was free and to begin the process of helping him write his memoir. The other purpose was to say good-bye to a few men I did not expect to see again due to their failing health.

25. Lichtenstein, "'Labor History' of Mass Incarceration," 5, 6.

26. David Blight, "Lecture 26—Race and Reunion: The Civil War in American Memory [April 24, 2008]," course titled the Civil War and Reconstruction Era, 1845–1877 (History 119). The full transcript is at http://oyc.yale.edu/transcript/567/hist-119, accessed Jan. 13, 2016.

27. Chinua Achebe, *Hopes and Impediments: Selected Essays, 1965–1987* (Oxford, U.K.: Heinemann, 1988), 148.

CHAPTER 4

Wandering through the Wisconsin Uprising

Stephen Meyer

On Friday, February 11, 2011, the newly elected Republican governor of Wisconsin, Scott Walker, to use his own phrase, "dropped the bomb," announcing Act 10, a new "budget repair bill" that would effectively end collective bargaining for the state's public employees. Not since Ronald Reagan's firing of striking air traffic controllers in 1981 had U.S. labor faced such a staggering assault. But the response of Wisconsin residents and their allies was no less historic. Soon thousands of people—then tens of thousands—converged on the Wisconsin state capitol in Madison. Thousands occupied and hundreds slept in "the people's house" for eighteen days. On the largest days of "the uprising," as the protests became known, well over a hundred thousand people surrounded the capitol and filled nearby streets. Although the protests and the recall effort they generated were unable either to stop Act 10 or to remove Walker from office during his first term, they produced a powerful new movement that has managed to score some victories and whose last chapter remains to be written.

Not surprisingly, the Wisconsin uprising inspired a cottage industry of books and articles that attempted to explain and assess these unprecedented events.[1] In this chapter, I seek to expand on these works by exploring my own minor role in the uprising through the lens of my experience as a labor historian and activist. On the whole, the uprising was and is a powerful example of both the opportunities and limitations of academic activism. As a historian and faculty member at the University of Wisconsin (UW)–Milwaukee, I served as a local resource on labor history for news outlets covering the uprising, defended activist graduate students from administrative sanction, and helped my students interpret the historical significance of events unfolding around them. Moreover, as a member of the Wisconsin Labor History Society, I assisted in the scholarly analysis of the mounting protests and in creating spaces for academics, activists, and artists to collaborate around a common cause. As important as these academic experiences were, however, the collaborations—and the protests themselves—reinforced just how small a part that other academics and I were playing in a much larger and more diverse movement. And the uprising transformed me, as well, not only shaping the course of my retirement but drawing me deeper into forms of anonymous rank-and-file activism that constituted the beating heart of Wisconsin's progressive response to Walker and his agenda.

My experience of the uprising was shaped by my early life. I was the first in my working-class family to attend college. I enrolled in 1960 but had too much fun and flunked out freshman year. After a four-year stint in the U.S. Air Force, I returned to college, but I did not become a good student until I began to study labor history, a discipline that meshed with my background. Somehow, I managed to be accepted to graduate school at Rutgers University, which had an incredible labor and social history faculty and a cluster of activist graduate students. I enrolled in its Comparative Labor History Program, where I specialized in Russian, British, and U.S. labor history. At Rutgers, history graduate students represented a core in the unionization drive for teaching assistants in the early 1970s. As we began to organize, the faculty collective bargaining chapter of the American Association of University Professors (AAUP) invited us to affiliate with them, and the graduate students agreed. I became secretary of the Rutgers AAUP chapter and the graduate student member of the collective bargaining team. In our first round of negotiations, we achieved a regular contract, health insurance, and a grievance procedure for graduate students. From then on, labor issues became embedded in my academic life.

In the early 1970s, the Anglo-American Labor History Conference brought together senior and junior labor historians from both sides of the Atlantic. Besides U.S. historians like David Montgomery and Herbert Gutman, who established the contours of the "new" labor and social histories, we encountered the ideas of many prominent British Marxist historians—E. P. Thompson and Eric Hobsbawm, in particular—who deeply influenced me and other historians of my generation, inspiring us to rethink how labor and social history could and should be done. They formed the basis of how I studied and wrote U.S. labor history.

With the exception of a five-year stint at the Illinois Institute of Technology (IIT), all of my education and teaching have taken place at public institutions, at both two-year colleges and universities, where I frequently encountered students with backgrounds similar to mine. While at Rutgers I taught introductory courses in European and U.S. history, worked with its labor studies program, and taught and developed curriculum for a labor studies program at a community college in Newark. After graduation I taught in a prison college program in New York and then taught in a two-year liberal arts college in Wisconsin, where the teaching load included working in another prison program. After serving four years as an academic migrant worker, I began a five-year stint in a tenure track appointment at IIT. From there, I moved to a joint appointment in history and labor studies at the University of Wisconsin–Parkside, directing a small labor studies program and teaching at the UW–School for Workers (a labor education extension program). At UW-Parkside, I taught various U.S. and European history and labor studies courses with rank-and-file union leaders and members; at the School for Workers, I likewise taught labor history and the elements of union administration. After sixteen years, I moved to UW-Milwaukee, where I taught undergraduate and graduate classes in U.S. and labor history until my retirement in 2011.

My research has always involved U.S. labor history. Taking heed of a David Montgomery comment that the history of workers and managers should be done together, my dissertation on the Ford Motor Company, which later became my first book, *The Five Dollar Day*, examines this interconnection through how Ford officials attempted to instill an industrial work ethic in a largely preindustrial workforce. My next major project began in the context of the academic culture wars of the Reagan years, which depleted readily available funding for social and labor history research, pushing me toward topics that would allow ready access to research in local sources. I chose to write a history of a left-wing union local at Allis-Chalmers, the largest Wisconsin industrial firm of the first half of the twentieth century. The resulting book, *Stalin over Wisconsin*, is a detailed shop-floor case study of the relations between workers and managers. My most recent book, *Manhood on the Line*, involves a concern about the inhospitable climate for women and African American men that arose out of a densely masculine shop culture among automobile workers.[2]

Knowledge derived from my teaching and research influenced how I engaged in service activities as well. As director of the UW-Parkside Labor Studies Program, I often served as the academic voice of Southeastern Wisconsin workers and their unions. In a midwestern state that saw many plant closings and much industrial relocation, I participated in programs on these issues, including at Allis-Chalmers, where I conducted videotaped interviews to preserve the history of the union local. In all of my academic work, especially in Wisconsin educational institutions, my labor expertise provided the knowledge and experience that resulted in my deep involvement in faculty governance. Before 2009, faculty members were the only public employees in Wisconsin legally barred from engaging in collective bargaining. Much of the rationale for this exclusion rested on the UW System's strong traditions of faculty governance, which were embedded in state law. At UW-Milwaukee, I served on the faculty senate, often on its seven-person executive committee. Both at UW-Parkside and at UW-Milwaukee, I learned that faculty governance often allowed a powerful voice on traditional labor issues such as wages, hours, and working conditions.

As a labor historian, some of my most important professional activities involved the Wisconsin Labor History Society (WLHS), which I helped found in 1981. Formed by a combination of Wisconsin union leaders and labor academics, the society brought together Wisconsin union members, progressive activists, and labor scholars around the history of workers and their unions. I was active in its annual conferences—giving presentations, serving as commentator for sessions, and chairing sessions—and, in more recent years, I served as a board member. In addition to the promotion of labor history, the society generally supports and lobbies for issues associated with Wisconsin unions and workers. Over the years, the WLHS has achieved legislation for the inclusion of labor themes in the Wisconsin social studies curriculum. It also commemorates annually the Bayview Massacre (a Milwaukee offshoot of Chicago's Haymarket incident), publishes a quarterly newsletter, and sponsors yearly labor history essay contests and projects for middle school and high school students and essay contests for college students. The WLHS conducts an annual labor history conference on a historical theme of topical interest to Wisconsin workers, often in union halls in Milwaukee, Madison, and elsewhere across the state.

By mid-February 2011, when Walker's dramatic actions stunned Wisconsin, my academic activism and general grounding in labor history and experience with labor issues prepared me for involvement in the struggle that would follow. But, just as my participation had its roots in my personal history, so too did Act 10 and the uprising reflect deeper currents in Wisconsin life. Despite the state's long association with twentieth-century progressivism—including the origins of the academic field of labor history, deep socialist and progressive political traditions, enlightened social and labor legislation, and public employee unionism—Wisconsin possesses a complex history of divided politics. The rise of conservative senator Joseph McCarthy during the 1950s, for example, coincided with the tenure of Milwaukee socialist mayor Frank Zeidler. In fact, since the heyday of socialism at the beginning of the twentieth century, a socialist occupied Milwaukee's mayoral office through 1960. In the twenty-first century, the continued bifurcated character of Wisconsin politics was revealed in tea partier Ron Johnson's defeat of the progressive Democratic U.S. senator Russ Feingold in 2010, an event that was followed two years later by the defeat of Wisconsin conservative icon Tommy Thompson by an openly gay Democrat, Tammy Baldwin.

In recent years, however, Wisconsin experiments with social legislation have shifted rightward. Several factors have shaped this shift, most importantly the Great Recession. As with other states in the industrial heartland, downsizing, plant closings and relocations, and concessionary givebacks have for years decimated Wisconsin's industrial core in Milwaukee and in small industrial cities, substantially weakening the collective strength of workers through their unions. But the economic crisis also further weakened other elements of Wisconsin's social structure. In the wealthier white Milwaukee suburbs, middle managers saw the decline in value of their most significant economic assets—their retirement accounts and their homes—as the U.S. economy went into a tailspin. "Out-state" rural Wisconsin suffered as a decades-long collapse of small family farms and plant closures in small, one-industry towns narrowed economic opportunities and deepened an already stressed rural economy. People from across the social spectrum—laid-off industrial workers, the upper rungs of the middle class, the always-stressed rural poor—were hurt and angry. And, moreover, they were jealous of those who did not suffer as much as they did. Wisconsin Republicans took advantage of this anger and capitalized on it with their antitax agenda. For many years, Republican governor Tommy Thompson offered small income tax givebacks—one or two hundred dollars—to taxpayers, cementing some of the white urban and rural poor to the Republican Party. More recently, the Republican public relations machine recast all public servants—from janitors to university professors—as public "takers" rather than as service providers. Republicans and their allies demonized public employees as analogous to the similarly despised (and often black) urban poor. Jealous and economically damaged, urban workers, the rural poor, and suburban middle managers now saw public servants and the urban poor as the enemy who benefited from their tax money.

This politics of resentment fueled Scott Walker's rise to the Wisconsin governorship. Before becoming governor, Walker had played on these economic and racial jealousies as the Milwaukee County executive, maligning both the disadvantaged urban poor and the more advantaged public employees. From the perspective of the white suburbanites who fled urban and black Milwaukee, both groups lived off the tax dollars taken from their pockets. The American Federation of State, County, and Municipal Employees (AFSCME) constantly refused concessions and thwarted Walker's efforts to reduce county taxes, increasing his antiunion leanings. AFSCME resistance to Walker's fiscal conservatism and to cutbacks stiffened his desire to break unions and enhanced his antiunion credentials. He eventually privatized and outsourced many public-service jobs. And Walker, a college dropout, resented and acted against another group of takers, the public school teachers, as well. Although teachers are not state employees, Act 10 applied to all teachers in public schools across the state.

In the 2010 gubernatorial election, Walker faced Democrat Tom Barrett, the mayor of Milwaukee. During his campaign, Walker alleged that a budget crisis existed in the capital, but he did not specify solutions or details to it beyond fiscal caution and conservatism. Consequently, many progressives who should have known better slept through the campaign. For example, the unions never energetically supported Barrett, who faced the same fiscal constraints of the Great Recession and wanted concessions from public employees to balance budgets. They should have known better given Walker's antiunion positions as Milwaukee County executive. But, in the past, the unions had accommodated themselves to whoever occupied the governor's office, either Democrat or Republican.

After the 2010 U.S. Supreme Court decision on *Citizens United v. FEC*, however, a new feature shaped the national and state political arena: virtually unlimited corporate money for political advocacy. Americans for Prosperity and the Wisconsin Club for Growth, two front groups influenced by David H. Koch and Charles Koch, poured millions of dollars into advertisements that saturated the Wisconsin airwaves in support of Walker and other Republican candidates for office. In the November 2010 election, Walker defeated Barrett with just 52 percent of the vote compared to Barrett's 47 percent, and the Republicans won a political trifecta: the Wisconsin governor's office, the senate, and the assembly. Although supposedly nonpartisan, Wisconsin's state supreme court also had a Republican orientation. In Wisconsin, one-party rule prevailed.

Throughout the 2010 campaign, Walker never publicly proposed the elimination of collective bargaining or the weakening of all public employee and teacher unions as a solution to what was in fact a fabricated budget crisis. After the election, hints of a totally new regime were in the air. At the time, Walker covertly told a wealthy donor of his intention to make Wisconsin a right-to-work state after he "divided" and "conquered" the labor movement. Initially, I suspect, Walker believed that he could simply issue an executive order, as did Indiana governor Mitch Daniels when he succeeded in eliminating public employee collective bargaining in 2005. But Wisconsin was different, and collective bargaining was solidly embedded in state law. Sworn in to office on January 3, 2011, Walker probably soon realized that he needed to develop specific legislation to weaken public employee unions.

After the election, Walker's mantra became "Wisconsin is open for business." When he arrived in the governor's mansion, Walker announced a $3.6 billion state budget deficit in the next biennium. Wisconsin state representative Mark Pocan noted that the amount was based on "$3.9 billion in new agency requests" and not actually on the new budget allocations.[3] On February 11, Walker announced his "budget repair bill," Act 10. This omnibus forty-six-page budget bill rewrote existing legislation to achieve significant budget cuts, to substantially alter Wisconsin public-employee relations, and to make Wisconsin law more business friendly.

Act 10 transformed labor relations for all levels of Wisconsin government—state, county, and municipal. The antiunion legislation targeted not only state employees, but all public employees. In addition to making serious cuts to the state budget, Act 10 attempted to weaken and finally to destroy public-sector unionism across the state. Specifically, the antiunion elements of the proposed legislation amended the Municipal Employment Relations Act and the State Employment Relations Act. Among its provisions was a prohibition against employers bargaining on "any factor or condition of employment except wages," and limiting wage negotiations merely to increases in the consumer price index. Moreover, it included two other especially burdensome requirements that undermined the very existence of unions. The first requirement not only called for the annual recertification of collective bargaining representatives but also demanded 51 percent of bargaining unit members (rather than the usual majority of those actually voting) for recertification. The second forbade state and municipal employers from deducting union dues from employees' earnings. Essentially, in accordance with this framework, a public employee union would have little reason to exist and to represent public workers.[4]

Moreover, state workers effectively suffered a significant reduction in their pay. Act 10 took money from public employees' pockets with the requirement that they pay half of the pension contributions, or 5.8 percent of their salaries, and 12 percent of their salaries for health insurance premiums, also adding co-payments to health plans. During my tenure of state employment, Wisconsin had some extremely lean budgets and state employees often accepted larger employer contributions for pension and health benefits instead of wage increases.[5] Following Act 10, the Institute for Wisconsin's Future calculated that the "typical state worker earning $40,000 a year lost $3,668 in take-home pay."[6] Since health insurance premiums were a fixed amount, lower-paid workers, especially custodial and office staff, bore the additional burden of losing a larger percentage of their income.

The Walker administration knew that this proposed law would receive widespread opposition. Unsurprisingly, Act 10 exempted only two public safety union groups, firefighters and policemen, who both have often supported Republican governors—with the latter being called upon to quell any public disturbances in reaction to the law. Further, the original proposal for the legislation included draconian features against any form of "concerted action" on the part of public employees. This provision specifically anticipated labor actions as a result of Act 10 and detailed sanctions in the event that the governor declared a state of emergency. Act 10 provided for the discharge of any public employee with an unapproved absence from work for "any three working days" during such a declaration. A public employee also faced discharge for participation in "a strike, work stoppage, sit-down, stay-in, slowdown or other concerted activities" that interrupted the "operations or services of state government." It specifically forbade "participation in purported mass resignations or sick calls."[7] Walker and his minions had reason to incorporate such drastic and oppressive language into the proposed legislation.

Walker's proposals moved far beyond the accepted political values of the state. They even stunned Republican allies. Ten days before the public announcement of Act 10, the Republican state senate majority leader, Scott Fitzgerald, informed fellow Republican and senate president Mike Ellis, that Walker wanted to "do away" with unions; Ellis responded: "Holy shit! I can't believe this."[8]

Although the full scale of the law's consequences was not immediately clear in the wake of Walker's public announcement, Wisconsin's public employees recognized the threat and quickly hit the streets. After the Friday announcement of Act 10, Wisconsin public employees began making plans to resist the unprecedented assault on their right to bargain collectively and to maintain their unions. On Monday, February 14, the first group to act was the Teaching Assistant's Association (TAA) at UW-Madison, formed in the mid-1960s as one of the first such unions in the country. Unlike the UW faculty, which still had little or no organization on many campuses despite the 2009 lifting of the organizing ban, the state's graduate employees possessed organizations that could propel and shape the resistance to the governor and legislature. For example, on my own UW-Milwaukee campus, which lacked a faculty union, the Milwaukee Graduate Assistant's Association and the local AFSCME chapter provided buses to transport some faculty the 70 miles to the state capitol. The Madison graduate students had planned a Valentine's Day campaign to lobby the governor with the presentation of cards that said "We ♥ UW. Don't Break My ♥." After AFSCME and the Wisconsin Education Association Council (WEAC), the main Wisconsin public school teacher's union, secured demonstration permits, an estimated crowd of two thousand attended afternoon and evening rallies and marched around the state capitol. The size of the crowds rapidly increased, especially on weekends.

The day after the initial demonstration, my partner, also a UW-Milwaukee historian, and I hopped in our car and headed for Madison to join the protest to challenge the elimination of our and other public employee rights. When we arrived, we greeted a crowd of ten thousand other like-minded public employees and their supporters outside the capitol. Inside, a group of three thousand protesters initiated what would become an eighteen-day occupation of the building. Although Act 10 exempted firefighters and police from the most draconian features of Walker's legislation, many from these groups soon joined the demonstrations to the cheers of the protestors. Another faculty colleague joined us the next day, and together we witnessed the crowd of protesters swell to twenty thousand. The chants we heard included, "What's disgusting?—Union busting" and "This is what democracy looks like!" Teachers also staged a walkout that shut down the Madison public school system, allowing teachers, students, and supporters to join the demonstrations. From that point on, large daily demonstrations surrounded the statehouse, particularly during the lunch hour and in the evening, when state offices closed. On weekends, the crowds commonly swelled to as many as sixty thousand and occasionally exceeded a hundred thousand people, filling the side streets leading to the capitol building.

Soon after the Madison demonstrations began, the Republican propaganda machine excoriated the protestors as "union thugs." On the contrary, anyone who saw the demonstrators in Madison witnessed a broad cross section of the men, women, and children of the Wisconsin population, including not just ordinary union members and their families, but supporters from many segments of the Wisconsin citizenry. Over the weeks of demonstrations, I saw among the demonstrators many public employees, K–12 teachers, public school students, and progressive small-business owners and farmers. Families were especially prominent in the crowds. Many young children carried signs or wore T-shirts proclaiming that they were "union thugs." The most inspiring protesters came from the firefighter and police unions, who chose to support the demonstrations despite the efforts of the Walker administration to divide them from their fellow unionized public employees.

The Madison demonstrations were surprisingly peaceful. Initially a few arrests occurred in the senate chamber when Republicans prevented the introduction of amendments to their proposed legislation, but peace prevailed even in the face of consciously provocative tea party counterdemonstrations—featuring conservative luminaries Andrew Breitbart and Sarah Palin. In both instances, the conservative Walker supporters constituted a small contingent of fewer than a thousand people at one of the statehouse entrances. They were overwhelmed by fifty or sixty thousand Walker opponents marching and chanting around the four blocks surrounding the capitol grounds. But the protests were not confined to Madison. On May Day, a yearly immigrant rights demonstration in Milwaukee swelled to a hundred thousand people. Demonstrations also occurred around the state at university campuses and at various state office buildings. Moreover, while one of the purposes of Act 10 was to eliminate the recently extended right of collective bargaining to faculty, the legislation prompted several out-state UW campuses to overcome resistance to unionization and to organize into the American Federation of Teachers. Several out-state UW campuses actually voted to unionize in the midst of the Madison demonstrations. In Milwaukee, frequent demonstrations occurred at Scott Walker's home in the Milwaukee suburb of Wauwatosa. In the first weeks of the uprising, hundreds of union demonstrators followed Scott Walker around the state, chanting and protesting whenever he spoke at a public or private event.

On February 17, after attempts to amend or soften the most draconian elements of the antiunion legislation failed, all fourteen Democratic state senators fled the state across the border to Illinois. In Wisconsin, a budget bill like Act 10 required a larger quorum for passage. With all Democratic state senators absent, the legislation could not move forward under normal procedures. The Republican majority in the senate called for state and other police officers to arrest and return the absconding Democrats to the state capitol. While some futile negotiations continued from Illinois, other Republican shenanigans ensued, including attempts to dock the senators' pay and stopping direct deposit of pay checks and insisting on personal appearance to pick them up. In Madison, assembly Democrats conducted continuous hearings to gather public testimony and many actually slept in the capitol to assure their testimony. Then, late at night on February 25, to shouts of shame from the gallery, the Republican majority in the Wisconsin Assembly finally passed Act 10 in under a minute. Subsequently, on March 9, Republicans stripped Act 10 of its fiscal elements, thereby eliminating the need for a larger senate quorum to pass the legislation, but they kept the antiunion and non-fiscal provisions in the legislation. As an impromptu demonstration gathered, they passed the bill eighteen to one, with less than the required two-hour notice for a senate vote. The next day, the assembly concurred and passed the revised collective bargaining bill. On March 12, Scott Walker signed the bill into law.

The fourteen Democratic senators, known by supporters as the Fabulous Fourteen, returned to Madison to the largest demonstration yet. When we heard that they might return, my partner and I once again headed for the Wisconsin capitol. Possibly as many as 150,000 people surrounded the building and filled the streets leading to the capitol. Walker and the Republicans succeeded in enacting the bill, but the resulting struggle left many Wisconsin citizens furious, and legal challenges slowed the act's implementation.

As a labor historian, I immediately understood the serious implications of Act 10 for Wisconsin employees, including my faculty and staff colleagues at UW-Milwaukee. As a member of the faculty senate, I began sending explanations of the implications of Act 10 to faculty colleagues on any email list available. Some faculty members responded to object to my flurry of emails, but many more praised my efforts. A handful of my more conservative colleagues also criticized these emails, which made me realize that pro-Walker Republicans might find my emails to constitute illegitimate use, but I always noted that I spoke from the perspective of my academic discipline of labor history. And in my emails I often noted an 1894 UW Regents policy (reaffirmed in 1994) of "sifting and winnowing" in the search for academic truth.

During the semester when the Wisconsin uprising began, I taught two undergraduate survey classes—one on U.S. labor history and the other examining U.S. history since Reconstruction. The demonstrations provided a genuine teaching moment, especially for the former class. Some students went to the demonstrations in Madison; a few even slept inside the capitol. In the broader survey, a couple of activist teaching assistants got into trouble for comments in their classes, prompting me to intercede on their behalf to the dean of the College of Letters and Science. Another departmental staff member generated a bit of heat for forwarding a faculty member's email about a demonstration during the summer statewide recall elections.

Besides emailing faculty colleagues, teaching classes, and marching around the state capitol, I engaged in other activities that employed my knowledge of labor history. On the UW-Milwaukee campus, students held rallies during which I briefly spoke about the labor implications of Act 10. The Milwaukee public radio station interviewed me about Act 10 and labor history; segments of this interview also were broadcast on National Public Radio. I challenged a *New York Times* labor reporter's premature conclusion about the labor loss in Wisconsin and a *Milwaukee Journal Sentinel* editor on the paper's uncritical stance on Walker and Act 10. I spoke about the Wisconsin events with reporters from foreign newspapers from as far away as Sweden and Portugal. Later, I also participated on academic panels at the North American Labor History Conference and the

Social Science History Association about the threats to public employee unionism in Wisconsin and other midwestern states.

In the midst of the Wisconsin's uprising, my partner and I took a long-planned spring break trip to the United Kingdom that revealed not only the international reach of the philosophy supporting Act 10 but also the potential power of workers to organize against such ideas and their representatives. We spoke on the Wisconsin events to a small group at the University of Cambridge. In the United Kingdom, as in Wisconsin, public employees were under assault from a resurgent conservative government and faced cuts in their budgets as a result of the Great Recession. British chancellor of the exchequer George Osborne even borrowed a phrase from the Scott Walker playbook, announcing, "Britain is open for Business." (Talk about an international capitalist conspiracy!) On a Friday evening, we attended *Woody Sez*, a musical biography of Woody Guthrie. At the end of the show, the performers encouraged the audience to attend a next-day demonstration in Hyde Park. Following these instructions, we witnessed a million people who came to London from across Britain to protest the savage cuts to public services. For some six hours, we saw lines of demonstrators—often with their union banners—still marching into Hyde Park. If the Madison uprising was impressive, this was genuinely awe inspiring for a single-day event. And Britain's March weather was much more accommodating than Wisconsin in February.

Returning to Wisconsin, we found that the struggle against Act 10 continued. The effort to slow the implementation of the law shifted to a Wisconsin Supreme Court election. The allegedly nonpartisan court had swung right after a recent election involving massive out-of-state advertising funds aimed at electing a conservative to the high court. Progressives had an opportunity to reverse this course by defeating David Prosser, one of the main conservative justices, who was up for reelection in early April 2011. JoAnne Kloppenberg, a Madison judge little known in the rest of the state, ran against Prosser. Once again, however, the outside money machine cranked up in support of a conservative justice. Nonetheless, initial returns revealed that Kloppenberg was ahead by slightly over two hundred votes. Then, the next day, around 7,500 votes mysteriously appeared amid considerable controversy in the Republican stronghold of Waukesha County. In May, Prosser was declared the winner by just over seven thousand votes. Despite Prosser's victory, however, his close Supreme Court election against a relatively unknown Madison candidate demonstrated how divided Wisconsin was and revealed the possibility of an electoral overturn of the right-wing Wisconsin political system.

In April, the Wisconsin Labor History Society held a conference on the theme of the state's progressive heritage that provided an opportunity for union members, activists, and scholars to consider and to assess the developments of the Wisconsin uprising. Though developed before Walker's antiunion campaign, the theme was prescient, contrasting the progressive past with the regressive present. As keynote speaker, the labor historian Leon Fink noted that the progressive

Wisconsin Idea "faces a political landscape bathed today in a combination of corporate greed, attacks on public welfare spending, and the retraction of long-established labor rights." I moderated a final session featuring David Newby, emeritus president of the Wisconsin AFL-CIO; Corliss Olsen, director of the UW School for Workers; and Frank Emspak, a retired School for Workers professor. The panel gave the featured speakers and the audience the chance to reflect on recent developments in Wisconsin. Newby most directly referred to the recent activism and demonstrations. Believing that the future of progressivism resided in the "re-creating and reorganizing of progressive political power" from "the immense energy and commitment and resolve across the state," he suggested that success might come from the effort to create a Democratic majority in the state senate through a proposed recall effort against the Republican state senators. Despite the potential of such an electoral route to change, however, he noted that the Democratic Party had become "more of a money machine." Without a progressive organization "to lead the tens of thousands who participated in the marches and rallies," he urged "'bottom-up' organizing" and local "self-organization" as the "key to a democratic future for Wisconsin." After the presentations, a lively audience discussion ensued, in a powerful manifestation of how the WLHS could bring together academics, union members, and labor activists.[9]

In late May, Prosser's Wisconsin Supreme Court victory had consequences for the legal developments surrounding Act 10. A Dane County judge ruled that the Republican senators had violated the state's open-meeting law in their rush to pass it, nullifying Act 10 and sending the issue to the Republican-dominated Supreme Court. During the deliberations over whether or not the Republican senators violated the open-meeting law, Prosser had allegedly throttled a fellow justice, Democrat Ann Walsh Bradley. The allegation fell within the jurisdiction of the Dane County sheriff, but, after accusations that he was biased because he had endorsed Prosser's opponent, his chief deputy investigated the incident. Eventually the charges were dropped, and the Wisconsin Supreme Court upheld Act 10.

In this context, calls for electoral recalls spread across the state. The Wisconsin state constitution requires that a state official be in office a full year before a recall can be conducted. Although a number of state senators became eligible for recall in 2011, recall proceedings against Scott Walker could not begin until January 2012. Recall elections required signed petitions from a number equaling no less than 25 percent of the votes cast in the original election. The recall elections began as the recall petitions were submitted. In mid-July 2011, a Green Bay Democrat won the first election. In early August, recall elections against six Republicans resulted in the loss of two senate seats. The Republicans retained the majority, but one moderate Republican, the only one to vote against the collective bargaining bill, held the balance of power in the senate. (Later he opposed a Republican bill to redistrict legislative boundaries for the future recall election of Walker.) Two Democratic senators also faced recalls but won handily.

In November 2011, the Walker recall effort began in earnest. Fearing its negative impact on the 2012 presidential election, the state Democratic Party opposed the recall, so two non-party affiliated progressive organizations—We Are Wisconsin and United Wisconsin (mainly a coalition of unions and other progressive groups)—led the recall campaign. Walker opponents needed around 540,000 signatures to get the issue on the ballot. On January 17, 2012, two weeks after Walker's first year in office, supporters of union rights filed over a million signatures to support the recall of the Wisconsin governor and almost 850,000 to recall the lieutenant governor, Rebecca Kleefisch, who had been elected separately. In addition, Walker opponents filed petitions for the recall of four other Republican senators, including senate majority leader Scott Fitzgerald. The huge number of signatures raised hopes for the success of a possible recall.

Enthused and energized, many recall supporters went door to door and staffed tables to gather signatures. At the end of the spring 2011 semester, I retired as a UW-Milwaukee faculty member, earlier than my planned retirement date the following year. I feared that my continued anti-Walker activities might lead to unwanted attention and complications. Before the recall, I had rarely been more politically active than to vote in primaries and general elections or make the occasional small donation to a political candidate. Now, I often occupied a table in the student union encouraging students, staff, and faculty to sign recall petitions. Some signature collectors faced the ugly side of Republican intimidation. For example, in Kenosha, a local Republican official attempted to drive into a table of volunteers gathering recall signatures, and on another occasion a faculty colleague gathering signatures and monitoring similar intimidation had a camera destroyed.

Wisconsin returned to the venomous political heritage of the 1950s, as Republicans reached back to the blacklist, made infamous across the nation by U.S. Senator McCarthy of Wisconsin. Although Wisconsin's open records law applied to recall petitions, allies of state Republicans scanned the signed petitions and posted them online to facilitate local political intimidation of Walker opponents. Anyone who signed a petition became persona non grata for political appointments or was politically marginalized even when participating "legitimately" in the political process. In June 2013, Walker himself appointed a student to the UW Board of Regents, only to revoke the appointment when the student's signature was discovered on a recall petition.[10] During the 2014 Wisconsin gubernatorial campaign, one conservative website posted the recall signatures, along with public records on political donations and criminal convictions, and even called for armed poll watchers to monitor the elections.

Near the end of April 2012, before the recall elections, the WLHS held another conference that centered on the Wisconsin uprising. As a WLHS board and program committee member and a cochair of the Milwaukee local arrangements committee of the Organization of American Historians (OAH, also meeting in the city at that time), I coordinated, with others, the two conferences and developed their themes and programs in ways that highlighted the uprising. The Labor and Working-Class History Association (LAWCHA) also met during the OAH conference. Given the intense national interest in the events in Wisconsin, LAWCHA scheduled multiple sessions concerning Wisconsin and labor history. The WLHS conference took place in the postal workers' union hall a few blocks from the OAH convention site; its theme was "It's Not Over: Reclaiming Wisconsin's Labor Heritage," which gave scholars and activists an opportunity to examine the recent assault on labor rights and possible means for resistance.

The incoming LAWCHA president, Shel Stromquist, provided the organization's keynote address, comparing the "Old Wisconsin Idea" of the Progressive Era with what he called the "New Wisconsin Idea" that had flowered in the wake of Walker's assault on labor. In particular, he noted that, while the old idea had relied on "experts and state policy," the new idea rested on "mobilization and direct action." Many other speakers also addressed the tactics and strategies of mobilization. Mike Konopacki, a political cartoonist, discussed how the depiction of bosses in a "humorous or derisive manner can often work to mobilize workers." Peter Rickman, an organizer for We Are Wisconsin, talked about the use of the new media and the blend of new and old media in the organization of the Wisconsin protests. Other activists related their experiences during the Wisconsin uprising: Charity Schmidt, a TAA member, urged activists and union members to remember the larger picture and greater inclusiveness; Muhammed Mahdi, from "Occupy the Hood" (an outgrowth of the Occupy movement), stressed involvement in community issues beyond the concerns of only union members; and Lane Hall, the originator of the Overpass Light Brigade (a group of local activists who used LED light displays with anti-Walker electoral slogans at highway overpasses in Milwaukee and around the state to focus attention and educate during the recall campaigns) described the group's activities. Chris Larson, one of the Fabulous Fourteen state senators, explained how his knowledge of new media (as a younger state senator) allowed him to serve as "messenger" to the outside world for the other senators in Illinois. In large part because of his activism during the uprising, he later became the state senate minority leader.[11]

One of the most significant presentations involved Brad Lichtenstein, a Milwaukee independent filmmaker. He had collected footage during the initial Walker gubernatorial campaign before Act 10 and the Madison demonstrations for *As Goes Janesville*, a documentary on the social impact of a General Motors plant closing in Janesville, Wisconsin.[12] In the course of his filming, he had encountered the then-candidate Scott Walker speaking with Janesville billionaire and donor Diane Hendricks. After Lichtenstein explained that the film would not be released for a year, Walker allowed Lichtenstein to film the exchange. Hendricks asked Walker when Wisconsin would become a right-to-work state. Walker responded that he first had to deal with the public employee unions as part of his "divide-and-conquer" strategy. At the WLHS conference session, Lichtenstein said that he believed in the open commons and that the film clip would soon be publicly available. In anti-Walker television advertisements, this clip became an important component in the campaign against the antiunion governor.

Unfortunately, but unsurprisingly in a post–*Citizens United* nation, a million signatures and the creativity, innovation, and energy of protestors were all trumped by money and duplicity in the recall elections. In the Democratic primaries for state senators, the Republicans ran "fake" Democrats funded by the Republican Party against real Democrats to muddy the waters and to drain their opponents' financial resources. In the gubernatorial Democratic primary, Milwaukee mayor Tom Barrett defeated Dane County executive Kathleen Falk, who had been the choice of many progressives and labor leaders. Scott Walker amassed almost $37.3 million compared to just under $6.6 million for Barrett. Most of Walker's money—54 percent—came from out of state, while Barret's campaign took only 29 percent of its funds from donors from outside Wisconsin. Walker's wealthy donors again funded a multimillion-dollar television campaign, a huge staff, and rallies around the state to defeat the Milwaukee mayor in the recall campaign. The money funded almost continuous attack advertisements against Barrett. Some of these ads argued that it was premature to recall a governor who had served only one year in office. In the end, Walker won the recall election with 53 to 46 percent of the vote, a percentage representing a 1 percent gain for Walker over the original election. The victory propelled Walker, now the darling of the Republican Right and of the Koch brothers, to the national political arena. Only one of the six Republican state senators facing recall lost. Despite the meager impact of the recall, the senate briefly lost its Republican majority until the resignation of a Democratic senator returned the majority to the Republicans.

After the 2012 recall victory, Walker faced the prospect of a 2014 election for his second term. Instead of the Milwaukee mayor, Walker now faced Mary Burke, a political novice and executive of the Trek Bicycle Corporation. He duplicated his prior electoral coalition and won "decisively among men, rural and suburban voters, married voters, older voters and regular churchgoers." Though the turnout was lower than during the recall, Walker defeated Burke 52 to 47 percent. Walker received 1 percent less than in the recall election; Burke received 1 percent more than Barrett had. Walker's victories were hardly landslides, yet one-party rule offered the chance for significant damage to Wisconsin's progressive tradition. He won with huge amounts of hidden outside money and tightly coordinated advertising campaigns. Walker was on a roll with three successive gubernatorial victories behind him in a little over four years, setting his sights on a campaign for the U.S. presidency in 2016.[13]

For Walker, the road to the Wisconsin governor's office involved a staggering depth and breadth of corruption. Two John Doe investigations (similar to grand-jury investigations to gather evidence of a crime or crimes) revealed the tip of the iceberg of his shady efforts to corrupt and to demean Wisconsin's electoral process. The first investigation focused on the use of public employees and resources in Walker's initial gubernatorial election; the second investigated the coordination between the Walker campaign and financial front groups that spent millions of dollars to aid the Walker cause, something specifically forbidden in Wisconsin. Walker's campaign, the Wisconsin Republican Party, and the financial organizations fiercely resisted the progress of the two inquiries, often claiming that the investigators were tainted Democratic Party partisans. Although Walker toned down his conservative rhetoric as he successfully fought the John Doe probes and sought reelection, the conservative steamroller continued its work in the background. Soon after his second inauguration, he returned to his confrontational posture and targeted two major opponents—private-sector unions and the liberal academics of the University of Wisconsin System.

Despite his assertion as late as December 2014 that right-to-work legislation would be a "distraction," soon after his inauguration he returned to his "divide-and-conquer" strategy.[14] The assault on private employees began when his Republican allies introduced right-to-work legislation back in early 2014. When the regressive legislation was formally introduced after Walker's inauguration in 2015, the labor movement again mounted demonstrations, though significantly smaller and less intense than in 2011. Weariness of continuous struggles against Republican one-party rule in Wisconsin limited the size and intensity of the protests. After being rushed through the legislature, Walker gladly signed the law.

The Walker administration then began an assault against the University of Wisconsin with a drastic change in its mission statement. As Jonas Persson, a writer with the Center for Media and Democracy (CMD), observed, the stated intent was to make the university more business friendly and to address "the state's workforce needs." The core principle of the UW mission was that "the boundaries of the university are the boundaries of the state." The Walker proposal eliminated references to "public service and improving the human condition." Most astonishing, it eliminated one line from the mission statement of the state university system: "Basic to every purpose of the system is the search for truth." This raised a firestorm of protest throughout Wisconsin, including from some members of his own party. The Walker administration immediately backtracked and claimed that the deletion of the UW mission statement was a "drafting error." Subsequently, his office claimed that the error was a "miscommunication" to his budget director. A CMD open-records request uncovered that Walker's chief of staff issued deletion instructions to the budget drafters and Walker's office press secretary essentially obfuscated and lied to the press about the effort, falsely assuring that "The final version of the language was not seen or approved by our office."[15] In the end, the popular outcry caused Walker to cave and to eliminate the proposed changes to the UW mission statement.

But the Walker and Republican budget proposal assault on the academy continued with a proposal to eliminate tenure and shared governance. These academic practices were mainly institutional policies, customs, and traditions in other states, but Wisconsin had taken the step of embedding them in state law. Under legislatively mandated shared governance, the faculty had "primary responsibility" for academic programs and for faculty personnel policies, sharing other authority with the administration. Currently rescinded, this powerful legislation had given enormous shared power to the UW faculty. Currently, the faculty role is merely to "advise" the administration. UW System committees have been delegated to develop and devise a new system for the UW Regents, now mainly appointed by Scott Walker.[16] But the new law severely limits the nature and scope of faculty power.

Moreover, in the wake of repeated budget cuts, Walker proposed massive additional cuts to an already underfunded UW System. Initially, Walker's proposal called for $150 million for each year of the biennial budget, or a total of $300 million; later, in response to widespread criticism, the Republican-controlled Joint Finance Committee reduced the amount to $125 million for each year, or a total of $250 million for each year of the biennial budget.[17]

By the summer of 2015, when Walker began what would become a brief run for the Republican nomination for president on an antiunion platform, he presided over a deeply divided state. In Wisconsin, his poll numbers fell sharply, an indication of the shallowness of his support. Many, including me, blame President Barack Obama for his failure to take a forceful public stand on the recall elections in support of the unions and public employees. Fearful of expending his political capital in a divided state, the president did not come to Wisconsin during the Madison protests. Although he attended Milwaukee's LaborFest in September during his 2008 presidential campaign and during the 2010 midterm congressional campaign, he appeared in Wisconsin only once in 2011, for a January event in the small town of Manitowoc before Walker's February announcement of Act 10. In 2012, Obama attended an event at Master Lock well before the Walker recall campaign began. Then, well after Barrett's loss to Walker in the recall, he again courted the labor vote for his presidential reelection campaign at a September 2012 rally. In the presidential election that year, Obama defeated Mitt Romney in Wisconsin with 53 to 46 percent of the vote. From the perspective of many uprising supporters, he cynically averted spending political capital that might well have changed the recall's outcome. At least in the short term, the recall's failure strengthened Walker's hand in Wisconsin and the wider antiunion movement spreading across the nation and the Midwest in particular.

*   *   *

The Walker counterrevolution against the Wisconsin Idea's progressive political and social values revealed many other consequences. Foremost was the insidious impact of big money in state and local political campaigns since the *Citizens United v. FEC* Supreme Court decision. The Koch brothers, through front groups such as the Wisconsin Club for Growth, Americans for Prosperity, and others, poured substantial amounts into the campaigns of Walker and the recalled Republican legislators. Also insidious in Wisconsin was the impact of the American Legislative Exchange Council (ALEC) and its covert manipulation of the legislative process. One Wisconsin survey of voting records for 2011–12 revealed many Republican legislators marched "lockstep" with ALEC. Sixty-one Wisconsin politicians—or 46 percent of the legislature—"voted with the ALEC agenda one hundred percent of the time." Another fourteen voted with it on a whopping 94 percent of votes.[18] When UW Madison history professor and future American Historical Association president William Cronon's "Wisconsin's Radical Break" essay was published as a *New York Times* op-ed, exposing ALEC's assault on Wisconsin political traditions, he aroused the ire of political groups who did open-records requests of his emails and successfully intimidated him into quiescence.[19]

Finally, as the Cronon incident indicated, the uprising not only lent itself to numerous opportunities for scholar-activists to become involved in their workplaces and communities but also laid bare the very real dangers associated with such involvement. Indeed, in making clear the vulnerability of academic institutions to conservative attack, it emphasized the necessity for scholar-activists to work within broad coalitions. And the very size and scope of the protests was humbling. Although my knowledge and experience allowed for an intervention into the Wisconsin turmoil, my role was minor compared to the roles others played. The real heroes of the Wisconsin uprising were the many thousands who marched and petitioned and continue to work against the regressive Scott Walker administration and its allies, revealing the extent to which social change requires organization at least as much if not more than the intervention of academics.

Notes

1. This chapter collects my experiences, thoughts, and impressions of the Wisconsin uprising from its origins in Walker's election through the recall effort and subsequent elections, from 2010 through 2015. Many of the political details may be found in Jason Stein and Patrick Marley, *More than They Bargained For: Scott Walker, Unions, and the Fight for Wisconsin* (Madison: University of Wisconsin Press, 2013); and John Nichols, *Uprising: How Wisconsin Renewed the Politics of Protest, from Madison to Wall Street* (New York: Nation Books, 2012). Other accounts focusing on the 2011 demonstration are Michael D. Yates, ed., *Wisconsin Uprising: Labor Fights Back* (New York: Nation Books, 2011); Mary Jo Buhle and Paul Buhle, eds., *It Started in Wisconsin: Dispatches from the Front Lines of the New Labor Protest* (London: Verso, 2011); and Erica Sagins, ed., *We Are Wisconsin: The Wisconsin Uprising in the Words of Activists, Writers, and Everyday Wisconsinites Who Made It Happen* (Minneapolis: Tasora Books, 2011). Almost daily accounts of the protests can be found at the Center for Media and Democracy's PRWatch website, www.prwatch.org/topics/wisconsin-protests. For a contrasting perspective on the role of scholar-activists, see Robert D. Johnston, "The Madison Moment: Labor Historians as Public Intellectuals during the Wisconsin Labor Crisis," *Labor: Studies in Working-Class History of the Americas* 9.2 (2012).

2. Stephen Meyer III, *The Five Dollar Day: Labor Management and Social Control in the Ford Motor Company, 1908–1921* (Albany: State University of New York Press, 1981);

Stephen Meyer, *"Stalin over Wisconsin": The Making and Unmaking of Militant Unionism, 1900–1950* (New Brunswick, N.J.: Rutgers University Press, 1992); Stephen Meyer, *Manhood on the Line: Working-Class Masculinities in the American Heartland* (Urbana: University of Illinois Press, 2016).

3. See Mark Pocan, "Walker's Trojan Horse," Wisconsin State Representative Mark Pocan, http://markpocanwi.blogspot.com, accessed October 1, 2014.

4. The detailed and complex original law, 2011 Wisconsin Act 10, March 11, 2011, is at https://docs.legis.wisconsin.gov/2011/related/acts/10.pdf. It included deletions and amendments to existing legislation that touched on state finances, collective bargaining, and compensation and fringe benefits of state employees.

5. "Summary of Provisions of 2011 Act 10," legis.wisconsin.gov, 895–98, 887, 888–89. As found at Internet Archive Wayback Machine, https://web.archive.org, March 11, 2013, accessed January 25, 2015. PDF copy of original in author's possession.

6. Institute for Wisconsin's Future, "The Price of Extremism: Wisconsin's Economy under the Walker Administration," Institute for Wisconsin's Future, Milwaukee, 2011.

7. 2011 Wisconsin Act 10, 37–38.

8. Stein and Marley, *More than They Bargained For*, 49.

9. See *Wisconsin Labor History Society Newsletter* 29.1 (summer 2011).

10. Karen Herzog and Patrick Marley, "Scott Walker Pulls Student's Regents Appointment over Recall Petition," *Milwaukee Journal Sentinel*, June 14, 2013, www.jsonline.com, accessed January 25, 2015.

11. On the April WLHS Conference, see *Wisconsin Labor History Society Newsletter* 30.1 (summer 2012).

12. PBS also broadcast *As Goes Janesville* (dir. Brad Lichtenstein, Kartemquin Films, 2012) as part of its *Independent Lens* series.

13. Craig Gilbert, "Walker Reproduces His Coalition—and His Victories—from 2010 and 2012," *Milwaukee Journal Sentinel*, November 5, 2014, www.jsonline.com, accessed September 10, 2015; and Jason Stein, "Walker Defeats Burke for 3rd Victory in 4 Years," *Milwaukee Journal Sentinel*, November 5, 2014, www.jsonline.com, accessed September 10, 2015.

14. Patrick Marley, "Walker Says Right-to-Work Bill Would Be a Distraction," *Milwaukee Journal Sentinel*, December 12, 2014, www.jsonline.com, accessed September 10, 2015; Jason Stein and Patrick Marley, "In Film, Walker Talks of 'Divide and Conquer' Union Strategy," *Milwaukee Journal Sentinel*, May 10, 2012, www.jsonline.com, accessed September 10, 2012.

15. Jonas Persson, "Emails Show Walker Chief of Staff Oversaw Changes to Wisconsin Idea," PRWatch, May 11, 2015, www.prwatch.org, accessed August 30, 2015.

16. Lincoln Caplan, "Scott Walker's Wisconsin and the End of Campaign Finance Law," *New Yorker*, July 21, 2015, www.newyorker.com, accessed January 25, 2015.

17. Julie Bosman, "2016 Ambitions Seen in Walker's Push for University Cuts in Wisconsin," *New York Times*, February 16, 2015, www.nytimes.com, accessed September 2, 2015.

18. Brendan Fischer, "WI GOP Marches Lockstep with ALEC Agenda, Voting Records Show," PRWatch, March 10, 2014, www.prwatch.org, accessed January 25, 2016.

19. William Cronon, "Wisconsin's Radical Break," *New York Times*, March 22, 2011; Mary Bottari, "Have You No Decency?," PRWatch, March 25, 2011, www.prwatch.org, accessed January 25, 2016.

CHAPTER 5

Immigrants in a Disaster Zone

Teaching, Learning, and Advocating Alabama's New Civil Rights Movement

Michael Innis-Jiménez

In 2011, many of Alabama's Latino and Latina residents were struck by two disasters, one natural and one manmade. On April 15 and April 27, 2011, tornadoes damaged and destroyed large swaths of West, Central, and North Alabama, including several immigrant neighborhoods. At the same time, a high-profile anti-immigrant bill, the Beason-Hammon Alabama Taxpayer and Citizen Protection Act, otherwise known as House Bill (HB) 56, was working its way through the state legislature. This self-proclaimed "Toughest in the Nation" anti-immigrant law, enacted in June, made everyday activities illegal for not only undocumented immigrants but also those people who interacted with them.[1]

The tornadoes and the law colluded to create a "perfect storm" that changed the state's physical, cultural, economic, and political landscapes. Like many other Alabamians, undocumented immigrants and their families lost their lives, their homes, and their property; but, unlike their documented neighbors, if they survived, they also feared arrest and deportation. Undocumented survivors could not easily access relief and aid readily available to the documented community, thus forcing them to rely even more on informal networks and the assistance efforts of preexisting advocacy organizations.[2] Even schools, often regarded as a refuge in moments of community crisis, became associated with the threat of family dislocation. As traumatizing as these events were, however, they also sparked a diverse group of Alabamians to forge a coalition capable of mounting significant public protests and pushing back against the state's resurgent nativism.

These twin disasters also had a powerful impact on my teaching. At the time, I was in my fourth year as an assistant professor of American studies at the University of Alabama in Tuscaloosa, one of the communities heavily hit by the tornadoes and the law. As a historian of labor, the working class, and Latino and Latina immigrants in the United States, I had long been interested in making meaningful connections between undergraduate students and community organizations, and I was already developing a service learning course titled "Immigration and Ethnicity in the South." Following the events of the spring and summer of 2011, I changed the focus of my course but not its objective. For the next three years, I taught the course with a focus on disaster and post-disaster experiences among immigrants to the U.S. South. This new focus included the experiences of immigrants and the reactions of advocates, service providers, and nativists. It was clear that immigrant Latinos in Alabama had experienced many hardships. My goal as a teacher and activist was to educate and link these historical experiences so that students could better understand, critically analyze, and share the significance of what was unfolding around them.

I first taught the course in the fall 2010 semester—only a few months before the introduction of HB 56 but following the rise of anti-immigrant rhetoric in the region. The course ran with ten undergraduates and five graduate students. The group of eight men and seven women included an African American man, a Cuban American man from Florida, and a Mexican American woman from Texas. My goal was to provide an immersion opportunity in a real-world environment. With a particular focus on Latino and Latina immigrants in Alabama, students participated in traditional class discussions, readings, and interactions with guest speakers from social-service and immigrant-rights organizations. The course's core was a twenty-five-hour community based service-learning project to help students better understand the historical and contemporary issues confronting immigrant Latinos and receiving communities.

Students chose organizations to work with from a list of immigrant-serving community partners that I provided. To enhance the learning opportunities and level of engagement, I had each student create a final project that included a written report and multimedia presentation about his or her affiliated organization and the service-learning duties he or she performed there. The vast majority of students worked with Latino and Latina children through an after-school tutoring program run by a local service provider. Although I was initially skeptical of the benefit to my students of spending their service-learning time as after-school tutors, it soon became clear during class discussions and final project presentations that the students participating in the after-school tutoring became more engaged and sought to learn more about the immigrant experiences of their charges and the families they came from.

The focus of my course changed significantly after the first year. When I had first taught the course, my focus had been on introducing students to first-wave Latin American immigrants, the immigrant experience in Alabama, and the challenges to service providers caused by a severe shortage in Spanish-speaking providers. My fall 2011 class had a much different feel. In many ways, the entire campus felt different. The previous regular term had ended early because of the devastation of the April 27 tornado. Although it did not hit campus, the tornado leveled several apartment complexes and neighborhoods, destroying a full 10 percent of Tuscaloosa's city and county housing. For whatever reason, the demographics of my course changed after that, as well. Of the twelve undergraduates and five graduate students enrolled in my fall 2011 course, all but two were women. Among the students were an African American man, an African American woman, and a Latina.

Early in the fall 2011 semester I posed the following question to my students: How did Alabama, a state where those of Latin American descent (including U.S.-born, naturalized citizens, legal residents, and undocumented immigrants) make up less than 4 percent of the population, become a hotbed of anti-immigrant rhetoric and legislation? Historically, some Alabama activists, religious leaders, and civil rights organizations have answered similar questions by pointing to the state's long history of violence and discrimination against people of color and those with contested whiteness, including African Americans, Italians, Southeast Asians, and Latinos. Others have focused on conservative white southerners' persecution complex, which imagined the South as a region whose peaceful existence was (and is) disturbed by the arrival of "outsiders." Students also learned how the recent economic downturn (like so many economic downturns before) had provided the political fuel to change the state's political landscape to one that demanded and made possible anti-immigrant legislation. After the Great Recession reached Alabama in December 2008, unemployment went from a late 2008 average of approximately 3.5 percent to a 2009 average hovering around 10 percent. What followed was an American hallmark during times of crisis: nativism and anti-immigrant legislation.

To return to my question to my students, whatever HB 56's precise origins, however, the law—first proposed in March 2011 and subsequently amended over the next year—had very few unintended consequences. It was designed to make everyday life difficult, even precarious, for anyone who "looked foreign" regardless of citizenship or immigration status. For example, the law made it a felony for undocumented immigrants to enter into "business transactions" with the State of Alabama. This part of the law emphasized that public servants could be charged if they conducted business with immigrants, including standard transactions dealing with driving and business licenses and even license plates. Montgomery County's probate judge posted a notice that anyone "conducting business transactions with any government office will be required to provide issuing officials proof of their United States citizenship or that they are a lawfully present alien in the United States." The notice emphasized that this requirement applied to "*ALL* transactions conducted in our office" (original emphasis).[3] Officials in the town of Allgood interpreted the law to limit the connection to city water to those who could prove "lawful presence," making potable water officially off-limits to undocumented immigrants. The state's most populous county, Jefferson, required proof of legal status to register and pay the taxes on a mobile home. Lack of a registration or tax decal could result in confiscation of the home.[4]

A more encompassing part of the law made *all* contracts between an undocumented immigrant and another person invalid. This meant that, at the state level, banks and car dealerships did not have to honor loan agreements and child support agreements were void, as were contracts with landlords and attorneys. One egregious example occurred in North Alabama. A used-car dealer repossessed the car of an undocumented immigrant despite the fact that the immigrant in question had not missed a payment. Although the law did not put the dealer's business license at risk for selling to "illegals," as he incorrectly claimed, it did invalidate the payment plan and sales contract. This immigrant had already paid nearly $3,000 of the $6,400 sales price.[5] The burden of these new restrictions fell not only on the immigrants themselves, but also on anyone who "looked foreign," in this context, meaning neither "white" nor "black" and non-English-speaking. At the same time, the law encouraged private businesses and public officials to "play it safe" by limiting their interactions with anyone whose skin color or speech threw their status into doubt.[6]

Although most of the provisions in HB 56 made life difficult, the law's attack on education offered a telling point in the anti-immigrant wave of the early twenty-first century. Assimilation starts—and has traditionally started—with education. In earlier immigration waves to the United States, boards of education, settlement houses, churches, and immigrant advocacy organizations initiated the assimilation process through the formal education of immigrants, including teaching English to adults. Although there have been various, and at times competing, reasons for assimilation, over the years many Mexicans, for example, had chosen to learn English to improve their social contacts and economic conditions. Education of immigrants in Alabama became a flashpoint for quite different reasons.

While Great Depression–era nativists demanded that Mexican immigrants learn English and work toward U.S. citizenship, Alabama's twenty-first-century nativists made the education of immigrant children and adults more complicated and much less inviting in order to encourage "self-deportation." To elevate anti-immigrant feelings in a state that had historically spent little money on public education of any kind, nativists promulgated the false perception that immigrant children drained money from public schools in a time of teacher layoffs and cuts to public education. However, the state's tax system made the vast majority of the public school funding dependent on state sales taxes, a tax burden shared by all who purchased products in the state.[7] Furthermore, the law required public schools to verify and report the immigration status of enrolling students and their parents. On September 29, 2011, the day after a federal judge ruled that the school reporting provision could go into effect, immigrant parents kept their kids out of school for fear they would be detained when picking up or dropping off their children.[8]

In this context, I sought to turn my course into a vehicle for both education and advocacy. Therefore, as part of my fall 2011 course, I required students to complete a project that engaged immigrant experiences or their community partner's role in disaster recovery. One of my goals was to build a post-tornado, post-HB 56 oral history collection with student-conducted, University of Alabama Institutional Review Board (IRB)–approved, interviews. Since the vast majority of my 2011 and 2012 students had experienced firsthand the Tuscaloosa tornados of April 2011, a few having lost homes, I expected a shared connection between interviewer and interviewee. I also expected hesitation by interviewees to sign the stringent IRB-approved consent forms and any other paperwork. With a few exceptions, most Latinos and service providers who the students approached agreed to be interviewed. Those interviewed in 2011 and 2012 included immigrants, Mexican Americans, public school teachers, pastors, and the Tuscaloosa city police chief. The majority of students in the classes, for their part, became passionate about improving recovery and everyday life for immigrants while showing dissatisfaction with the actions of state lawmakers.

One of the most important events in firing this passion was a rally in nearby Birmingham, Alabama, on November 21, 2011. Students and I traveled the forty-five minutes from Tuscaloosa to Birmingham for what was billed as a rally to kick off a statewide immigrant-rights campaign. The campaign was part of a public education initiative sponsored by a consortium of civil rights, immigrant advocacy, and labor organizations called One Family/One Alabama. Although I expected a crowd and a "pep rally" atmosphere, I was not prepared for the scale and emotion of the event. We were outside along with about 2,200 people who arrived too late to get inside the city's iconic two-thousand-seat Sixteenth Street Baptist Church, where in 1963 four African American girls had been murdered by a Ku Klux Klan bomb in the midst of the campaign to desegregate the city.

The location was intentional. Indeed, a public battle had already been raging over the appropriation of the civil rights movement's moral authority. A week earlier, Alabama governor Robert Bentley had criticized activists who linked early twenty-first-century immigrant rights in Alabama to the legacy of the state's 1960s civil rights movement. In public comments the governor argued that "It's really somewhat of an insult to the four little girls that were killed in that bombing in Birmingham and the people who were beaten here at the bus station and those that lost their homes and their churches were bombed. It's a disservice to them and an insult to them that went through that movement."[9]

As the event testified, however, Bentley's efforts backfired. African American community leaders, including the church's pastor, suggested that Sixteenth Street host the rally to emphasize the importance of African Americans joining with Latinos in fighting against Alabama's newest injustice, a racist nativism codified in the new anti-immigrant law. One after the other, we witnessed prominent civil rights leaders, politicians, and members of the general public step up to the pulpit to speak about the importance of joining together, pushing back against Alabama leaders, and fighting discrimination in Birmingham and across the state. Terri Sewell, U.S. representative for the 7th District of Alabama, announced the beginning of a "new chapter in this war" on civil rights. Birmingham mayor William Bell linked the 1960s to the current struggle: "I am here to tell you that just as we fought in the past, we will fight now to overcome this injustice." Birmingham City Council president Roderick Royal pointed fingers: "We will say no to Robert Bentley. We will say no to [state senator] Scott Beason. We will say no to [state representative Micky] Hammon. And we will say no to every reincarnated George Wallace in the state of Alabama." Speaking from the pulpit to the crowd in and outside of the church, U. W. Clemon, a civil rights activist and Alabama's first African American federal judge, called for unity as he repeated the famous slogan of the Industrial Workers of the World, "an injury to one is an injury to all," demonstrating (even perhaps unconsciously) the link between the labor movement and movements for black and immigrant rights, past and present.[10] He told Birmingham's veteran civil rights activists, the "foot soldiers" of 1960s Birmingham, to put their "marching shoes back on" and to fight back against the oppression of immigrants in Alabama. The excitement in the crowd was palpable as cheers and tears filled the sanctuary and the street.

On that night, Alabama's governor and legislative leaders awoke a sleeping giant.[11] The state's anti-immigrant political climate, defined by rights advocates as one powered by the "politics of hate," created an impressive alliance that evening and an energy that linked organizations as well as people. The National Association for the Advancement of Colored People (NAACP), the League of United Latin American Citizens (LULAC), the United Farm Workers (UFW), the Service Employees International Union (SEIU), the AFL-CIO, Greater Birmingham Ministries, the Southern Poverty Law Center, Alabama Appleseed, the Hispanic Interest Coalition of Alabama, the Birmingham City Government, and several other organizations joined in loud opposition to the wave of anti-immigrant rhetoric and legislation in Alabama and the rest of the U.S. South.[12] In addition, numerous national labor and civil rights advocates and icons, including Dolores Huerta from California and Representative Luis Gutiérrez of Chicago, actively supported the campaign.

But the law also attracted significant criticism from within Alabama's business community, especially from farmers, construction company managers, and service industry operators. An August 24, 2011, *Wall Street Journal* article, published after the bill had passed but before the law went into effect, highlighted the disconnect between conservative legislative leaders and employers who depended on immigrant labor. According to the article, business leaders were already complaining about the dire economic consequences and the possibility of farmers and small-business owners going under. HB 56 was causing worker shortages within "agribusiness, the state's biggest industry, and sectors such as construction, which is charged with rebuilding the tornado-hit city of Tuscaloosa." The state's agriculture commission reported that "squash, tomatoes and other produce [were] rotting in the fields."[13] Moreover, enforcement of the law resulted in embarrassing incidents in which foreign-born executives at two of the state's highly prized car manufacturing plants were detained.[14] This combined pressure—from activists and from within the business community—ultimately resulted in the weakening of the act and the overturning of several of its key provisions.[15]

The twin disasters of 2011 were devastating to many immigrants and their communities, but a host of Alabamians came together in their wake not only to heal but to fight longstanding inequalities and new policies that targeted some of the state's most vulnerable residents. As a university professor living and working in one of the affected communities, I had the opportunity to design a course that allowed students to move from building a conceptual and analytical framework to making personal connections to a diverse group of new people in their community and across the state. This framework and web of connections revealed both structures of power (often unevenly applied) and ongoing examples of movement building to contest those same structures. Although the vast majority of my students showed a desire and willingness to continue working with and for immigrant communities through advocacy or continued volunteer work with local service providers, I cannot know the course's long-term impact on my students' lives. However, I can say that it transformed me. In particular, it revealed the ways in which engaged teaching and scholarship can take moments of trauma and disempowerment and change them into opportunities for students, educators, and their allies to not only better understand but also confront the use of power in their own lives.

Notes

1. For more on HB 56 and public reactions to it, see Jennifer E. Brooks, "'No Juan Crow!': Documenting the Immigration Debate in Alabama Today," *Southern Cultures* 18.3 (2012): 49–56.

2. Meredith Hoffman, "Alabama Tornado Victims Fear Immigration Crackdown," *New American Media*, May 29, 2011, http://newamericamedia.org, accessed March 23, 2013.

3. Quoted in Joan Friedland, "Turning Off the Water: How the Contracting and Transaction Provisions of Alabama's Immigration Law Make Life Harder for Everyone," *Immigration Policy Center Special Report* (Washington, D.C.: Immigration Policy Center, November 2011), 5–6, www.immigrationpolicy.org, accessed January 31, 2016.

4. Friedland, "Turning Off the Water," 6.

5. Southern Poverty Law Center, "Alabama's Shame: HB 56 and the War on Immigrants," Southern Poverty Law Center, January 2012, www.splcenter.org, accessed April 4, 2014.

6. For a detailed analysis of HB 56's contracts provision, see David P. Weber, "Restricting the Freedom of Contract: A Fundamental Prohibition," *Yale Human Rights and Development Law Journal* 16 (2013): 51–103.

7. For more on the economic effects of anti-immigrant legislation in Alabama, see Samuel Addy, "A Cost-Benefit Analysis of the New Alabama Immigration Law," Center for Business and Economic Research, Culverhouse College of Commerce and Business

Administration, University of Alabama, January 2012. Report available at http://cber.cba.ua
.edu, accessed April 2, 2014.

8. For a brief example of the effects of HB 56 in the public-school classroom, see Jeremy
B. Love, "Alabama Introduces the Immigration Debate to Its Classrooms," *Human Rights*
38 (2011): 7.

9. "Governor Bentley Says New York Times Editorial Is 'an Insult,'" WVTM13, November
17, 2011, www.alabamas13.com, accessed January 30, 2012.

10. For more on this slogan, its labor movement origins, and its importance to organizers, see Ben Hanford, "What's the I.W.W. Preamble For?," *Coopers International Journal*
16.8 (August 1908): 476–78.

11. Eric Velasco, "Hundreds Rally at Sixteenth Street Baptist to Protest Alabama's Immigration Law," *Birmingham News*, November 21, 2011; "On the Rise in Alabama," *New
York Times*, November 13, 2011. For a video recording by the Alabama Coalition for Immigrant Rights of parts of the event (not including Clemon's remarks), see www.ustream.tv/
recorded/18672392, accessed November 29, 2011. For more detailed remarks by Clemon
on the immigration law and civil rights, see www.youtube.com/watch?v=okxowDLDsak,
accessed April 7, 2014. For more on the links between the African American civil rights
movement in Birmingham and the HB 56 battles, see Kevin R. Johnson, "Immigration
and Civil Rights: Is the 'New' Birmingham the Same as the 'Old' Birmingham?," June 1,
2012, *William & Mary Bill of Rights*, 2012; UC Davis Legal Studies Research Paper No.
300, http://ssrn.com, accessed March 5, 2013.

12. Jamie Winders, "Representing the Immigrant: Social Movements, Political Discourse, and Immigration in the U.S. South," *Southeastern Geographer* 51.4 (2011): 596–614.

13. Miriam Jordan, "Alabama Immigrant Law Irks Business," *Wall Street Journal*, August
24, 2011, www.wsj.com, accessed September 1, 2011.

14. Ed Pilkington, "Alabama Red-Faced as Second Foreign Car Boss Held Under Immigration Law," *Guardian*, December 2, 2011, www.theguardian.com, accessed December
3, 2011.

15. Ben Winograd, "Out of Legal Options, Alabama Files Petition at Supreme Court,"
January 13, 2013, Immigration Impact, http://immigrationimpact.com, accessed March 4,
2013; David Noriega, "Alabama's Draconian Anti-Immigrant Law Dies with a Whimper,"
BuzzFeed News, October 13, 2014, www.buzzfeed.com, accessed January 23, 2014.

CHAPTER 6

Remembering the 1911 General Transport Strike in Liverpool

Sam Davies

The year 2011 marked the centenary of the Liverpool General Transport Strike, one of the most serious and prolonged disputes of Britain's pre-1914 labor unrest. It provoked not only the civil authorities to bring in police reinforcements but also the Home Office to send in troops and to position a gunboat in the River Mersey. Indeed, in the words of one historian, during the summer of 1911 "Liverpool in some eyes came near to a revolution."[1] One hundred years later there were many diverse efforts to remember and celebrate this seminal event in Liverpool's labor history, including those of one group of historians and labor and trade union activists of which I was a part. This chapter examines these efforts, bringing out the great rewards that can be made in terms of taking history beyond the academy and into the labor movement and in plugging the past into the present to both educate and inspire.

Commemoration in International Context

The commemoration of labor history anniversaries of course has a long history in itself. From a very narrowly academic viewpoint, there is no reason that historians should take note of anniversaries at all, yet for a wider public they have meaning, as much emotional as anything else. They bring the past back to life, but more than that they inevitably make us think about the present, to compare now with then. For the twenty-first-century labor movement in particular, this is often an uncomfortable process, as the comparison seldom flatters the present. Yet the remembering of past struggles, past victories, and even past defeats can be both instructive and inspiring for labor activists today.

This was brought home to me very clearly by a visit to the United States. In a plenary session at the 2009 Labor and Working-Class History Association (LAWCHA) conference in Chicago, LAWCHA president Michael Honey reflected on publishing his book, *Going Down Jericho Road*, during the fortieth-year commemoration of the assassination of Martin Luther King Jr., who died while supporting striking sanitation workers in Memphis, Tennessee. Honey made an impassioned call for labor historians to celebrate and commemorate significant anniversaries of labor struggles in their localities, precisely as a way of questioning and galvanizing the present-day labor movement. This was underscored by a tour of Chicago's meatpacking district, now long gone but still commemorated by the Union Stock Yard gate, and then by a visit to the Haymarket Memorial, both arranged by the conference organizers. The significance of the latter for the present day was illustrated vividly upon hearing of the conflicts between the Chicago police force and labor activists over what exactly should be represented on the Haymarket Memorial before it was dedicated in 2004—whose history was this anyway?[2] But, as a scholar and as a resident of Liverpool, I found it thought-provoking that, by comparison, so little of the labor history of my city seemed to be commemorated by such public monuments. This was even more striking given that a Labour History Museum in Liverpool had been short-lived, established under the aegis of the Labour Council in 1986 but closed by the subsequent Liberal Democrat administration. The upcoming centenary of the 1911 strike seemed like an appropriate opportunity to address this disparity.

Why 1911?

There are particular reasons why the events of 1911 have a special resonance for Liverpool. The events of that year in the city were of course part of a much wider outbreak of industrial unrest that swept across Britain in the period, famously identified by historian George Dangerfield in 1935 as one of the main causes of what he called the "strange death of Liberal England."[3] It is no accident that as the centenary approached there was renewed interest in Dangerfield's book—for many years rather unfashionable in emphasizing the political, social, and industrial conflicts of pre-1914 Britain.[4] Historians in Britain and elsewhere recognized the significance of the centenary through a number of events and publications, as well.[5] Yet, for Liverpool, 1911 was and still is of heightened significance for a number of reasons.

First, the nature of Liverpool's working class meant that a strike uniting the city's many transport-based, unskilled, and mainly casual workers was a defining moment in its history. There had been an earlier movement of the skilled trades in the city, and in fact Liverpool boasted the earliest trades council in Britain, established in 1848. There had also been socialist organizations such as the Social Democratic Federation, Fabians, and Independent Labour Party active in the city from the 1880s. In a local economy dominated by activities associated with the port, however, the difficulties in organizing the vast numbers of the unskilled were manifold. The "new unionism" of the late 1880s had seen the first significant attempts in organizing dockers and seafarers in Liverpool, only for the employers' counteroffensive of the 1890s to almost completely reverse any gains. So it was that 1911, which saw the permanent unionization of the unskilled for the first time, marked a significant turning point.

Second, religious sectarianism had notoriously divided the Liverpool working class and been an obstacle to industrial and political organization. Only two years before, the city had been scarred by an outbreak of vicious sectarian violence between Protestants and Catholics over the summer of 1909. The future Labour leader, Ramsay MacDonald, in the wake of a by-election swung against Labour by sectarian issues, pronounced in 1910 that "Liverpool is rotten and we had better recognise it."[6] Thus it was extraordinary to see Protestant and Catholic workers marching together on Bloody Sunday, August 13, 1911. On that day, a crowd of eighty thousand assembled in the city center in support of the strike, and hundreds were hospitalized after an unprovoked attack by police and troops; two days later troops fired on a crowd in a dockside district of the city, killing two men and wounding thirteen others.[7] Less than three months after that, the political fruits of this unity seemed to have been delivered, when the Labour Party won seven seats in the city council elections, having previously only ever won single seats on three separate occasions. As noted elsewhere, this was far from the end of sectarian politics in Liverpool, with Labour failing to win control of the council until as late as 1955, but nevertheless 1911 again marked a significant watershed in this regard.[8]

Finally, the repressive response of the government and local authorities to the events of 1911 was particularly marked in Liverpool. There was violence across the country, especially around the period of the national railway strike in mid-August, but the police and military response in Liverpool was particularly ferocious. This reached a peak on Bloody Sunday, and the two fatalities the following week were not the only ones during the 1911 strikes, as four days later another two men were shot in Llanelli, South Wales.[9] The state response in Liverpool, however, was distinctive in reflecting a deep contempt for the city's working class. From a local policeman saying that the "people of these parts are not Englishmen, they are savages," to the Liverpool head constable, singling out "roughs from the adjoining Irish district" as the cause of trouble, to Home Office officials who dismissed a written protest about police brutality as "an Irish Petition . . . characterised by Irish vagueness and largeness of heart" that "might be treated with Anglo-Saxon phlegm and laid by," all demonstrated an anti-Irish and peculiarly anti-Liverpool prejudice.[10]

Remembering 1911

This history of conflict and contempt was the context then for the centenary celebrations of 1911 in Liverpool. There was no unified organizing body for this endeavor; instead, many different organizations and individuals became involved, and numerous events and publications were arranged. The particular strand of this activity that I focus on here centers on a number of academic historians and labor activists who became involved in a Labour History Group established by the Trades Union Congress North West (TUCNW) in Liverpool in 2011. Some of this group had been involved in the 1980s Labour History Museum already mentioned, and they cohered around the planning of the new Museum of Liverpool (eventually opened in 2012). They formed an unofficial labour lobby on the community advisory body, seeking to have labor history as best represented as possible in the museum, while not hiding their ultimate aim of reestablishing a separate labor history museum in the city. It was this group that began to plan for the 1911 centenary.

So many people were involved in this effort over time that it seems impertinent to highlight the role of particular individuals, but it is impossible to explain the process without doing so.

On the academic side, Ron Noon and I, both based at Liverpool John Moores University (LJMU), were involved with the centenary events.[11] Our joint commitment to what might now be called public history was hardly recent and had always been geared toward working with the labor movement. As long ago as 1980, for instance, we joined other colleagues to produce *Merseyside in Crisis*, a book that placed the desperate economic and social crisis facing Liverpool at that time within its longer historical context.[12] We sold five thousand copies of this book, primarily through direct sales at over a hundred trade union and Labour Party branch meetings. We later also produced *Genuinely Seeking Work*, an analysis of mass unemployment on Merseyside in the 1930s, as well as a pamphlet commissioned by the Post Office Workers' Union on productivity deals.[13] Other initiatives included my article on the Liverpool Docks Dispute of 1995–98, and Ron Noon's work with the Merseyside Construction Safety Campaign (a body organized by various unions) in reviving interest in the writings of the local syndicalist Fred Bower, resulting in a pamphlet and a public ceremony in 2004 to commemorate the centenary of the occasion when Bower and Jim Larkin (a Liverpool-born socialist and trade unionist) buried a socialist message to a future society under the foundation stone of the Anglican cathedral.[14] In all these activities, the aim was to work with the labor movement to make available whatever historical knowledge and research skills we had; the 1911 celebrations were a continuation of this aim.

On the other hand, of course, such efforts were possible only if sections of the labor movement were amenable to them. Many organizations and individuals have been involved in these collaborations over the years, but in the context of the 1911 events, a number of individuals were involved. Alan Manning, then the regional secretary of TUCNW (now retired), was crucial in throwing his organization's weight behind the activities. Also central to the group were two activists with a long history of involvement in the labor movement, and whose great experience and wide circle of local contacts were invaluable in planning the activities. Now retired, Eddie Roberts was a Transport and General Workers Union (TGWU) activist at Dunlop's Speke plant in the early 1960s before he joined Ford's (Halewood), where he became a steward and later convener in the Paint, Trim and Assembly plant. In 1970, he became the regional TGWU official for the Association of Clerical, Technical and Supervisor Staffs (a division of the TGWU) and then in 1977 became the regional TGWU organizer for District 6 (Merseyside). Tony McQuade, also now retired, was a shop steward at British Leyland site 2 (Speke) from 1970 until the plant's closure in 1977, becoming eventually chairman of the TGWU 6/612 branch. Eventually known as the unemployed branch, the TGWU 6/612 played a pivotal role in establishing the Merseyside Trade Union, Community and Unemployed Resource Committee, of which Tony was vice president. From 1984 to 2009 he was a regional industrial organizer for the TGWU (which later formed part of Unite, now Britain's largest union). Without the involvement of these and other labor activists, the centenary commemorations could not have taken place.

Searching for the Human Side of Labor Conflict

In planning the centenary commemoration, we quickly confronted the decision of where to focus our efforts. On the one hand, we were fortunate enough to have a substantial literature published on 1911 on which to draw, including studies concentrating specifically on the police and on the significance of syndicalism in the strikes.[15] One obvious focus for any commemoration was Bloody Sunday and the succeeding days of unrest in mid-August 1911, but new research was needed, especially to bring out the human side of these conflicts. A detailed examination of the local press and the *Manchester Guardian* and the *Times*, and several trips to Kew to review the Home Office records in the British National Archives, provided new insights into these tumultuous events; some of our discoveries have since been published.[16]

One of the most striking features that emerged from this research was the scale and ferocity of the police and military repression that Liverpool experienced. From the wanton batoning of the crowd on Bloody Sunday, to the wholesale arrests made during the succeeding riots, the harsh prison sentences handed down in peremptory court hearings, and the widespread use of troops and firearms culminating in two fatalities, the city was under siege by the authorities. This in turn led to our looking into who were the hospitalized and arrested victims of this crackdown, which revealed that a wide cross section of mainly working-class men, women, and children suffered, across sectarian divides.

Eventually, we focused our attention on the two men shot, Michael Prendergast and John W. Sutcliffe, and they became the centerpiece of the commemoration. Their deaths occurred on the evening of Tuesday, August 15, 1911, when a convoy of vans holding convicted prisoners after the events of Bloody Sunday was dispatched to Walton Gaol on the northern outskirts of the city. Passing through the Vauxhall district, the convoy was attacked by some of the local populace, whereupon troops opened fire, killing the unfortunate Prendergast and Sutcliffe. In all, ten men, three women, and two children were hospitalized, nearly all of them coming from the very near vicinity, part of a crowd of local residents in a strongly working-class area near the docks where casual, unskilled labor was the norm. There were significant discrepancies between the press reports immediately after the event and the statements made at the subsequent inquest on the two deceased; there were also discrepancies between the testimony of the military and police and that of the civilians who gave evidence. The military witnesses alleged that they had come under ferocious attack from the crowd, justifying their opening fire. There were no soldiers hospitalized, however, and civilian witnesses said that most of the crowd were bystanders who had come out of their houses to see what was going on. When asked whether they had orders to shoot to kill, the soldiers provided only evasive answers, none of them denying the allegation outright.[17]

Further research into Michael Prendergast revealed that he was a Roman Catholic docker, at the time of his death aged twenty-nine according to his gravestone, although some newspaper reports claimed he was thirty.[18] He lived at 37 Steel Street, on the opposite side of Vauxhall Road from Lamb Street, just across the Leeds–Liverpool Canal, with his sister, Marcella, and her husband, Henry King, a railway porter. Also living in the house was a boarder named William Murphy, who may have been related to the others because he was later buried in the same grave with them. Prendergast's family can be traced back in the census returns in the north end of Liverpool to the 1860s, with both his maternal and paternal grandparents recorded as being born in Ireland. Very little else of his life can be discovered, especially as there seems little possibility of tracing any direct descendants of Prendergast, since all the occupants of his household met tragic ends soon after his own. His brother-in-law, Henry, died as a corporal in action in France in 1918; the boarder, Murphy, had died earlier in January 1914; and no fewer than two nieces and a nephew are also recorded on his headstone as dying in infancy. His sister, Marcella, barely outlived them all, dying in November 1919 according to burial records.

Rather more can be found out about the other fatality, John W. Sutcliffe. He was a twenty-year-old Catholic carter, who according to the 1911 census lived at 6 Hopwood Street with his uncle, Dennis Lennon, a master carter, and his aunt, Ellen. Also living in the household was another of John's uncles, William Murphy, again a carter, and his seven-year-old cousin, Nellie Brown. The fact that Sutcliffe was Catholic is significant as it belies a commonly held view repeated in some of the earlier studies of 1911 that it was "a Catholic docker and Protestant carter" who had been killed. This myth was first recorded in print in Harold Hikins's 1961 essay on the strike, in which Hikins attributes the information to a living survivor of 1911 who he interviewed.[19] This myth suits the narrative of how sectarian divisions had been broken down, with both sides of the sectarian divide being able to claim a martyr, but it is patently untrue. Sutcliffe was baptized in the local Catholic church, St. Sylvester's, and buried in Ford Catholic cemetery. Both sides of his family can be traced back to the 1850s resident in the north end of Liverpool, and the grandparents of his Catholic mother, Catherine (née Murphy), were Irish born. On his paternal side, however, there were Protestant connections, as his father, Charles, was born a Protestant but converted to Catholicism on marriage. Thus the Lennons and Browns that John Sutcliffe lived with might well have been Protestant, as well, although his aunt Ellen was presumably one of the Catholic Murphys. In turn, two further traditional views of Liverpool are challenged. Sutcliffe's parents "mixed marriage" shows that the sectarian divide at a personal level was not perhaps as absolute as it has sometimes been made out to be. At the same time, it has been said that many if not most carters in Liverpool were Protestants, but clearly this was not the case with Sutcliffe.[20]

Our sense of the human tragedy of Sutcliffe's death deepened as we traced some of his living descendants. Ellen O'Shaughnessy, a granddaughter of John's sister Ellen, was traced through her relations in Canada via a genealogy website. She was still living in Liverpool and was interviewed as part of the research. Maureen Harrison, Joan Dwyer, and Patricia Woods, three granddaughters of John's younger brother, James R. Sutcliffe, came forward themselves when they saw publicity of the centenary events, and provided much additional knowledge. Ellen's branch of the family had no knowledge of their antecedent's tragic end, whereas the other branch was not only well aware of it, but also corroborated the account given in the press by their great-aunts of John Sutcliffe only going out to close the shutters on his uncle's house during the disturbance. They also provided fascinating details of James Sutcliffe, who had been away at sea at the time of his brother's death. An undated letter to his wife while away at sea sometime later (probably around 1919, as he refers to numerous deaths due to the "Spanish flu"), on writing paper headed with a crucifixion scene, shows him to have been a loving husband. Even more poignant, his merchant marine papers record that he had a tombstone tattooed on his left arm, which may have been in memory of his dead brother.

The Centenary Commemorations

Armed with the results of our research, we set about crafting and organizing the commemorations. As the group's first contribution to the centenary commemorations, over the summer of 2011 the TUCNW published a handsome, well-illustrated pamphlet, *1911 and the Liverpool General Transport Strike*. Five thousand copies of this pamphlet were distributed to affiliated members of the TUCNW. As the centenary of the shooting of Prendergast and Sutcliffe approached, a meeting was organized near the shooting site at the Eldonian Village Hall on

Vauxhall Road. The venue was significant, as it lies in the heart of the dockside working-class district in which the two men lived. Although much of the low-quality housing had been demolished in the intervening century, the Eldonian estate itself is the result of a remarkable project to preserve some of the original community by building new homes on the site.[21] Well over a hundred people attended the meeting, including local Labour MPs and city councilors, labor and trade union activists, and some of John Sutcliffe's descendants. The meeting was chaired by Eddie Roberts, and a number of speakers commented on the events of a hundred years previously and their relevance to the present. They included Ron Noon and me from LJMU; Tony Mulhearn, one of the Labour councilors barred from office in the 1980s because of the council's fight against the policies of the Thatcher government; and Tony McQuade. Local musicians Alun Parry and Ian Prowse played, and the meeting concluded with a communal rendering of "Solidarity Forever." BBC Television filmed the event, with footage appearing in a documentary film on the shootings that was broadcast in November 2011.[22]

Other activities linked to the labor movement came out of the research on 1911, especially in relation to the first national railway strike, which formed the backdrop to the events in Liverpool. The two main trade unions representing railway workers today were also keen to commemorate this significant turning point in their own histories. The president of the Rail, Maritime and Transport Workers (RMT), Alex Gordon, organized a one-day conference on the strike in November 2011 at the Peoples' History Museum in Manchester, at which I presented a paper. In May 2012, the train drivers' union, the Associated Society of Locomotive Engineers and Firemen (ASLEF) held its annual assembly of delegates in Liverpool. The union's regional organizer, Colin Smith, after attending the centenary meeting, asked Ron Noon and me to address the assembly on the strike. Both unions stressed the relevance of bringing history into the present and counterposing it with problems facing trade unionists today. The response from union members at both events was enthusiastic.

In 2012, the TUCNW Labour History Group agreed to erect a plaque at the site of the shootings. The Casa, a bar and social center for the labor movement in Liverpool established by dockers sacked in the long lockout of 1995–98, organized the manufacture of the plaque, for which the support of Casa director Tony Nelson was vital. As already noted, most of the original buildings along Vauxhall Road where the shootings took place had been demolished, but at the corner of Hopwood Street (now Gem Street) still stood the building that in 1911 housed a pub. On its wall Tony McQuade affixed the commemorative plaque, which reads as follows:

1911 TRANSPORT STRIKE

At this site on 15th August 1911 John W. Sutcliffe
A 19-year old carter was shot dead by British troops during

the Liverpool Transport Strike.
Further up Vauxhall Road Michael Prendergast a
30-year old docker was also fatally injured.
Many others were injured including women and children.
On behalf of all working-class people we remember the
sacrifices they made fighting for trade union and political rights.

The plaque was unveiled on Saturday, August 18, 2012, by Len McCluskey, the general secretary of Unite. A large crowd again packed the Eldonian Village Hall to commemorate the lives and deaths of Michael Prendergast and John Sutcliffe. The meeting was introduced by Ron Noon, and descendants of John Sutcliffe were again present to hear me trace the men's family histories. Len McCluskey and Eddie Roberts also spoke, stressing the importance of remembering the history of trade union struggles, but also pointing out the vital issues confronting the labor movement today. Local singer Alun Parry sang two labor songs, and actor Jamie Vere performed a dramatic reconstruction of the 1911 events. This meeting also ended with the singing of the IWW song, "Solidarity Forever."

Finally, it is necessary to point out that the response to the 1911 commemoration was not always positive. Just as some academics do not see public history as a proper activity for a "professional" historian, there are also those in the labor movement who are suspicious of the intrusion of "academics" into the world of labor. This was exemplified most clearly in conversations on the website of a local radical magazine, *Nerve*. After its coverage of the 1911 centenary event and other commemorative meetings, some online comments criticized the involvement of academics, in some cases drawing a value-laden distinction between "historians" on the one hand and "activists" on the other. Apart from a few abusive comments that the magazine removed from the site, much of the conversation raised valuable issues. As one contributor put it, "automatically branding anyone who is an historian or 'academic' as being 'ivory-tower' and against rank and file militancy is mistaken. What was positive about the 'Bloody Tuesday' commemoration at the Eldonians was it brought together different strands of the labor movement and working-class activists, both those who have fought and done us proud for many years, and those new to the struggle."[23]

We posted elsewhere in the discussion our own response to the debate:

We organised the event to commemorate the 1911 shootings because they are an important part of the working-class history of Liverpool which have [*sic*] received very little attention before, and they were also a great injustice which has never been righted. The intention was to deliver a respectful, serious and comradely tribute to the men who died, to do honour to them and the working-class community of which they were a part, and to remind the trade union and labour movement of today of the significance and importance of these events of 100 years ago. Whether we succeeded or not in doing this can only be judged by those who attended the event—but for our own part we felt truly moved and inspired by the response of the audience, summed up by the magnificent singing of "Solidarity Forever" at the end.[24]

Moreover, a powerful sense that the past continues to repeat itself in our present intruded on our research and activities around that time. For instance, only two days before the unveiling of the 1911 plaque, thirty-four striking miners at the Marikana mine in South Africa were shot dead by police, and at least seventy-eight others injured. A minute's silence in honor of the South African fatalities was held at the opening of the 2011 event in Vauxhall, and it was impossible for those in the Liverpool audience not to draw a parallel to the events of a century earlier. The inescapable fact is that workers in struggle still face powerful, even brutal, opposition internationally.

In the background of the 1911 commemoration throughout, there was yet another present-day issue that could not be ignored. In October 2012, the results of the independent enquiry into the 1989 Hillsborough tragedy, when ninety-six Liverpool football fans died, were announced. They confirmed that culpability for the deaths lay with the police and other authorities providing security for the match, and that there had been a systematic campaign to hide the truth, to vilify the dead fans, and to place blame on the dead. Most notoriously, four days after the 1989 disaster, Kelvin MacKenzie, editor of the *Sun*, a British tabloid newspaper owned by Rupert Murdoch, splashed "THE TRUTH" across the front page, with three smaller headlines underneath: "Some fans picked pockets of victims," "Some fans urinated on the brave cops," and "Some fans beat up PC giving kiss of life" (the last refers to alleged assaults on a policeman while he was attempting to resuscitate a victim). All these allegations were later proven to be untrue and to have been planted by the police.[25]

Another glaring example of the way in which people from Liverpool have been unfairly maligned is from 2004, when Boris Johnson, then a Tory MP and currently mayor of London, wrote in the *Spectator* that by holding a two-minute silence in the city in remembrance of Ken Bigley, a Liverpool citizen who had been killed as a hostage in Iraq, Liverpool was displaying a disproportionate "outpouring of sentimentality."[26] Moving from the particular to the general, he went on to say that Liverpudlians "see themselves whenever possible as victims, and resent their victim status; yet at the same time they wallow in it . . . they cannot accept that they might have made any contribution to their misfortunes, but seek rather to blame someone else for it, there by [*sic*] deepening their sense of shared tribal grievance against the rest of society." As evidence for this, he castigated "Liverpool's failure to acknowledge, even to this day, the part played in the [Hillsborough] disaster by drunken fans at the back of the crowd who mindlessly tried to fight their way into the ground that Saturday afternoon. The police became a convenient scapegoat, and the *Sun* [*sic*] newspaper a whipping-boy for daring, albeit in a tasteless fashion, to hint at the wider causes of the incident."[27] Johnson was forced to make a groveling apology, but his sentiments eerily echoed comments made a century ago about Liverpudlians, noted earlier in this chapter, of "savages," "roughs," and "Irish vagueness and largeness of heart." For the "Liverpool Irish" of 1911, substitute the "scousers" of the twenty-first century. As William Faulkner wrote, "The past is never dead. It's not even past."[28]

Going Forward

The Prendergast and Sutcliffe plaque is one of the few monuments dedicated to the city's labor history—more needs to be done. For the future, it was decided by the TUCNW Labour History Group that an annual Prendergast and Sutcliffe lecture on labor history would be organized to commemorate the events of 1911. Labor historian Tony Lane delivered the first lecture in October 2013 on the Seamen's Reform Movement, again held at the Eldonian Village Hall. The second lecture, on the life and times of the Liverpudlian syndicalist Fred Bower, was presented by Ron Noon at the Bluecoat Chambers in December 2014. The TUCNW group also collaborated with the Dublin-based 1913 Committee in commemorating the centenary of the 1913 Dublin lockout, holding a joint public meeting in Liverpool on the connections between the Liverpool and Dublin labor movements. Ron Noon and I also annotated the 2015 republication of Fred Bower's 1936 classic, *Rolling Stonemason*.[29] Finally, members of the TUCNW group were involved in establishing Merseyside Trade Union and Labour Heritage in 2013, with trustees drawn from representatives of local trade unions, museums, and universities. Its aim is to preserve the history of trade unionism and the labor movement in the area through an oral history project, and it has the support of many local and national trade union leaders and activists.[30] There was again a trans-Atlantic impetus to this initiative—while attending the conference honoring Shelton Stromquist on which this collection of essays is based, my visit to the Iowa Labor History Oral Project archives inspired me to endeavor to bring about something similar in Liverpool.

The 1911 centenary in Liverpool stimulated a broad range of activities in the city and was instrumental in bringing historical issues to a wide audience. The 1911 centennial activities outlined in this chapter are an attempt to combine serious historical research and genuine popular engagement, with a focus on the labor history of the city. More than anything else, it is also an attempt to connect the past with the present. Consideration of the problems, and the achievements, of the early twentieth-century labor movement helps stimulate discussion on the current state of labor.

Notes

1. Harold Hikins, "The Liverpool General Transport Strike, 1911," *Transactions of the Historic Society of Lancashire and Cheshire* 113 (1961): 169; Eric Taplin, *Near to Revolution: The Liverpool General Transport Strike of 1911* (Liverpool: Bluecoat Press, 1994), 12.

2. Details of LAWCHA conference from "Program: Race, Labor and the City: Crises Old and New, Roosevelt University, 430 S. Michigan Avenue, Chicago, Thursday, May 28–Sunday, May 31, 2009," electronic copy provided to author by Michael K. Honey from the personal collection of Erik Gellman. Honey's book is *Going Down Jericho Road: The Memphis Strike, Martin Luther King's Last Campaign* (New York: W. W. Norton, 2008). Regarding the contested commemoration of Haymarket, see James Green, *Death in the Haymarket: A Story of Chicago, the First Labor Movement and the Bombing that Divided Gilded Age America* (New York: Pantheon, 2006), 274–320.

3. George Dangerfield, *The Strange Death of Liberal England* (London: MacGibbon and Kee, 1966).

4. See, for instance, John Garrard, "One of the Most Vivid and Indeed Genuinely Witty Works of History Ever Written: *The Strange Death of Liberal England*," *North West Labour History* 31 (2006–7): 7; John Callaghan, "The Edwardian Crisis: The Survival of Liberal England and the Rise of a Labour Identity," *Historical Studies in Industrial Relations* 33 (2012): 1–23.

5. Centenary events included the following: the Colloque International "A la redé-couverte de la Grande Fièvre Ouvrière, 1911–14," Université Paris 3, Sorbonne Nouvelle/Université Paris 13, Paris Nord (2011); the "Near to Revolution? 1911 Centenary Conference," Liverpool John Moores University (2011); and the RMT public meeting, "Great Unrest: 100 Years since the First National Railway Strike—Fighting Unions 1911 and Today," People's History Museum, Manchester, 2011. Centenary publications included special themed editions of *Historical Studies in Industrial Relations* (vol. 33, 2012) and of *Labour History Review* (vol. 79, 2014).

6. Ramsay MacDonald quoted in Ross McKibbin, *The Evolution of the Labour Party, 1910–1924* (London: Oxford University Press, 1974), 14.

7. Fred Bower, *Rolling Stonemason: An Autobiography* (London: Jonathan Cape, 1936), 196.

8. On the subsequent political development of Labour, see Sam Davies, *Liverpool Labour: Social and Political Influences on the Development of the Labour Party in Liverpool, 1900–1939* (Keele, U.K.: Keele University Press, 1996). On the limitations of the advances of 1911, see John Belchem, "Radical Prelude: 1911," in *Liverpool: City of Radicals*, eds. John Belchem and Bryan Biggs (Liverpool: Liverpool University Press, 2011), 14–40, esp. 25–36; but for a more positive assessment, see Mark O'Brien, "Liverpool 1911 and Its Era: Foundational Myth or Authentic Tradition?," in Belchem and Biggs, *Liverpool*, 140–58.

9. On the Llanelli deaths, see Deian Hopkin, "The Llanelli Riots, 1911," *Welsh History Review* 11 (1983): 488–515; R. Geary, "Tonypandy and Llanelli Revisited," *Llafur* 4 (1987): 34–45; J. Edwards, *Remembrance of a Riot: The Story of the Llanelli Railway Strike Riots of 1911*, (Llanelli, U.K.: Llanelli and District Civic Society, 2010); Tim Evans, "The Great Unrest and a Welsh Town," *International Socialism* 131 (2011), http://isj.org.uk, accessed 17 Jan. 2016.

10. *Manchester Guardian*, 17 Aug. 1911; National Archives, Public Record Office, Kew, Home Office, 45/10656/212470/141; National Archives, Public Record Office, Kew, Home Office, 45/10657/212470/398.

11. Ron Noon was a senior lecturer in history at Liverpool John Moores University until his retirement; I am professor of history at the same institution.

12. Merseyside Socialist Research Group, *Merseyside in Crisis* (Manchester: Manchester Free Press, 1980).

13. Merseyside Socialist Research Group, *Genuinely Seeking Work: Mass Unemployment on Merseyside in the 1930s* (Liverpool: Liverpress, 1992).

14. Sam Davies, "History in the Making: The Liverpool Docks Dispute 1995–96," *North West Labour History* 21 (1996–97): 67–72.

15. Jane Morgan, *Conflict and Order: The Police and Labour Disputes in England and Wales 1900–1939* (Oxford, U.K.: Clarendon Press, 1987), 164–75; Barbara Weinberger, "The Summer of the Great Unrest," in *Keeping the Peace? Policing Strikes in Britain, 1906–1926* (New York: Berg, 1991), 69–102; Bob Holton, "Syndicalism and Labour on Merseyside, 1906–14," in *Building the Union: Studies on the Growth of the Workers' Movement: Merseyside, 1756–1967*, ed. H. R. Hikins (Liverpool: Toulouse Press, 1973), 121–50; Bob Holton, "The Transport Strikes of 1911," in *British Syndicalism 1900–1914* (London: Pluto Press, 1976), 89–110.

16. See Sam Davies, "'Crisis? What Crisis?': The National Rail Strike of 1911 and the State Response," *Historical Studies in Industrial Relations* 33 (2012): 97–125; Sam Davies and Ron Noon, "The Rank and File in the 1911 Liverpool General Transport Strike," *Labour History Review* 79 (2014): 55–81.

17. *Times*, 1 Sept. 1911; *Manchester Guardian*, 1 Sept. 1911; *Liverpool Daily Post and Mercury*, 1 Sept. 1911.

18. He was also recorded as twenty-nine in the 1911 census, but according to baptismal records, the only Michael born to his parents Robert and Anne was born on 31 July 1878, which would have made him thirty-three at the time of his death. It is possible that this Michael was an earlier child who had died in infancy. Prendergast's and his parents' names were at different times also recorded as "Pender" or "Pendergast," causing even greater ambiguity. All this shows the problems of using census and birth, marriage and death records, so his age of twenty-nine must be accepted with some reservations.

19. Hikins, "Liverpool General Transport Strike, 1911."

20. On the alleged Protestantism of carters in Liverpool, see Phillip Waller, *Democracy and Sectarianism: A Political and Social History of Liverpool 1868–1939* (Liverpool: Liverpool University Press, 1981), 253; Paul Smith, "'A Proud Liverpool Union.' The Liverpool and District Carters' and Motormen's Union, 1889–1946: Ethnicity, Class and Trade Unionism," *Historical Studies in Industrial Relations* 16 (2003): 2–5; but see 10–11 for evidence that some carters were Catholics.

21. On the history of the establishment of the Eldonian village, see Jack McBane, *The Rebirth of Liverpool: The Eldonian Way* (Liverpool: Liverpool University Press, 2008).

22. "Inside Out North West," dir. Laurence Inwood, broadcast 7 Nov. 2011, www.bbc.co.uk, accessed 17 Jan. 2016. See also "Liverpool's Fatal 1911 Riots Remembered," 16 Aug. 2011, BBC News, www.bbc.co.uk, accessed 17 Jan. 2016.

23. Comment posted by Luke to Jeremy Hawthorn, "Two Workers Shot Dead by Soldiers in 1911 Are Honoured," *Nerve*, 24 Aug 2011, www.catalystmedia.org.uk, accessed 17 Jan. 2016.

24. Comment posted by Sam Davies and Ron Noon to Jeremy Hawthorn, "Two Workers Shot Dead by Soldiers in 1911 Are Honoured."

25. See Michael White, "Hillsborough Disaster: A Case of Class Injustice?," Politics Blog, *Guardian*, 18 Oct. 2011, www.theguardian.com, accessed 17 Jan. 2016.

26. Boris Johnson, "Bigley's Fate," *Spectator*, 16 Oct. 2004, http://archive.spectator.co.uk, accessed 17 Jan. 2016.

27. Ibid., "'Sorry' Johnson sent to Liverpool," BBC News, last update 16 Oct. 2004, http://news.bbc.co.uk, accessed 17 Jan. 2016.

28. William Faulkner, *Requiem for a Nun* (New York: Random House, 1951), 1:3.

29. Fred Bower, *Rolling Stonemason: An Autobiography*, annotated and introduced by Ron Noon and Sam Davies (London: Merlin Press, 2015 [1936]).

30. Progress on this project has been held up by illness, affecting both Ron Noon and me, from 2015 and onward, but activities likely will revive under the auspices of the TUCNW Labour History Group.

PART II

Connecting Classrooms and Communities
Education, Outreach, and Engagement

Connecting Classrooms and Communities

Education, Outreach, and Engagement

Matthew M. Mettler

Educators interested in pursuing meaningful roles that connect classrooms and communities, especially those that span academia and the labor movement, face significant challenges. They must find employment in a difficult and increasingly corporate environment with few labor-focused employment opportunities and in which academic administrators view signs of labor activism as a liability. Once employed, educators often must divide their time to meet obligations in teaching, research, publishing, service, and their personal lives. Those fortunate to secure academic employment must also overcome the distrust that has unfortunately but understandably soured relations between labor unions and intellectuals. Finding or creating a niche to work effectively as an engaged educator is no small task. Despite these obstacles, innovative and passionate teachers often strike this balance with grace. The five chapters in this section illustrate these possibilities, highlighting the relationships, organizations, and spaces in which teachers build dynamic communities and connections to students and working people.

This section opens with reflective autobiographical essays from two prominent labor historians for whom engagement in the labor movement and local community has been central to their work as teachers. In "The Great Unspoken: Teaching and Learning Working-Class History from the Seminar Room to the Union Hall," James R. Barrett looks back on his more than thirty years at the University of Illinois. He underscores the many contributions labor historians have made through their scholarship and teaching, especially when connected to worker outreach and engagement in local conflicts and struggles. Turning his attention to the evolution of his graduate seminar in working-class history, Barrett shows how an earlier focus on class and unions has been displaced, in part, and enriched by greater attention to race, ethnicity, gender, and sexuality. This shift provides for new understandings of class and points to the need for scholars and teachers to explore workers' individual experiences and emotional lives.

Peter Rachleff's "Teaching Labor History on the Middle Ground: Connecting the Campus, the Union Hall, and the Community" expands our definition of the classroom. Rachleff, who taught labor and African American history to undergraduate students at Macalester College, emphasizes the pedagogical and political benefits of teaching on the "middle ground"—those creative spaces in which people from different walks of life share common experiences and build connections. Rachleff and his colleagues in particular turned to the arts, film, and theater to connect liberal arts students, union activists, and community members. Rachleff also has helped to create these middle grounds through Untold Stories, a community-based labor history program, and through his cofounding of the East Side Freedom Library (in Saint Paul, Minnesota), an educational and cultural center for labor history and contemporary social justice struggles.

Educators' unions, a growing sector of the labor movement, are important vehicles for education and political engagement as well. Such engagement has expanded into higher education to include establishing unions of professors (from the tenured to contingent faculty) and of graduate students, battling attacks on higher education, and defending shared governance. Historian Susan Breitzer turns our attention to the latter in "The Difference a Union Makes: Graduate Employee Activists' Engaged Scholarship and Their Working Lives." Breitzer, who helped form the Campaign to Organize Graduate Students (COGS) at the University of Iowa in the 1990s, interviewed former leaders of COGS, asking how their time with the union influenced their professional and personal lives. Her chapter presents a rare glimpse of activists who have sought to balance their identities as graduate students, scholars, employees, union members, and teachers, showing how their COGS experience was an important education itself, solidifying commitments to engaged scholarship and teaching. Unions in higher education may well become a vital link between academia and the labor movement in the twenty-first century.

The final two chapters in this section explore the history and educational work of two important midwestern public university-affiliated labor education programs. In "Making History Every Day: The Iowa Labor History Oral Project and Popular Education," the director of the University of Iowa Labor Center, Jennifer Sherer, presents an approach to teaching labor history drawn from her experience as a labor educator. At the center of this work is the landmark Iowa Labor History Oral Project, which the Iowa Federation of Labor initiated in the 1970s to document the experiences of workers across the state. Workers encountering these oral histories in classrooms or union halls not only learn about Iowa's labor history, but they gain a clearer view of the contemporary workplace and organizing challenges they face; this process subordinates narrative and historical context to stimulate activism in the present and future by drawing on commonalities between present and past. Sherer chronicles the history and educational ambitions of the project, detailing the creative ways in which the center uses this rich resource in educational outreach to workers.

In "The Polk School: Intersections of Women's Labor Leadership Education and the Public Sphere," Emily E. LB. Twarog examines the transformative role of a multiday residential labor school, both for the female participants and for herself. As director of the Regina V. Polk Women's Labor Leadership Conference (known as the Polk School), Twarog discusses its origins, recounting Polk's legacy as a union organizer, and assesses the school's impact on newer generations of women in a changing labor movement. The program helps emerging leaders gain specific organizational skills and, even more importantly, reach new levels of confidence and commitment to organizing. Twarog also describes how her involvement in the Polk School has expanded her role as a labor scholar and educator, offering the rewards of a larger public role.

The essays in this section show the value of tapping into hidden histories for *teaching* labor and working-class history. Barrett concludes his chapter with a suggestion that labor and working-class historians consider directing their research toward the largely "hidden history" of the personal and emotional lives of individual workers. Researching and writing this hidden history, as Barrett notes, presents significant methodological challenges. Workplace experiences and the impact those experiences have on personal aspirations and emotions constitute a common denominator that students of all ages and backgrounds can share and discuss. Teachers and labor educators, including the five collected here in part 2 of *Civic Labors*, find creative ways to facilitate these discussions and explorations. As Sherer stresses, oral histories work well as an educational tool precisely because they bring the personal and emotional experiences of workers to the surface, enabling participants to relate to one another and to labor's history. At its best, this process of establishing common ground and fostering learning—whether in a college classroom, a labor center, a union hall for graduate student workers, a theater, or a public library—nurtures the confidence, relationships, and longer-term perspective that social movements require.

CHAPTER 7

The Great Unspoken

Teaching and Learning Working-Class History from the Seminar Room to the Union Hall

James R. Barrett

As working-class history has matured (not to say grown old), labor historians have accumulated stacks of articles and blogs on scholarship, including long discussions of a continuing "crisis" in working-class history.[1] In fact, the contribution in terms of scholarship has been enormous, though it seems to be less widely acknowledged lately than it once was. Although the impact is often ignored in broader assessments of U.S. historiography, scholars aiming to write "from the bottom up" have transformed the narrative by establishing the role of common people in creating this history.[2] The field continues to evolve and to attract interest with some of the most creative recent work taking a more global perspective.

Interestingly, however, while the research and writing of working-class history continues to generate vigorous debate and growth in the field, with some notable exceptions and in private conversations, we talk much less about teaching.[3] This is a mistake. When we teach this subject, what are we teaching, to whom are we speaking, and what are they learning? How can we reach a broader public? These questions are, or should be, part of an ongoing conversation. The perspective here is distinctly personal, but my object is frankly prescriptive: what can scholars in the field do to make working-class history a part of life in their communities and, in the process, continue to vitalize the field, thereby ensuring its future? One argument, implicit throughout, is simply that these efforts have at least as much, perhaps more, to do with teaching and outreach broadly defined as with research and writing. Another is that for all the discussion of globalism and world history, it is important to, as the old Swedish socialist motto has it, "dig where you stand." The most meaningful teaching and outreach work is still done locally with less flash but more effect. Consulting and writing for the national AFL-CIO leadership are certainly important, but these suggest a different model of change, one focused on the top, rather than the bottom. The opportunities for change at a local level remain impressive; in addition, these are all close to our homes and schools and often in the hands of working people themselves. What we can offer is a greater understanding of the integrity and significance of working lives, the contributions of working people to our society, and, perhaps in the process, some lessons for the transformation of that society.

This chapter first addresses the many venues for working-class history and its diverse audiences. Labor historians' attention remains focused too much on publication and conference presentations, not enough on bringing this vital history to a larger and more socially diverse audience. Next I take up a case study of one seminar in working-class history in order to show how changes in scholarship have reshaped what we teach and to consider how the implications of these changes have redefined what we mean by the term "working-class history." Judging from the involvement of my own students, this academic work is often closely linked to activism. I close by suggesting a very different vantage point from what we are used to in writing and teaching, a "hidden history" of working people that largely remains to be explored. Much of the best working-class history has been created through a focus on the local workplace and community; the next frontier may well be the even more intimate world of the individual—identity, personal relationships, and emotions. Considering the working-class subject as an individual as well as a member of the collective may change our perspective in terms of our writing, teaching, and activism within our local communities.

Our Audiences

Our own university and college students absorb most of our teaching time and energy. The class composition varies, of course, depending on the institution, and rising tuition rates tend to reduce diversity, but at large state schools they are still likely to come from various class, ethnic, and racial backgrounds. One thing students tend to have in common, however, is that most know little about working-class history. In this regard, the most important venues may not be labor history courses at all, but rather large survey classes organized with the working-class experience—work, community, organization, and conflict—at their core. In some ways, it is more challenging and significant to organize the entire story of the United States around the experiences and agency of working people. This is one reason I have always welcomed the chance to teach large survey courses. It is possible and important to reinterpret the whole story from a working-class perspective.[4] But campus teaching goes on not just in formal classes, but also in spaces that are not necessarily political or labor oriented—study groups, political organizations, and ethnic studies programs. Over the three decades I taught at the University of Illinois at Urbana-Champaign, the working-class history course, as it has elsewhere, has always been a magnet for students in anti-sweatshop and labor support movements, and this element of teaching drew me into support for such movements.

At Illinois the constituency has indeed changed for the undergraduate course in working-class history, and the enrollments have undoubtedly diminished. An anecdotal sampling of colleagues at other large, mostly state institutions suggests great variation on this score, but some diminution of enrollment in such courses was not unusual.[5] In the 1980s and 1990s, my one-semester American Working-Class History course was always filled to capacity with a waiting list and a number of students auditing. Given the demographics of the student body, most students were white, but many came from working-class backgrounds, and the course always enrolled a number of Latina, Latino, and black students. Some of these students entered the AFL-CIO's Union Summer program or took part in reform movements in the Chicago Teachers Union (the Coalition of Rank and File Educators) and similar groups.[6] I make no claim that this particular course produced activists, but it was part of a broader experience for many students who went on to labor activism of one sort or another.

To the degree labor history enrollments have declined, there are undoubtedly many reasons for this. It is difficult to judge how much this decline is part of the more general deterioration in enrollments and majors being observed in most history departments; the general shift from the humanities and social sciences to business and other "applied" courses has likely taken a toll. But there is some reason to think that labor history declines have had their own dynamic, as well. Sharply rising tuition rates make it more difficult for blue-collar students, a common constituency for these courses, to get to the university. The kind of "diversity" that gets a lot of lip service these days from administrators seems not to embrace the student's class background. The hostile political climate in the country might make such courses look a bit subversive. Presumably, they are. Conservative students are likely to view with skepticism a course that takes seriously class inequality and the resulting conflict. Indeed, the political center of the undergraduate population may well have shifted to the right over the past three decades.

At Illinois the rise of ethnic studies courses and majors, a process I have been involved with from the beginning of my career, has resulted in fewer students of color enrolling in labor history courses. Discussing race and class is problematic in such courses when the students are overwhelmingly white. Over the past twenty years, Latina and Latino students have been the best organized and most active on labor issues at Illinois. Many come from working-class families in Chicago and around the state. Students of color are naturally interested in their own communities' histories, the stories of their people. We need to remind everyone, however, that for most of these students, a working-class history course that is sensitive to issues of racial and ethnic difference *is* their history.

Students in elementary and high school classrooms represent an even larger constituency. Heavily unionized public school teachers are often in search of curriculum and ideas related to the history of common people, a view of U.S. history from the bottom up. The most ambitious curriculum project nationally was undoubtedly the U.S. Department of Education Teaching American History grant program (2001–11) that provided substantial resources to mount institutes and workshops on a wide range of topics, including working-class history in its various forms. Under this grant, I worked with the American History Teachers' Collaborative in Urbana-Champaign as well as with a variety of Chicago teachers' programs run through the Newberry Library over the past twenty years. Sessions included predictable topics like Haymarket and the Pullman Strike as well as technology and management from the perspective of workers, the social historical context for Upton Sinclair's *The Jungle*, the Irish and American labor, and other workshops and seminars dealing with race and class. While these grants have now run their course, with little hope for anything like them in the near future, school districts and teachers' unions continue to organize programs dealing with labor history. Most often, the teachers or curriculum specialists come to us, but there is no reason we should not approach school districts with proposals.

Union-initiated Labor History in the Schools programs have helped to facilitate curriculum workshops on the subject. State and regional labor history societies have been active in this area for some time, and the Illinois Labor History Society has been something of a model in this regard. The Labor and Working-Class History Association (LAWCHA) has a committee devoted to these efforts. The Champaign County AFL-CIO has in the past organized such a committee that worked with school districts and teacher union officials to buy labor history books for school libraries and to organize workshops on labor history topics, although the interest in such programs has fluctuated with changes in labor leadership. The point here is that if you feel it is important for working-class history to be part of the school curriculum, there are opportunities to make this happen.[7]

I leave aside the many programs specifically designed for union members and other working-class people. These offer a connection some labor historians have pursued throughout their careers, but this route is beginning to fade. Some of this activity has been related to labor education programs at institutes around the country, but those programs themselves are in decline. Many have been under attack over the past twenty years. This is often the result of simple budget cutting, but they have also been casualties of a shift in the discipline of industrial relations research and teaching that views what used to be "labor" institutes largely in terms of "human capital" and stresses corporate needs rather than labor needs. When the attacks come, it is usually the labor education side of the industrial relations enterprise that suffers most. But this does not mean that unions themselves are uninterested in educational efforts generally or labor history in particular; many seem to be looking for help from sympathetic scholars.

Labor teach-ins, once common—especially in the Midwest, where they often sprang up in the midst of the strikes and lockouts of the 1980s and early 1990s—have also been receding. During the Local P-9 struggles with Hormel in the 1980s and the lockouts and strikes at the Staley, Firestone, and Caterpillar plants in Decatur, Illinois, in the early 1990s, a series of teach-ins facilitated strike support activity and also helped place these local conflicts in a global context that made them more understandable to those involved.[8] Recent attacks on public employee unions, particularly in the Midwest, have spawned similar activities, and the links between these more recent struggles and those in other periods of right-wing attacks might be of particular interest to public employees today. A variant to the labor teach-in, in which workers (more often union leaders) appear on panels at academic conferences, is not quite the same thing. Such panels greatly enrich academic conferences and at least interject contemporary labor realities into academic settings, but they often remain fairly remote from the communities and local organizations involved in the actual conflicts. Small, local events built around the experiences of working people in the community have tended to be successful and represent another way to bring peoples' own history back to them.

One logical explanation for the rarity of labor teach-ins these days is simply that strikes, which have often been the occasion for such events, have all but disappeared in the United States. The most spectacular conflicts, like the 2012 Chicago Teachers Union (CTU) strike, tend to be among public workers. Historians of the working class should be seeking connections with these newer movements.

At Illinois my study and teaching of working-class history and my daily engagement with labor activism have always been connected. Here, at a large, heavily unionized campus, several distinct but allied movements have emerged. One, of course, has been the graduate employees organizing since the late 1980s, which produced the Graduate Employees' Organization (GEO), which is affiliated with the American Federation of Teachers (AFT), the Illinois Federation of Teachers, and the AFL-CIO. Like most unions, but more successfully than most, GEO has been engaged in almost constant organizing and in 2009 led a successful strike against threats to graduate student tuition waivers. Pro-union faculty provided a broad range of support to enforce the strike, guarded against victimization, and educated the campus community around the issues. The culture that has developed around GEO has helped change the atmosphere on campus and offer encouragement and direct support to other labor activists. The Service Employees International Union local led a weeklong strike in 2012, and union faculty picketed with custodial and food service workers. In response to the chancellor's call for service to the community's poor, union faculty organized a food drive to provide assistance but also to publicize that many families of full-time service workers were living at or below the poverty level.

Finally, the Illinois faculty has begun to move on its own behalf. Encouraged by the successful AFT–American Association of University Professors (AAUP) organizing drive among faculty at the University of Illinois at Chicago (UIC), by our own successful GEO here in Urbana-Champaign, and most recently by the remarkable rank-and-file and community strike by the CTU, faculty in Urbana-Champaign have gained the confidence to challenge the growing corporate atmosphere on campus. A joint AFT-AAUP campaign won collective bargaining rights for non-tenure-track faculty in spring 2014. The campaign among tenure-track faculty has attracted considerable support, particularly in the humanities, fine arts, social sciences, and ethnic studies and other interdisciplinary units, but is likely to take much longer. For the past twelve years or so, we also have had a Campus Labor Coalition, in which delegates from the various groups on campus, including the faculty, meet monthly and in emergency situations to compare notes and plan activities in support of one another. Campus strikes have been more successful as a result of this cooperation.[9] This thriving campus labor environment has contributed to a successful living wage campaign, an active Jobs with Justice chapter, strike support for teachers and other groups, and a variety of educational efforts in the broader community.

Opportunities also abound for approaching the broader "public"—for want of a better term—through a range of media. In my own community, labor activists have sustained a weekly *World Labor Hour* on WEFT 90.1 FM, our community radio station, underwritten by the Champaign County AFL-CIO and some local unions. Discussions of working-class history are often central to the programming and have included a number of faculty and graduate students working in the field. If this seems too ambitious, historians might offer a regular "Labor History Minute" or occasional short programs on public or community radio, community television, or other venues. I often hear complaints about the lack of labor programming on public radio and television, but I am not sure many labor historians are approaching their local stations with ideas for such programming. Labor historian and activist Peter Rachleff has made it a point to write for local labor papers in the Minneapolis–St. Paul area. Union publications would often be glad to have the occasional history column. The *Public Eye*, our own alternative newspaper in Urbana-Champaign, frequently covers labor events and news. The Independent Media Centers that emerged from the World Trade Organization protests of the 1990s continue to thrive in many cities and towns, and these are logical venues for this sort of activity and other labor history programming.

This kind of teaching, broadly defined, which relates more closely to labor and other social justice movements than much of our work can present a dilemma: whatever her or his personal commitments, a professional historian is not in precisely the same business as other colleagues and comrades in such movements who are dedicated to generating the sort of literature that will allow them to win their struggles, often against enormous odds. Historians of the working class can not only take part in such movements as individuals, but also lend their research, writing, and teaching skills to supporting them. But the usual standards apply: the arguments need to be reasonable and based on evidence. This is literally a balancing act, and I have no easy solution. As I suggest throughout this chapter, I believe that, if there is a problem in this area of our lives, scholars are not holding back from such movements because of this concern. Rather, it is that they could be far more engaged in such movements that are gestating all around them.

The roots of what we came to call the new labor history lay in the social and political movements and the remarkable rank-and-file upsurges of the late 1960s and 1970s. The more recent past has brought a general crisis not only to the organized labor movement in the midst of its precipitous decline, but also to working-class families trying to survive. Wealth is increasingly concentrated at the top, benefits disappear, work is intensified, and wages and living standards plummet. Seldom have social class differences and inequality been more apparent, certainly not since the 1920s.[10] This makes some academics' relative disinterest in social class appear all the more perverse. The realities of class may be disappearing from the pages of history texts, but they are only too apparent for most working-class families in the United States. This is not a moment to abandon a class analysis of U.S. history; it is a time when this perspective is more valuable than ever.

What difference could such engagement make for social justice movements? It is not an easy question to answer, and certainly the potential for such efforts should not be overstated. But at the very least, this sort of teaching can provide a historical perspective on vital contemporary movements. This kind of activist teaching can help working people understand what is happening to them. It can also demonstrate the long legacy of working-class protests, some of which succeeded, and their relationship to the sort of social, political, and economic changes needed in the United States and throughout the world today. On the negative side, it is as important to recognize and understand defeats as the rare victories. For understandable reasons, historians of the working class seem to spend less time and effort on this part of the narrative.

My experience is that opportunities to talk about history within this context are all around us and that many of the human targets of today's wars against working people are eager to hear about it. It would be foolish not to recognize the intellectual challenges facing working-class history and the political challenges to the movements that inspired and sustained it. The point here, however, is that the opportunities for making a connection between the academic work and the lives of working people abound in a great variety of settings. The question in large part is one of will on the part of the field's practitioners.

From Class to "Identities" in the Seminar Room

As significant as each of our constituencies is, the people who are most important to the survival of the academic field and its necessary transformation over time are our graduate students. One way to capture the "crisis" in the field is to simply look at what is happening in seminar rooms where working-class history is being interpreted by the next generation of scholars. Since a systematic survey of such seminars is beyond the scope of this chapter, I offer a case study, a graduate seminar that appears to be not too different from what has been happening in many such courses over the past three decades. Thus, a case study of History 492, Comparative Working-Class History, an example of the work in one classroom, team-taught by myself and the Russian labor historian Diane Koenker over a period of almost thirty years at the University of Illinois at Urbana-Champaign.

The tradition of teaching and learning working-class history through comparative study is old. The ideological and political background of labor history lent itself to such an international approach.[11] All historians make assumptions. One of these in working-class history has been that while each society was different in many ways, there were common characteristics to industrial capitalism across the boundaries of nation states and thus, common characteristics to working-class life and the movements that workers created to deal with the exigencies of the system. Courses in labor history taught in unions and working-class organizations were based on this assumption, as were Workers Education Association courses in the United Kingdom and comparable trade union and labor college classes in the United States and elsewhere. Long before we started talking about "transnational history," assumptions regarding capitalism and the class experiences it shaped led working-class history teachers and students to cross national boundaries in order to make some rather bold comparisons. For this much, it seems, we have still to thank Marxism, which has always been inherently international in scope and comparative in method. The idea that capitalist societies exhibit comparable characteristics has been hard-wired into this approach to history, and this assumption has encouraged an international approach.

An early example of this approach at the postgraduate level was the Centre for the Study of Social History and its program in Comparative Labor History at the University of Warwick. Established by E. P. Thompson in 1968 and lasting until the late 1990s, the program drew students and visiting faculty from around the world but especially from the United States and other parts of the English-speaking world.[12] The older generation represented in this volume are connected with this tradition through Thompson and David Montgomery. Some in the younger generation are connected to it through seminars at Iowa, Illinois, and elsewhere that were shaped by teachers like Thompson. When Montgomery, the first in a series of visiting U.S. professors at the center, returned to the University of Pittsburgh in 1970, he established a working-class history program there and taught seminars that often employed comparative reading and research.

This was the model we had in mind when Diane Koenker and I established a seminar and preliminary exam field in comparative working-class history at Illinois in 1986.[13] Although comparative seminars on a range of topics have since become common, the labor seminar was the first of these at Illinois. The early versions of this course focused on key themes in the field in the 1970s and 1980s and employed a comparison between the United States, Russia, and Western European societies, particularly England, France, and Germany. Since then, the seminar has evolved, reflecting changes in the field itself, our own research, and the student composition of the course. Most students these days come with little or no political experience, and those with political experience often come from social movements focused as much or more on race and gender than on labor.

The seminar has always started with several weeks on key concepts—which used to mean various conceptions of class formation—in order to provide an over-all framework for discussion. Most of the remaining sessions focused on work, family and community, unions and strikes, aspects of working-class culture, and characteristic forms of radical working-class politics. The question of American exceptionalism provided a focus for our comparative analysis. We also set most of the readings around the late nineteenth and early twentieth centuries. In the beginning, our units of comparison were capitalist nation-states—initially the United States, prerevolutionary Russia, Great Britain, and France—but over time we devoted increasing attention to distinctions between capitalist and socialist societies, economies, and cultures.

One change in the course stimulated by colleagues working in other fields and by the rise of "world history" has been a fitful integration of new geographic and conceptual perspectives—notably, colonial labor in various settings.[14] In general, however, the seminar has continued to be explicitly comparative and to focus primarily on the societies, though perhaps less on the nation-state itself, of Western Europe, Russia, and the United States.

Changes in the theory and scholarship led to changes in the seminar. Over the years, a variety of "subjectivities"—gender, of course, and race, but also sexuality and ethnicity—have tended to crowd out discussions of class as a broad category of analysis rather than simply yet another form of identity. Much of the discussion interrogates the concept of class in relation to these other forms of identity that students employ to explain workers' lives and behavior. Increasingly, feminist readings tended to decenter the workplace and direct students' attention to the domestic sphere and to engender older problems like class formation, the transformation of work processes, and shop-floor relations. We eventually talked as much about reproduction as production, and the archetypal worker in this seminar was as likely to be a woman factory worker or domestic servant as a brawny miner or steelworker.[15] To take the discussion from the global to the personal, we began to focus on forms of working-class personal narrative. These encouraged students to consider the significance of social class and these other forms of identity at a personal level and the more subjective dimensions of this experience—emotions and personal relationships. This focus has seldom translated into dissertations on the personal worlds of workers, but I think the consideration of this subjective side of working-class experience has at least reminded writers to consider the personal along with the collective.

When Diane and I sat down recently to evaluate the seminar, we realized that, in a course on working-class history, we had largely neglected the transformation of unions and the evolution of that characteristic form of working-class protest, the strike. This problem led us to think a bit more about what it is that labor historians do and what we have to offer other scholars and the broader public—a question always worth asking.

Why did History 492 change so much over the years, and what does this mean in terms of the evolution of the field? In part, of course, themes in the seminar have changed because research in working-class history has changed, but how? An inclination to press outward from factory and union was internal to the field from the very beginning of the new labor history. E. P. Thompson, David Montgomery, and those of us following them recognized in workers' lives a dynamic that went far beyond workplace and union. In seeking to expand the view of workers' lives and to capture their experiences in diverse settings, Thompson, Shel Stromquist, and other "new labor historians" have emphasized the pervasiveness of class, that is, the idea that class permeated and shaped all aspects of working-class life, not only work and labor organization.[16] In the process, the scope and subject matter of the field expanded exponentially. One way, then, to understand our focus on many more dimensions of working-class life over the years—family life, youth culture, consumption and style, even personal identity and relationships—is as an effort to grasp the broader significance of social class.

But the shift that has occurred since the 1980s goes deeper. When we started this seminar, most labor historians employed similar frameworks, asked similar questions, and relied on similar sources. A few readings on a given topic could convey the range of scholarship at the given time and suggest some bases for comparison and contrast. Many of the "new labor historians" of the 1970s and 1980s shared a common perspective and vocabulary drawn heavily from the "looser" version of Marxism and socialist humanism championed by scholars like E. P. Thompson.[17]

Over the past twenty years, as a result of postmodern theory, the decline of the labor movement, and perhaps also some crisis of confidence regarding the concept of class itself, this influence has become increasingly more diffuse. The typical subjects of the new labor history's workplace-community studies—labor protest, the politics of work, urban communities, and working-class politics—have often receded, displaced to some degree by a greater emphasis on social difference within working-class populations, especially issues of race, ethnicity, gender, and sexuality. In the process, class is sometimes viewed simply as one of several simultaneously held identities. Our circumscribed realm of shared assumptions has shrunk a bit; the field has become more complicated, contested, and dispersed. We direct our students to widely diverging approaches, methodologies, and voices. Subjects that once might have seemed marginal to the narrative have emerged as central. Current graduate students, who come with experiences and perspectives different from our own, are part of this process of reshaping the seminar.

This appears to be happening well beyond the confines of the History 492 seminar room. In the process, what we understand by the term "working-class history" has been transformed. Historian Liz Faue has argued that most historians of the working class remain "grounded in nineteenth century theories of class" and "have given primacy to productive relations as both the determinant and dominant source of class consciousness and conflict."[18] Yet this course's evolution suggests we are now talking about class in a very different and much broader way than "nineteenth-century theories"—traditional Marxism. Indeed, working-class history seems particularly "porous" in relation to new themes and theory. Perhaps for this reason, the seminar—and student interest in it—persisted and we continued to organize it along comparative lines. This in itself seems significant. While we may well have changed our ways of thinking about it, we have not abandoned the concept of social class, the idea that material inequality shapes peoples' lives and actions and, in turn, holds the possibility of change in these societies. Class remains an important way of understanding the historical experience of poor and working people.

Are we past debates over "class" among the many forms of identity? Few historians of the working class would argue today that class is simply more important or dominant. Indeed, one might argue that a key problem in working-class history and certainly in the contemporary United States is precisely that class identity has been weaker than other forms of identity, namely race, religion, and gender. The argument here is not that our courses and lectures should ignore all this, but rather that we have, in fact, not solved the historical problem of the articulation between such identities. And in cases where considerations of race, ethnicity, and gender have crowded out older but important questions, it seems legitimate to revisit some of these—work, strikes, working-class politics—with the various forms of identity and experience, including class, in mind.

Likewise, the seminar's continuing adherence to a comparative approach suggests that we still make some assumptions about the characteristics of capitalism, industrialism, and patterns of working-class life as we move from one society to another. Without common characteristics between social organization and workers' behavior, what have we to compare? Many of today's historians of the working class are less fixed in their assumptions than we were when we hatched the idea for this course, but we still share some of them. I cannot demonstrate the typicality of our seminar experience, though my impression from speaking to colleagues is that it is not unusual. At the least, it would be a good idea for us to take teaching in its many settings and audiences as a worthy focus of our future discussions about the field.

The most recent incarnation of this seminar still included the material on personal narrative and certainly emphasized the diversity of working-class experience and social difference within laboring populations. But it also returned to themes of working-class organization and protest. Consumption and child rearing are vital subjects, but so are labor organization and strikes. There are distinctive characteristics of working-class life and experience that are different from those of middle-class people and elites. We lose track of these distinct characteristics and experiences at the risk of losing the rationale for working-class history as an essential field of study.

For my own doctoral students and others I have worked with, I think the connection between this intellectual world and various forms of activism is often taken for granted. Some have gone directly into union organizing or labor education work. Others who have taken up tenure-track academic jobs remain active in their unions and AAUP chapters. Many are members of the Labor and Working-Class History Association and help on its projects. Several work with unionized teachers in professional development programs. We reach out to our diverse audiences each in her or his own way.

The Hidden History of the Working Class

By definition, working-class history has focused on the collective—the community, social movement, union, or crowd, and it has evolved in the United States and elsewhere in a distinctly materialist context, influenced by Marxism and social science methods. But what would the story look like from the personal perspectives of the common people who constitute our subjects? While recent approaches have stressed the global character of working-class history, our next challenge may well involve the individual. We need to raise the subjective side of our subjects' historical experience—identity and personality, personal relationships, and emotions—and I believe we need to do so in the very heart of a materialist approach to social history. What Robert Orsi has called the "inner history" of common people remains largely unexplored in working-class history.[19]

Part of the problem, of course, is one of sources, but so far we are not looking very hard. Case files—for criminal or civil legal actions, for social service agencies, for employers—may be read against the biases of the middle class and professional people likely to be overseeing such settings, and they often contain a wealth of data on personalities and relationships. Continued analysis of popular culture—song lyrics, for example, can suggest values and feelings. Clues to the intellectual and spiritual lives of common people might be embedded in religious ritual or prescriptive texts and religious practice itself. Above all, personal narratives—the autobiographies, letters, and interviews of workers, which are too often seen simply as empirical *sources*, might be read with working-class subjectivities in mind—personal identity, relationships, and emotional responses to life experiences. Working-class autobiography, for example, is a distinct genre with its own characteristics and potential.[20]

Why is this important? First, there is the matter of motivation. We assume the significance of emotion and the importance of personal relationships in explaining our own behavior, yet we seldom consider these explanations for the people we study. When we consider the factors shaping social movements, is it too much to ask how the more personal dimensions of working peoples' lives shape their political activism, the movements they created, and the changes they made in their societies?[21]

But there is a more important reason. The individual looms large in explaining the evolution of bourgeois society, but the individuality of working-class people is seldom acknowledged. To some degree this is a natural tendency given the collective character of the phenomena that interest most social historians, but the effect of this can be to objectify our subjects. In acknowledging the significance of personal experience, we invest working-class people with a humanity often denied them in their own societies and times.

Often associated with postmodern theories and methods, the subjective side of history has often been counterposed to the more traditional concerns of labor historians—work, material inequality, and protest. Why? Might it not enrich our work on these and other subjects to consider our blue- or white-collar actors not simply as atoms or as cogs in a great social and political machine but also as individuals with their own affective lives? Why is it not possible to consider the role of emotions, personality, and intimate personal relationships in the motivations of working people? Emotions may seem a world away from most labor history frameworks, but it is safe to assume that they played a role of some importance in the lives of these people.

Class was and still is not only a material, social, and cultural, but also a profoundly emotional experience. What we call class consciousness involved not only social and political aspirations, but also a world of hurt, resentment, envy, and anger and also more positive emotions like love and pride. As Richard Sennett and Jonathan Cobb observed many years ago, the deepest injuries of class may not be on the surface but rather "hidden" in peoples' personal lives.[22]

We say that we are interested in the mentalities of common people, but without coming to terms with their private lives, it will be difficult to understand their motivations and their experience of class. What does this have to do with researching and teaching working-class history? First, if we remain interested in common people and their everyday lives, surely this includes family life, relations between the sexes, and religious ideas and practices that were often at the very heart of working-class communities in the United States. Second, a consideration of such factors might not only provide students a more accurate portrayal of working-class life but also allow them, especially working-class students, to see themselves reflected in the history we ask them to consider. Perhaps more importantly, we might ask whether and in what ways our own personal experiences shape what we choose to study and how we go about teaching.[23]

This need not entail a retreat from the big questions about power in society. In fact, it might be difficult for students and readers to understand what was and is at stake in this history, let alone workers' motivations in trying to make social and political change, without considering our subjects as real people and how our own identities and experiences shape our understandings of them. In this sense, to return to the language of an earlier generation, the personal is indeed political.

Notes

Thanks to Jenny Barrett and the editors for their comments on an earlier version of this essay. The essay is dedicated to Shel Stromquist, who has embodied the best of working-class history as a field of study and as a vocation.

1. For an internal discussion of the crisis, see the long exchanges concerning a "backlash against labor history" on the H-Labor Listserv, www.h-net.org/~labor, June–July 2006 and April–May 2007.

2. David Brody, "The Old Labor History and the New: In Search for an American Working Class," *Labor History* 20 (winter 1979): 111–26. Neither *American History Now*, revised edition, edited for the American Historical Association by Eric Foner and Lisa McGirr (Philadelphia: Temple University Press, 2011 [1997]), nor *A Century of American Historiography*, edited by James M. Banner Jr. (Boston: Bedford/St. Martin's, 2010), include essays on labor and working-class historiography. Earlier editions of the Foner-McGirr volume contained an essay on labor history; this has been dropped in the 2011 edition.

3. One major exception is the discussion on teaching labor history often on the agenda at the annual Midwest Labor and Working-Class History Conference, organized by graduate students at Iowa, Illinois-Urbana, Illinois-Chicago, and other midwestern universities.

4. This is not a new idea, of course, it was the concept behind the American Social History Project and its enduring narrative. Christopher Clark, Nancy Hewitt, Nelson Lichtenstein, Susan Strasser, Roy Rosenzweig, Joshua Brown, David Jaffee, Bruce Levine, and Stephen Brier, *Who Built America? Working People and the Nation's Economy, Politics, Culture, and Society*, 2 vols., 3rd ed. (Boston: Bedford, 2008). The point here is that the broadest audience for such an approach focused on working-class people might come in survey rather than labor history courses.

5. On May 16, 2014, I emailed about twenty senior labor historians, people who had been teaching such courses for some time, regarding labor history course enrollments. I heard back from about a dozen. While enrollment in graduate courses tended to be stable in most places, as it has been at Illinois, the situation in undergraduate courses was more mixed. These enrollments had remained even in about half the schools and declined in the other half. Some of these had at one time been quite large courses; others had always been smaller enrollment seminar-type courses.

6. Union Summer is an AFL-CIO internship program in which participants are introduced to the labor movement through educational programs and union organizing campaigns.

7. The most comprehensive site for labor history curriculum and related materials for teachers may be Rosemary Feurer's excellent "Teacher's Page" at her Labor History Links at www.laborhistorylinks.org, accessed June 15, 2015.

8. On the Staley lockout and related conflicts that made central Illinois a "war zone" in the early 1990s, see Stephen Ashby and C. J. Hawking, *Staley: The Fight for a New American Labor Movement* (Urbana: University of Illinois Press, 2009); Stephen Franklin, *Three Strikes: Labor's Heartland Losses and What They Mean for Working Americans* (New York: Guilford Press, 2001). On the Hormel conflict see Peter Rachleff, *Hard-Pressed in*

the Heartland: The Hormel Strike and the Future of the Labor Movement* (Boston: South End Press, 1993).

9. For further details, see "Campus Labor and the Corporate University: A LaborOnline Forum," July 9, 2013, Labor and Working-Class History Association, http://lawcha.org, accessed July 9, 2013.

10. The share of total U.S. income going to the top 1 percent of wealth holders has more than doubled between 1976 and the present. It appears that the staggering economic and social inequality in the United States between the 1970s and early twenty-first century has grown considerably over the course of the recovery from the 2008–9 recession. See Emmanuel Saez, "Striking It Richer: The Evolution of Top Incomes in the United States," updated with 2009 and 2010 estimates, at http://elsa.berkeley.edu, accessed June 11, 2015.

11. E. J. Hobsbawm, "Labor History and Ideology," in *Workers: World of Labor* (New York: Pantheon Books, 1984), 1–5.

12. On the Warwick program and its relationship to the earlier tradition of workers' education in England, see Peter Searby et al., "Edward Thompson as a Teacher: Yorkshire and Warwick" in *Protest and Survival: Essays for E. P. Thompson*, edited by John Rule and Robert Malcolmson (London: Merlin Press, 1993), 1–23.

13. The following discussion of the Illinois seminar in comparative working-class history is based in part on James R. Barrett and Diane P. Koenker, "The Saga of History 492: The Transformation of Working-Class History in One Classroom," *Labour/Le Travail* 61 (spring 2008): 181–213. I thank Professor Koenker and colleagues at *Labour/Le Travail* for permission to reproduce some of this material here. An earlier version was presented at the "Working-Class Worlds: Local and Global Perspectives on Labor History" conference at the University of Iowa. The original article includes an appendix with syllabi and preliminary examination questions from the course.

14. See, for example, David Roediger and Elizabeth D. Esch, *The Production of Difference: Race and the Management of Labor in U.S. History* (New York: Oxford University Press, 2012), 98–135; Dipesh Chakrabarty, "Communal Riots and Labor: Bengal's Jute Mill Hands in the 1890s," *Past and Present* 91 (1981): 140–69; Jonathan Hyslop, "The Imperial Working Class Makes Itself 'White': White Labourism in Britain, Australia, and South Africa before the First World War," *Journal of Historical Sociology* 12.4 (1999): 398–421; Frederick Cooper, *Decolonization and African Society: The Labor Question in French and British Africa* (Cambridge: Cambridge University Press, 1996).

15. Alice Kessler-Harris, "Treating the Male as Other," *Labor History*, 34 (spring 1993): 190–204; Joan Scott, "On Language, Gender, and Working-Class History" and "Women in The Making of the English Working Class," in *Gender and the Politics of History* (New York: Columbia University Press, 1988), 53–67 and 68–91; Sonya Rose, "Class Formation and the Quintessential Worker," in *Reworking Class*, edited by John R. Hall (Ithaca, N.Y.: Cornell University Press, 1997), 133–68.

16. Brody, "Old Labor and the New"; Shelton Stromquist, "Perspectives on the New Labor History: The Wisconsin School and Beyond," *International Labor and Working Class History* 39 (spring 1991): 81–88; Leon Fink, "John R. Commons, Herbert Gutman, and the Burden of Labor History," *Labor History* 29 (1988): 313–22.

17. On the relationship between Thompson's "looser" notion of class formation and the rise of the "new labor history," see James R. Barrett, "An Awkward Fit: The Making of the English Working Class and the 'New Labor History' in the United States," *Historical Reflections/Reflexions Historiques* 41 (spring 2015): 7–18.

18. Elizabeth Faue, "Reproducing the Class Struggle: Class, Gender, and Social Reproduction in U.S. Labor History," *Amerikanische Arbeitergeschicte Heute*, edited by Irmgard Steinisch, special issue, *Mitteilungsblatt des Instituts für soziale Bewegungen* 25 (2001), 47–66, 47. See also Elizabeth Faue, "Retooling the Class Factory: United States Labor History after Marx, Montgomery, and Postmodernism," *Labour History* 82 (May 2002): 109–19.

19. Robert Orsi, *The Madonna of 115th Street: Faith and Community in Italian Harlem, 1880–1950* (New Haven, Conn.: Yale University Press, 1985), 150–51. My volume of essays around these themes, *History from the Bottom Up and the Inside Out: Essays in Class, Race, and Identity*, is in press (Duke University Press).

20. Kathryn Oberdeck, "Popular Narrative and Working-Class Identity," in *Labor Histories: Class, Politics, and the Working-Class Experience*, edited by Eric Arnesen, Julie Greene, and Bruce Laurie (Urbana: University of Illinois Press, 1998), 200–229; James R. Barrett, "Was the Personal Political? Reading the Autobiography of American Communism," *International Review of Social History* 53.3 (2008): 395–423; Diane P. Koenker, "Scripting the Revolutionary Worker Autobiography: Archetypes, Models, Inventions, and Markets," *International Review of Social History* 49.3 (December 2004): 371–400; Mary Jo Maynes, *Taking the Hard Road: Life Course in French and German Workers' Autobiographies in the Era of Industrialization* (Chapel Hill: University of North Carolina Press, 1995); George Steinmetz, "Reflections on the Role of Social Narratives in Working-Class Formation: Narrative Theory in the Social Sciences," *Social Science History* 16.3 (fall 1992): 489–516; Carolyn Steedman, *Landscape for a Good Woman: The Story of Two Lives* (New Brunswick, N.J.: Rutgers University Press, 1987).

21. For work that employs issues of sexuality and other personal considerations in analyzing working-class radicals, see Kathleen A. Brown and Elizabeth Faue, "Social Bonds, Sexual Politics, and Political Community in the US Left, 1920s to 1940s," *Left History* 7 (2000): 9–45; Kathleen A. Brown and Elizabeth Faue, "Revolutionary Desire: Redefining the Politics of Sexuality of American Radicals, 1919–1945," in *Sexual Borderlands: Constructing an American Sexual Past*, edited by Kathleen Kennedy and Sharon Ullman (Columbus: Ohio State University Press, 2003), 273–302; James R. Barrett, "Revolution and Personal Crisis: William Z. Foster and the American Communist Personal Narrative," *Labor History* 43.4 (fall 2002): 465–82, reprinted in Kevin Morgan, ed. *People of a Different Mould? Studies in Communist Biography* (Geneva: Lang, 2004); Barrett, "Was the Personal Political?"

22. Richard Sennett and Jonathan Cobb, *The Hidden Injuries of Class* (New York: Random House, 1972).

23. See, for example, James R. Barrett, "The Blessed Virgin Made Me a Socialist Historian: An Experiment in Catholic Autobiography and the Historiography of Race and Class," in *Faith and the Historian: Catholic Perspectives*, edited by Nick Salvatore (Urbana: University of Illinois Press, 2007), 117–47.

CHAPTER 8

Teaching Labor History on the Middle Ground

Connecting the Campus, the Union Hall, and the Community

Peter Rachleff

For more than three decades I have taught labor history in Saint Paul, Minnesota. While my primary base has been Macalester College, a private liberal-arts college, my most dynamic work has bridged the divides between the academy and the wider community in which it is located. Whether the goal of a particular project has been to educate college students, trade unionists, working people in general, immigrants, or the public at large, I have found that creating spaces that constitute middle grounds make it possible to connect these constituencies, which in turn creates the most productive learning environment.

Individual institutions, regardless of their expressed goals, have often resisted and even undermined the construction of such spaces and the connection of such constituencies. In their own ways, colleges and union halls tend to discourage the presence of "outsiders" in their spaces. In the years I taught at Macalester, the college built a brick and wrought-iron wall around the campus and introduced a security system at the library that served as a checkpoint for anyone who appeared not to "belong." While most union halls provided less formal obstacles to entrance, visitors typically found nuanced, cultural challenges to feeling welcome, such as the presence of smoke and beer, the hearty camaraderie of years of friendship, the formalities of *Robert's Rules*, the skeptical gaze. These dynamics led me, over the years, to see myself as "marginal" wherever I went. But, particularly after hearing a brilliant talk by Harvard sociologist Charles V. Willie, I understood the potentiality of marginal locations as sites of creativity and innovation. And so I thought of myself as trying, from the margins, to create a middle ground, a meeting place, where institutions and constituencies might overlap.[1]

In 1983, my second year at Macalester, I was approached by Lauren Brockway, a public employee union activist in the American Federation of State, County, and Municipal Employees (AFSCME) with an idea for a labor history film series. In retrospect, I think she hatched her idea from her own experiences of marginality. Women were not yet fully accepted into the workplace or the labor movement, as evidenced by the struggle of bank tellers in Willmar, Minnesota, for union recognition in the late 1970s, and by Lois Jensen's early 1980s sexual harassment lawsuit against Eveleth Taconite Co. and the United Steelworkers' of America (USWA). Lauren was also an activist in the radical Minnesota support network for the Irish struggle for independence, which pushed her to the margins of the mainstream labor movement but also fueled her interest in labor's past, when transnational solidarities and militancy were closer to the heart of the movement. Lauren suggested screening films in a major campus venue on winter Saturday afternoons, followed by audience discussions. She organized a planning committee of local labor activists, whose primary responsibility was to build the audience. This was my introduction to a network of women and men who would become central to my life and work over the next thirty-plus years.[2]

We called the series *The Power In Our Hands: The History of the American Worker*. I was able to leverage space on campus, an unattractive but spacious science hall. We included a mix of documentaries and dramatic films, and we recruited scholars and activists to be discussion leaders. A local graphic artist produced our poster, which signified on William Balfour Ker's 1906 engraving "From the Depths." The science hall held 250, and we nearly filled it for eight successive Saturdays. Much of the energy in the room came from local anti-plant-closing activists, who had been influenced by the health-and-safety leader of the Oil, Chemical, and Atomic Workers' Union, Tony Mazzocchi, anti-concessions activists from the United Auto Workers' Union (UAW), and union democracy advocates, particularly from Teamsters for a Democratic Union. The film and discussion series became a space in which progressive Macalester students and local labor activists, men and women who identified with *Labor Notes* and its sobriquet of "troublemakers," met one another and shared ideas.[3]

Looking back after thirty years, I recall three specific events and individual participants from that series that illustrate the educational and political potential of projects that bring together mixed audiences—across generations, across institutional locations, across experiences. These events contributed both to the learning of labor history and to the ongoing evolution of labor activism in the Twin Cities. They also suggest the complex ways that a conversation between the past and the present is critical to the teaching of labor history.

I led the postshow discussion of our opening film, *The Wobblies*. One of the first people I called on was a tall, senior gentleman wearing a flannel shirt and suspenders. He hauled himself to his feet with two canes, and began, "when I was in the Seattle General Strike . . .". You could have heard a pin drop. He explained that he had moved to Minnesota in the 1920s to work in the north woods and that in the 1930s he had participated in the unionization of the logging camps and sawmills by the International Woodworkers of America and the formation of the Congress of Industrial Organizations (CIO). His point was to encourage us to understand how the Wobblies had planted the seeds for the labor upheaval of the

Great Depression. I scurried to secure his name and phone number. His name was Carl Winn. Later that spring, I brought him into my Macalester labor history class. He prefaced his remarks by telling the students that his only formal education was a GED and that he had never thought that he would be in a college classroom, let alone address one. He explained to the students that he had joined the IWW while working in logging boom sites in the World War I–era Pacific Northwest. When he described how he and his fellow workers put log rafts together, he took off his shoe to show where he had had cleats on his soles for walking on logs in the rapidly moving water. Carl also explained to the students how he had lost a finger in a crush of logs. He brought the past to life for these students.[4]

Another Saturday we featured the 1942 documentary, *Native Land*. The film drew extensively on the transcripts of the U.S. Senate LaFollette Civil Liberties Committee, which had heard the testimony of southern union organizers and workers in the late 1930s. Narrated by the legendary African American actor, vocalist, and activist Paul Robeson, the film careens back and forth from images of waving U.S. flags to hooded Ku Klux Klan thugs. The planning committee had invited Carl Ross, the former district organizer for the Communist Party and a victim of McCarthyism, to make some comments and lead the post-film discussion. After Carl's remarks, an audience member rose to his feet with a memorable comment: "Along with other local labor activists, I was convicted under the Smith Act in 1941 and sent to Sandstone Prison. You Stalinists never lifted a finger to defend us." He was referring to leaders of Minneapolis Teamsters Local 574, who were connected to James Cannon and Leon Trotsky. There was nothing "academic" about the nontheoretical discussion that ensued in the science hall.

All of us present, including my students, got a crash course in the impact of political factionalism in the history of the Minnesota Left. Labor activists who had stuck with the Communist Party in the Great Depression and World War II saw those who had allied with Leon Trotsky as bitter enemies, and vice versa. This enmity had contributed to damaging splits within the labor movement and had undermined struggles that had needed solidarity. The audience also felt the palpable intensity with which these conflicts had not only raged half a century before, but also continued to have salience for men and women who saw themselves on the Left. Yet the lessons offered in this discussion did not stop there. Carl Ross clearly moved the audience when he publicly apologized and said that the Communist Party had been wrong not to defend the members of the Socialist Workers Party in 1941. A few years later, several of those present in the audience that day would work with Ross on his Twentieth-Century Radicalism project at the Minnesota Historical Society. These films and discussions were suggesting that knowing and understanding labor's "untold stories" could make it possible to step beyond the limitations that had been contained within these stories.[5]

On another afternoon in the film series, an audience member stood to make a statement about the present rather than ask a question about the past. Bud

Schulte had worked for years at Iowa Pork Processors in South Saint Paul and was a member of United Food and Commercial Workers (UFCW) Local P-4. He and 210 fellow workers had recently decided to strike rather than accept the significant wage cuts that their employer had proposed. Bud was not just asking us to learn or understand his story; he was asking us to *get involved*. Audience members passed a hat for funds and circulated a sign-up sheet to assist with picket duty. When Iowa Pork management leafleted Saint Paul's predominantly African American neighborhood in an effort to recruit black strikebreakers and generate racial conflict on the picket lines, some of us produced our own leaflets that we took door-to-door. Over the next weeks, each postshow discussion included a progress report on the strike and the collection of monetary and human resources.

In the following year, our experiences in the middle ground created in that science hall would inform the development of support activities on behalf of the striking Hormel workers in Austin, Minnesota. Planning committee members, audience members, workers, retirees, and students came together as the Local P-9 Support Committee, and I served as its chairperson. Our shared knowledge of labor's untold stories expressed in those films, our shared experience of the Iowa Pork strike, and our solidarity in support of those strikers, schooled us for involvement in the Hormel strike. Our work as the P-9 Support Committee would serve as a template for eighteen other solidarity committees that would organize across the United States and shape the meaning of that struggle.[6]

Teaching, learning, and contributing to labor history became mutually enforcing processes for workers, students, retired labor activists, and trade unionists. In Austin, the Hormel strikers not only revisited the history of their union progenitor, the Independent Union of All Workers, but also interwove the stories of 1930s packinghouse worker activism in Fort Dodge, Mason City, Cedar Rapids, and Ottumwa. Local P-9's motorcycle brigade of roving pickets deliberately followed the very routes taken by their predecessors half a century earlier. In the Twin Cities, meetings of the P-9 Support Committee included presentations on labor history, with particular attention paid to the militant building of unions in the 1930s, from epicenters in Minneapolis and Austin north to Fargo and south to Omaha, spreading across Iowa and Wisconsin, and from packinghouse worker cores to other manufacturing, retail, and service sector workers. Local P-9 generated a cohort of speakers, many of whom spoke to college classes throughout the Midwest, including my own. This new energy and interest began to shape a cycle of scholarship. Although the Hormel strike and related struggles were defeated, this middle ground of solidarity activism proved fertile for the production of a new comprehension of labor history and creative thinking about the labor movement's future.[7]

In the fall of 1997, I collaborated with Beth Cleary, associate professor of dramatic arts and dance at Macalester College, in her staging of Clifford Odets's 1935 play, *Waiting for Lefty*. Determined not to present this play as a curious historical artifact, Beth placed *Lefty* in the present, cast women and actors of color in historically white male roles, and contextualized the play with three short pieces from the 1930s, which broadened its racial and gender terrain: Langston Hughes's *Limitations of Life*, a satirical riff on the film *Imitation of Life*; H. F. V. Edward's *Job Hunters*, set in a Harlem unemployment office in 1931; and a movement piece Beth created with women students, which she based on Meridel Le Sueur's novella, *Women on the Breadlines*.[8]

After these intellectual table setters, *Lefty* opened with Harry Fat, the corrupt union boss, delivering his self-serving monologue. But he was interrupted by waves of characters in contemporary union jackets who swept over the forty-five-degree raked stage (a sharply slanted ramp), carrying signs protesting not only the taxi drivers' union's timidity but also the dominance of white, male characters in the original play. A new cast was negotiated on the spot, with new cross-racial and cross-gender casting now employed, and then the play proceeded. Audiences paid rapt attention as the story unfolded, and its penultimate scene shocked many, when actors leaped from seats in the audience to harangue Harry Fat, bemoan Lefty's death, and urge a wildcat strike. At its end, a Mother Jones character emerged to distribute "Solidarity Forever" song sheets to the audience, who were encouraged to stand and sing along with the cast. The union members sang it by heart, which was very moving to the actors. The song was a living historical document at the end of the production, and the only credible alternative to the historically infamous ending of its premiere New York City production, where the actors called for a strike and members of the theater audience rushed out into the streets.

In preparation for the play, Beth exposed her cast to historical and contemporary labor activism. She brought Manny Fried from Buffalo for a residency. A playwright, actor, and union activist (mostly in the United Electrical Workers), Manny had acted in the original New York City production of *Waiting for Lefty*. Although he was in his eighties in 1998, he was still active, and he not only reminisced but pushed student actors through intensive vocal and physical exercises. His commitments and vigor testified to a long life of labor activism and theater training.[9]

In the summer before the *Lefty* production, United Parcel Service (UPS) workers waged a dramatic strike to turn part-time jobs into full-time jobs, and the media largely represented them as a youthful workforce, the labor militants of the future. When young workers struck several suburban Cleveland McDonald's just as *Lefty* rehearsals were beginning, the buzz among the cast was palpable. I heard student actors say, "Those workers are our age—we could be making history." Several local members of the International Brotherhood of Teamsters on strike at UPS held a series of discussions with the cast, communicating their passion and energy to the actors. When the play went up, it was often UPS strikers who were the first audience members to rise for "Solidarity Forever." Other local labor activists wearing union jackets—AFSCME, UAW, BMWE, UTU, USWA, UFCW—also leaped to their feet. They were excited to see cast members wearing their unions' jackets in the scenes in which they enacted the "contemporary" interventions in the play. Here, in this darkened theater, a middle ground had taken shape.

In tandem with the preparation of the play, I offered a new course: "The U.S. in the 1930s: The Great Depression and New Deal." A core group of the *Lefty* actors and stagehands took it, as did another dozen or so students attracted to the topic. The actors brought their rehearsal experiences into our classroom, while they brought their enhanced knowledge of the 1930s into rehearsals, where they shared this with other cast members. After providing an overview of the period, my course dug deeply into social and cultural history. We relied on a body of lively new scholarship, such as Liz Cohen's *Making a New Deal*, Robin Kelley's *Hammer and Hoe*, Barbara Melosh's *Engendering Culture*, and Michael Denning's *The Cultural Front*. Our attention ranged from long-term changes in class, racial, gender, and ethnic formations and identities in the first three decades of the twentieth century and the particular challenges that the Great Depression posed, to the ways that activists engaged them in their efforts to mount responses to the Depression and the ways that artists and cultural workers constructed and employed art in the 1930s. We toured Saint Paul's City Hall, which was completed in the early 1930s and brims with the aesthetics of that era. We of course read *Waiting for Lefty* and other period plays, such as *One Third of a Nation* and *It Can't Happen Here*, looked at New Deal visual art, and listened to popular music, from Aaron Copland to Paul Robeson and Billie Holiday.[10] In discussion we also explored parallels and connections between the 1930s and the late 1990s, as well as the ways that cultural work can be organized around political goals. All the students in the class attended the production of the play, which came at the very end of the semester, and many of them participated in the postshow discussions that followed each performance and brought students into interaction with the union activists and working people who also attended.

Six years later, a friend returned from the Great Labor Arts Exchange and asked that I look at a video of a concert performance of a new labor musical–jazz opera. I loved everything about this new piece, *Forgotten: The Murder in the Ford Rouge Plant*, written and composed by Steve Jones, and I began to consider how I might use it in my labor history work at Macalester and in the community. Jones uses *Forgotten* to retell events in 1937, when Lewis Bradford, a Methodist minister turned union organizer and radio host (his *The Forgotten Man's Hour* ran against Father Coughlin's anticommunist *Hour of Power* on Detroit area radio stations) died mysteriously in the Ford Rouge plant, then the world's largest factory. Having run afoul of Harry Bennett, Ford's henchman, Bradford was found in a remote area of the plant on November 30, 1937, his skull fractured. Although the company doctor termed his death an accident, union activists and his own family always suspected murder. Steve Jones—who was Bradford's great-nephew—used this mystery as the basis for an opera about workers' struggles to organize in the Great Depression.[11]

I asked my Macalester colleague, music professor and choral director Bob Peterson, if he would be interested in directing this musical and in co-teaching a new course with me in the spring 2005 semester, Telling Labor's Story through Music. Bob was not only willing, but, as we got deeper and deeper into the project, he forgot our agreed-upon goal of a "concertized production" (no sets, lights, or costumes) and set his—and soon our—sights on a fully staged production performed by Macalester students at the end of the semester.

The course was open to students with no prior knowledge of labor history or experience in musical performance. We required every student to participate in some way in the ultimate staging of the musical, whether performing or produc-ing publicity, taking tickets, or working backstage. The course gave students an introduction to U.S. labor history and the current challenges faced by working people, while maintaining a focus on the place of music and song in working-class culture and the labor movement more broadly. In class, Bob taught a range of historically situated genres that revealed the expressive and strategic power of the languages of music. We proceeded chronologically, from slave work songs to hip hop, with a particular focus on the 1930s. Course readings ranged from LeRoi Jones's *Blues People* to Tricia Rose's *Black Noise*, Ruth Glasser's *My Music Is My Flag* to Robbie Leiberman's *My Song Is My Weapon*. Our most illuminating resource proved to be Benjamin Filene's *Romancing the Folk: Public Memory and American Roots Music*. His argument about the impossibility of the quest for "authenticity" in folk music became a framing device for the students' exploration of their own abilities to cross class lines and play blue-collar workers on stage. It also informed our appreciation of Steve Jones's eclectic musical score for *Forgotten*, his strategy of hailing the 1930s musically while communicating to contemporary audiences with contemporary arrangements and sounds.[12]

With support from Macalester, Bob and I were able to travel to Detroit to see a professional production of *Forgotten*, directed by Elise Bryant and performed by unionized musicians and actors. The support also allowed us to bring guest presenters to our class and cast. Benjamin Filene was director of the Museum and Exhibits Division of the Minnesota Historical Society, and his guest presentations to the class made him a part of the project's extended family. We enticed composer Steve Jones to Saint Paul to work in a rehearsal with the cast and once more to see the production. Illinois public intellectual and folksinger extraordinaire Bucky Halker (who holds a doctorate in American studies from the University of Min-nesota) provided an in-class presentation on how he approaches working-class music as a living legacy, meant to be revised through each performance. Bucky performed a concert that brought his ideas to the wider campus community and raised interest in our *Forgotten* effort.[13]

Most importantly, we were able to form a partnership with UAW Local 879 at the Saint Paul Ford truck assembly plant. This local had been the home base for the P-9 Support Committee twenty years earlier, and its leaders had been prominent activists in the Hormel struggle. They were receptive to connecting with the Macalester students, and the background work students were doing for the *Forgotten* production was a perfect fit for a collaboration. To me, it was vital that students have a sense of the work performed in an auto plant and also that they get to know autoworkers. The Ford plant had been closed to tours since September 11, 2001, but the union shop chairman worked to gain access for us and then led our tour himself. We also attended a union meeting and, with the assistance of the local leadership, had several focus group discussions with workers at the union hall. These experiences had a big impact on the students. The students realized that autoworkers also perform work that is largely unseen by the public, and, in the context of Ford plant closings nationally, imperiled. (Indeed, this plant would close permanently five years later.) The students and workers engaged in conversations about the significance of unionization, on the one hand, and the ways it was being undercut by neoliberalism and the North American Free Trade Agreement, on the other. The Ford workers became interested in the students' work on *Forgotten* as a way to represent workers' lives, and the histories of mortal threat faced by workers choosing to organize. This project had become a meeting place for workers and students, a middle ground that throbbed with energy and ideas.[14]

The play was performed twice, for free, one night in the college's concert hall and a second at the union hall. On both occasions we played to a full house. Some student audience members went to the union hall, and some union members came to the college. We were pushing against deep institutional boundaries on all sides. The audiences were enthusiastic, and the student performers were moved—and inspired to quite terrific performances. Composer Steve Jones, who attended the performance at the college, was knocked out by what had started out to be a "concertized" production by young people standing behind music stands. It rocked. And it moved. And it was followed by lively discussions with audiences—and among cast and course members. And it would continue to be referenced by its participants for years to come.

The *Lefty* and *Forgotten* projects had created middle grounds, spaces where students and workers met, shared ideas and experiences, and were challenged and inspired. In these spaces, labor history came to life. Some participants were not merely educated, they were transformed. Some have become union members, organizers, and staffers today; one is the staff person for the Minnesota Fair Trade Coalition and the musical director of the Saint Paul Labor Chorus; some are community organizers, teachers, actors, directors, writers, arts instructors, and arts administrators, with an understanding of labor history "from the inside." At the same time, workers from UPS, Ford, the University of Minnesota, and other workplaces were engaged by these college-based productions about working people. The productions placed workers' experiences in new contexts. These projects embraced this logic of teaching, learning, and making labor history by mingling workers, students, trade unionists, and social-justice activists, and by promoting conversations between the past and the present.

I'd like to add another set of experiences to this consideration of the construction of middle-ground spaces for the teaching and learning of labor history. Beginning in 1998, under the auspices of a well-established local nonprofit, the Friends of the Saint Paul Public Library, a committee of academics, trade unionists, labor educators, and racial-justice advocates have come together annually to plan a series of labor history programs called Untold Stories. Each year, we have organized eight to twelve events—readings, lectures, panels, films, singalongs, and tours (sometimes on foot, sometimes by bus)—from mid-April to late May. Most feature local presenters and take place in neighborhood branches of the public library system, with the occasional use of a college campus, a union hall, a church, or a theater. These spaces have become middle grounds.

Each year's program has a unifying theme. The 2014 theme was "Memory and Place," for instance. Previous themes have included "Food Workers in the Global Economy" and "The Meaning of Freedom 150 Years after the Emancipation Proclamation." The organization provides valuable staff support and funding for brochures, travel expenses, and small honoraria for out-of-town presenters. A network of organizations—unions, academic departments, and historical societies—helps build audiences and promote programs. Up to about five hundred people attend Untold Stories each year, including high school and college students, trade unionists, rank-and-file workers, retirees, bibliophiles, and avid learners of all ages. Discussions are lively, provocative, and sometimes contentious.[15]

Untold Stories operates on multiple levels. By providing a public platform for authors, scholars, and student researchers, the program reintroduces workers and unions in the context of dominant historical and cultural narratives. Untold Stories provides spaces for those who know "the secret"—that the United States is not a classless society and that workers have often organized and acted on their own behalf—to meet one another. At times, as with the support that emerged out of the 1984 film series for striking packinghouse workers in South Saint Paul, communities form in these spaces and participants move from learning about history to taking part in contemporary activities and projects that will be deemed history in years to come, such as the state public employees' strike of 2001, the University of Minnesota clerical and technical workers' strike of 2003, and the immigrant rights march of 2006.

A great variety of presenters have contributed to the quality of this series. Outstanding labor scholars have presented, including David Montgomery, Jeremy Brecher, Nan Enstad, Tiya Miles, Michael Denning, Will Jones, David Bacon, Heather Thompson, and Biju Mathew. Audiences have heard from novelists and poets, filmmakers and photographers, high school students and MacArthur "Genius" Awardees. Local scholars, self-taught historians, and trade unionists have provided powerful presentations. Programs have celebrated the completion of a labor history mural in the Saint Paul Labor Center (painted by Tacoumba Aiken and Keith Christensen) and the one-hundredth anniversary of Woody Guthrie's birth (a concert performed by Darryl Holter and Larry Long). Untold Stories has explored the experiences of Latino sugar beet workers, African American Pullman porters and dining car waiters, Eastern European immigrant steelworkers living in company housing in Duluth, public school teachers, railroad workers, cigar makers, Native American communities, teamsters, packinghouse workers, iron miners, Civilian Conservation Corps workers, immigrants from all over the world, and more.[16]

The Untold Stories program has demonstrated that the middle ground of labor history can be mobile. Each year, Dave Riehle's tours are the most popular learning opportunities. I first met Dave during the 1984 film series when he was working as a railroad trainman. A year later, he would be my co-strategist in the P-9 Support Committee, and over the ensuing decades we would work together on many projects. Dave became a locomotive engineer, president of his United Transportation Union (UTU) local, a published labor historian, and a frequent guest speaker in my Macalester classes. When we launched Untold Stories, Dave piloted a new program: labor history tours of Saint Paul. Under his direction, students, teachers, workers, retirees, and social-justice activists have explored by bus or on foot the local experiences of the Great Northern Railroad strike of 1894, the founding of the IWW in 1905, Jewish labor history, African American labor history, the Minneapolis Teamsters' strikes of 1934, and more. This mix of participants have walked, listened, observed, and talked to each other, forming new relationships along with new ideas. Being in this kind of a space encouraged participants to consider the layers of relationships between the past and the present. Interviewed for a local community newspaper ten years ago, Dave explained: "Labor history is inherently subversive; it tells people that things don't have to be the way they are." When asked why people seem to know so little about the past, he continued: "People don't know much about the present, either. They don't know why things are happening to them, why we are in Iraq, why their wages are falling. But people figured those things out once, and they can again."[17]

Untold Stories has never been an exercise in nostalgia or simple celebration. Its planners have constructed this middle ground as a space within which difficult experiences can be examined and analyzed. In May 2014, Untold Stories offered a "Whiteness in Plain View" discussion in the public library of a predominantly white middle-class neighborhood. There were two presenters: Chad Montrie, a history professor from the University of Massachusetts–Lowell, who at the time was making a documentary film inspired by James Loewen's *Sundown Towns*; and Molly Hynes, a local high school sophomore who had just won first prize in the state History Day contest for her poster board, "Racism in Our Hometown." Chad showed a trailer from his film-in-progress, a ten-minute segment that examines the historical processes by which two very different Minnesota communities, Austin (the home of Hormel meatpacking) and Edina (an upper-class suburb of Minneapolis) had become exclusively white. Molly's project (developed with another Cretin–Derham Hall sophomore, Emily Voigt) detailed the responses in 1931 of white neighbors in south Minneapolis when an African American family, headed by Arthur Lee, a World War I vet and postal worker, moved in—and the direct action taken by postal workers to defend the Lee family. The seventy-five mostly white people who crowded into the library meeting room launched an impassioned discussion that belied all conventions of "Minnesota Nice." They were serious about understanding racism, white supremacy, whiteness, and resistance, and how it shaped their own lives. At the end of the discussion, Greg Poferl, a former postal worker who is now a high school history teacher and the advisor to Mollie and Emily, invited the audience to become involved in dedicating a monument to the Lee family and the postal workers who defended them in front of the very house that had been the scene of such drama more than seventy years ago. With Greg and his students in the lead and a cohort of postal workers engaged, Untold Stories audience members signed on to contribute to the funding of an historical marker at the Lee home and to attend the August 2014 opening at the University of Minnesota's Nash Art Gallery of an exhibit about this story. One might even say that these efforts were taking the Lee family story out of the realm of the "untold" and into the annals of local history.[18]

All of these projects, then—the film and discussion series, the P-9 Support Committee, the labor history courses that rely on theater or music or both, the public history series sponsored by the Friends of the Saint Paul Public Library— have created middle grounds that are particularly fertile for the teaching and learning of labor history. They share certain features: they occur in public, whether labor spaces or public libraries, or even college spaces to which the public has been invited; the participants represent diverse social and generational experiences; their titles and themes promote a conversation between the past and the present; the programs do not shy away from contradictions, controversies, and conflicts; on occasion, these projects can inform action on the part of the people who are participating.

I do not want to position myself as an all-knowing architect of these projects. As Marx wrote in the third of his "Theses on Feuerbach" (1845), "the educator must himself be educated." Despite my excellent education, I did not start out understanding what I have been laying out for you. My participation in these projects over the past thirty-plus years has taught me the value of a constructed middle ground for the teaching and learning of labor history. Given what I have learned, I have turned my attention to a major new project: the creation of a labor and immigration history center on Saint Paul's East Side, what my cofounder, Beth Cleary, our board, and I are calling the East Side Freedom Library. We are a new nonprofit corporation housed in an historic Carnegie library building on the East Side.[19]

For more than 150 years, this neighborhood has been home to immigrant working-class families. Previously from Europe, currently from the U.S. South, Central America, Southeast Asia, and East Africa, men and women have come here to work in manufacturing, construction, transportation, and, now, services. Generation by generation, immigrants have built the East Side: housing, churches, unions, and cultural and political organizations. Andrew Carnegie, ironically, provided the funds for the construction of this handsome 1917 public library, which is now being reinvented by a devoted labor historian. Now the East Side Freedom Library (ESFL) is its steward, and we are seeking to restore and renovate the building, fill it with books and educational resources, and develop programming that will facilitate the telling of immigrants,' migrants,' and workers' histories.

The ESFL will contain thousands of volumes focused on labor, African American, and immigration history, and on political economy and community organizing, as well as thematically aligned fiction, poetry, and drama. The collection begins with my own books, but it will also include much of David Montgomery's personal library, Sal Salerno's collection of proletarian fiction and poetry, and donations from historians and scholars including David Roediger, Paula Rabinowitz, Donna Gabaccia, Paul Buhle, and Allen Ruff. Our holdings include an international Black Art collection on permanent loan from Beth Cleary and me, as well as an extensive collection of art books discussing the artists themselves or the forms, periods, and movements to which they contributed. The Chinese American jazz saxophonist, composer, and activist Fred Ho, gave his collection of books and records to the ESFL before his death in spring 2014. The Hmong Archives, a twenty-year-old project in Saint Paul, whose holdings bear witness to the immigration of tens of thousands of Southeast Asian immigrants to the Twin Cities, will join us. We have an embarrassment of riches.

The East Side Freedom Library intends to build on the iconic significance of this historic building, a long-time middle ground. It is the one building on the East Side that has been used by every immigrant group, at times providing a space in which people mingled across racial and ethnic lines. At the same time, we intend to highlight the building as a site in which new immigrants will be welcomed, their cultures honored, their stories heard. With the support of the Knight Foundation's Art Initiative, we are commissioning silk screens to proclaim "Awaken to the Work of Freedom for Yourself and All Beings" in twelve languages, from Ojibwe and Dakota, Norwegian and Italian, to Hmong and Karen, a mural that will represent the peoples of this neighborhood, and library tables to be codesigned by immigrant artisans. We will also be videotaping discussions among the artists that will become the first installment of our storytelling projects and archives.

While the library's main floor reading room and built-in shelves will remain largely as they have been, the ESFL plans significant renovations to the downstairs spaces to serve as a home for "StoryWorks." We will create a performance space, adaptable to multiple uses, including community meetings, workshops, yoga classes, film screenings, and discussions. We will upgrade the staff break room into a catering-quality kitchen so that event participants can share food as well as stories and ideas. And we will transform the downstairs office into a space that can serve the housing needs of possible artists and teachers-in-residence. These changes can shift the inner life of this historic building and make it the kind of middle ground that fosters the teaching and learning of labor history in ways that involve the ostensible "students" as the creators of new knowledge.

The ESFL is already working with unions, churches, and immigrant and social justice organizations, as well as the Minnesota Historical Society, the Minnesota Humanities Center, the Friends of the Saint Paul Public Library, the University of Minnesota's Immigration History Research Center, Metropolitan State University's Institute for Community Engagement and Scholarship, the public schools, and local colleges and universities to develop programs for learners of all ages. In its first few months of operation, the ESFL has hosted programs marking Juneteenth, Frederick Douglass's 1852 Fourth of July speech, the election to national office of the president of the Saint Paul Federation of Teachers, and the history of the Labor Day holiday. We are also hosting a community-based theater production and an avant-garde jazz concert, and we are planning workshops on the history of Farmer-Laborism on the East Side, the experiences of immigrants with commons-like spaces in their countries of origin, and the dynamics of recent child immigration. Through the Saint Paul Public Schools Adult and Community Education program, I will be offering the History of Minnesota Labor and the History of Immigration to Saint Paul as six-week courses. I also will be mentoring local junior and senior high school students as they develop History Day projects, and retired college professors will offer their guidance to neighborhood students in the college and scholarship application process.

On our newly emerging middle ground, the East Side Freedom Library will foster border-crossing of all sorts: across generations, by training young people to conduct oral history interviews of seniors; across ethnic and racial lines, by conducting storytelling workshops that lead to public programs in which participants listen to each others' stories; by developing a finding-aid system that will encourage students of, let's say, Chicano history, to also consider resources in, let's say, African American or Asian American history; by linking visual art and music to the social histories of specific communities; by encouraging white people to reconsider their experiences and histories through the lenses of immigrant history, and by encouraging immigrants and people of color to reconsider their experiences through the lenses of class. There are conceptual borders we want to breach, as well: those between the past, the present, and the future; those between the production and consumption of knowledge; and those between education and entertainment. My former colleague, friend, and mentor Elder Mahmoud El-Kati, in his remarks at the Frederick Douglass event, called the ESFL "an intermediary educational institution, filling a great need." It is truly a middle ground, where participants can learn, grow, and create not just knowledge, but themselves.

Notes

Thank you to Barbara Fields for the ways she reorganized my thinking about "in-between" spaces in her masterful *Slavery and Freedom on the Middle Ground: Maryland during the Nineteenth Century* (New Haven, Conn.: Yale University Press, 1984). Thanks also to Beth Cleary for her editorial interventions in this essay, and the editors of this volume for their vision, support, and patience.

1. See, for instance, Charles V. Willie, *Oreo: A Perspective on Race and Marginal Men and Women* (Wakefield, Mass.: Parameter Press, 1975).

2. *The Willmar 8*, DVD, directed by Lee Grant (1981; California Newsreel, 2007); *A Matter of Sex*, directed by Lee Grant (1984); *North Country*, DVD, directed by Niki Caro (Warner Brothers, 2005).

3. William Balfour Ker, "From the Depths" (1906), accessed September 15, 2014, www.loc.gov; Les Leopold, *The Man Who Hated Work and Loved Labor: The Life of Tony Mazzocchi* (White River Junction, Vt.: Chelsea Green, 2007).

4. *The Wobblies*, DVD, directed by Stewart Bird (1979; Docurama, 2006). The archives of the Minnesota Historical Society contains a great oral history interview with Carl Winn, and his role in the birth of the CIO in northern Minnesota in the 1930s is discussed in Jerry Lembcke and William Tattam, *One Union in Wood: A Political History of the International Woodworkers of America* (New York: International Publishers, 1983).

5. *Native Land*, DVD, directed by Dudley Murphy (1942; Criterion, 2007); John Haynes, *Dubious Alliance: The Making of Minnesota's DFL Party* (Minneapolis: University of Minnesota Press, 1984); Bryan Palmer, *Revolutionary Teamsters: The Minneapolis Teamsters' Strikes of 1934* (Chicago: Haymarket Press, 2014); Carl Ross, ed., *Radicalism in Minnesota, 1900–1960: A Survey of Selected Sources* (Saint Paul: Minnesota Historical Society Press, 1994).

6. Peter Rachleff, *Hard-Pressed in the Heartland: The Hormel Strike and the Future of the Labor Movement* (Boston: South End Press, 1993).

7. Shelton Stromquist and Marvin Bergman, eds., *Unionizing the Jungles: Labor and Community in the Twentieth Century Meatpacking Industry* (Iowa City: University of Iowa Press, 1997); Roger Horowitz, *Negro and White, Unite and Fight: A Social History of Industrial Unionism in Meatpacking, 1930–1990* (Urbana: University of Illinois Press, 1997); Rick Halperin, *Down on the Killing Floor: Black and White Workers in Chicago's Packinghouses, 1904–1954* (Urbana: University of Illinois Press, 1997); Staughton Lynd, ed., *We Are All Leaders: The Alternative Unionism of the Early 1930s* (Urbana: University of Illinois Press, 1996); Staughton Lynd, *Solidarity Unionism: Rebuilding the Labor Movement from Below* (Chicago: Charles H. Kerr, 1992).

8. The Hughes and Edward plays are reprinted in James V. Hatch and Ted Fines, eds., *Black Theater U.S.A.* (New York: Free Press, 1973); Meridel Le Sueur, *Women on the Breadlines* [1977], is reprinted in her *Ripening: Selected Work*, edited by Elaine Hedges, 2nd ed. (New York: Feminist Press, 1990); Clifford Odets, *Waiting for Lefty*, reprinted in *"Waiting for Lefty" and Other Plays* (New York: Grove Press, 1966).

9. On the original New York production of *Waiting for Lefty*, see Colette Hyman, *Staging Strikes: Workers' Theater and the American Labor Movement* (Philadelphia: Temple University Press, 1997); Michael Denning, *The Cultural Front: The Laboring of American Culture in the 1930s* (New York: Verso Press, 2011); Emanuel Fried, *The Dodo Bird* (Buffalo, N.Y.: Labor Arts Books, 1972); and Emanuel Fried, *Drop Hammer* (Buffalo, N.Y.: Labor Arts Books, 1977).

10. See Lizabeth Cohen, *Making a New Deal: Industrial Workers in Chicago, 1919–1939* (New York: Cambridge University Press, 1990); Robin D. G. Kelley, *Hammer and Hoe: Alabama Communists during the Great Depression* (Chapel Hill: University of North Carolina Press, 1990); Barbara Melosh, *Engendering Culture: Manhood and Womanhood in New Deal Public Art and Theater* (Washington, D.C.: Smithsonian Institute Press, 1991); and Denning, *Cultural Front*. Arthur Arent, *One Third of a Nation*, 1938; John C. Moffitt, based on a Sinclair Lewis novel, *It Can't Happen Here*, 1938.

11. Steve Jones, *Forgotten: The Murder at the Ford Rouge Plant*, CD, 2005, www.forgottenshow.net; Alan Brinkley, *Voices of Protest: Huey Long, Father Coughlin, and the Great Depression* (New York: Vintage, 1983); Donald Warren, *Radio Priest: Charles Coughlin, the Father of Hate Radio* (New York: Free Press, 1996).

12. Leroi Jones, *Blues People: Negro Music in White America* (New York: Morrow, 1963); Ruth Glasser, *My Music Is My Flag: Puerto Rican Musicians and Their New York Communities, 1917–1940* (Berkeley: University of California Press, 1995); Robbie Lieberman, *My Song Is My Weapon: People's Songs, American Communism, and the Politics of Culture, 1930–1950* (Urbana: University of Illinois Press, 1989); Tricia Rose, *Black Noise: Rap Music and Black Culture in Contemporary America* (Middletown, Conn.: Wesleyan University Press, 1994); Benjamin Filene, *Romancing the Folk: Public Memory and American Roots* (Chapel Hill: University of North Carolina Press, 2000).

13. Bucky Halker, *Don't Want Your Millions* (Revolting Records, 2000), CD, and *Welcome to Labor Land* (Revolting Records, 2002), CD.

14. I've discussed the inner dynamics of UAW Local 879 in a paper I presented at the North American Labor History Conference in 2013, "From Racism to International Solidarity: The Journey of UAW Local 879, 1980–1995." I am revising this paper for publication.

15. The printed brochures for each year's Untold Stories can be found on the website of the Friends of the Saint Paul Public Library, accessed September 15, 2014, www.thefriends.org.

16. Accounts of many of these programs can be found in the electronic archives of Workday Minnesota, a project of the University of Minnesota's Labor Education Service (see www.workdayminnesota.org, accessed September 15, 2014).

17. Brian Kaller, "Labor Historian Leads Unusual Tour," *Pulse of the Twin Cities*, May 11, 2005, accessed September 15, 2014, pulsetc.com.

18. You can view the trailer for Chad Montrie's video at http://vimeo.com/77610411. For more on the Lee story, see Steve Brandt, "Site of Racial Showdown in Minneapolis Heading to National Register," *Star Tribune*, July 24, 2014, http://startribune.com, accessed February 1, 2016.

19. Karl Marx, "Theses on Feuerbach," in *The Marx-Engel Reader*, edited by Robert C. Tucker, 2nd ed. (New York: W. W. Norton, 1978 [1972]), 143–45.

Peter Rachleff, "Learning from David Montgomery: Worker, Historian, Activist," *New Politics*, summer 2012, http://newpol.org, accessed February 1, 2016. For more information on the Freedom Library, see the Facebook page for East Side Freedom Library (our initial name) and http://eastsidefreedomlibrary.org, accessed September 15, 2014.

CHAPTER 9

The Difference a Union Makes

Graduate Employee Activists' Engaged Scholarship and Their Working Lives

Susan Roth Breitzer

Higher education teaching and academic scholarship is inherently a value-laden endeavor, something historian Matt Mettler acknowledges in his work as a teacher and scholar. When he teaches about potentially politically charged issues like poverty or "the structural issues that create wealth inequality," Mettler takes care to include sources that convey viewpoints opposed to his own. Therefore, he sees his role as a teacher and activist as not just providing his students with "politically motivated material, but giving them the proper contexts," that enables them to weigh all evidence in an objective manner.[1] This acknowledgment is far from uncommon, against a backdrop of declining tenure-track opportunities and pressure to produce, which gives nearly every pedagogical and scholarly decision the potential to make or break a career. Yet for Mettler and many of his colleagues who were active in their graduate employee union while completing their doctoral work at the University of Iowa, making these decisions may involve considerations other than career advancement. Rather, these graduates, as they pursue their careers, seek to incorporate greater engagement into their scholarship and teaching.

Engagement, broadly defined, involves reaching out to some sort of public in order to generate a greater awareness of the real-life issues that one's teaching and scholarship address. But what makes one an engaged scholar and teacher? To be sure, one's choice of graduate program, areas of specialization, faculty influence, personal backgrounds, and experiences as union or community activists are important elements. For a cohort of graduate students from the University of Iowa, their involvement as founders and activists in their graduate employee union, COGS (Campaign to Organize Graduate Students) proved to be a transformative experience in the making of engaged scholars.

Numerous other major universities, such as the University of Illinois at Urbana-Champaign, New York University, Yale University, and the University of California–

Santa Barbara, are settings for comparable stories of struggles to achieve a union.[2] However, because each graduate employee union is different, focusing on COGS, which to date is the only graduate employee local of the traditionally blue-collar United Electrical, Radio, and Machine Workers of America (UE), illustrates how predominantly middle-class graduate students can allow themselves to be shaped by involvement with an unabashedly militant union.[3] This chapter, therefore, is a case study of a cohort of former graduate employee union activists with the UE Local 896-COGS who pursued doctoral studies at the University of Iowa during the union's formative decades. In it, I look at the ways in which union activism shaped not only the graduate careers of the people I interviewed, but their subsequent teaching, scholarship, and professional choices, as well.

The interviewees are about a dozen of my activist colleagues who attended the University of Iowa between the mid-1990s and the end of the first decade of the 2000s. Although this largely self-selected group is limited in diversity, these interviewees are hardly monolithic in background. They began graduate school at the University of Iowa at different ages and stages of life and with varied work and educational backgrounds. As a result, their previous work and life experiences significantly shaped their views about class, economic status, and work, and, to varying degrees, how such views were influenced by considerations of race or gender. Their activism in the graduate employee union movement at the University of Iowa came during the union's formative period, from the first (unsuccessful) COGS campaign through the early period after the first contract. Although nearly all the interviewees were involved with COGS in some formal way, from organizing to serving as officers, a few chose not to hold office but instead shaped union policy through less formal influence. The most notable examples of this informal influence were the efforts of John Scott and the late Paul Young to ensure that the COGS Coordinating Committee (its version of an executive board) would include a unity officer and an international student representative (held, whenever possible, by a minority and international graduate student, respectively), ensuring that antidiscrimination was built into the union's governing structure.[4]

After completing their graduate education and time with COGS, the participants of this study took a number of different paths. Although various factors informed their divergent paths and professional choices, ranging from the timing of their degree completion to family considerations, all of their postgraduate lives have been shaped to varying degrees by their participation in COGS. Despite their various commitments, their continued sense of engagement generally outweighs the differences. In particular, all have managed to maintain their identities as activists, even while respecting new limitations on activism imposed by professional status and family obligations. In addition, some have both reified and reshaped their activist identities by devoting their professional lives to the labor movement rather than to the academy.

Background to Graduate Union Involvement

These distinct histories of engagement took place against a backdrop of an un-precedented surge in graduate employee organization during the 1990s. Much of this new organizing was rooted in the significantly increased use of graduate and adjunct faculty labor for teaching that began in the 1980s. This shift away from a major role for full-time tenure-stream faculty was accompanied by exponential growth of the administrative side of universities and increased attacks on faculty tenure during a period of massive expansion of higher education in the post–World War II decades. Although faculty organizing for the protection of profes-sional status and academic freedom dates back to the founding of the American Association of University Professors (AAUP) in 1915, graduate employee organiz-ing was relatively late in emerging, with the first successful independent graduate employee union organizing at the University of Wisconsin–Madison in 1969.[5] But for that union, as for other graduate employee unions that followed, organizing a union would prove to be much easier than getting university administrations to the bargaining table.

For the next couple of decades, graduate employees organized around the country on a handful of campuses, almost exclusively at public universities. They encountered near-universal administrative resistance to recognition and legal decisions that disallowed graduate employee organizing on the basis that the primary graduate identity was that of a student, not an employee.[6] At the same time, the impetus toward organizing was affected by changing graduate student demographics. These included a growing proportion of older students entering graduate programs, coupled with a marked upsurge in the percentage of teaching and research duties performed by graduate employees and declining postgraduate employment prospects. These factors not only challenged the traditional "ap-prentice" model of graduate work but also spurred a new upsurge in graduate organizing efforts.[7]

Graduate employees' stepped-up organizing efforts encountered many obsta-cles, beginning with laws that blocked graduate union recognition and graduate collective bargaining. In states where graduate employees were legally classified as students, these unions had to mount legal battles for union recognition. At some schools, most infamously the University of Illinois, the battle for collective bargaining continued even after organizers secured recognition in state courts of their employee status as a legitimate bargaining unit.[8] But beyond legal challenges, nearly every graduate employee union faced the task of persuading its members to identify as workers as well as students and professionals, when it became clear that cultivating this worker identity was vital to each union's effectiveness. Cultivating this identity was never a simple matter, however. It was affected, for better or for worse, by the relationship with the international union with which graduate students had chosen to affiliate. There were even cases in which the parent union was slow or reluctant to acknowledge the desired autonomy of their graduate employee chapter or to respect the graduate unionists' knowledge of their own workplace.[9]

Although there was no apparent effort in Iowa to exclude graduate assistants from the state's Public Employment Relations Act (PERA), this larger struggle for recognition as workers shaped the experience of the COGS activists.[10] UE District 11 president Carl Rosen has pointed out in his account of working with COGS that, although the UE was new to organizing in an educational setting, veteran activists would come to understand that the graduate workers were scarcely different from other workers when it came to workplace issues ranging from wages to fair treatment. Rosen has also pointed out that what attracted Iowa graduate students to the UE, which in the last few decades has organized far beyond its base in heavy industry, was its traditions of rank-and-file democracy, comparative autonomy for its locals, and active member participation. Although after certification there would be adjustments on both sides, in the nearly two decades of COGS's existence, the group's enthusiastic embrace of UE's brand of unionism not only has contributed to COGS's effectiveness as a union but has also had a profound shaping effect on its activists.[11]

The perspectives of the group of interviewees have been shaped by their individual personal, educational, and activist backgrounds. Even class background proved to be more malleable in terms of how class is understood. Although most claimed a middle-class background, that identification was primarily a cultural matter for those who came from highly educated but not necessarily affluent backgrounds.[12] A few had what would be generally recognized as working-class backgrounds, including Deborah Herman, the daughter of a blue-collar family, who was the first in her family to complete college. John Scott's working-class consciousness was shaped both by his upbringing in a working-class black community in Detroit and by his long career as a leftist activist.[13] Regardless of each participant's class background, his or her consciousness was molded in a variety of ways that often included previous political or community activism that would influence their later involvement with COGS and beyond, whether it was Eric Fure-Slocum's previous community organizing or Scott's long activism with the political left.[14]

For all of these graduate activists who applied their previous experiences and skills to graduate union organizing, Iowa was their graduate program of choice. The strong labor history program and the opportunity to work with certain professors attracted the majority of historians.[15] Among those who took less typical paths to Iowa, Scott was one of the many graduate students whom his sister, Kesho Scott, a renowned sociology and American studies professor at Grinnell College (and whose own doctorate is from the University of Iowa), encouraged to attend Iowa for graduate school.[16] For some, such as Mettler and Jennifer Sherer, the path to Iowa was less direct and was shaped by intellectual, professional, and financial considerations, the last of which included the draw of a strong graduate employee union.

During their graduate years at Iowa, many activists worked as teaching assistants in a variety of disciplines, especially the history graduates, a number of whom taught one or more of the Issues in Human History series of courses. This gave them opportunities to design courses within certain parameters, granting them greater teaching autonomy than teaching assistants for survey courses enjoyed. For some, the issues courses would provide their first opportunities for engaged scholarship and teaching.[17] Beyond teaching, a couple of Iowa graduates held labor-education-related assistantships: Herman had a University of Iowa Labor Center assistantship that was sponsored by the AFL-CIO and open to children of active or retired members of AFL-CIO unions; and Sherer's work with the center in a part-time position led to her postgraduate career in labor education.

During the nearly two decades that this cohort pursued graduate studies at the University of Iowa, they would play a variety of roles, formal and informal, in the early history of COGS. These ranged from the first COGS campaign that ended in defeat in 1994, to a period of victory in a union recognition election and securing a first labor contract, to a second generation of activism in the new century. Participants' level of involvement varied and was shaped by factors that ranged from the length of time spent at Iowa to the stage of their graduate work. Even initial contact with COGS came about for varied reasons. For Herman, a conflict over her advisor's efforts to push her to drop the second assistantship she held with the University of Iowa Labor Center in addition to her teaching assistantship led not only to a change of advisors and majors, but to her first contact with the union; her voluntary participation would eventually include serving as its president. Others began more casually with meeting attendance, which led to deeper involvement. For Sherer, involvement began with attending general membership meetings, which led to her becoming a departmental steward, which involved both organizing and adjusting employee grievances. Then, following a period of readjusting of the union's governance structure, she became vice president for organizing. Word of mouth and personal invitations also played an important role in bringing in key activists, including Heather Kopelson, who eventually became campus chief steward of COGS. Some, such as Scott, largely avoided formal office, instead playing more informal roles, ranging from advocating choosing the UE over the American Federation of Teachers (AFT) in the second COGS campaign, to ensuring that nonwhite and international students' concerns remained central to the union's policies and actions. A few participants deepened their involvement with the UE and with the local labor movement beyond COGS, whether through convention attendance or as paid or volunteer summer organizers for other UE campaigns, or even as temporary or permanent UE staff.[18]

The majority of the interviewees experienced the early post-certification years of COGS, which included the tough negotiations for the first contract and the accompanying fight to get the university's broad nondiscrimination policy written into the graduate employee contract. Most also witnessed the revisions of the COGS constitution after the first contract and the streamlining of the union administration from three copresidents to a single president and a vice president for organizing. In this they were assisted by representatives from UE Local 1111, which represented the nearby Allen-Bradley plant, whose bargaining unit structure was surprisingly similar to that of the Iowa graduate workforce.[19] But even for those who served in COGS leadership roles following the reorganization, it was a continual work in progress to build and consolidate the union. By 2003, when the union was fairly well established, Mettler recounted that it was increasingly difficult to get people to run for union offices, a situation that possibly reflected the comparative complacency that can set in. However, Mettler added that COGS was nonetheless able to recruit suitable people, and he volunteered more than once during his graduate career.

Maintaining, and even improving, collectively bargained gains similarly did not cease to be a challenge for COGS, as illustrated by the efforts to secure tuition waivers and to defeat a proposed step system of pay. In some instances, as Sherer recounts, compromise was necessary, albeit always "compromising up." This was most evident when COGS, in response to administrative intransigence against the long-sought tuition waivers for all graduate assistants, instead bargained significant wage increases that made a difference at a time of stepped-up tuition increases.[20] Activists also resisted administrative efforts to introduce a step system of pay. This would have allowed departments to pay their graduate assistants according to the number of years they had been teaching, a move that the union opposed because of the potential for this to create division within the bargaining unit and for departments to hire less experienced teaching assistants over more advanced graduate students.[21] Some of the activists, however, were around to see union victories that included significant improvements in the already hard-won graduate employee health insurance plan and increased tuition waivers in subsequent contracts negotiated in the mid-2000s, finally achieving 100 percent tuition coverage with the 2011–13 contract.[22]

Throughout COGS's storied early history, most of its activists were graduate employees in a traditionally (and still predominantly) blue-collar union, and following the successful chartering, COGS activists consciously endeavored to be part of the larger UE, whether through participating in district and national conventions, assisting in non-COGS organizing, or representing UE in labor solidarity events. In doing so, they participated with full awareness of being part of not only the graduate employee union movement, but also of the 1990s revival in Iowa of the UE, which had disappeared from the state after the McCarthy-era attack on leftist industrial unions. Even during the first, unsuccessful COGS

campaign, which began in 1993, COGS activists considered UE affiliation only
to reject it, partially because, at the time, the UE was just getting reestablished in
Iowa. Other considerations included the UE's then lack of experience organizing
in an educational setting, as well as strong pressure from many activists in favor
of the Service Employees International Union. But as Dennis Deslippe recalls,
some COGS activists nonetheless strongly supported the traditionally militant
UE, and by 1995 the union's growing successes in organizing beyond its traditional
blue-collar constituency, as well as its visible support for the graduate employees'
cause, made it the affiliate of choice for the second, successful COGS campaign.

The positive difference COGS made in study participants' graduate working
lives included material gains such as dramatic improvements in base salaries,
tuition coverage, and health insurance over the first decade of the 2000s.[23] The
union also helped in addressing day-to-day workplace issues, even in departments
that were generally union-friendly, because periodic issues still remained to be
worked out with individual faculty, usually involving computation of work hours
and questions of overwork.[24] Beyond these tangible improvements, COGS's rank-
and-file participatory structure and encouragement of active member participation had other salutary effects. As David Colman recalls, by bringing together
graduate students from different disciplines, the union helped foster friendships
across departmental lines that might not otherwise have formed. For Colman, this
unity was "one of the great things about it . . . and probably still is."[25] But another
of the most significant and lasting intangible benefits that COGS provided for
its participants was a raised consciousness that would shape the interviewees'
subsequent teaching, scholarship, and professional choices.

Postgraduate Career Paths

Most of the graduates interviewed for this study followed the traditionally expected pursuit of an academic career, holding positions in institutions ranging
from a flagship state university to a small Catholic college. Some have achieved
coveted tenure-track positions. Others still seek stable, long-term employment
while weighing alternative options, including working full-time for organized
labor. Along the way, most have maintained the "labor consciousness" gained as
graduate employee union activists, whether as non-tenure-track faculty seeking
greater equality with their tenure-track colleagues, or as tenure-stream faculty
with graduate assistants of their own.[26] These varying career paths would ultimately shape the extent and limitations of the engaged scholarship and teaching
each would pursue and practice, as well as how much each would be pushing (or
not) to change the academic system. Understandably, those who chose careers in
labor activism or whose academic careers have remained in the contingent faculty
track would have greater investment in seeking change, even as contingency created its own limitations for activism. But those who did achieve tenure-stream

positions have maintained no less of a labor consciousness, often including active support for other campus workers' struggles.[27]

For every person interviewed, the timing of completion of doctoral work and personal circumstances affected their postgraduate paths, especially in light of the steadily declining number of full-time academic positions over the first decade of the twenty-first century. But even for those who graduated in the early 2000s, the path to the tenure track could be circuitous and uncertain. For example, Jason Duncan held a series of short-term positions and nearly gave up before landing his current tenure-track job at Aquinas College. Similarly, Michael Innis-Jiménez went from a short-term position to a tenure-track position at a unionized William Paterson University in New Jersey, only to leave it for an opportunity at the non-union University of Alabama for, among other reasons, a more research-friendly teaching schedule.

For nearly all activists, timing of marriage and family formation had a greater impact on career progress than even gender. Those scholars who married and became parents early in their careers often faced difficult choices. Notably, a number of the men have followed their spouses when it made sense, rather than adhere to the traditional gender expectations, consciously accepting the challenges of being a dual–academic career couple.[28] For Innis-Jiménez and Kopelson, who are married to each other, the University of Alabama relieved them of the dilemma facing too many academic couples by hiring both of them to tenure-track positions, in American studies and history, respectively.[29] Others have not been as fortunate, and a lingering unsettledness can affect not only career paths but also decisions regarding the very public engagement and activism that shape the identity of the engaged scholar and teacher. For Mettler, greater involvement in public activism has been limited by his current lack of settlement as a contingent faculty member. As he points out, "it's really difficult to be an activist when . . . you are constantly moving around" with "no sense of rootedness." But even for those who have become the most settled in their lives, personal circumstances, including stage of life and family formation, may have caused shifts and or re-evaluation of priorities. For example, for Colman, new fatherhood caused him to reevaluate the possibilities of full-time activism: "there's a moment in life when . . . political activity is no longer as central to your life as it was before."

Whether out of choice or because of the difficult job market, some COGS alumni quickly pursued a plan B career choice that was often a hybrid of academia and the labor movement. For Jennifer Sherer, who served a term as COGS president, her postgraduate career grew out of a graduate assistantship at the University of Iowa Labor Center, whose mission is "to provide educational programs and research support to Iowa's working people and their organizations." Sherer started when the center was short-staffed due to budget cuts, and she helped fill those holes by applying her union experience as vice president for organizing and then as president of COGS. She became vital to the operation of the center, which offered her a full-time staff position in 2005. Sherer recalls that after careful consideration about what this would mean for her academic career, "I did eventually apply and was hired . . . with the understanding that at some point I was going to take a leave of absence to eventually finish my dissertation." Sherer's concern about finishing acknowledged a certain ambivalence regarding giving up her academic identity, even when an attractive and meaningful alternative career presented itself.

Similarly, Herman and Julie Schmid, both past presidents of COGS, chose careers with the AAUP, where they work or have worked in high-level positions. Both decided to abandon pursuit of a traditional academic career soon after completion of their doctoral studies, as had Sherer. Schmid finished her doctorate with an awareness of the hypercompetitive job market for English PhDs that was further shaped by her labor activism. As a result, she began her alternative career when she moved to Portland, Oregon, for her husband's job and attained the position of executive director of the Portland State University AAUP chapter. She then worked at the national AAUP's Department of Organizing and Services from 2002 to 2008, before moving to Madison, Wisconsin, to organize for the AFT. In 2013 she was appointed executive director of the national AAUP. Shortly after Herman completed her doctoral studies, she recognized the unique challenges her interdisciplinary doctorate presented. So with guidance and encouragement from Ryan Downing, the UE field organizer for COGS, she took a staff position with the Teaching Assistants Association at the University of Wisconsin—the oldest graduate employee union in the United States and a local of the AFT. Then, when she realized that long-term employment in Madison was something of a moon shot, she took a position with the AAUP at the University of Cincinnati. For both Sherer and Herman, full-time organizing has put them in regular contact with full- and part-time faculty, even if they are no longer in the classroom as academics themselves. Herman, in particular, has come to appreciate the necessity of balancing sometimes conflicting identities as academics and as workers, pointing out that these dual identities as union activists and professionals are to be acknowledged rather than denied, and that no one is 100 percent one or the other.

Postgraduate Activism and Scholarly Engagement

Regardless of their career paths, the previous experiences of all of the interviewees as COGS activists have shaped their views of what lies at the heart of this chapter: engaged teaching and engaged scholarship. For some, work as labor educators or as labor organizers has involved what is by definition engaged teaching—educating workers toward union consciousness and effective union building. As director of the University of Iowa Labor Center since 2008, Sherer oversees a number of local and regional worker education programs. As executive director of the University of Cincinnati chapter of the AAUP, Herman taught "structural analysis" to labor leaders to help them adapt to changing situations and structures and move beyond getting stuck in modes and structures of leadership that may be well-suited to organizing a union but not appropriate for day-to-day union administration.

Those who pursued traditional careers in academia used the tools of their disciplines to pursue greater engagement in their teaching and scholarship. That included trying to bring their extended knowledge of labor and working-class history into "regular" history courses, as well as using greater creativity in shaping specialized courses.[30] Innis-Jiménez titled his course about blue-collar occupations Dirty Jobs and shaped the material to echo the popular "reality" show of the same name as a way of reaching out to the predominantly middle-class undergraduate population at the University of Alabama. Likewise, Fure-Slocum used familiar themes by titling a course about the history of the post–World War II U.S. political economy Walmart America. Having taught a variety of courses at Ramapo College, Colman has been fortunate to regularly teach Social Issues, a course that brings in concepts of "race, class, gender, and other categories that help shape inequalities of power." Beyond traditional courses, Innis-Jiménez has also reshaped the increasingly popular service learning that combines classroom instruction and community service to raise student consciousness regarding recent Latino and Latina immigration in Alabama at a time of stepped-up anti-immigration measures.[31]

The forms of engaged scholarship that COGS alumni practice is similarly broad. While still graduate students, Herman and Schmid coedited the 2003 *Cogs in the Classroom Factory: The Changing Identity of Academic Labor*. This book of essays on graduate employee and faculty organizing situates COGS in a period of significant expansion in graduate organizing, a surge that has shown no sign of stalling despite encountering increased opposition from public and private universities alike.[32] Both editors saw the necessity of such a volume amid the growing number of studies on organization in higher education at a time when most publications addressing the erosion of the tenure track were written by and about faculty and especially adjunct faculty. As a result, most addressed neither the graduate student movement nor the role the larger labor movement played in relation to faculty organizing. Schmid, in particular, highlighted the importance of a book that addresses graduate organization in response to the higher-education crisis and that is "written by people who were part of that movement."

Beyond publications specifically devoted to the topic of scholarly engagement and academic activism, some of the doctoral and postdoctoral research of this group of interviewees addressed class and labor issues but examined topics that could not be classified strictly as labor history. This reflects an increasingly common trend among labor historians to move away from union histories to the lived experiences and identities of working people, which frequently include considerations of race, class, and gender. Their scholarship ranges from Mettler's efforts to show the applied functions of labor research to John McKerley's demonstration of the ways that labor history can open doors to other aspects of working-class life. As a result of his involvement with COGS, Mettler was inspired to write about the Cold War–era trials of its parent union, the UE. Mettler's dissertation then addressed the postwar appropriation of industrial psychology by the United Auto Workers (UAW). His study challenges traditional assumptions regarding a shift in industrial unions such as the UAW toward greater bureaucracy and examines the more complex ways in which postwar unions adapted.

For many of the Iowa graduates interviewed, their research interests have evolved even beyond rethinking the traditional institutional focus on labor history. Although McKerley, like many of his colleagues, was first attracted to the Iowa history department for its strength in labor history, he admitted, "Ironically, I didn't stay a labor historian." This change in focus emerged partially from his growing self-consciousness as a southerner, which led to an interest in the history of race and to a more intensive study of African American history, which in turn shaped his doctoral work on the Missouri Democratic Party's failed effort to enact statewide, legal black disfranchisement in the early twentieth century. Similarly, Innis-Jiménez's published doctoral work, *Steel Barrio: The Great Mexican Migration to South Chicago, 1915–1940*, reflects his training as a labor historian but focuses more on urban and immigration history than on labor history.[33] Sometimes the purpose of the scholarship is to challenge the privileging of certain kinds of evidence over others. This motivates Kopelson's proposed effort to challenge the privileged place of written documentation, when it comes to researching historically marginalized groups, members of whom have been less likely to leave written records. Occasionally research brings in the personal background of the authors, such as Colman's current work on the crack and urban hip-hop culture of the New Jersey area in which he grew up. Finally, engaged scholarship may take on alternative forms to traditional publications, with a prominent example being Innis-Jiménez's curating of a special exhibit at the Museum of the New South in Charlotte, North Carolina, on Latino migration to the U.S. South.

Although these scholars have produced work that is often cutting-edge, they would caution that neither the variety nor the originality of subject matter or approaches is enough to make the scholarship "engaged." Rather, when shaping a research agenda, scholars may face a choice between great scholarship that advances one's individual career and a willingness to go out on a limb to produce scholarship that goes beyond displaying one's individual prowess as a scholar. The latter choice—according to McKerley—is key to the scholarly engagement that transcends the boundaries between the academy and the larger world. McKerley, whose projects include a coedited book that emerged from the Birmingham Civil Rights Institute's Oral History Project, admits that it is sometimes a tough choice between revising his doctoral work and engaging in his oral-history-related work that allows his scholarship to "touch people in more concrete ways." He is furthermore emphatic that truly engaged scholarship should be about amplifying the voices of subjects who may have historically been rendered voiceless. For Kopelson, engaged scholarship is closely tied to engaged teaching, involving both thinking in multiple perspectives and the ability to "look at the layers of meaning and experiences beyond what is visible on paper." Herman and Schmid see the greatest value in the kind of scholarship that can raise consciousness in its audience and motivate them to action.

All of my interviewees acknowledge that there are limits to engaged scholarship and teaching, especially the latter, as teaching involves a necessarily unequal relationship between instructor and student. Kopelson explains that "since the teacher is in a position of authority, telling students what they should think in one way or another" constitutes taking unfair advantage of this authority. Rather than teach students how they should think about the issues, therefore, Kopelson emphasizes that engaged teaching "should get students to examine the world around them critically" and to carefully evaluate what they might encounter. Similarly, as his teaching career has advanced, Colman no longer assumes that his students will come away from his classes with viewpoints similar to his, nor that they necessarily should.

For the engaged scholar, even without the cautions pertaining to teaching there is sometimes a fine line between engagement and activism. For Fure-Slocum, this recognition includes "a sense of . . . integrity when it comes to sources and how one uses these" so that "our immediate political ends aren't going to shape how we use the sources." McKerley points to precedents for this problem in the history of leftist scholarship, which has supported his assertion that "engaged scholarship shouldn't be propaganda." He takes guidance from renowned labor scholars such as E. P. Thompson, Herbert Gutman, and David Montgomery, who experienced the pressures of left-wing orthodoxy and reached the same conclusion that "you could be a committed left-wing scholar by being a good scholar," with scholarly excellence itself serving as a guard against line crossing.

Aside from the question of whether there are or should be limitations to engaged scholarship remains the question of how much of a difference engaged teaching and scholarship can make. Here the responses have been as varied as the respondents. Most who have pursued traditional academic careers have recognized the mind-opening potential of their work as well as the reality that this effect is more likely to be at the micro rather than the macro level. Although Kopelson declines to speculate about whether engaged teaching can really create change "on a grand scheme of things," she asserts that "it can certainly open up individual understanding" and change students' individual worlds. Similarly, Colman emphasizes that even raising the consciousness of individual students is important and productive, adding that doing so is "critical, especially amid the rapid changes in higher education away from traditional learning." On the other hand, those who chose to make their careers in organized labor recognize the potential impact of teaching and scholarship, but also their limitations. Schmid notes that, while books can be important to the educational and consciousness-raising process, what has really made a difference for the academic workers she represents is "an organized effort, at the campus level, [and] at the state level."

Conclusion: Public Activism and Bringing Justice Home

Apart from those who have devoted their professional lives to the labor movement, many who are in more conventional faculty careers have continued to
remain active on behalf of a variety of social justice issues, most of which involve
local activism and even personal politics. David Colman, for example, played
a leading role in fighting for better working conditions for Ramapo College's
food service workers, the majority of whom were Haitian immigrants. Others
have taken their activism into the greater public arena, bringing their intellectual commitments to bear on the areas of activism they pursue. Innis-Jiménez's
work with Alabama's immigrant rights movement is just one example. Similarly,
Kopelson's activism with the Alabama Birth Coalition's effort to decriminalize
midwife-attended home births and midwives is geared toward raising awareness
of the class and racial issues involved.

Without a doubt, public activism can be complicated by contingent faculty
status. For Mettler, this means being up-front about his scholar-activist identity while accepting the caveats doing so entails. While he is grateful that there
is "still a climate where I can be a scholar-activist" yet "not be discriminated
against in the job market," he recognizes the limits of this sense of surety and
is somewhat pessimistic about whether this situation can continue, given the
increased corporatization of universities and the faculties' decreasing power vis-
à-vis administrators when it comes to the very hiring decisions that protect the
academic freedom making engaged teaching and scholarship possible. Similarly,
Fure-Slocum, a long-term non-tenure-track professor, points out the risks and
rewards of bringing justice home in his effort to seek greater parity for non-tenure-
track faculty in areas ranging from regularity of teaching assignments to access
to college resources, an effort that reflects a larger, often rear-guard, struggle for
non-tenure-track faculty equity at colleges and universities across the country,
in response to the increased use of contingent faculty.

This cohort of Iowa doctoral students concludes that their previous labor activism
with COGS was a worthwhile activity that has unquestionably shaped their career
path and permitted them to incorporate a deeper social consciousness into their
work. For those working in the labor movement, this influence has been profound.[34]
Even those who graduated in the midst of the steep decline in the academic job
market have thus far maintained the raised consciousness that continues to shape
their working and scholarly lives. While not all have elected to engage in a balancing act between dual identities as academics and activists, all have used their dual
identities in their professional lives to push and even transcend the boundaries between the academy and the "real world," boundaries that have become increasingly
permeable. And the unique experience of being graduate assistants in a blue-collar
union known for its democratic structure and militancy has provided them with
a perspective that continues to shape their professional lives.

Notes

1. Matthew M. Mettler, telephone interview by the author, February 24, 2014. All succeeding Mettler quotations and information are from this interview.

2. Eric Dirnbach and Susan Chimonas, "Shutting Down the Academic Factory: Developing Worker Identity in Graduate Employee Unions," Richard Sullivan, "Pyrrhic Victory at UC Santa Barbara: The Struggle for Labor's New Identity," and William Vaughn, "Are You Now or Have You Ever Been an Employee?: Contesting Graduate Labor in the Academy," all in *Cogs in the Classroom Factory: The Changing Identity of Academic Labor*, edited by Deborah M. Herman and Julie M. Schmid (Westport, Conn.: Greenwood, 2003), 91–116, 139–50, 152–69; GESO (Graduate Employees and Student Organization), "About GESO," accessed September 30, 2014, http://geso.org/about; Graduate Employees' Organization, University of Illinois at Urbana-Champaign, "History," accessed September 30, 2014, www.uigeo.org/history; Charles Huckabee, "NYU Graduate Employees Vote to Unionize," December 12, 2013, http://chronicle.com.

3. Susan Roth Breitzer, "More than Academic: Labor Consciousness and the Rise of UE Local 896-COGS," in Herman and Schmid, *Cogs in the Classroom Factory*, 71–90.

4. John Scott, interview by John W. McKerley, Iowa Labor History Oral Project, Coralville, Iowa, February 5, 2014. All succeeding Scott quotations and information are from this interview.

5. "History of the AAUP," AAUP, accessed August 28, 2014, www.aaup.org; "TAA History," Teaching Assistants' Association, accessed October 7, 2014, www.taa-madison.org/; Julie Schmid, telephone interview by the author, March 11, 2014; all succeeding Schmid quotations and information are from this interview; Vincent Tirelli, "Beyond the Campus Gates: New Trends with Old Twists—The Personal Is Still Political," *Workplace: A Journal for Academic Labor* 1 (1998): 100–102. All opinions expressed in the Schmid interview are solely those of the interviewee, and do not represent the views or policies of the AAUP.

6. Scott Henkel, "Working Conditions and Learning Conditions After the National Labor Relations Board's *Brown University* Decision," *Workplace: A Journal for Academic Labor* 12 (2005): 44–53; David Montgomery, "Foreword: Preserving Our Independence, Acting Together," in Herman and Schmid, *Cogs in the Classroom Factory*, xii–xxi.

7. Dirnbach and Chimonas, "Shutting Down the Academic Factory"; Julie M. Schmid and Deborah M. Herman, "Introduction: The Changing Identity of Academic Labor," in Herman and Schmid, *Cogs in the Classroom Factory*, 1–9.

8. "History," Graduate Employees' Organization, accessed January 15, 2016, www.uigeo.org/history; Vaughn, "Are You Now or Have You Ever Been an Employee?"

9. "Exposing Concessions by 'Reform' Caucus at California Grad Employee Union," September 15, 2014, accessed January 15, 2016, www.dailykos.com; Kate Burns and Anthony M. Navarette, "Cannibals, Star Trek, and Egg Timers: Ten Years of Student Employee Organizing at the University of California," *Workplace* 1 (1998): 76–81; Sullivan, "Pyrrhic Victory at UC Santa Barbara"; James Thompson, "Unfinished Chapters: Institutional Alliances and Changing Identities in a Graduate Employee Union," in Herman and Schmid, *Cogs in the Classroom Factory*, 123–33; Philip Zwerling, "Union Organizing at the University of California," *Workplace* 7 (June 2001): 163–64.

10. "COGS: A Brief History of Your Union," COGS UE Local 896, University of Iowa, accessed June 23, 2014, http://cogs.org/history.

11. Ibid.; Breitzer, "More than Academic," 73–87; Ryan Downing and Jennifer Sherer, eds., "Always Organize: Clippings from the UE Local 896-COGS COGNITION Archive,"

Workplace 6 (December 2000): 72–82; Carl Rosen, "Afterword: Classroom, Lab, Factory Floor: Common Labor Struggles," in Herman and Schmid, *Cogs in the Classroom Factory*, 197–98; Julie Marie Schmid, "What's Next: Organizing after the COGS Union Affiliation Vote," *Workplace* 1 (1998): 85–88; Schmid, "Update from the Labor Movement Trenches: COGS-UE Local 896's Second Contract and the Power of Collective Action," *Workplace* 3 (April 1999): 69–70.

12. Jennifer Sherer, telephone interview by the author, March 12, 2014. All succeeding Sherer quotations and information are from this interview.

13. Deborah Herman, telephone interview by the author, May 6, 2014. All succeeding Herman quotations and information are from this interview.

14. Eric Fure-Slocum, telephone interview by the author, January 16, 2014. All succeeding Fure-Slocum quotations and information are from this interview.

15. Telephone interviews by the author: Heather Kopelson, March 31, 2014; Dennis Deslippe, January 26, 2014; Jason Duncan, February 20, 2014. All succeeding Kopelson, Deslippe, and Duncan quotations and information are from these interviews, respectively.

16. Grinnell College, "Kesho Scott," accessed June 26, 2014, https://www.grinnell.edu/users/scottk1.

17. Fure-Slocum interview; John W. McKerley telephone interview by the author, January 16, 2014. All succeeding McKerley quotations and information are from this interview.

18. McKerley interview; Mettler interview.

19. Rosen, "Afterword," 197–98.

20. "COGS: A Brief History of Your Union."

21. Kopelson interview.

22. "COGS: A Brief History of Your Union."

23. Ibid.

24. McKerley interview.

25. David Colman, telephone interview by the author, April 23, 2014. All succeeding Colman quotations and information are from this interview.

26. Colman interview; Deslippe interview; Duncan interview; Fure-Slocum interview; Michael Innis-Jiménez, telephone interview by the author, January 26, 2014 (all succeeding Innis-Jiménez quotations and information are from this interview); Kopelson interview; Breitzer, "More than Academic," 71–72, 87.

27. Colman interview; Fure-Slocum interview; Herman interview; Mettler interview; Schmid interview.

28. Fure-Slocum interview; McKerley interview.

29. Kopelson interview.

30. Duncan interview; Fure-Slocum interview.

31. See also Innis-Jiménez, chapter 5 in this book.

32. Montgomery, "Foreword," xii–xvi; Scott Jaschik, "Union Impact and Non-Impact," *Inside Higher Ed*, October 8, 2013, accessed January 15, 2016, www.insidehighered.com.

33. See Michael Innis-Jiménez, *Steel Barrio: The Great Mexican Migration to South Chicago, 1915–1940* (New York: New York University Press, 2013).

34. Fure-Slocum interview; Herman interview; Sherer interview.

CHAPTER 10

Making History Every Day

The Iowa Labor History Oral Project and Popular Education

Jennifer Sherer

According to Virgil Bankson, it was one morning in the early 1930s when workers on the kill floor of the Ottumwa, Iowa, Morrell meatpacking plant first "agreed they was going to stick together." Then, about "five, ten minutes to eight," his coworker Clarence Poncey sat down.

> [He] had his sixteen cattle skinned, and he got a bucket, and he set down on it. The boss come over to him and says, "What's the matter, Clarence?" Clarence says, "When that hand gets around to eight o'clock, I'll start skinning that beef." The boss says, "You can't do that. You're fired." Clarence says, "Fine."
>
> Then the other four floorsmen quit working, and boy, it just shook that boss to pieces. The superintendent come up there, and he says, "What's your problem?" The floorsmen say, "We are not going to be drove no more." "Well," he says, "I'd like to talk to you about this." "Okay," the workers say, "We'll go back to work. We'll meet you in the dining hall after work."
>
> So when the day was over, the superintendent thought just these four floorsmen was going to come down and talk to him. *But the whole gang went down.* You never heard a meeting like that one. But I'll tell you, we ended up with 64 cattle an hour from then on until way long time after we got the union. That was the first time I ever got into a meeting, really, when there was any action taken. From then on that give us younger guys a lot of spunk, you know.[1]

This story, taken from a much longer interview with Bankson (long-time chief steward of Local 1 of the United Packinghouse Workers of America), provides a glimpse of the rich archive of oral histories that the Iowa Labor History Oral Project has made available to historians, educators, and the public. The excerpt also illustrates one of the many ways oral histories are reshaping how my colleagues and I teach labor history at the University of Iowa Labor Center. By way of introducing a story like Bankson's in a labor education class, we would typically ask students to consider specific questions while reading the passage. What problems were workers dealing with in this situation? What did workers decide, say, or do in this situation? And what values, beliefs, or hopes motivated their actions?

Regardless of a class's primary "subject," discussions of oral history excerpts almost always begin with students seeing themselves in others' stories, finding ways to relate an oral history account to their own experiences of work and union membership or leadership. In many cases, answers to a question like "What values, beliefs, or hopes motivated workers' actions?" can generate lengthy discussion of what kinds of "union values" have motivated students' involvement in their own unions or communities, or even their own attendance at a labor education class. In many cases, we would then ask students to analyze specific organizing strategies and tactics workers employed in the situation. Related questions might include the following: How successful were workers' attempts to solve a particular problem? How did workers try to change the balance of power in their workplace? What specific steps did workers take to build strength as a group? In the process, students inevitably reflect on whether and how such dynamics are at work in their workplaces and unions today—related to the still-familiar problem of unsafe line speeds in industrial settings, or parallel struggles for control of working conditions that arise in any occupation.

In a class focused on legal rights or more broadly on labor history, we might ask students to consider what Bankson means when he says "until a long time after we got the union," revealing that the story he tells here took place before he and his coworkers had organized a formal union or had the ability to bargain legally binding contracts. At this point, introduction of new information about the passage of the National Labor Relations Act (NLRA) shortly after the events in this story took place could give way to further questions about how organizing might have differed before and after such a law was in place, as well as what this example of pre-NLRA organizing might teach us today about the roots of workers' power, or how tactics have changed over time.

This chapter is an outgrowth of my own ongoing journeys of engagement with labor history, popular education, and the Iowa workers who become my students (and my teachers) in labor education classes. It is also an attempt to reflect on the historical origins and contemporary implications of a local legacy of engaged practice that has evolved from relationships among key figures and institutions in Iowa's labor history. These unique forms of long-term engagement among labor leaders and scholars have sustained a massive, multi-decade, statewide labor oral history project that is and will continue to be a boon to labor and working-class historians for generations to come. At the same time, project records show that although project leaders developed ambitious goals for taking labor history public—or at least introducing it into a few Iowa public schools— these goals were frustrated at every turn and ultimately abandoned. The project has nonetheless gone on to contribute significantly to labor history education in Iowa, but with audiences of adult workers rather than high school students, and in popular education settings rather than in public schools. Finally, this chapter is an expression of hope that new opportunities to engage current and future generations of workers might yet tap the project's potential to become part of broader, transformative educational initiatives.

The stories at the center of this essay take place in relation to my current workplace, the University of Iowa Labor Center. Our center reaches over two thousand union members each year in Iowa and neighboring states through noncredit continuing-education programs. These include residential multiday courses on campus and off-campus classes held in union halls, labor temples, public libraries, and other spaces around the state, in sessions varying in length from one hour to several days. Like many university-based labor programs established after World War II, Iowa's labor education program—initially housed within the University of Iowa Bureau of Labor and Management—emerged in an era when "industrial relations" was ascendant as an academic field of study and when public institutions, including universities, were enlisted to support the development of stable collective bargaining relationships and of the professionalization expected of labor leaders engaged in increasingly bureaucratized and legalistic interactions with management.[2] Like similar programs established at public universities during this period, the bureau's initial offerings to union members focused primarily on "traditional union activities" such as negotiations, contract enforcement, and union administration—subjects that Barbara Byrd and Bruce Nissen categorize in their 2003 nationwide survey of labor education programs as "union maintenance" courses. Like other similar programs, the center's teaching areas have expanded over the years to encompass what Byrd and Nissen categorize as "union-building" subjects such as "organizing the unorganized, membership mobilization, outreach, and developing internal union vitality."[3] Most recently, labor center programming has expanded to include "workers' education" more broadly, and efforts to reach populations beyond those in traditional unions to address the reality that the vast majority of U.S. workers cannot hope to access education about workplace rights and labor issues through membership in traditional labor organizations.

At least since 1975, when it became an independent unit, the University of Iowa Labor Center has consciously maintained what Gregory Mantsios, long-time director of the City University of New York's Joseph S. Murphy Institute for Worker Education, characterizes as an "empowerment approach" to worker education. Mantsios defines such an approach as one that "encourages students to analyze economic and political institutions and to see their personal world in the context of historical change, institutional contradictions, and social issues."[4] Today the center's motto, "Building the labor movement through education," reflects this orientation. Mirroring growing international interest in the role of participatory education in people's movements from the 1970s onward, labor educators in Iowa's program have been heavily influenced by models of popular education intended to foster transformational learning rooted in students' lived experience.

The work of Myles Horton serves as a touchstone for many popular educators working in the labor movement today. Horton founded the Highlander Center in Tennessee in the 1930s as part of his lifelong efforts to develop adult education and participatory research as sources of leadership and strategic problem solving within social movements. From the 1930s to the 1960s, Highlander education programs provided labor and civil rights movement leaders and activists with "a place to think and plan and share knowledge." In Horton's words, popular education in the context of social movements is transformative in its creation of new linkages among experience, learning, and action: "The people who come to the workshops have a lot of knowledge that they don't know they have. Highlander gives them a *chance* to explore what they know and what some people we bring in as resources can share with them. Then they have to go back home and test what they learn in action" (original emphasis).[5] Brazilian popular educator Paulo Freire's work within Latin American people's movements has provided a related theoretical framework for contemporary labor educators.[6] In his *Pedagogy of the Oppressed* (first published in English in 1970), Freire famously delineated his notion of praxis—"reflection and action upon the world in order to transform it"—as a consciously dialectical approach to adult education that, like Horton's, uses student experience and critical analysis as starting points for transformative action.[7]

In popular education settings, oral histories can become a powerful pedagogical tool, especially when they offer firsthand reflections on experiences that are distant in time but highly familiar to students in other ways, in some cases because of shared geography or work in a particular industry or occupation, but most often because of experience with a similar type of workplace or organizational problem. In labor education classes, stories in which narrators encounter such problems in their roles as local officers, front-line stewards, or rank-and-file activists become especially resonant. A story such as Bankson's might be selected for use in a class not primarily because it depicts a straightforward victory or clear resolution to a problem, but because it distills moments of decision or action, hints at motivating hopes or beliefs that guided workers' choices, or identifies contextual or organizational factors that made workers' responses to a problem possible. Placing students in dialogue with such stories of worker struggles to solve everyday problems (and thereby transform their workplaces and worlds) can allow today's workers to situate their own experiences in relation to history, and the history-making choices they themselves make every day.

Labor center educators are fortunate to be able to draw from an enormous local archive of labor oral histories to use in such classroom settings. Launched in the early 1970s by the Iowa Federation of Labor (Iowa's state federation affiliated with the AFL-CIO), the Iowa Labor History Oral Project (ILHOP) was built around a formal partnership between Iowa labor leaders and academics, educators, and librarians affiliated with Iowa universities and with the State Historical Society of Iowa. From 1977 to 1984, the project placed full-time interviewers in the field to conduct oral history interviews with union leaders and rank-and-file activists, and to collect available historical records and documents. Additional interviews were conducted on an ad hoc basis through the early 1990s, and the collection today includes over eleven hundred oral history interviews and over eight hundred linear feet of records held in the Iowa Labor Collection at the State Historical Society library. The collection has served as the basis for numerous scholarly articles, dissertations, and monographs, and continues to provide a model for others attempting to "properly establish" labor oral history collections.[8] Labor historian Shelton Stromquist has described ILHOP as "one of the most impressive collections of interviews with workers in the country."[9]

ILHOP emerged in tandem with a much larger oral history movement that took shape in the late 1960s and 1970s alongside surging interest in social history.[10] A national Communications Workers of America (CWA) oral history project housed at the University of Iowa had provided a local model for successful university-union partnership in the collection of labor oral histories from 1968 to 1972.[11] However, ILHOP was also unique in its origins and scope. The project was initiated and led by the Iowa Federation of Labor, AFL-CIO (hereafter IFL), particularly IFL executive officers Jim Wengert and Mark Smith. Wengert, IFL secretary-treasurer and later president, "took leadership in finding funding and in creating a distinguished advisory committee" to oversee ILHOP, while Smith— first as a university labor educator and subsequently as IFL secretary-treasurer and then as president—took charge of implementing early phases of the project.[12]

ILHOP's founders articulated goals extending far beyond merely creating a high-quality oral history archive. Accounts of ILHOP's origins reveal both preservationist and ideological aims, and reflect labor leaders' consciousness of the contested institutional terrains on which the production of history and the practice of education take place. One version of ILHOP's origin story features a 1973 conversation between Wengert and International Association of Machinists Grand Lodge representative Bill Fenton following the death of a mutual friend. Realizing that their conversation would likely constitute the only ephemeral record of the man's contributions as a trade unionist led them into conversation about the possibility of preserving the stories of other Iowa labor leaders.[13] Another ILHOP origin story recalls a moment when Wengert learned that the Newton, Iowa–based Maytag corporation, whose workers had waged a series of historic struggles over the decades, was donating its papers to an archive. Wengert viewed this announcement as another illustration of why unions urgently needed to tell and preserve their own stories, so that employers would not control the state's history. Relating this story in a 2014 public talk, IFL secretary-treasurer emeritus Jan Laue summarized the IFL's persistent view that "ILHOP is an affirmation that workers' life experiences are worthy of recording; what workers did and do at work is important at an individual as well as at a societal level. If the story of the industrial titans is all we have, our history is distorted and incomplete."[14]

ILHOP was funded directly by Iowa union members via the IFL, which for over two decades supported interview collection and transcription through dues collections. A special monthly one-cent per capita assessment to establish ILHOP was approved by IFL convention delegates in 1976.[15] The Teamsters and United Auto Workers (UAW), although not affiliated with the IFL, made occasional voluntary contributions to the project, with the understanding that its scope would encompass the histories of all Iowa unions.[16] The funding primarily supported hiring of project staff—professional oral historians and transcribers—and travel and equipment expenses associated with recording the interviews. Aside from a one-time $6,000 grant from the National Historical Publications and Records Commission in the 1970s, ILHOP's work was for over twenty years solely supported by the Iowa labor movement, with total contributions likely totaling over a half-million dollars.[17] Librarians at the State Historical Society of Iowa later processed, indexed, and cataloged the collection with the support of a major grant from the Institute of Library and Museum Services.

ILHOP's thirty-plus-year track record of facilitating deep engagement between academic historians and labor unions can be traced to its founding structures. The advisory committee IFL officers convened to oversee the project intentionally included representation from labor leaders, university-based historians, and eventually librarians from the State Historical Society of Iowa. The labor center played a central role in facilitating these relationships, and center staff members— first Mark Smith, then Lynn Feekin, and eventually Roberta Till-Retz—served as ILHOP project directors and chairs of the advisory committee. Along with representatives from the center and the IFL, the founding advisory committee included leaders of several Iowa unions and historians from four Iowa universities.[18] Awareness of history as a human creation and education as an ideological act permeate early ILHOP records, which reveal that the project's founders were from the outset intensely focused on the potential educational use of the interviews. The audience to be educated was invariably described as "young people," or more specifically, students in Iowa public schools. ILHOP founders considered the creation of educational materials on Iowa labor history to be the project's raison d'être, and early IFL communications about the project consistently emphasized this point. A one-year update printed in a 1978 issue of the *Iowa AFL-CIO News* explained to Iowa union members "that's why we are doing this project. To write the book, make the film, provide the teaching materials, or whatever it takes to make young people understand our heritage and contributions."[19] At a later stage of the project, ILHOP interviewer Merle Davis continued to assure the advisory committee that while in the field conducting interviews, he had found local union leaders "to be enthusiastic about our work. Most people I met realized the value of the project and of the need to educate the children, the public, and themselves."[20]

Records of initial ILHOP Advisory Committee meetings further confirm that broad educational aims were priorities for project leaders, who explained at a 1979 meeting "that the materials would be collected and made into a book which hopefully can be sold to the public schools so children could learn about unions."[21]

Three years later, ILHOP leaders continued to emphasize that "a primary target is the public schools, in order to bring a labor perspective into public education," and committee members engaged in lengthy discussions of how ILHOP materials might best be packaged for widespread use by public school teachers.[22] In 1983, the committee reiterated that the two "major goals of the project" were "development of a series of labor history units" for secondary schools, and "publication of a popular book," but that the first goal remained the "higher priority."[23] That same year, new committee member Shelton Stromquist, who had recently joined the history department faculty at the University of Iowa, volunteered to coordinate work of a subcommittee assigned to assess "how labor is treated in some representative high school history texts, widely used in Iowa school systems" as a prelude to developing new Iowa labor history materials for high school teachers. The subcommittee's assessment confirmed ILHOP leaders' suspicions about the lack of attention labor history received in public schools, finding the "general presentation of American labor history" in textbooks to be "woefully inadequate."[24]

Although the desire to impart knowledge about labor's past and present value to young students continued to animate labor leaders' visions for ILHOP, these visions proved difficult to realize. By all accounts, attempts to develop and introduce ILHOP curricular materials into public schools were fraught with challenges.[25] Advisory committee members were conscious from the outset of the difficulty of introducing new curricular materials, and they discussed seeking assistance on "targeting the right areas and presenting the material in a readily usable form." They also anticipated that introduction of a labor history curriculum might face both practical and political barriers, acknowledging that "teachers are inundated with materials which various groups, including business, want them to incorporate into their courses."[26] By the end of 1983, planned meetings with social studies teachers to discuss these challenges had been "postponed due to scheduling difficulties."[27]

ILHOP leaders nonetheless pursued the first, and "higher priority" of their "major goals" in 1983 by commissioning faculty from the Purdue University College of Education to produce what was intended to be the first of three modules in a high school curriculum based on ILHOP interviews.[28] The resulting module included lengthy excerpts from oral history transcripts, along with suggested discussion questions and writing prompts and an audiotape containing three selected interviews.[29] Advisory committee members were critical of the pilot module from the start, first soliciting individual feedback from the three university historians on the committee, then meeting in a joint session to review the entire manuscript and suggest numerous editorial changes, including complete revision of the section intended to place interview excerpts in context.[30] Even after this extensive revision process, committee members remained dubious about the module's utility; it was, they agreed, too long and lacked crucial features such as internal titles and subheadings, a detailed table of contents, and identifying information such as interviewees' communities of origin, all of which they worried would limit its use by classroom teachers.[31] Despite having engaged a representative of Iowa's Department of Public Instruction to serve on the ILHOP Advisory Committee, labor leaders found it difficult to secure commitments from school districts and teachers to use the pilot module. IFL secretary-treasurer Mark Smith was charged with contacting social studies coordinators in school districts to explore opportunities to pilot the first module of the ILHOP curriculum.[32] Smith reported in 1986 that after contacting "six or seven school districts," only one, in Iowa City, had responded positively.[33]

A second module developed in 1987 underwent similarly extensive scrutiny from the committee, whose members displayed an ambitious commitment to developing high-quality instructional materials that would be both historically accurate and accessible to teachers and students.[34] By 1991, a final version of the curriculum had been further modified by an ILHOP subcommittee led by Mark Smith and ILHOP field interviewer Merle Davis and reviewed by a group of Des Moines high school teachers.[35] Smith reported that the new package had "now been successfully piloted in the Des Moines school district" and was being distributed to central labor councils across the state, which were charged with "pursuing implementation in their school districts."[36] Apart from the Des Moines teachers who had worked with Smith personally, however, few adopted the curriculum, and there appeared to be no practical way to introduce the materials on a school-wide or district-wide basis in other locations. Most teachers were reluctant to experiment with untested materials, especially on a subject unfamiliar to them.[37] Ultimately, hopes that ILHOP materials would be used to introduce labor history into Iowa public high schools were never realized on any widespread or sustainable basis.

Pursuit of the committee's second major goal—"publication of a popular book"—yielded far greater success. In 1986, at the same time that ILHOP leaders were seeking teachers to pilot the first high school curriculum module, Shelton Stromquist proposed moving forward with drafting a book manuscript "built around a core of edited transcripts from the best interviews in the collection." Committee members approved Stromquist's proposal and "generally welcomed the idea of this project and of creating something from the project which would be available to union members and the public."[38] The resulting volume, *Solidarity and Survival: An Oral History of Iowa Labor in the Twentieth Century*, was published by the University of Iowa Press in 1993. The IFL purchased bulk quantities of the book for distribution and discounted sale to union members, giving the book a wide audience among at least one generation of Iowa labor leaders. Stromquist in turn arranged for royalties from the book to be returned to the IFL for use in funding the oral history project. Since the 1990s, ILHOP and accompanying labor collections in the Iowa State Historical Society have continued to enjoy heavy use from academic labor historians, and *Solidarity and Survival* remains popular with Iowa labor activists, many of whom learn of the book at IFL or labor center events.

The aims of ILHOP's founders reflect acute consciousness of public education and historical memory as contested terrains for the labor movement, and an impulse to mobilize intellectual and institutional resources on this terrain on their behalf. Visions for ILHOP, however, devoted little attention to the education of union members themselves. This may stem from the fact that labor leaders presumed that union members were already being exposed to union culture, values and traditions through firsthand experience in their own unions or, for a subset of union leaders, through attendance at labor education programs. While workers were not the intended primary audience for ILHOP, they have nonetheless become ILHOP's greatest beneficiaries. Indeed, to return to where our story began, oral histories have become potent pedagogical tools for those of us at the center working to develop a labor education praxis for the twenty-first-century labor movement. In *Pedagogy of the Oppressed*, Paulo Freire famously critiques what he characterizes as a traditional, authoritarian "banking" model of education, in which professional educators, who possess and attempt to control knowledge, aim to "deposit" new information into the minds of students who are presumed to "know nothing" of the subject at hand. Arguing that "Liberation is a praxis: the action and reflection of men upon their world in order to transform it," Freire urges educators committed to liberation to "abandon the educational goal of deposit-making and replace it with the posing of the problems of men in their relations with the world."[39]

Posing problems of workers in their relations to the world and engaging them in reflection upon these problems in preparation for action to transform their workplaces and communities is the essential mission of labor education. However, educators dedicated to "generating consciousness and transforming power relations" while working within the context of existing educational institutions and labor organizations can expect to confront practical challenges. These include tensions between the urgent need to reflect on problems in relation to student experiences, and the equally urgent and legitimate expectations of students and union program sponsors to receive valuable "deposits" of unfamiliar, technical content, quantifiable new knowledge, or immediately applicable skills.[40] Opportunities to teach labor history in labor education settings are in this sense both abundant and limited. Chances to incorporate historical examples or provide historical "context" arise in nearly any core labor education class on subjects ranging from collective bargaining to health and safety or the legal rights of union stewards. On the other hand, in settings where educational objectives are tied to the desires of participants and organization leaders to address specific urgent challenges, extended periods of time to consider labor history can be difficult to come by. And when labor history is requested as a course topic, it can easily become instrumentalized. Stephen Brier, executive producer of the labor-focused *Who Built America?* multimedia curriculum, notes that labor history as presented to union members often tends to emphasize only "the institutional history of trade unions, focusing narrowly on the organization of established unions and the broader national structures" of the AFL and CIO. Decades' worth of new work in labor and working-class history has succeeded brilliantly in placing workers at the center of U.S. history, but generally without attending to how workers might also be placed at the center of labor history education.[41]

Among contemporary labor educators, the image of a "spiral" has become a well-known means of conceptualizing the process through which popular education beginning from a "point of departure" rooted in everyday experience can create spaces for transformative learning and lay the groundwork for future action. A class or workshop designed using these principles typically begins by drawing on student experience, then moves from this center point by encouraging students to identify patterns among their experiences, and finally to contextualize experiences in relation to new knowledge or theories introduced to the group by educators, peers, new texts, or other sources. The spiral image evokes the centrality of student experiential knowledge as a starting point, while dialogue among educator and students moves from this point outward along a spiral-shaped path, connecting student experiences with new information and reflections. The expectation is that the spiral eventually broadens to connect existing experience with the wider world, as students engage in activities or discussions designed to practice, plan, or strategize on how to apply new knowledge and understanding to social problems in daily life.[42]

As we struggle to create spaces where this type of transformative worker education can take place, oral history excerpts have come to figure more and more prominently in our twenty-first-century classrooms. One or several short passages from interviews might feature in an introductory session of a multiday residential education program for emerging union leaders. Or segments from oral histories might be presented as the basis for discussion of the roles of shop floor leaders in a class focused on the duties of union stewards. And in a labor history class for a central labor council or young workers group, we often introduce segments of interviews from across multiple decades and industries and then engage with students in identifying and analyzing particular themes. Oral history interviews have also proven an important means of confronting the perennial challenge of engaging students in participatory learning in multiunion education programs, where an educator's first task is to quickly establish a collaborative atmosphere among students who often enter the classroom as strangers. Hailing from a diverse range of unions and occupations, participants may find it difficult at first to identify points of commonality with others in the room. Elaine Bernard, executive director of the Harvard University Labor and Worklife Program, reflects on this challenge in a useful description of her favorite icebreaker to use with new classes of union leaders who are meeting each other for the first time in multiunion educational settings. In this exercise, paired participants each tell about a "union moment," which Bernard defines as "an incident that has a profound effect on the individual and demonstrates to the participant (often for the first time) the power of democratic, collective action." In keeping with the classic popular education spiral, the exercise starts with what participants know: their own experiences.

The second stage of the exercise then moves the class to gather and reflect on their personal experiences, identifying patterns and seeking insight into broader questions about collective experiences with work, society, and union leadership. Bernard describes that when pairs share their narratives with the larger group, "we note that in spite of the diverse personal histories and stories, there are common elements to all the tales. They are all accounts of groups in action dealing with issues of economic and social justice and dignity." From here, participants may be challenged to consider how their new insights can be put to work in their own unions. Bernard says she ends the exercise with "a challenge to the group to consider how to . . . create more participatory, empowering union moments for all of their members," having acknowledged that "it's these experiences that transform members into activists and build unions."[43]

Such an exercise is a favorite of mine, as well, especially for groups of experienced leaders who often have lived through decades' worth of "union moments" but had little time to reflect on them in settings where these moments can be seen for what they are: the collective actions through which working people transform work, society, and the course of history. Yet facing this same classroom challenge with groups of new union members or emerging leaders—who arrive to class with a lifetime's worth of relevant experiences but far less union experience and thus fewer (if any) identifiable "union moments"—can be even more daunting. This particular challenge has contributed to new approaches to teaching labor history and drawing on oral history interviews over the past decade at our center. In these settings, carefully selected oral history interview excerpts serve as the "union moments" that we work with students to analyze, compare, and learn from. Over time, educators at our center have cultivated an internal archive of dozens of such excerpts, from which we often select stories to engage a particular group of students in placing firsthand accounts of historic worker actions in dialogue with critical analysis of familiar, contemporary problems.

A final example, this one from an ILHOP interview with one of Virgil Bankson's coworkers, Ethel Jerred, further illustrates how oral histories can bring students' lived experience into relation with historical "union moments." Here, Jerred recounts how during World War II she became one of the first eighteen women hired into what had traditionally been regarded as "men's departments" in the Morrell plant. "Some men were bitter. Some men weren't," Jerred recalls, and she felt pressure to prove "we could be just as respectable as the wives at home. Our husbands was in the service, and all we wanted was our wages for a good day's work." She narrates her introduction to the union by recalling her first conversation with the local president:

> I was a person who knew nothing about unions. I'd always worked where the boss told me what wages I would draw and what hours I would work. I don't think there was over five women on the packing floor, and Ed Filliman, president of the union, come up to me . . . and he said, "Would you like to join the union?" . . . And I said, "Well, what will it cost?" And he said, "It'll cost you fifty cents to join and fifty cents a month." Well, that was a lot of money then, and I said, "Well, what will I get out of it?" because I'm Swede and I'm a little tight, and I want to know what I'm going to get out of my money. And he started to tell me about job security. . . . And I let him go on and on. I got to thinking about the fifty cents, and I said, "No, I just don't believe I want to. I think I can find someplace else to put my fifty cents." And he said, "Well, sister, I'll tell you one thing. If you want us to cooperate with you, you better cooperate with us." And so, I figured, well, I'll give it a try. I said, "Okay, I'll sign up."
> He was the greatest inspiration to we women, because after the five of us women had signed up, he said, "All right. We have a steward for men in here. I think you women ought to elect a woman to be your spokesman." A woman is a little reluctant to go to a man . . . because things were still a little fuzzy about women working in these areas. "Then, if . . . any problems come up, when we go out to meet with the company your person that you've elected . . . will go out with us." And guess who was elected. . . . I didn't know very much then, but I was willing to learn, and I learned a lot from this man.[44]

Jerred's recollection of this turning point in her life represents a "union moment" familiar enough that, as Freire puts it, students will "easily recognize the situations (and thus their own relation to them)." Like other favorite selections from ILHOP interviews, what Freire would call the "thematic nucleus" of Jerred's account possesses the educational virtue of being "neither overly explicit nor overly enigmatic."[45] Indeed, I have learned from our students that, for many of them, this account's status as a representative example of women's wartime movement into industrial employment is, on first reading, mostly beside the point. Instead, most students (of both sexes) are initially drawn into dialogue with Jerred's account of her conversation with the local president who first asks her to join the union, precisely because they can immediately recognize their "own relation" to this familiar conversation. Some are drawn to recalling conversations that accompanied first encounters with their own unions, and the considerations or motivations that accompanied their decisions to become dues-paying members. Others want to share examples of their own successes in welcoming new hires into their unions, or of more frustrating conversations with coworkers who have chosen to remain nonmembers and not pay union dues. In multiunion discussions of this excerpt, students not only recognize themselves in Jerred's story, but also begin to discover that their peers in workplaces across our "right-to-work" state have similar experiences to share.

Only after students have recognized and expressed their own relationship to the story—drawing clear connections between their experience of "here and now" and the "there and then" Jerred describes—does further unpacking of this story's complexities go forward. Further discussion of her conversation with the union president might analyze his approach to asking her to become a union member and also cultivating her as a leader. We might eventually explore questions about how such conversations occur in today's workplaces, how new members or leaders are identified and recruited, and what representative membership and leadership mean in the context of democratic organizations. Only at this point might the discussion begin to spiral outward to encompass the broader historical context in which this conversation occurs, the tensions Jerred observes as a woman first breaking into the "men's departments," and the simmering internal divisions the union president is presumably trying to keep from undermining solidarity within his union. Many students can recognize themselves in this aspect of the story as well, and the "generative theme" of a divided workplace often gives way to discussion of challenges associated with contemporary divisions—along lines of gender, race, ethnicity, age, immigration status, job classification, or other categories germane to student experience. Depending on the setting, we as educators may at some point introduce additional information about Jerred, who goes on to lead historic postwar struggles to retain women's jobs, dismantle sex-segregated classification systems, and seek equal pay, eventually mobilizing other women behind ground-breaking Title VII lawsuits to contest discriminatory actions by both her employer and the union in which she had by then become an important leader.

Before engaging in a classroom discussion of Jerred's historic role, however, it is important that students have first listened to her recount a conversation with which they are all familiar. Unlike "union moments" narrated by textbook authors, films, or instructor lectures, oral history excerpts introduce the past to today's workers as narrated by their own peers. Seeing counterparts from earlier time periods as agents of historical change encountering familiar, day-to-day challenges allows students to begin to see themselves as agents of their own histories, engaged in distinct, though related, struggles. At the same time, it is undeniably important that the sources of such stories are identified as part of ILHOP, deemed historically significant by the "authority" of the academic institutions and educators who collect, preserve, and present them. Engaging with stories told by historical counterparts with whom they can easily identify as peers, then considering why and how these stories have been considered important enough for permanent preservation in a nationally recognized oral history collection, can reconfigure students' relationships to the past as well as the present, enabling recognition that they and their coworkers are indeed making history every day. As one student put it in an anonymous labor center course evaluation in 2014, exposure to labor history "opened my eyes that the labor movement is far from over—it is a constant fight that will never end." Other more typical student comments on classes that incorporate ILHOP examples often note new senses of "pride" in realizing "how much labor history took place in Iowa (and started in Iowa)" or rededication to "keep up the fight in order to stop a return to the bad times." Such student responses affirm that encounters with oral history can indeed introduce workers to the ongoing praxis in which they "simultaneously create history and become historical-social beings."[46]

Conceived as an intense, prolonged, and radical attempt to listen closely to Iowa workers, ILHOP has arguably begun to exceed its founders' original education goals by finding a ready audience among new generations of Iowa union members. Although ambitious hopes that the project might also interest those outside the labor movement in listening more closely to labor's stories remain largely unrealized, ILHOP has nonetheless enabled transformative dialogue within labor's ranks, across generations, and among workers. And ILHOP has more history to write. A new round of ILHOP interviews began in 2014, and a reconvened ILHOP advisory committee consisting of labor leaders, historians, educators, and librarians is beginning to consider future directions for ILHOP and the labor collections in an age of "digital humanities" and new approaches to public history. Discussions about how best to engage broader audiences with ILHOP are being informed by over a decade of student interactions with ILHOP interviews in labor education classrooms, where the interviews continue to help workers identify, confront, and strategize around real-world problems.

In arguing for the potential of labor education to transform workers' relationships to history and their own making of it, it is important not to overstate labor education's impact or to ignore its many limitations. Even at the peak of its reach, labor education in the United States was never able to directly engage more than a small segment of the working class. In an era of declining union density and austerity in higher education, university-based labor education programs have shrunk in size and number, while education departments in many national or international unions have all but disappeared. Remaining programs retain varying missions, not all of which include worker education as a central function.[47] And where such programs continue, they may operate under a wide array of institutional constraints. Finally, labor educators must remain aware that they cannot themselves create or lead social movements; instead, they must do their best to recognize opportunities to work within such movements when and as they emerge, while in the meantime living the contradictions of working both "inside and outside" the systems they hope to transform.

Despite these challenges, labor education should be regarded as one essential component of the labor movement's potential revitalization. Indeed, no social movement in U.S. history has ever succeeded without some form of popular education engaging people in realizing their transformative, problem-solving potential to remake their worlds. Labor historian Nelson Lichtenstein argues that today the "fate of American labor is linked to the power of the ideas and values that sustain it."[48] If this is so, then little could be more important than nurturing the fragile spaces in which workers come together to reflect on, interrogate, and articulate what labor values are or should be, to encounter old ideas and generate new ones, and to shape collective hopes and dreams into the historic actions of tomorrow.

Notes

1. Virgil Bankson, interview by Paul Kelso, October 18, 1978, transcript, Iowa Labor History Oral Project (ILHOP), State Historical Society of Iowa Library, Iowa City, quoted in Shelton Stromquist, *Solidarity and Survival: An Oral History of Iowa Labor in the Twentieth Century* (Iowa City: University of Iowa Press, 1993), 100.

2. See Everette J. Freeman and Dale G. Brickner's description of labor education's "modern period" in "Labor Education: A Growth Sector in a Stagnant Industry," in *The Re-Education of the American Working Class*, edited by Steven H. London, Elvira R. Tarr, and Joseph F. Wilson (New York: Greenwood Press, 1990), 3–19, 6–9.

3. Barbara Byrd and Bruce Nissen, *Report on the State of Labor Education in the United States*, Center for Labor Research and Education, Institute of Industrial Relations, University of California, Berkeley, 2003, 13–14.

4. Gregory Mantsios, "Worker Education: Developing an Approach to Worker Empowerment," in London, Tarr, and Wilson, *Re-education of the American Working Class*, 36–49, 47. Essays in that volume and elsewhere categorize competing schools of thought in labor education as either "instrumentalist" (focused on maintaining the status quo and reproducing existing union institutions) or "ideological" (focused on critical thinking and analysis of social realities as a basis for transformative or even revolutionary social change), although in reality most labor education straddles these categories, both in programmatic structure and course content. Further, this inevitably false dichotomy may obscure that there is no educational stance that is neutral or "nonideological."

5. Myles Horton, *The Long Haul: An Autobiography* (New York: Teachers College Press, 1998), 148.

6. Paulo Freire, *Pedagogy of the Oppressed*, translated by Myra Bergman Ramos (New York: Herder and Herder, 1970). See also Myles Horton and Paulo Freire, *We Make the Road by Walking: Conversations on Education and Social Change* (Philadelphia: Temple University Press, 1990) for an extended dialogue between Horton and Freire exploring the similarities and differences between their own pedagogies and popular education within U.S. and Latin American social movements.

7. Freire, *Pedagogy of the Oppressed*, 36.

8. Jim Strassmeier, "Messages from Our Past: Recordings on Labor and Workplace in the Oregon Historical Society Oral History Collection," n.d., Oregon Historical Society, in the author's possession.

9. Shelton Stromquist, *Solidarity and Survival*, ix.

10. Rebecca Sharpless, "The History of Oral History," in *History of Oral History: Foundations and Methodology*, edited by Thomas L. Charlton, Lois E. Myers, and Rebecca Sharpless (Lanham, Md.: AltaMira Press, 2007), 9–32.

11. ILHOP founding documents suggest that the CWA project served as an important precedent. An initial proposal for ILHOP noted that "The [University of Iowa] Center for

Labor and Management has some limited experience in Oral History projects. It super-vised a 12 volume Oral History project of the Communication [*sic*] Workers of America and itself conducted some interviews with Iowans in the Quad City area" ("Background information for members of the Advisory Committee for the Iowa Labor History Oral Project," n.d., Iowa Labor History Oral Project Records, State Historical Society of Iowa Library, Iowa City, hereafter ILHOPR). According to John Schacht, who worked on the CWA project, UI labor education program director Tony Sinicropi had attracted the CWA-funded oral history project to the UI, where, from 1968 to 1972, UI staff coordinated the recording and transcription of eighty-nine interviews with CWA members from across the country (Schacht, "American Labor and Working Class History at Iowa: Part I," *Books at Iowa* 53 [1990)]). Sinicropi became director of Iowa's labor education programs (part of the UI Bureau of Labor and Management at the time) in 1963. See also "Anthony V. Sini-cropi, NAA President 1991, Interviewed by Jim Oldham, June 3, 1993," National Academy of Arbitrators History Committee Interview, accessed June 12, 2014, www.naarb.org.

12. Roberta Till-Retz, "Notes for Presentation at Opening of ILHOP Grant Ceremony," lecture, State Historical Society of Iowa Library, Iowa City, January 10, 2000.

13. Ibid.

14. Jan Laue, "Documenting the History of Women in Politics," lecture, University of Iowa Public Policy Center "Women in Politics" conference, Iowa City, April 18, 2014.

15. Delegates raised the ILHOP per capita assessment to two cents in 1977. The per capita rate later increased to three and then four cents for a brief period of time in the early 1980s, when the bulk of interviewing was conducted, then reverted to two cents (Till-Retz, "Notes for Presentation at Opening of ILHOP Grant Ceremony," 5).

16. Records indicate that at the project's outset, Teamsters contributed $225.24 per month to ILHOP and the UAW pledged to contribute $1,000 per year (Minutes of Iowa Labor History Oral Project Advisory Committee Meeting, October 21, 1997, ILHOPR), although correspondence suggests that in later stages of the project, funding commit-ments from non-affiliated unions were not always honored (James W. Wengert to Charles Gifford, April 22, 1983, ILHOPR).

17. Till-Retz, "Notes for Presentation at Opening of ILHOP Grant Ceremony," 5. As of 1990, the IFL had contributed $253,900 to the project from the special per capita levy, and Iowa Teamster and UAW unions had contributed an additional $15,000 (Mark Smith to John Schacht, September 24, 1990, ILHOPR).

18. The founding advisory committee included Iowa leaders from the Communica-tions Workers, Teamsters, and United Auto Workers unions and history faculty from the University of Iowa, Drake University in Des Moines, Iowa State University, and the University of Dubuque (later union representatives on the committee came from the American Federation of Grain Millers, National Association of Letter Carriers, and the United Food and Commercial Workers). See "Background Information for Members of the Advisory Committee for the Iowa Labor History Oral Project," n.d., ILHOPR, and Till-Retz, "Notes for Presentation at Opening of ILHOP Grant Ceremony," 4. Mark Smith (who later served as an IFL officer, where he maintained a leadership role in ILHOP), chaired early ILHOP advisory committee meetings held in 1976 and 1977. After Smith left the Iowa Labor Center to become IFL secretary-treasurer, the role of project director fell to center director Lynn Feekin, and then to center educator Roberta Till-Retz. A full listing of committee members, including those who served at later stages of the project, is in the "History of Labor in the United States" curricular module printed by the Iowa Federation of Labor, AFL-CIO (1991), ii.

19. Paul Kelso, "Nears End of First Year: Labor History Project Interviews 150," *Iowa AFL-CIO News* 7 (1978): 2.

20. Merle Davis, "Iowa Labor History Oral Project Report of Progress, June, 1982–April, 1983," April 19, 1983, ILHOPR.

21. Notes from Iowa Labor History Oral Project Advisory Committee Meeting, February 16, 1979, 3–4, ILHOPR.

22. Minutes of Iowa Labor History Oral Project Advisory Committee Meeting, May 26, 1982, 2–3, ILHOPR.

23. Minutes of Iowa Labor History Oral Project Advisory Committee Meeting, April 19, 1983, 1, ILHOPR.

24. Memo to Iowa Labor Oral History Advisory Committee from Shelton Stromquist, Ellis Hawley, and Fred Adams, October 25, 1983, in author's possession.

25. The IFL also attempted to introduce labor history to a subset of high school students during this period through sponsorship of an essay writing and scholarship contest, which was structured around the required reading of a self-published volume on U.S. labor history that the IFL had commissioned from Jack Flagler, a former director of the UI Center for Labor and Management. (The IFL commissioned a new version of the book from author David Colman, a University of Iowa doctoral candidate studying with Stromquist at the time; shortly after that books publication in 2000, the essay contest was phased out.) Although these projects overlapped in time, the scholarship program was not part of ILHOP, and the published volumes did not draw directly on oral history interviews. When in February 1989 the Iowa State Historical Society published a "Labor in Iowa" issue of its *Goldfinch* magazine for young readers, the IFL engaged in a similar effort to encourage elementary school students to use the issue in their classes. Bundled copies of the magazine were distributed in some Des Moines schools and were made available to central labor council leaders, who in some cases made efforts to introduce them to teachers in their communities. In that 1989 issue, "Voices from the Past" features short excerpts from ILHOP interviews. David M. Colman, *A History of the Labor Movement in the United States* (Iowa Federation of Labor, AFL-CIO, 2000); "Labor in Iowa," *Goldfinch* 10 (State Historical Society of Iowa, 1989); Mark Smith telephone conversation with the author, July 3, 2014.

26. Minutes of meeting of Iowa Labor History Oral Project Advisory Committee, April 19, 1983, 2, ILHOPR.

27. Minutes of meeting of Iowa Labor History Oral Project Advisory Committee, October 29, 1983, 1, ILHOPR.

28. Ibid. At an October 29, 1983, meeting, the committee decided to hire Sam and Lulla Shermis, social studies curricula consultants from Purdue University, to "work up a prototype" of an instructional module.

29. Lulla and S. Samuel Shermis, *Unemployment and the Rise of Organized Labor in Iowa*, Iowa Federation of Labor, AFL-CIO, 1986.

30. Ellis W. Hawley to Mark L. Smith, letter September 11, 1985; Fred Adams to Mark Smith, letter September 20, 1985; Ralph Scharnau to Mark L. Smith, letter September 11, 1985. All in ILHOP Records, University of Iowa Labor Center

31. Minutes of meeting of Iowa Labor History Oral Project Advisory Committee, March 6, 1986, 2, ILHOPR.

32. Roberta Till-Retz to ILHOP Advisory Committee, letter March 11, 1986, ILHOPR.

33. Minutes of meeting of Iowa Labor History Oral Project Advisory Committee, April 29, 1986, 1, ILHOPR.

34. Minutes of meeting of Iowa Labor History Oral Project Advisory Committee, January 16, 1987, 2–3, ILHOPR.

35. *The History of Labor in the United States—Focus: The Iowa Experience*, Iowa Federation of Labor, AFL-CIO, 1991.

36. Minutes of meeting of Iowa Labor History Oral Project Advisory Committee, February 20, 1991, 1, ILHOPR.

37. Mark Smith telephone conversation with the author, July 3, 2014.

38. Minutes of meeting of Iowa Labor History Oral Project Advisory Committee, April 29, 1986.

39. Freire, *Pedagogy of the Oppressed*, 66.

40. Rick Arnold, Bev Burke, Carl James, D'Arcy Martin, and Barb Thomas, *Educating for a Change* (Toronto: Doris Marshall Institute and Between the Lines, 1991), 26.

41. Stephen Brier, "Putting Working People Back at the Center of U.S. History," in London, Tarr, and Wilson, *Re-Education of the Working Class*, 217–24, 217.

42. See Arnold et al., *Educating for a Change*, and Bev Burke, Jojo Geronimo, D'Arcy Martin, Barb Thomas, and Carol Wall, *Education for Changing Unions* (Toronto: Between the Lines, 2002), 56–57.

43. Elaine Bernard, foreword, in Burke et al., *Education for Changing Unions*, ii.

44. Ethel Jerred, interview by Merle Davis, October 5, 1981, transcript, ILHOP, quoted in Stromquist, *Solidarity and Survival*, 129.

45. Freire, *Pedagogy of the Oppressed*, 107.

46. Ibid., 91.

47. See Byrd and Nissen, *Report on the State of Labor Education in the United States*, 14, 65–67.

48. Nelson Lichtenstein, *State of the Union: A Century of American Labor* (Princeton, N.J.: Princeton University Press, 2002), 275.

CHAPTER 11

The Polk School

*Intersections of Women's Labor Leadership Education
and the Public Sphere*

Emily E. LB. Twarog

In 1976, Regina V. Polk, an organizer with Chicago's largest Teamster local, introduced a resolution on behalf of the Teamsters Women's Council to the 21st Constitutional Convention of the International Brotherhood of Teamsters (IBT). The
resolution called on the international union to "launch an intensive organizing
campaign directed at those areas of the labor force in which women are concentrated." The resolution went on to point out that although increasing membership
was one goal, another was promoting "greater participation of women members
at every level of the [IBT]."[1] The resolution was adopted.

Polk was twenty-six years old and had only been a union organizer for a year.
Polk's relationship with the union's Local 743 began when she worked as a hostess
at the Red Star Inn. She contacted the local in an effort to organize her coworkers. When she was fired for organizing, Local 743's leadership was so impressed
with her energy and people skills that they hired her as a staff organizer. In spite
of the continued hyper masculinity of the 1970s—particularly in the IBT—Polk
was able to gain the respect of labor leaders throughout Illinois. Her organizing
vision was a direct response to the changing demographics of the U.S. workforce
in the late 1970s and into the 1980s. "Since 1970, the proportion of all women
in the labor force increased from 43 percent to nearly 60 percent," with women
entering clerical and service sector jobs in unprecedented numbers.[2] Meanwhile
men's workforce participation declined during the same period as manufacturing
jobs gave way to mechanization and the global workforce. Over the past generation, more than 40 percent of union members were women and nearly one-third
were people of color. Yet, only 21 percent of lead union organizers were women.[3]
Nor do women hold many leadership positions in unions where they constitute
a large majority of the membership. For example, although 52 percent of the
American Federation of State, County, and Municipal Employees are women,
only 38 percent of women are in top leadership.[4] At the local level, the percent-
ages are typically much lower.[5]

As traditional blue-collar job growth stagnated, women workers made up for the lag by joining the expanding world of entry-level clerical and service sector jobs.[6] Unlike industrial and production line jobs, these jobs were historically nonunion and filled by a predominately female workforce who did not connect with the popular perception of "working class." In their view, they had little in common with working-class men, whose physical labor drove the manufacturing economy, and the "hard hats" who built the nation's infrastructure. The cultural construction of work depended on a gendered division of labor that framed office work as distinctly separate from manufacturing and construction trades. The categorization of jobs by sex was among one of the most common and overt cases of workplace discrimination. The Equal Employment Opportunity Commission banned this in 1968, but many newspapers ignored the ban and continued to segregate job classifieds by gender. The U.S. Supreme Court reinforced the ban when they ruled against sex-typing jobs in the 1973 decision against the Pittsburgh Press.[7]

For Polk, organizing clerical workers represented the next moment in time for the U.S. labor movement. In 1975, Polk joined the ongoing campaign to organize clerical workers at medical insurance giant Blue Cross–Blue Shield, which dragged on for two years. In the end, with the help of Polk and another female organizer, the workers voted to unionize. Her experience organizing women clerical workers reinforced what the labor movement was up against in the changing workforce. In a letter to the IBT Central States Council, Polk wrote: "Whether we like it or not, clerical workers continue to cling to an image of themselves which is different from that of blue-collar workers. Though conditions and wages speak to the contrary, these workers conceive of themselves as 'middle class' rather than 'working class.' A clerical worker can be in a job that is less skilled and pays less than a warehouseman, yet still feel 'superior' in the office setting."[8]

Six years after she was fired from her job at the Red Star Inn, Polk was selected to give the keynote speech at Local 743's annual Steward's Seminar. Polk's sobering address highlighted the many challenges facing organized labor as well as the benefits of unions to all workers. "The message to our members and the public should go on to say that unions are needed today as ever. . . . As long as there is discrimination against *anyone*—unions are needed. As long as women make 59 cents for every dollar that men make—unions are needed."[9] Many in the union saw in Polk the potential to be the local's first female president.

On the evening of October 12, 1983, Polk boarded a commuter plane bound for Carbondale, Illinois, to attend a meeting of the Illinois Jobs Coordination Council that would address new ways to fund retraining programs for workers who lost their jobs due to plant closings and layoffs.[10] Flight 710 took off from Chicago's Meigs Field despite the pilot's concerns about electrical problems. In the midst of a thunderstorm, the pilot signaled trouble to the Federal Aviation Administration's radar agency in Kansas. Ten minutes later, the small commuter jet "disintegrated" as it "skidded along the ridge three miles east of Pinckneyville [in] . . . southwestern Illinois."[11] All ten people aboard the plane died, including Polk at the age of thirty-three.

Polk's death underscored the dismal representation of effective women leaders in the U.S. labor movement. Shortly after her death, Tom Heagy, Polk's husband and a wealthy banking executive, founded the Regina V. Polk Fund for Labor Leadership. Later, Heagy directed the settlement from a wrongful death suit with the airplane company, augmented by donations from friends and colleagues of Polk, to establish the Regina V. Polk Scholarship Fund for Labor Leadership. Its board of trustees consisted of representatives of IBT Local 743, Joel D'Alba (Polk's good friend and well-regarded Chicago labor lawyer), Illinois labor leaders, and others familiar with Polk's efforts. The fund was established to educate women union members on the basics of union leadership as well as to educate students interested in working in the labor movement. The endowment has funded two programs since its founding in 1984—DePaul University's Regina V. Polk High School Program, which provides organized labor education curriculum to more than three thousand Illinois high school students annually, and the Regina V. Polk Women's Labor Leadership Conference (also known as the Polk School).

This chapter examines how Polk's impressive legacy and the leadership training program established in her name encourages and nurtures democracy through access, agency, and power to the public sphere.[12] The University of Illinois at Urbana-Champaign's School of Labor and Employment Relations–Labor Education Program (LEP) is the institutional home of the Regina V. Polk Women's Labor Leadership Conference. The mission of the Polk School is to develop the leadership skills of women union members by helping them find and develop their voice and build their confidence in order to take on leadership roles in their unions.

The chapter is also my story and how I found the only tenure-track job in the United States in which my fifteen years of work in the food service industry and five years as a server and union steward in an upscale restaurant actually helped me get a job in the academy. Examining these two stories side by side, this chapter concludes with a deeper look at an academic program that refutes *New York Times* columnist Nicholas Kristof's cry that professors are not engaged in public life.[13] Indeed, it is the mission of the job itself.

The Polk School

Regina Polk's vision permeates the school. Each woman accepted into the program, which runs for three consecutive days once a year, receives a copy of Polk's 1981 Steward's Seminar speech and is asked to sign a contract affirming her commitment to full attendance and participation. During the conference itself, women live, learn, eat, and sleep together at a retreat location removed from the hustle and bustle of their daily lives. The school serves two purposes. First, it offers a program that helps women identify and cultivate their leadership skills regardless of prior experience. Second, it is designed to be a safe space where women can share with one another their challenges, perceptions, and beliefs about gender and work that motivate their leadership ambitions.

Women come from all sectors of the economy, with a recent jump in public-sector enrollments. One of the strengths of the school is its diversity: women of different races, ethnicities, sexual orientation, occupations, ages, and lengths of union membership attend. The Polk School imposes few limitations for eligibility: the school is open to all women workers—union and nonunion. The large majority of women who participate are granted scholarships that cover the cost of instruction and room and board. The disadvantage of the scholarship model is that women are eligible to attend the school only once on scholarship, in order to allow other women to attend.

The Labor Education Program (LEP) at the University of Illinois at Urbana-Champaign is an interdisciplinary program with a mission of extension teaching and scholarly and applied research. When I was hired as a LEP faculty member, I also became the director of the Polk School.[14] Our outreach for the Polk School is driven in large part by LEP's teaching relationships within the Illinois labor movement. We distribute printed brochures to local unions and union leadership in the LEP database. An electronic version of the brochure is emailed to our entire database, which includes Polk alumnae and all the rank-and-file workers who have previously attended a LEP class. In addition to mailings and email blasts, we promote the school throughout the year at all the classes we teach. Most recently, the Polk School has entered the social media world; our Facebook page posts school updates as well as news and information on issues of race, gender, sexuality, and work.[15]

One of the unique aspects of an outreach strategy that relies on LEP's network is the Polk School policy of accepting only rank-and-file union members into the program. We do this since union staff often have access to trainings that rank-and-file workers do not. On the few occasions when we have set aside this rule, we witness rank-and-file women tending to defer to their staff person. This deference limits a woman's opportunity to find her voice and to craft her own leadership vision, thus the rule remains in force.

The curriculum itself provides a reason we have not directed considerable energy to outreach into the "alt-labor" workforce. Although the school's curriculum changes every few years, the classes often focus on the nuts and bolts of contract unionism, such as collective bargaining, filing grievances, and enforcing a union contract. As a result, the school draws more from a traditional union base that benefits from these important skills.[16]

The Polk School ran its first multiday, residential program in 1988. At the time, women's union membership was increasing, but an uptick of women in leadership positions did not follow. Union officials claimed this was because women were not interested in leadership positions, while also maintaining that there were no institutional barriers to women running for union office. The reality, however, is that local union leaders gain their skills through participating in the activities offered by their local union—attending meetings, taking training classes, doing political work, and moving through the ranks of the local leadership positions such as grievance handler, steward, or health and safety representative.[17] Yet, unions were doing little to encourage involvement of women into the business of running the union. According to a 2004 study commissioned by the AFL-CIO's Executive Committee Working Women Council and presented to the AFL-CIO Executive Board, women's leadership on a local level remained disproportionate to the percentage of women members because unions do not take intentional steps to open leadership doors to women.[18] The Polk School is one example of women's labor education that seeks to open those doors for women in their unions.

During the 1970s, at a moment when faculty and students in the nation's colleges and universities were agitating for the establishment of women's, ethnic, and racial studies departments, the numbers of workingwomen were on the rise. Women union members founded the Coalition for Labor Union Women in a declaration of labor feminism not seen since the 1940s, and a new generation of university women labor educators began advocating for labor education programs directed at women.[19] The first set of women's schools was led by Barbara Wertheimer, the founder of Cornell University's Institute for Women and Work, with the support of Lois Gray, then associate dean and director of Extension and Public Service at Cornell's School of Industrial and Labor Relations, and Joyce Kornbluh, founder of the Program on Women and Work at the University of Michigan. Through the University and College Labor Education Association (UCLEA), these three held the first women's summer school in 1976. Within a few years, four summer schools affiliated with UCLEA were organized around the country using the AFL-CIO's geographical mapping of the United States, Canada, and Puerto Rico. In addition to the UCLEA schools, various U.S. and Canadian universities and unions began organizing women's conferences and summer schools in the 1970s.[20]

The pedagogical approach of contemporary women's schools, including the Polk School, is deeply influenced by popular education methods. Rather than relying on traditional hierarchical and Socratic teaching methods, instructors teach basic leadership skills by turning to role-playing activities, small group projects, and classroom discussions, driven by workers' own lived experiences and facilitated by one or more instructors. The education model is based on action, with an approach that is learner centered, experience based, and participatory, leading to individual and collective change.[21] It is this back and forth that helps foster an environment of public intellectualism. Furthermore, the integration of popular education methods into a skills-based curriculum defines the relationships that continue beyond the three-day school, helping to broaden the relationship between faculty and student, and between university and community, which I explore below.

Public Universities as Historically Community Spaces

In five years as a labor studies professor, I have experienced interactions with students that bring to life the importance of the university as a community space. At the 2015 Polk School graduation ceremony, a graduate told the assembled women that she once took a weeklong communications course with me as part of her union's leadership program held each summer on the campus of the University of Illinois at Urbana-Champaign. It was that experience, she commented, that gave her confidence to become more involved in her union. A few months later, during a leadership class I was teaching for the United Steelworkers' Women of Steel program at the university, an alumna of the Polk School credited her training at Polk with her new position on her local union's negotiating committee. For many women who attend union leadership schools at the university it is their first time taking a course on a college campus. They bring their campus experiences back to their own communities, emboldened and empowered to bring activism and needed changes.

By housing the Polk School and LEP, the University of Illinois at Urbana-Champaign fulfills its historical mission as one of the original land grant universities established after President Lincoln signed the Morrill Act in 1862. Under the Morrill Act, such universities were founded on the premise that higher education should "democratize" by moving away from a liberal arts emphasis and by making "higher education more available and accommodating to the men of the field and of the machine."[22] In 1885, Illinois Industrial University was renamed the University of Illinois, and by 1967 the university reorganized into a system with campuses in Urbana-Champaign, Chicago (the Circle Campus, located on Navy Pier), and a medical center (Chicago). In 1982, the latter two campuses merged to become the University of Illinois at Chicago, an urban research university. In 1995, Sangamon State University (established in 1969) was brought into the fold as the University of Illinois at Springfield, with the Urbana-Champaign campus serving as the flagship.

Eighty years after the founding of the university, the Illinois labor movement initiated a resolution calling on the University of Illinois to establish an institute that would serve the workers of Illinois in much the same way that the campus was serving the needs of the agricultural industry and business fields. At the sixtieth annual Illinois State Federation of Labor convention in October 1942, the Milk Wagon Drivers Union Local 753 of Chicago introduced Resolution 96: "'The workers, both during the war [World War II] as well as in post-war planning, are confronted by situations of such magnitude that call for expert and detailed knowledge and advice in order that equality and justice be done for the workers in meeting their problems,' and that the State University of Illinois 'does give a similar service in advising and aiding the farmer in the solution of his problems.'"[23]

By 1946, the Institute for Labor and Industrial Relations opened its offices on the campus of the University of Illinois at Urbana-Champaign, with the responsibility for "fostering, establishing and correlating resident instruction, research and extension work on labor relations."[24] Within two years, the extension program was working in twenty Illinois communities and had established a residential summer school program with the United Steel Workers of America (USWA, now USW).[25]

A university-based institute for labor relations was not unique to the University of Illinois. In fact, by 1946, public and private universities and colleges across the country were opening labor education programs, with forty-six campuses engaged in labor education from research to hosting summer programs to (most commonly) engaging in regional and statewide extension programs. Labor education proved to be a new and exciting direction for many institutions of higher education that served to provide a link between elite institutions and the community. As New Deal economist and labor educator Caroline F. Ware highlighted in her 1948 study of labor programs in the United States, the need for courses in labor-management relations, union administration, and worker education grew. Industrial relations became "a recognized and important field for research and teaching." In the post–World War II period, when the nation had the highest rates of unionization, labor unions were "widely accepted as a segment of the total community." Utilizing the benefits and resources of public universities allowed industrial relations to flourish, as labor educators used the agricultural extension model to expand their statewide networks.[26] In short, the establishment of labor education programs was widely seen as an avenue to link the university to the general public.

Programs like the Polk School open the university to the general public. When the Polk School was founded, the trustees opted to place the program at a public university with a long-standing commitment to labor education extension. Similarly, in 1947, the USWA District 7 (Indiana and Illinois) chose the University of Illinois at Urbana-Champaign as the site for their annual summer program. And, years later, the American Federation of State, County, and Municipal Employees (AFSCME) also established a summer school on the campus.[27]

When these programs first ran, professors from various campus departments taught in the summer schools in Urbana-Champaign. This collaborative teaching approach declined over time. Today, most faculty on campus do not even know the programs exist. This is one example of the isolationism encouraged by the narrow parameters used to define tenure-worthy work. The reprioritization of campus funds means that labor education programs are shoehorned into sociology programs or social work schools if not eliminated all together. Today there are only a handful of industrial relations schools that offer undergraduate and graduate programs along with labor extension.[28]

Access to Women's Leadership Education

With more women in the workforce, there has been an interest in scholarly research examining the importance and impact of women's labor education on leadership development. The research largely examines either women's labor union leadership or efforts to organize women into unions.[29] Here I focus on the former. Industrial relations scholars tend toward interdisciplinary approaches and typically publish in U.S. and U.K. industrial relations journals. As is true in many fields, a focus on gender is often neglected, but there is growing interest in issues of gender and leadership, especially given the persistent reality that the number of women in leadership positions lags behind that of their male counterparts, despite the fact that women are the fastest growing group of unionized workers.[30]

In the early 1980s, the U.S. Bureau of Labor Statistics officially ceased collecting data on women's participation in unions. Despite this missing data set, scholars are finding ways to measure women's union participation. Scholars Gary Chaison and P. Andiappan, from the United States and Canada, respectively, performed foundational research on gender and leadership in unions. Having studied Canadian unions and their leadership structures, they published a series of influential articles in the 1980s examining the barriers to women advancing in local union leadership. As they noted in one of their earliest studies, "demand for equality on the job has prompted the demand for equality within the union. A continuing and very visible sign of inequality is the inability of women to attain a 'fair share' of union governing positions."[31] A critical contribution of their work is the recognition that "women must first become active in local unions before they can attain influential and visible union positions." Chaison and Andiappan push that conclusion further by "exploring the relative importance of the barriers to participation as seen by both male and female union officers."[32] Labor studies scholar Ruth Needleman argues that "female involvement at every level of . . . decision-making will strengthen the trend within organized labor that historically has advocated greater rank-and-file participation, greater internal democracy, [and] more collective and community-oriented practices"—we'll return to this quotation later.[33] Similarly, one group of scholars argues in their study of Massachusetts unions that increased women's leadership positively affects "policies concerning such issues as sexual harassment, child care, and pay equity."[34]

In 1992, Helen Elkiss, the founding director of what was then known as the Polk Workshops (now the Regina V. Polk Women's Labor Leadership Conference), surveyed a hundred women who had attended the first four schools from 1988 to 1992. Elkiss's goal was to "quantify the move, if any, into upper level union leadership positions . . . and to identify barriers that women face when seeking to move into union leadership positions."[35] The survey response was an astounding 50 percent: fifty-one Polk alumnae responded to the mailed survey. Almost half of the respondents were between forty-one and fifty years old, and 31 percent were in their thirties. A third of the respondents were mothers, almost half of whom had school-aged children living at home. A little more than half of the respondents self-identified as "white," and 31 percent identified as "black." By far the majority of the respondents were long-time union members with over a decade of union experience. Based on these and other demographic responses, Elkiss "concluded that the profile of an active union woman with aspirations to union leadership is a white, middle-aged single woman with either no children or grown children who has not only completed high school but attended some type of college courses."[36]

Elkiss's study found that over 50 percent of the participants listed "family time constraints" as a barrier to greater leadership; "lack of self confidence" and "need more union education" came in second and third, respectively.[37] Additionally, under the category "Other," thirteen participants listed additional barriers including, "racism, too tough to break into the 'old boys' network,' not enough leadership positions available, male co-workers harass active women, and women face physical limitations." Based on Elkiss's research, Needleman's vision of a more democratic and inclusive union is still a mirage. In fact, Elkiss likens the barriers to women's union leadership to the corporate glass ceiling: "access to top level local and international/national union positions is often closed due to reasons similar to those that lead women to 'bump their heads' on the glass ceiling in the executive suite."[38] The bottom line is that inequality is persistent within the labor movement despite the organizational mission to fight for the rights of all workers. Unions are not immune from the consequences of social and cultural realities of racism and sexism.

The recognition that unions as organizations need to act in a transformative manner that leaves behind the "enduringly patriarchal" in order to make space for a more diversity-friendly union seems to have reached the upper echelons of the labor movement: the AFL-CIO is formally committed to diversity.[39] However, women workers continue to flock to women's labor leadership schools because they need access to skills training but are not getting it through their unions. One of the most relevant studies for labor educators is the 2008 study by scholars Michelle Kaminiski and Elaine K. Yakura. Building on the existing literature that identifies a lack of leadership and the aforementioned barriers, Michelle Kaminski and Elaine Yakura identify four essential steps to leadership for women workers. They observe that women who pursue and attain leadership positions in unions often move through four distinct phases of development: 1) finding one's voice, or "understanding oneself as a person with power in an organizational setting," 2) developing basic skills, which might mean "working on a committee, taking workshops . . . or learning a technical skill that is central to the union," 3) figuring out the politics, or understanding "how things really get done in the union," and 4) setting your own agenda by "initiat[ing] and lead[ing] projects that others carry out." In suggesting interventions to assist women at each stage of development, Kaminski and Yakura themselves note the importance of women's summer schools for those seeking to "develop basic skills."[40]

The Polk School is dedicated to helping each year's participants achieve the first two phases. In 2015, two colleagues and I began a long-term survey of Polk alumnae. Below is a representative sample of the open-ended comments by Polk alumnae, reaching back over the past twenty years that demonstrates the Polk School's relevance with the leadership development process outlined by Kaminski and Yakura:

- "After Polk, I was fired up and determined to stand up for my rights as a Union member. No more would [the] administration bully me or create acts of . . . intimidation against me."
- "I got more involved in local politics to help give a voice to Union workers in my community."
- "It re-energized me and made me feel that as a woman, I can do anything."
- "Polk helped me with my confidence"
- "The most significant impact Polk has on my activism is that of self esteem and courage to stand up for what is right in the workplace."[41]

Labor Educators as Public Intellectuals

Labor educators have a unique position within academia. As a tenure-track faculty member, I am expected to publish scholarly articles and books, teach undergraduates, and contribute to the vitality of the university community. I am also expected to be able to show up at a union hall and energize and engage a classroom of fifty union apprentices who just came off a ten-hour workday while I teach a one-time, four-hour class on labor history. In a sense, I need to be bilingual; I must be able to move seamlessly from one identity to another in order to engage my audience.

My identity as a scholar is linked to my work as an educator in the public sphere. It drives my pedagogical approach in both the traditional university classroom as well as in my research and peer-reviewed publications. Most labor educators at university-based labor education programs are not tenure-track faculty. In many programs, there are two faculty categories. The first category is labor educators whose sole job is extension teaching to workers (nonunion and union); typically, labor educators have a master's degree or equivalent teaching experience as union staff. The second category is tenure-track faculty members with PhDs in industrial relations or in intersecting humanities or social sciences fields; these people are tasked with traditional teaching expectations in addition to research and writing for peer-reviewed journals and presses. The teaching and research expectations of faculty at the Labor Education Program in the School for Labor and Employment Relations at the University of Illinois at Urbana-Champaign fall into both categories. This puts tenure-track and tenured labor educators in an ideal position to engage as public intellectuals. I would argue it is our civic duty as scholars and educators of labor and working-class studies to push us beyond the turrets of the ivory tower and engage and comment on contemporary debates and struggles.[42]

When I began graduate school, I was thrilled to be in an interdisciplinary program called Work, Race, and Gender in the Urban World at the University of Illinois at Chicago. I was leaving my work as a community organizer to dedicate myself to teaching, or so I thought. By the time my graduate work was ending, I found myself isolated and adrift. I was frustrated with a discipline that studied workers yet seemed wholly disconnected from actual workers. I often considered leaving academia to return to my union waitressing job. In fact, I was more likely to earn more and have better benefits at the hotel than in many academic jobs.[43] But it was not the fear of unemployment as much as the fact that labor historians are so ensconced in their ivory tower that they often do not see people at work, struggling, and organizing. As it turns out, I got my storybook ending. I get to teach workers how to find and use their voice. And I get to use my voice to teach the public about work, oppression, and organizing.

The founders of the School for Labor and Employment Relations likely did not imagine a women's leadership development curriculum that includes confidence building through yoga, worker visits to the university archives, and debates on the relevance of feminism to the labor movement.[44] Yet this model of the university as a community space is exactly what land grant universities should be doing. And it is what teacher-scholars can do. As historian and labor educator Daniel Gilbert makes clear, "the conditions and political economy of intellectual work by university-based intellectuals are central terrains of social struggle in the contemporary age of neoliberalism."[45] To date, the United States still lacks a clear vision for gender justice in the workplace, especially when it concerns public policies that support working parents, the advancement of women in electoral politics, and gender equity in the boardrooms as well as in labor unions. The Polk School is training women to take on these challenges by helping them find their voice and build their confidence.

Notes

1. Reprinted in Terry Spencer Hesser, *I Am a Teamster: A Short, Fiery Story of Regina V. Polk, Her Hats, Her Pets, Sweet Love, and the Modern-Day Labor Movement* (Chicago: Claremont Press, 2008), 63.

2. Marlene A. Lee and Mark Mather, "U.S. Labor Force Trends," *Population Bulletin* 63.2 (June 2008): 4.

3. Amy Caiazza, *I Knew I Could Do This Work: Seven Strategies that Promote Women's Activism and Leadership in Unions* (Washington, D.C.: Institute for Women's Policy Research, 2007), 1; Lee and Mather, "U.S. Labor Force Trends," 3–6..

4. Lee and Mather, "U.S. Labor Force Trends," 4; Caiazza, *I Knew I could Do This Work*, 1.

5. Gary Chaison and P. Andiappan, "Profiles of Local Union Officers: Females Versus Males, *Industrial Relations* 26.3 (September 1987): 281–83.

6. An excellent example of this shift is the documentary film *Fast Food Women*, directed by Anne Lewis Johnson (Appalshop, 1991).

7. On legislative action against sex-segregated help wanted ads. See Nicholas Pedriana and Amanda Abraham, "Now You See Them, Now You Don't: The Legal Field and Newspaper Desegregation of Sex-Segregated Help Wanted Ads, 1965–75," *Law and Social Inquiry* 31.4 (fall 2006): 905–38.

8. Hesser, *I Am a Teamster*, 59.

9. Ibid., 109–10.

10. Jim Strong, "Regina Polk Fund," *Chicago Tribune*, March 12, 1984.

11. "10 Killed as Illinois Commuter Plane Crashes in Thunderstorm," *New York Times*, October 13, 1983.

12. For more on this see Nancy Fraser, "Rethinking the Public Sphere: A Contribution to the Critique of Actually Existing Democracy," *Social Text* 25/26 (1990): 56–80; Daniel A. Gilbert, "The Generation of Public Intellectuals: Corporate Universities, Graduate Employees and the Academic Labor Movement," *Labor Studies Journal* 38.1 (March 2013): 33–34.

13. See Nicholas Kristof, "Professors, We Need You!," *New York Times*, February 15, 2014.

14. I was honored to inherit the position in 2011 when Polk's second director Helena Worthen retired from the university.

15. Started in 2011, the Facebook page had over three hundred likes as of fall 2015. There is usually an uptick in traffic on the page in the spring as preparations for the school get underway.

16. I use the term "alt-labor" as a shorthand to include non-majority union organizing efforts, such as the "Our Walmart" campaign, workers' centers, and the various service sector movements around the country that encompass the fight for a higher minimum wage. While the importance of including women from alt-labor organizations has gotten a lot of attention, the curriculum of the Polk School is oriented primarily for women with collective bargaining agreements. As a result, we do not do much outreach to women in alt-labor organizations. However, it does not mean that they will not be considered for a scholarship upon applying. For a discussion about a renewed focus moving forward for women's summer schools to educate workers in alt-labor organizations, see Emily E. LB. Twarog, Jennifer Sherer, Brigid O'Farrell, and Cheryl Coney, "Labor Education and Leadership Development for Union Women: Assessing the Past, Building for the Future," *Labor Studies Journal*, March 2016.

17. Gary Chaison and P. Andiappan, "An Analysis of the Barriers to Women Becoming Local Union Officers," *Journal of Labor Research* 10.2 (June 1989): 149–62; Helen Elkiss, "Training Women for Union Office: Breaking the Glass Ceiling," *Labor Studies Journal* 19.2 (summer 1994): 25–42.

18. AFL-CIO, "Overcoming Barriers to Women in Organizing and Leadership: Report to the AFL-CIO Executive Council, March 2004," http://dpeaflcio.org, accessed September 30, 2015.

19. The term "labor feminism" was coined by historian Dorothy Sue Cobble, *The Other Woman's Movement: Workplace Justice and Social Rights in Modern America* (Princeton, N.J.: Princeton University Press, 2005); for more on the history of CLUW, see Silke Roth, *Building Movement Bridges: The Coalition of Labor Union Women* (Westport, Conn.: Praeger, 2003).

20. For more on the evolution of women's labor education, see Joyce L. Kornbluh and Mary Frederickson, eds., *Sisterhood and Solidarity: Workers Education for Women, 1914–1984* (Philadelphia: Temple University Press, 1984). For a study of the contemporary

state of women's labor education in the United States, see Twarog, Sherer, O'Farrell, and Coney, "Labor Education and Leadership Development for Union Women."

21. Many labor educators root their pedagogical approach in the work of Highlander Center's founder Myles Horton and Brazilian scholar-activist Paulo Freire; see Myles Horton and Paulo Freire, *We Make the Road by Walking: Conversations on Education and Social Change* (Philadelphia: Temple University Press, 1991); and chapter 10 in this volume.

22. Scott Key, "Economics or Education: The Establishment of American Land-Grant Universities," *Journal of Higher Education* 67.2 (1996): 198.

23. Milton Derber, "A Brief History of the Institute of Labor and Industrial Relations," 1987, unpublished manuscript (in author's possession), 1.

24. Ibid., 8.

25. Caroline F. Ware, "Trends in University Programs for Labor Education, 1946–1948," *Industrial and Labor Relations Review* 3.1 (1949): 56.

26. Ibid., 63.

27. Derber, "Brief History of the Institute of Labor and Industrial Relations," 41–49.

28. The most visible schools that include all the original elements of the earlier industrial relations schools are the University of Illinois, Cornell University, Rutgers University, and Pennsylvania State University. The United Association for Labor Education is currently conducting a state of the field study.

29. See Charlotte Yates, "Challenging Misconceptions about Organizing Women into Unions," *Gender, Work, and Organization* 13.6 (2006): 567–84, for an excellent example of literature on the gender and union organizing.

30. Yates, "Challenging Misconceptions about Organizing Women into Unions," 566.

31. Gary Chaison and P. Andiappan, "Characteristics of Female Union Officers in Canada." *Relations Industrielles/Industrial Relations* 37 (1982): 765–77.

32. Chaison and Andiappan, "Analysis of the Barriers to Women Becoming Local Union Officers," 150.

33. Ruth Needleman, "Women Workers: A Force for Rebuilding," *Labor Research Review* 1.11 (1988): 1.

34. Dale Melcher, Jennifer L. Eichstedt, Shelley Eriksen, and Dan Clawson, "Women's Participation in Local Union Leadership: The Massachusetts Experience," *Industrial and Labor Relations Review* 45.2 (1992), 268.

35. Elkiss, "Training Women for Union Office," 28. Elkiss was a tenured professor at the University of Illinois at Urbana-Champaign's Institute for Industrial Relations and Research and director of the Labor Education Program's Chicago office. She is also the only female professor to be tenured in this Labor Education Program to date.

36. Elkiss, "Training Women for Union Office," 28.

37. Only 8 percent cited child care as a barrier. For a recent analysis on gender and caregiving, see Rhacel Parreñas and Eileen Boris, *Intimate Labors: Cultures, Technologies, and the Politics of Care* (Stanford, Calif.: Stanford Social Sciences, 2010).

38. Elkiss, "Training Women for Union Office," 34, 26.

39. See AFL-CIO Executive Council, "Resolution 7: A Diverse and Democratic Labor Movement," AFL-CIO Constitutional Convention, 2009, www.aflcio.org, accessed September 30, 2015; Gill Kirton and Geraldine Healy, "Transforming Union Women: The Role of Women Trade Union Officials in Union Renewal," *Industrial Relations Journal* 30.1 (1999): 31.

40. Michelle Kaminski and Elaine K. Yakura, "Women's Union Leadership: Closing the Gender Gap," *WorkingUSA: The Journal of Labor and Society* 11 (December 2008): 463–64.

41. Emily E. LB. Twarog, Helena Worthen, and Judy Ancel, "Polk Impact Study 2015," manuscript.

42. For a good commentary on our "civic duty," see Robert D. Johnston, "The Madison Moment: Labor Historians as Public Intellectuals during the Wisconsin Labor Crisis," *Labor: Studies in Working-Class History of the Americas* 9.2 (summer 2012): 7–24.

43. Joe Berry, *Reclaiming the Ivory Tower: Organizing Adjuncts to Change Higher Education* (New York: Monthly Review Press, 2005)

44. The Institute for Labor and Industrial Relations changed status from an institute to a stand-alone school at the university in 2010, becoming the School of Labor and Employment Relations.

45. Gilbert, "Generation of Public Intellectuals," 33.

PART III

Bridging Scholarship and Activism
Paths of Engagement

Bridging Scholarship and Activism

Paths of Engagement

Kristen Anderson

To be both a scholar and an activist is in some ways to live in two worlds. Activists by definition are fighting to accomplish change in the world. They presumably seek research that can be applied practically to achieve their goals. Their struggle may leave them little time for reflection. Academics, on the other hand, devote considerable time to reflection and theoretical work, sometimes neglecting the practical application of their research entirely. Academics aim for some level of objectivity, often interpreted to mean they should not take sides in conflicts they study. Activists, in contrast, are overtly partisan. A vast gulf appears to separate the two, with the real-world trenches of the activists on one side and the ivory tower of the academics on the other.[1]

Instead of accepting this as inevitable, we might begin to find ways to work productively with this apparent gap. Social movement scholars David Croteau, William Hoynes, and Charlotte Ryan refer to this division as "the creative tension between thinking and action, between theory and practice." They do not see the divide between the worlds of the activist and the scholar as unbridgeable, arguing instead that "both activism and theory . . . are diminished by the failure to integrate the two."[2] Similarly, the part 3 contributors illustrate that scholarship and activism need not be separate worlds. Some of the best scholarship is shaped by engagement, and some of the most effective activism is informed by scholarship. This does not mean, however, that scholars seeking to engage in activism do not face significant challenges; these chapters also illustrate many of the difficulties of this type of work. Nevertheless, the essays highlight the great value that engaged scholarship holds for our research, our lives, and our society.

Engaged scholarship requires patience, risk, and experimentation. Engagement by definition takes time—relationships with communities and organizations are not built overnight. Academic structures set up to reward traditional scholarship generally value neither the process nor the results of this relationship building. Similarly, the publications that academics are expected to create, whether for hiring, tenure, or promotion decisions, are neither generally pitched to a wide audience nor designed for practical application. Scholars wedded to more traditional ideas about academic work frequently assume that academics engaged in activism sacrifice their objectivity, producing research that lacks "serious" purpose.

Misunderstandings stemming from these different goals and incentives can make forming relationships between scholars and activists difficult, as well. Activists are sometimes suspicious of the motives of academics, worrying that their research serves primarily to advance their own careers and perceiving the work of even well-meaning academics as disconnected from the real world. As community organizer Saul Alinsky put it, "the word 'academic' is synonymous for 'irrelevant.'"[3] The authors in this section have experimented and persisted, seeking ways to make their scholarly lives and work relevant to wider audiences and wider concerns.

The contributors to part 3 display a variety of approaches to combining scholarship and engagement. In "Launching the Kalmanovitz Initiative: A Labor Historian's Labor History," Joseph A. McCartin describes the ways in which he was able to combine activism with his position as a labor historian at Georgetown University. In particular, McCartin explains his role in the creation of a labor initiative at Georgetown, the Kalmanovitz Initiative for Labor and the Working Poor, and the achievements of that initiative, which included facilitating both conversation and collaboration between various labor representatives and incubating new ideas, such as Georgetown's Just Employment Policy. McCartin points out that this level of engagement requires institutional and personal commitments of time and resources. He was not able to teach or research in the same ways he had previously while working on the initiative. But the kinds of teaching and research he did undertake were in many ways more meaningful to him because of the engagement they involved.

Colin Gordon's "My Life as a Wonk" demonstrates the two-way relationship that can exist between scholarship and engagement, pointing to a range of different ways he works as an engaged scholar. Gordon describes how his traditional academic study of urban decline in St. Louis became useful to present-day residents as they debated future urban policies regarding schooling and housing. He further describes how his involvement with the Iowa Policy Project led him to rethink the direction of his own scholarship. By producing work in nontraditional formats that is designed to reach a large audience, Gordon has been able to make his research more useful to present-day policy discussions than most academic historical writing.

In "'The Soul Puts Together Its Pieces': Lessons from the Casino Floor," Susan Chandler discusses the research that went into her book, *Casino Women*, as well as her quandary about whether to become an academic or remain an activist. Her background as an activist spurred her desire to do work like *Casino Women—*

which examines the grass-roots organizing efforts of the Culinary Union in Las Vegas. Chandler concludes that engaged scholarship has great benefits, both professionally and personally. She was able to raise issues important to her state and share her research with her students, but the engagement her research involved also meant that she was living a more joyous and committed life.

Kim E. Nielsen's "Disability and Labor Activism: The Pains and Joys of Coalitions" examines the difficulties that disability and labor activists have faced when working together. While both groups are interested in ensuring safe working conditions for all laborers, she notes that labor activists' emphasis on disability as a tragedy to be eliminated can be alienating for disability activists who do not see their lives as tragic. Nielsen examines the role that conceptions of disability played for both labor and disability activists in the twentieth century. But this gap need not be unbridgeable; scholars and activists of labor and disability have much to learn from each other. By working together, they could develop a better understanding of the historically constructed nature of both disability and work, leading to the possibility of a movement that aims to achieve safer and more just work environments for everyone.

Finally, Stephanie Luce's "Engaged Scholarship and the Living-Wage Movement" demonstrates clearly the synergy between scholarship and engagement. Luce describes her involvement as a researcher with the living-wage movement in Los Angeles and the ways in which this experience shaped her future career. Not only did she continue to be involved with living-wage campaigns in other cities, but her academic research shifted as well to focus on this topic. Luce conveys the frustrations of academics who enter the world of activists—issue campaigns are often primarily ideological rather than based on research, and opponents insist on oversimplifying the issues involved. Scholars must accept that the best-reasoned argument does not always win. Nonetheless, Luce argues that researchers can make important contributions to movements, not just in terms of producing research to meet the short-term goals of a campaign, but in analyzing campaigns on a larger scale that can help movements formulate and pursue larger goals.

Taken together, these essays illustrate both the challenges of engaged scholarship as well as the substantial gains for both research and activism from such collaborations. These authors demonstrate that there can be a real synergy between activism and scholarship. The research we do as scholars can have policy implications. The work we do as activists can cause us to rethink the direction of our research. Scholarship can influence or lead to activism. And activism can lead to or influence scholarship.

This is a heartening message for scholars who worry that their work might not be meaningful or have an impact on the real world. Academic work might not have such an impact automatically, but we can choose to shape our careers in ways that bring us closer to that goal. We can choose to become genuinely engaged with the communities we study, building real relationships and partnerships across the activist-academic divide. We can find publication venues that let our work reach a larger audience. We can pursue research that speaks to the larger policy discussions of the day. The contributors to part 3 demonstrate how—with enough effort, commitment, and creativity—we might leave behind the artificial isolation of the "ivory tower" and pursue a life of scholarship shaped by engagement.

Notes

1. On the struggle over objectivity in the historical profession, see Peter Novick, *That Noble Dream: The "Objectivity Question" and the American Historical Profession* (New York: Cambridge University Press, 1988).

2. David Croteau, William Hoynes, and Charlotte Ryan, introduction, in *Rhyming Hope and History: Activists, Academics, and Social Movement Scholarship* (Minneapolis: University of Minnesota Press, 2005), xi–xviii, xii, xiii.

3. For a discussion of some of the difficulties of combining scholarship and activism, see David Croteau, "Which Side Are You On? The Tension between Movement Scholarship and Activism," in Croteau, Hoynes, and Ryan, *Rhyming Hope and History*, 21–32, 21. See also Croteau, Hoynes, and Ryan, introduction.

CHAPTER 12

Launching the Kalmanovitz Initiative

A Labor Historian's Labor History

Joseph A. McCartin

In late August 2006, my academic career took an unexpected turn when I accepted an invitation to meet with my president, John J. DeGioia of Georgetown University. I had no idea then why President DeGioia asked me to his office. But I suspected it might have to do with the student-labor solidarity agitation that had been roiling Georgetown's Washington, D.C., campus for several years by that point. DeGioia had just defused the most recent wave of agitation by helping arrange for a subcontracted janitorial service provider to drop its opposition to recognizing a union among its employees. As it happened, I knew most of the student activists who had been pressuring DeGioia's administration on this and other labor issues; many of them had taken my labor history classes. I assumed that DeGioia probably wanted my opinion on where campus labor issues now stood.

As that meeting approached, I thought about how much my career as a labor historian at Georgetown had been shaped by the encroachment of "real-world" labor issues into campus life. I had arrived at Georgetown in 1999 having taught at the University of Rhode Island and the State University of New York College at Geneseo. The prospect of moving to Georgetown was attractive to me, not only because it was a great university located near the archives where I did most of my research, but because the place was founded by the Society of Jesus—the Jesuits—the same Roman Catholic order that had founded the College of the Holy Cross, where I had studied as an undergraduate. Jesuits had helped change the course of my life at Holy Cross. I entered college as a premed chemistry major. But my exposure to liberation theology and Catholic social teaching helped redirect my interests. I switched my major to history, joined the Jesuit Volunteer Corps after graduation, and became a community organizer with the Texas Association of Community Organizations for Reform Now (ACORN). That experience had in turn led me back to graduate school, to the study of labor history, and ultimately to Georgetown.[1]

I arrived at Georgetown during a period of intense student activism on the campus, activism that perhaps played an indirect role in my hiring. Two weeks after my campus interview in January 1999, a student anti-sweatshop movement that had been building on campus for a year reached a boiling point. On February 5, 1999, thirty students staged a sit-in in the offices of President DeGioia's predecessor, Father Leo J. O'Donovan, SJ. After an eighty-six-hour standoff, the students won the creation of a Georgetown University Licensing Oversight Committee, which was charged with ensuring that no apparel carrying the school logo was made under sweatshop conditions. Thereafter, the students pressed the university to publicize the identities and locations of all factories that made apparel with the Georgetown logo.[2]

The History Department search that took place during those tumultuous weeks produced a most unusual result. My friend Michael Kazin, then at American University, and I were both hired from the same search. Michael's first book was an exemplary work of labor history, but he solidified his identity as a pathbreaking political historian with his second book, *The Populist Persuasion*.[3] According to the *Chronicle of Higher Education* story on our hiring, both Michael and I had "wowed the search committee," and the university had found a way to hire us both when a senior colleague announced he would retire within a year of our arrival.[4] But I knew that such a complex deal had to be approved by the university's highest authorities, and I was grateful that Georgetown's students were in the process of making such a powerful case for labor reform at precisely the moment when university officials were considering my candidacy.

Those same students helped break me in as a teacher at Georgetown. Among the students in my first labor history class at Georgetown in the fall of 1999 were Laura McSpedon and Andrew Milmore, leaders of the students' labor group, the Georgetown Solidarity Committee (GSC). McSpedon, it turned out, had an influence among youthful labor activists that reached far beyond the Georgetown campus. She had participated in the AFL-CIO's Union Summer program in 1997. Influenced by that experience, she had returned to campus that fall and cofounded the GSC (with students Ben Smith and Gabe Kramer). The organization began to raise awareness about sweatshop production, participating in a campaign against Guess jeans. The next year, McSpedon, along with Tico Almeida from Duke, helped convene the founding meeting of a new national organization that knitted together campus-based student anti-sweatshop groups, United Students Against Sweatshops (USAS).[5] During my first year on campus, McSpedon and her colleagues were pushing for the enactment of a code of conduct for apparel manufacturers, demanding that Georgetown help replace the ineffectual Fair Labor Association—a group convened by the Clinton administration that promised to police overseas labor standards for universities—with a more vigilant group that the anti-sweatshop activists were in the process of forming, the Worker Rights Consortium (WRC). Thanks to the tireless work of the GSC and Georgetown's enlightened administrators, the university became a charter member of the WRC.[6]

As McSpedon and other founding members of the GSC graduated and moved on, others took their places, and as the enrollments in my labor history classes grew, so too did the number of GSC activists I encountered. They were a smart and independent bunch who did not need or seek faculty mentors. They ran a nonhierarchical, democratic organization, and they were not afraid to take bold action, although they were careful to do so only after they had laid the proper groundwork and could then act strategically to win important, tangible gains. I admired their work, all the more so when, after winning the creation of the WRC, they turned their attention to the plight of low-wage campus workers. By 2003 they had begun a campaign to win a living wage for all campus workers, whether employed by the university directly or by its contractors.

The campaign reached its crescendo in the spring of 2005, when Georgetown students engaged in a hunger strike in an effort to win the living-wage policy they sought. Many of the leaders of that hunger strike had been students in my labor history class during the action. Although I was not their adviser, I admired their passion and strategic sense. In the end, they won a very progressive policy from the university that not only endorsed the living wage, but also recognized the right of all campus workers to organize, whether they were employed directly or subcontracted. But, true to their ideals, the students did not rest contented with this victory, which they believed would be meaningless unless the workers unionized to secure their gains. GSC students immediately followed with a campaign during the 2005–6 academic year demanding card-check union recognition for campus janitorial service workers, insisting that President DeGioia pressure the janitorial services company to recognize the union since a majority of workers had signed union authorization cards. Although DeGioia did not want to force the janitorial contractor to abrogate his right to a secret ballot election, he worked toward a compromise solution. By the summer of 2006, the janitors won their union. This controversy had just been settled when DeGioia asked to see me.

Had I worked at another university or for a different person, I might have expected that President DeGioia was summoning me to complain about the students who had been pressuring him or to enlist me to plead his case to them. Although I had not met one-on-one with DeGioia before, I knew enough about him to dismiss these possibilities. Having earned a philosophy doctorate at Georgetown, he taught a course on the ethics of globalization and thought deeply about social justice. DeGioia had been a protégé of Father Timothy Healy, SJ, who had led Georgetown in the 1970s and 1980s and who had been a prominent U.S. defender of Bishop Óscar Romero of El Salvador. DeGioia carried on Healy's spirit. Named the first non-Jesuit president of Georgetown University in 2001, DeGioia delivered an inaugural address summoning the university to make social justice a cornerstone of Georgetown's mission even if doing so would "sometimes make us uncomfortable."[7] His enlightened response to the discomforting student protests of 2005–6 had demonstrated that he was prepared to live up to this summons.

Not only did DeGioia not criticize the student activists when we met, he expressed his hopes that Georgetown might now begin to take up a position of leadership on labor issues going forward. DeGioia explained that he had spent the summer thinking about labor and conferring with people he respected, including AFL-CIO president John Sweeney and Jack Joyce, the recently retired president of the Bricklayers Union. This thinking deepened his conviction that Georgetown could assume a leadership position on labor issues, building on its own experiences, its connection to the Jesuit order, and Catholic social teaching about workers' rights. He asked me if I would work with him to help realize this vision.

As DeGioia outlined his thinking, I was aware of the difficulties I would encounter if I accepted his invitation. Policy making on labor issues seemed mired in gridlock, and it was difficult to imagine what progress might look like as inequality surged and changes in the economy and workforce were making existing labor policies obsolete. The labor movement itself was not only losing strength and influence, it was more divided than it had been since the formation of the AFL-CIO in 1955. The Roman Catholic Church, whose progressive social teachings on labor DeGioia wanted to engage, seemed to have relegated workers' rights to a secondary level of concern at that moment in its history. Nor were university-based labor centers proliferating and thriving. The University of Notre Dame was in the process of reducing the Higgins Labor Research Center to a labor studies program, while labor centers at public universities were under increasing attack from antiunion forces. Added to all of this was a personal issue: I was struggling to finish a book, the publication of which would be delayed if I accepted DeGioia's invitation.

Nonetheless, I was too intrigued by President DeGioia's vision and inspired by the serendipitous chain of events that brought me to this juncture to say no.

Planning a Labor Initiative at Georgetown

In the fall of 2006, when I began working on what we first called the "Georgetown Forum on Economic Justice in the Global Economy," I had no idea what form the labor initiative should take. But, knowing that we wanted to build something that engaged "real world" practitioners, not only academics, we reached out first to union leaders in a series of one-on-one consultations to ask them what issues they believed a university labor center ought to engage. President DeGioia brought together a number of these leaders for a dinner in March 2007 that allowed us to probe further. The dinner confirmed three things for us. First, Georgetown could convene people who might not otherwise come to the same table. Among those at that first dinner were AFL-CIO president John Sweeney and his predecessor, Tom Donahue. Although their relationship had turned acrimonious when Sweeney ran against Donahue for the AFL-CIO presidency in 1995, at our table they chatted amicably and contributed their ideas. We also learned that there were limits to our convening ability. We could not invite leaders from unions affiliated with Change to Win, which had split from the AFL-CIO in 2005. There was simply too much animosity resulting from that recent fracture. Most significantly, we realized just how difficult it would be to find a potential funder for the work we wanted to do. Although they were enthusiastic about our plans, the union leaders had no leads on potential funders.

Funding a labor initiative was difficult in part because we never considered seeking money from unions. Even had the unions offered help (they had their own pressing financial problems, especially after the 2005 split), we believed their money would compromise our credibility and independence, which ultimately would benefit neither party. The same logic held for businesses. Corporate support might not only compromise our independence but also encourage antiunion corporations to seek to improve their public relations through a well-placed donation.

It took months, but an answer to the funding problem finally emerged. President DeGioia and his chief consultant, Susan Frost, met in the summer of 2007 with Louis Giraudo, a successful San Francisco businessman with progressive leanings. Giraudo had built a fortune by turning a family business, Boudin, the San Francisco sourdough bakery, into a large and profitable chain. Giraudo was an active Catholic, former chairman of the board of the Jesuits' University of San Francisco, and a donor to Georgetown, which his children attended. Moreover, he was known and respected by labor leaders of all stripes. The Boudin chain proudly boasted that it was unionized, the AFL-CIO had previously recognized Giraudo with an award, and Giraudo had developed a friendship with the instigator of the Change to Win split, President Andy Stern of the Service Employees International Union (SEIU), having mediated an agreement between SEIU and two Bay-area hospitals in November 2005.[8] Although Stern had not been invited to the 2007 planning dinner, DeGioia had come to know and respect him during SEIU's campaign to organize Georgetown's subcontracted janitors. We were determined to avoid taking sides in the AFL-CIO conflict with Change to Win, and the naturally diplomatic Giraudo not only understood this, but he welcomed the opportunity to do what he could to lessen tensions between the rivals.

At DeGioia's request, I began meetings in September 2007 with Giraudo, Stern, other labor leaders and practitioners, and Georgetown colleagues.[9] I quickly realized how difficult it would be to create a model for our initiative that was true to Georgetown's identity as a research university and yet responsive to the desires of Giraudo and his friends in labor to develop an institution whose influence would not be merely academic. It took months for me to find the right balance.

On February 4, 2008, I presented DeGioia and Giraudo with a draft plan for our labor initiative, which accounted for Giraudo's wish that it engage live labor issues. I suggested we adopt a clinical model by drawing on the experience of Georgetown's law school, a respected leader in clinical legal education. It was a learning-by-doing model that I felt would promote student education and faculty engagement while also supporting good ideas emerging in the fields of labor relations and worker organization.

DeGioia and Giraudo liked the concept, but before committing fully to the plan, they asked me to set up a demonstration project to test it. Over the next eight months I devised and implemented a two-track pilot project. One track aimed to create plans for a co-op employment agency for immigrant day laborers in northern Virginia, to be built in collaboration with the Laborers' International Union of North America (LIUNA). The other track aimed to convene union leaders, pension plan experts, congressional staffers, and progressive investors to outline an agenda dealing with the growing crisis in retirement security and union pension funds.

As it turned out, neither track played out as we expected. Unfortunately, the first scheduled convening of the retirement security project took place on October 3, 2008—two weeks after the bankruptcy of Lehman Brothers as Congress debated the Toxic Asset Relief Program (TARP), which was signed that very day by President George W. Bush. Chaos enveloped the financial markets during our gathering, further complicating an already complex issue. Giraudo and another businessman in attendance, private equity investor Leo Hindery Jr., left the table repeatedly during the discussion to tend to their businesses as markets melted down. The ongoing instability of the financial system in the weeks that followed and the complexity of the issues involved led us to suspend scheduling a follow-up meeting. Meanwhile, the work we did on the day laborer co-op project was shelved when our LIUNA partner was suddenly transferred, depriving the project of its principal community supporter.

The sidetracking of these projects taught us the importance of finding the right collaborators and reminded us that, even when we planned well, forces beyond our control could affect our work. With that in mind, DeGioia and Giraudo negotiated the final terms of a gift agreement in May 2009 to fund Georgetown's labor initiative. Giraudo arranged for the gift to come through the Kalmanovitz Charitable Foundation, a Bay-area foundation, on whose board he sat and to whose assets he had contributed. We in turn adopted the name of the foundation, which had been established by the estate of Paul Kalmanovitz, a Polish Jewish immigrant entrepreneur who had made a fortune as the owner of Pabst Blue Ribbon. On July 1, 2009, Georgetown's Kalmanovitz Initiative for Labor and the Working Poor (KI) officially opened its doors.

The Kalmanovitz Initiative's Early Days

The initiative's launch came at an awkward time for me. I was just beginning a sabbatical funded by fellowships from the Woodrow Wilson International Center for Scholars and the American Philosophical Society. My plan had been to finish my book *Collision Course: Ronald Reagan, the Air Traffic Controllers, and the Strike that Changed America* before August 2011, the thirtieth anniversary of the 1981 strike of the Professional Air Traffic Controllers Organization (PATCO), whose story it told. Launching the initiative led me to miss that writing deadline.

The problem was not simply that I had to devote so much time to the work of launching the Kalmanovitz Initiative. It was also that this work contrasted so sharply with the experience of writing my book. At times the contrast was so stark as to be disorienting. Writing immersed me in the past, while the initiative pulled me into the present; writing required time alone, while the initiative demanded a seemingly endless stream of meetings, calls, and emails. I divided my days between these two very different projects, but at times I felt that their gravitational forces were pulling me in opposite directions, each of these commitments making me less able to fulfill the other as well as I would have liked.

Among the things that made the initiative work satisfying despite the difficulties was that it allowed me to take part in a true team effort, something that I could not experience writing or teaching. Many great partners joined me in defining and driving the work of our initiative. I first turned to former students, most of whom were veteran campus labor activists: Maya Zwerdling, a leader of the 2005 hunger strike, helped coordinate our pilot project; Zack Pesavento, another hunger striker, helped set up our website; Sarah David-Heydemann, another student-labor activist, came on as my first assistant. I was equally fortunate in recruiting senior colleagues. In an especially crucial hire, I persuaded Jennifer Luff to turn down a teaching opportunity at another university to become our director of research. She was uniquely well qualified, possessing a doctorate in American studies, a deep knowledge of labor history, and nearly ten years of union experience with the Steelworkers, SEIU, the AFL-CIO, and Change to Win.

During our first six months, Jennifer Luff and I concentrated on introducing our initiative to unions and other allied organizations in Washington and defining our mission. We believed that developing the KI's mission in consultation with these groups would ensure the relevance of our work. We knew we lacked the resources to be a policy shop like the Economic Policy Institute or the Center for American Progress. We also lacked access to the sort of tax-supported funding stream that allowed the UCLA Labor Center and the University of Oregon's Labor Education Research Center to become such successful organizations. Had we placed our founding gift in an endowment, it would have yielded only $50,000 per year in operating funds, so we were forced to begin spending these resources immediately. Whatever role we defined for our initiative, we needed a plan to make it financially sustainable.

Three things complicated our efforts. The most pressing was union politics. As it happened, we opened our doors in July 2009, when union infighting was especially bitter.[10] Ongoing animosity between Change to Win and the AFL-CIO and a growing controversy around Andy Stern's leadership of SEIU made it more difficult for us to establish ourselves as an independent entity willing to work with any union. When Richard Trumka succeeded John Sweeney as president of the AFL-CIO in September 2009, we tried to create an event that might bring the rivals together. President DeGioia presented an honorary doctorate to Sweeney two weeks after Trumka succeeded him. We wanted to invite Change to Win leaders, including Stern (once a deputy of Sweeney's in SEIU) to that ceremonial event but discovered that was impossible. The Sweeney event was a poignant tribute to a distinguished union career, but it failed as a diplomatic opening and confirmed how strained interunion relations remained.

Andy Stern became an especially divisive figure during our first years as a result of controversies that developed within SEIU and between SEIU and UNITE HERE.[11] Outside observers accused Stern of taking sides in a leadership struggle within UNITE HERE in an effort to capture the Amalgamated Bank, which that union controlled. These allegations further marginalized Stern in the world of his fellow union presidents. Meanwhile, he placed one of his union's largest locals, United Healthcare West, under trusteeship when its president, Sal Rosselli, refused to cooperate with the international union's efforts to take more control of healthcare bargaining. A near civil war erupted among California's unions in response to the Stern-Rosselli feud, one that affected us on the other side of the continent. We hoped to hire Fred Feinstein, former general counsel to the National Labor Relations Board (NLRB) as our policy adviser. But after Feinstein issued a legal opinion defending SEIU's trusteeship in January 2010, it became impossible to hire him without being seen as taking sides, so we went in another direction.[12]

As we navigated explosive union politics, we also encountered significant inertia among unions as they awaited a big breakthrough in the first eighteen months of the Obama presidency. Most union staffers we met with during our first year were focused on passing the Employee Free Choice Act (EFCA), which would allow unions to avoid difficult elections and win recognition if a majority of workers signed authorization cards. The exclusive focus on that bill seemed unwise, yet voicing doubts about it was nearly impossible in those months when its passage seemed possible.[13] The death of Massachusetts senator Ted Kennedy in August 2009 and the subsequent victory by Republican Scott Brown in a special election to fill Kennedy's seat on January 19, 2010, effectively shelved EFCA. But well into 2010, unions continued to wait on the Obama administration. Some hoped that Obama's White House Task Force on the Middle Class, led by Vice President Joseph Biden, would devise a string of executive actions affecting federal procurement and other policies that could tilt the economic landscape in the unions' favor. Only after the Republican sweep of the midterm elections of 2010, which denied labor any chance for the big breakthroughs it had sought, did we find that unions had much interest in the work of our small clinic.

Up to that point, when unions approached us it was usually in furtherance of their own preformulated plans. SEIU's Capital Strategies division, for example, wanted us to help secure a Ford Foundation grant for the creation of experimental "healthcare development financial institutions," designed to combine community development, health care delivery, and labor-standard-setting functions.[14] The prospect of claiming a portion of a Ford Foundation grant to fund our overhead was tempting. But the project was outside our competency, and considering it helped us see that becoming a pass-through for other groups' foundation grants would prevent us from defining our own mission.

Refining Our Mission

It took at least two years of trial and error for us to refine our mission in light of the resources we had at our disposal, the specific attributes that we possessed, and the possibilities of our historical moment. We realized that what made our initiative unusual among other university-based labor research centers was its unique combination of characteristics: its origins in a history of student activism; its small size; the historical training of its key staff; its location in Washington, D.C.; and its rootedness in the nation's oldest Catholic university, one well-known for its facility in promoting interreligious dialogue. We made a conscious effort to leverage our distinctive attributes and to turn our weaknesses, including our small size and short history, into strengths.

By 2011, changes in the larger context within which we operated made it easier for us to refine this mission. Between March 2010 and March 2011, a palpable mood change took place within the labor movement. Andy Stern stepped down as SEIU president and Mary Kay Henry defeated his chosen successor, Anna Burger, in May 2010. Henry's leadership softened divisions among the unions, and a number of AFL-CIO unions began collaborating with Change to Win's Strategic Organizing Center. Having settled into office, Richard Trumka meanwhile made clear that he wanted the AFL-CIO to engage large ideas. He began reaching out to academics, inviting Nelson Lichtenstein to address the March 2010 meeting of the AFL-CIO's Executive Council.[15] The Republican landslide in the midterm elections of 2010 only accelerated the opening to new conversations within the labor movement. When the newly elected governor of Wisconsin Scott Walker ignored massive protests and rammed through Act 10, stripping most of his state's public employees of their collective bargaining rights in March 2011 (see chapter 4), union leaders knew they had entered a dangerous new era, and they were increasingly open to new ideas.

These events created new opportunities for our initiative. Most immediately, they provided us with a more prominent platform. In the midst of the Wisconsin turmoil, I was invited to address a meeting of the AFL-CIO Executive Council on March 2, 2011. Only days earlier, on February 26, seventy thousand protesters had flooded Madison and hundreds occupied the state capitol building. A handful of Democratic state senators went into hiding in an effort to deny Walker the legislative quorum he needed to pass his sweeping bill, and on the morning I came to the council meeting, the remaining members of the Wisconsin senate had voted to fine the missing senators for their absence. As the Wisconsin standoff reached a fever pitch, the leaders of the AFL-CIO's constituent unions seemed both alarmed and hopeful. All were painfully aware of the magnitude of the threat Walker represented. Yet they were clearly encouraged by the backlash his attack had stirred among union supporters in Wisconsin and beyond. Before introducing me, Trumka offered his executive council a brutal assessment of recent trends. The executive council was a notoriously independent group composed of the top officers of the federation's constituent unions, who were easily tempted to place the fortunes of their individual unions ahead of those of the movement as a whole. Lest any recalcitrant executive council members believe that Walker represented an isolated threat, Trumka showed them charts that spoke to labor's long-term problems. He left no room for doubt that the movement's future was bleak if those trends were not reversed.

Following Trumka's presentation, I told the union leaders the story of another AFL-CIO Executive Council meeting that had taken place under similarly dramatic circumstances thirty years earlier, on August 3, 1981. That morning in 1981, as the air traffic controllers of PATCO walked off their jobs in defiance of federal law, President Ronald Reagan issued an ultimatum, giving them just forty-eight hours to call off their strike and promising to permanently replace them if they did not heed him. The story I told was fresh in my mind because I had just finished drafting it for my book.[16] The PATCO showdown was an important turning point for labor, I reminded the union leaders. It seemed to me that some day people might look back on the standoff with Walker as another turning point. What kind of turning point it would be was partly in their power to shape, I believed. "By raising the issue [of collective bargaining] in the way that he has, the governor has, whether he realizes it or not, done you a favor," I said. "Suddenly you have an opportunity to engage people on this question as you have not been able to do in a generation: to explain why unions are necessary; why they are vital in a democracy; and to do it in a way that connects to peoples' realities. Walker has given you an opportunity to make a case that you haven't had an opportunity to make on the national stage in a while: a case not just for trade unionism, but for who and what we are as a democracy."[17]

Subsequent events showed that making that case was easier said than done. Walker not only withstood labor's efforts to recall him from office; he used his confrontation with unions as the springboard for a short-lived presidential bid. Nonetheless, the Walker phenomenon was clarifying.

My talk to the AFL-CIO Executive Council marked an end to the rollout phase of our initiative, and the increasingly embattled state of unions and collective bargaining symbolized by Walker's rise helped both galvanize my colleagues in the Kalmanovitz Initiative and develop constituencies for our work that extended beyond the university. In that context we fleshed out a three-point mission: developing an educational program rooted within but reaching beyond Georgetown; using our university's unique convening power to help build new networks of knowledge and activity; and incubating new solutions to the problems that workers were facing.

Our educational mission was easiest to define. Jennifer Luff taught classes on the history of organizing and on oral history, and I taught labor history. But we were determined that our educational offerings extend beyond the classroom. Thus, Luff recruited students to collaborate with her in developing an impressive online archive on the history of the Justice for Janitors movement in Washington, D.C. The website that came out of this multiyear project included oral history interviews with janitors, organizers, and employers, curated photos and documents, related academic articles, and an interactive map and timeline.[18] It was a model of worker-centered digital history.

Importantly, we decided to forego establishing a labor studies major or minor at the outset to avoid entangling our work too deeply in university bureaucracy. Instead, we developed nontraditional educational opportunities that we hoped would introduce new influences into Georgetown's campus culture. Our first program was an outreach effort to the day laborer community in Washington, D.C., which built on thinking we had developed in our pilot project. This program saw students go out twice a week to visit the street corners where Spanish-speaking immigrants congregated, waiting to be picked up by prospective employers. The students taught English to the workers, helped the workers report incidences of wage theft to a local legal clinic, and in the process learned a great deal about the struggles of low-wage immigrants. Many who participated in that program went on to take part in an alternative spring break program we devised called Worker Justice DC. They spent their spring breaks living in a youth hostel in the city and getting introduced to a wide array of workers' problems and a full range of organizations combatting those problems on both the national and local levels. By 2013 we developed a paid summer fellowship that gave students an intensive two-month introduction to organizing. In 2014 we added a paid research fellowship. By offering a modest monthly stipend, we were able to ensure that at least half of our fellows were students of color. (Thanks to the outreach efforts of our coordinator, Nick Wertsch, and our Salvadoran-born office administrator, Jessica Fernanda Chilin, some were also undocumented.)

In our public events we strove to broaden peoples' thinking on what constituted the twenty-first-century labor question. We brought science-fiction novelist Cory Doctorow, author Barbara Ehrenreich, and newspaper columnist Eugene Robinson to talk about labor and its intersection with their work. We invited U.S. poet laureate Philip Levine to conduct a poetry workshop that included both students and campus workers.[19] We invited the controversial performance artist

Mike Daisey to make his first public statements since the radio program *This American Life* exposed as a fabrication parts of his famous "Mr. Daisey and the Apple Factory" monologue on Chinese Foxconn workers—an event that triggered valuable discussion of the role that art ought to play in struggles for justice.[20] And we hosted Pulitzer Prize–winning investigative journalist Amy Goldstein in a yearlong residency in which she mentored our student researchers even as she wrote a book on the disappearance of good jobs from the nation's heartland.

Our educational mission also included partnering with community organizations to research the problems of the working poor in Washington, D.C. We collaborated on reports about failed job training programs and the scheduling practices of retail sector employers. And we undertook selected commissioned studies utilizing the research experience of our graduate students, such as a report analyzing trends in the "on-demand" economy for a major union.

Our efforts to develop a convening capacity were aided both by our location in Washington and by the institutional culture of Georgetown University. The university takes great pride in its history of bringing people together. Its Latin motto, *Utraque Unum* (both made one), is drawn from a line in Saint Paul's letter to the Ephesians that alludes to the Holy Spirit's work reconciling division. In the wake of the Civil War, Georgetown adopted blue and gray as its school colors to symbolize this reconciling spirit.[21] We drew on this *Utraque Unum* tradition to define our initiative as a place that could bring diverse constituencies together: rival unions looking for a neutral venue and facilitator, academics and practitioners with shared interests, incipient networks that needed a hub, heterogeneous groups that sought dialogue. We strove to convene people in ways that not only fostered dialogue but promoted action.

Giving substance to this role, we hosted the founding meeting of several new networks. These included the Labor Research Action Network (2011), whose annual meeting we hosted each year through 2015, and the Alianza Nacional de Campesinas (2012), a national network of farmworker women. In collaboration with the Labor Network for Sustainability and its director Joe Uehlein, we hosted a series of roundtable dialogues among unionists and environmentalists, which by 2014 had grown to include fifty participants. In a similar vein, we recruited Marc Bayard, a longtime labor veteran, to help us mount a series of high-level discussions on the state of African American workers, bringing black trade unionists together with civil rights activists such as the Reverend William Barber II, leader of the Moral Monday movement in North Carolina, and Derrick Johnson, the leader of the Mississippi National Association for the Advancement of Colored People (NAACP).

We also promoted networking between academics and practitioners in more traditional conferences. One, hosted in partnership with the journal *Labor: Studies in Working-Class History of the Americas*, led to a volume that explored the impact of the Great Recession in light of historical precedents.[22] Another, a collaboration with the Joseph S. Murphy Institute for Worker Education and Labor Studies of the City University of New York, led to a book that evaluated policies aimed at helping low-wage workers.[23] In our most ambitious conference sponsorship, we teamed with Sherry Linkon to host the first joint meeting of the country's two largest labor studies organizations, the Labor and Working-Class History Association and the Working-Class Studies Association, in May 2015. Small convenings were equally rewarding. Jennifer Luff initiated a series of after-hours discussions for union staffers who wanted intellectual stimulation and a place where they could share ideas without running afoul of organizational politics or interunion rivalries.

But our most difficult work went into developing a capacity to incubate new ideas. Key to that work was our inauguration of a practitioner fellowship, aimed at bringing labor activists and practitioners to campus for periods of reflection and creative thinking. We offered our fellows modestly funded sabbaticals that allowed them to take a leave from their day jobs for three to four months. We provided them with office space and research support, and connected them with potential allies at Georgetown and in Washington who could help them develop initiatives they had no time to flesh out in their demanding jobs. In effect, they acted as both clients for our clinic and as visiting experts whose ideas ended up influencing our direction. The policy director we hired in 2010, Katie Corrigan, led our work in this area. A former director of the Sloan Foundation–funded project Workplace Flexibility 2010, and an adept networker and strategic planner, she helped our fellows devise their plans. Over its first three years, the program helped a number of talented practitioners seed important work. Immigrant rights lawyer Edgar Aranda-Yanoc developed new techniques for combatting wage theft in northern Virginia; union staffer Michelle Miller teamed with web activist Jess Kutch to launch a new online worker advocacy tool, Coworker.org; the founding director of the Los Angeles Alliance for a New Economy (LAANE), Madeline Janis, laid the groundwork for Jobs to Move America, a campaign to build better, cleaner transit systems with union jobs; Saket Soni of the National Guestworkers Alliance planned a national campaign around contingent labor; Joe Uehlein of the Labor Sustainability Network laid plans for an ongoing labor-environmental table meant to foster greater collaboration between two communities often at odds; Erik Forman of the Industrial Workers of the World worked on ideas for organizing fast-food workers; community organizer Hilary Klein of Make the Road New York developed plans for a multicity car wash workers' organizing campaign; Donald Cohen of In the Public Interest developed plans for a campaign against the privatization of public jobs. Unquestionably, we learned more from these fellows than they did from us. Their residencies kept us and our students engaged with the new thinking that has been bubbling up within and around the labor movement in recent years.

We tried to contribute to that new thinking with our own idea as well, an effort to improve the lot of low-wage workers on college campuses. Following the hunger strike by student labor activists in 2005, Georgetown adopted its Just Employment Policy, guaranteeing workers a living wage, access to a range of university benefits, and the right to organize, whether they were employed by the university directly or by its contractors.[24] As we researched the practices of other universities, we concluded that Georgetown's policy was among the most progressive in the country and we resolved to promote it on other campuses.

Our confidence in that policy had been bolstered by seeing how effectively it worked to help solve three labor issues on Georgetown's own campus. When Georgetown's dining hall workers, employed by Aramark, one of the largest food service contractors in the country, began organizing a union in 2010, the company initially resisted their effort.[25] The university responded by reminding Aramark that Georgetown's Just Employment Policy required campus contractors to respect their workers' rights to organize. In response, Aramark scaled back its resistance and formally recognized the union on April 7, 2011.[26] A year later Georgetown's adjunct professors began organizing. Instead of fighting that effort, as many other universities were doing, Georgetown cited its Just Employment Policy and took a position of neutrality toward the effort, ultimately recognizing the union in May 2013 after an NLRB-supervised election.[27] And when the university learned that another campus food service provider was found to be systematically denying workers overtime pay, it pressured the contractor to agree to regular audits of its campus payroll.[28]

Encouraged by these outcomes, we began promoting the Georgetown model. In 2013 we engaged Georgetown's Harrison Institute for Public Law in this project. The institute's director, Bob Stumberg, put law students to work crafting a portable, legally sound version of the Just Employment Policy that we could disseminate widely. Kalmanovitz staffers Nick Wertsch, Vail Kohnert-Yount, and Alex Taliadoros began offering workshops about the policy on other campuses, focusing first on the twenty-eight-school network of Jesuit colleges and universities. Spreading the policy will not be easy, we know. But we hope to take advantage of the fact that the world's most prominent Jesuit—Pope Francis—has spoken out forcefully in favor of an economy of dignity and inclusion. If the model gains traction on other Jesuit campuses, we hope to disseminate it beyond the Jesuit network to other institutions of higher learning, religious and secular alike. The Georgetown model has already been cited as a precedent to be emulated by Brandeis University students as they push for enactment of a similar policy on their campus.[29]

But our most ambitious incubation effort reached well beyond the university world. It grew from an invitation Richard Trumka extended at the 2011 AFL-CIO Executive Council meeting, asking us to help labor think about its future. In an effort to promote a constructive dialogue about labor's future, we framed a project we called Bargaining for the Future. It focused on promoting discussion of a crucial aspect of labor's current crisis that was receiving insufficient attention. It was common to attribute labor's crisis to a failure to organize the unorganized, an inability to increase union density, and a troublesome set of labor laws that made organizing difficult. But the organizing problem was in large part related to a larger problem: collective bargaining as it developed after World War II was simply breaking down. Labor needed to learn how to bargain in a world in which once–vertically integrated corporations were disaggregating into lengthening supply chains, spinoffs, and franchises.[30] As financial markets drove that disaggregation, workers became detached from long-term employment relationships under this new form of capitalism and labor markets increasingly became casualized. Unless labor figured out how to bargain in this new environment, organizing was bound to fail. Jennifer Luff, Katie Corrigan, Seth Newton Patel, and I interviewed a range of labor activists and experts and collaborated on a working paper making our argument: "Bargaining for the Future: Rethinking Labor's Recent Past and Planning Strategically for Its Future."[31] We presented it to union leaders at a meeting on Georgetown's campus in April 2013, and over the following three months we used the paper to structure a series of discussions that involved dozens of academics, union staffers, worker rights organization leaders, and a diverse array of activists and experts.

To crystallize a concrete project based on these discussions, we turned to the master organizer, Stephen Lerner, who joined our initiative as a fellow in 2013. Architect of SEIU's Justice for Janitors campaign, Lerner had long argued that conventional collective bargaining was dying. If organized workers are to regain power, Lerner contends, they need to reach beyond their immediate employers to force the nation's real financial powers to the bargaining table, just as janitors in the 1990s reached beyond their immediate employers to pressure those who truly held the power to define labor conditions in the hypercompetitive building service industry—wealthy building owners—to support union demands.

We were convinced that one place where collective bargaining was ripe for the application of these insights was the public sector. In response to the Great Recession and Wisconsin-style attacks on their very existence, some public sector unions had begun developing creative bargaining strategies in partnership with community organizations in which they crafted bargaining demands that served the common good as much as the needs of union members.[32] These strategies sought to put new issues on the public-sector bargaining agenda: getting taxpayers' money back from banks and Wall Street firms that had manipulated interest rates and induced cities into bad financial deals; lifting standards for private-sector workers; preserving public services that are vital to improving the quality of life of communities; and fighting privatization in order to protect the public interest.[33] We believed that our initiative was uniquely well positioned to help generalize this emerging model.

We formed a planning committee that included Lerner, who was already advising these experimental bargaining efforts; Donald Cohen, director of In the

Public Interest; Saqib Bhatti, who now directs ReFund America; representatives from SEIU, the American Federation of State, County, and Municipal Employees (AFSCME), the American Federation of Teachers (AFT), and the National Education Association (NEA); and representatives from the nation's largest community organization networks, including Jobs with Justice and the Association of Californians for Community Empowerment (ACCE).[34] We planned a national conference that would pull in academics, and representatives from local unions and community organizations from California, Illinois, Minnesota, Ohio, Oregon, Washington, and Wisconsin, states that seemed ready for action. From the conference we hoped would emerge a new network of labor and community organization collaborators who would together pioneer new ways of bargaining.

Our "Bargaining for the Common Good" conference took place at Georgetown on May 21–22, 2014, and attracted 140 participants. It generated enthusiasm and triggered follow-up meetings in the states, as unions began collaborating with community allies in developing demands for 2015 bargaining sessions.[35] Many participants told us that it was our conference that got labor and community organizations in their communities to begin planning together. Although it is too early to assess the success of the project, some participants, such as members of the Fix LA Coalition, achieved big breakthroughs with their campaigns by implementing Common Good principles and leveraging connections developed at our convening.[36]

"Bargaining for the Common Good" confirmed for us that we could play a useful incubating role. A network of the sort that emerged from our May 2014 meeting would have been difficult for unions alone to assemble. Although SEIU, AFSCME, AFT, and NEA have begun working together on an increasing number of projects, rivalries among the unions persist, as do tensions both between key locals and their parent national organizations, and between unions and community organization allies (who often feel a power imbalance in their relationships with unions). As an outside entity, our initiative was able to function effectively as an intermediary. We also were able to contribute a vision to the larger project that drew on the pioneering work of the unions themselves and infused it with the perspectives of scholars whose research related to the project. By hosting "Bargaining for the Common Good" in our neutral space, not owned by any union or community organization, we were able to help launch a truly shared project. The Kalmanovitz Initiative had finally come into its own.

Looking Back and Looking Ahead

This work changed the course of my career. Most practically, it led me to devote less time to classroom teaching and the practice of the historical craft and more time to raising money, managing a staff, and developing programs and initiatives. My learning curve was steep and in some ways costly. Although Georgetown granted me a course reduction for each semester I have worked on this initiative,

I have had to scale back scholarly work that I love. I did finish my PATCO book, but work on a new project has been slow. I miss the archives. At the same time, the work described here has taught me things I never could have learned had I continued on the path I was following ten years ago. My engagement with contemporary labor issues and practitioners has clarified the arc of labor history over the past forty years for me, and that will no doubt affect my future scholarly work.

I am acutely aware of how exceptional and fragile this opportunity has been. The Kalmanovitz Initiative was made possible by a conjuncture of developments that could not have been anticipated and might not be replicable. The passion of Georgetown's student-labor activists, the leadership of a progressive university president determined to revive and update Roman Catholic social teaching on labor, the support of an unusually farsighted donor, and the help of many colleagues made this work possible. The disappearance of any of those enabling factors could cause it to fold, and midway through the seventh year its longer-term sustainability is still uncertain.

In the end, this work has given me back much more than I have given to it. I realize that someone with better organizational, managerial, and fund-raising skills might have accomplished more with this remarkable opportunity. But circumstances have entrusted the responsibility to me. So I have simply tried to make the most of it, knowing that, like the subjects of my historical work, I can only imperfectly comprehend the story I am living.

Notes

With thanks to Diane Reis, Elisa McCartin, and Mara McCartin, who encouraged me; Georgetown History Department colleagues who supported me; John J. DeGioia and Lou Giraudo, who made the work possible; and to the many who joined me in shaping the Kalmanovitz Initiative for Labor and the Working Poor, including Paul Adler, Marc Bayard, John Beck, James Benton, David Blitzstein, Denise Brennan, Bob Bussel, Jesslyn Cheong, Jessica Fernanda Chilin, Katie Corrigan, Pedro Cruz, Patrick Dixon, Susan Frost, Taylor Griffin, Sam Halpert, Sara David Heydemann, Joe Hower, Harry Kaiser, Michael Kazin, Vail Kohnert-Yount, Stephen Lerner, Sherry Linkon, Jennifer Luff, Ruth Milkman, Rachel Milito, Jim Morlath, Michael Paarlberg, Seth Newton Patel, Zack Pesavento, Matt Porterfield, John Russo, Bob Stumberg, Alex Taliadoros (to whom I'm also grateful for his editing of this chapter), John Tremblay, Nick Wertsch, and Maya Zwerdling.

1. For more on what led me to Georgetown, see Joseph A. McCartin, "*Utraque Unum*: Finding My Way as a Catholic and a Historian," in *Faith and the Historian: Catholic Perspectives*, edited by Nick Salvatore (Urbana: University of Illinois Press, 2007), 165–85.

2. Olivia Ensign, "Georgetown University Students Campaign against Sweatshops, 1997–1999," Global Nonviolent Action Database, February 15, 2010, http://nvdatabase.swarthmore .edu, accessed January 17, 2016.

3. Michael Kazin, *The Populist Persuasion: An American History* (New York: Basic Books, 1995). Kazin's first book was *The Barons of Labor: The San Francisco Building Trades and Union Power in the Progressive Era* (Urbana: University of Illinois Press, 1987).

4. Courtney Leatherman and Scott Heller, "Georgetown Hires 2 in Labor History," *Chronicle of Higher Education*, June 18, 1999, A50.

5. McSpedon went on to become national field organizer for Jobs with Justice. On USAS, see Christopher Kelly, "Students Against Sweatshops," in *Living the Catholic Social Tradition: Cases and Commentary*, edited by Kathleen Maas Weigert and Alexia K. Kelley (Lanham, Md.: Rowman & Littlefield, 2005), 175–96; and Liza Featherstone, *Students Against Sweatshops: The Making of a Movement* (London: Verso, 2002).

6. Pietra Rivoli, *The Travels of a T-Shirt in the Global Economy: An Economist Examines the Markets, Power, and Politics of World Trade*, 2nd ed. (Hoboken, N.J.: John Wiley, 2009), 127–30.

7. President John J. DeGioia, "Inaugural Address: Engaging the Tensions, Living the Questions," Georgetown University, October 13, 2001, www.georgetown.edu, accessed January 17, 2016.

8. The agreement ended a strike at the California Pacific Medical Center and averted one at St. Luke's. Representative Nancy Pelosi, "Pelosi Applauds Agreement to End CPMC Strike, Commends Giraudo," press release, November 10, 2005, http://pelosi.house.gov, accessed January 17, 2016.

9. If he was aware of it, Stern refrained from mentioning my criticisms of his leadership style, published that year. Andy Stern, *A Country That Works: Getting America Back to Work* (New York: Free Press, 2006); Joseph A. McCartin, "The Andy Stern Riddle," *New Labor Forum* 16.2 (November 2007): 169–73.

10. Steven Greenhouse, "Infighting Distracts Unions at Crucial Time," *New York Times*, July 8, 2009; Nelson Lichtenstein and Bill Fletcher Jr., "SEIU's Civil War," *In These Times*, December 2009, http://InTheseTimes.com, accessed January 17, 2016.

11. UNITE HERE is a labor union that merged two existing unions, UNITE (Union of Needletrades, Industrial, and Textile Employees) and HERE (Hotel Employees and Restaurant Employees International Union).

12. Steve Early, *The Civil Wars in U.S. Labor: Birth of a New Workers' Movement or Death Throes of the Old?* (Chicago: Haymarket Books, 2011); "Former NLRB General Counsel Feinstein Criticized Over Legal Opinion Written for SEIU," *Daily Labor Report*, January 22, 2010, A16.

13. For my views on the EFCA fight, see Joseph A. McCartin, "Democratizing the Demand for Workers' Rights: Toward a Re-Framing of Labor's Argument," and "Reply to Lance Compa and Sheldon Friedman," *Dissent*, 52.1 (winter 2005): 61–66 and 70–71; and Joseph A. McCartin, "Scholarly Controversy: Labor Rights as Human Rights? Probing the Limits of Rights Discourse in the Obama Era: A Crossroads for Labor and Liberalism" and "Reply to Lance Compa, Richard McIntyre, and Gay Siedman," *International Labor and Working-Class History* 80 (fall 2011): 148–60 and 184–88.

14. The Ford Foundation ultimately did give a $200,000 grant to SEIU to fund work on this idea, which soon evolved into a new entity called Vital Healthcare Capital, a social impact lender. On Vital Healthcare Capital, see vitalcap.org, accessed January 19, 2016.

15. At the AFL-CIO Executive Council meeting on March 1, 2010, Lichtenstein critiqued labor's dependence on the Democratic Party. A version of his talk is published as "Labor's Role in the Obama Era: A Troublesome and Unreliable Ally?," *Dissent*, June 7, 2010, www.dissent magazine.org, accessed January 17, 2016.

16. Joseph A. McCartin, *Collision Course: Ronald Reagan, the Air Traffic Controllers, and the Strike that Changed America* (New York: Oxford University Press, 2011), 290–94.

17. Joseph A. McCartin, "Turning Points: An Address to the AFL-CIO Executive Council," March 2, 2011, cited at James Parks, "Wis. Protests Are Watershed Opportunity for Working People," AFL-CIO, March 26, 2011, www.aflcio.org, accessed January 17, 2016, and available at Georgetown University, https://georgetown.box.com, accessed January 17, 2016.

18. *Justice for Janitors DC: A Digital History*, Kalmanovitz Initiative for Labor and the Working Poor, http://georgetownlaborhistory.org, accessed January 17, 2016.

19. At the conclusion of his term, a reporter asked Levine: "what is the most interesting thing that happened to you this year since you became U.S. poet laureate?" Levine responded: "First, I'd have to say it was a visit to Georgetown University's Kalmanovitz Initiative for Labor and the Working Poor. I didn't know there were still little groups of people coming to college to learn how to make our society more equitable and democratic." Quoted in Peter Armenti, "Poet in Motion: Levine Discusses his Tenure as Laureate, the State of his Craft," *From the Catbird Seat: Poetry and Literature at the Library of Congress* (blog), Library of Congress, April 6, 2012, http://blogs.loc.gov/catbird, accessed January 17, 2016.

20. Eric Wemple, "Mike Daisey Tells Georgetown of His Apple Story: 'The Essential Idea Is True,'" *Washington Post*, March 19, 2012, www.washingtonpost.com, accessed January 17, 2016.

21. Robert Emmett Curran, *A History of Georgetown University*, vol. 1, *From Academy to University, 1789–1889* (Washington, D.C.: Georgetown University Press, 2010).

22. Leon Fink, Joseph A. McCartin, and Joan Sangster, eds., *Workers in Hard Times: Nineteenth-Century Panics to the Twenty-First Century Great Recession in International Perspective* (Urbana: University of Illinois Press, 2014).

23. Stephanie Luce, Jennifer Luff, Joseph A. McCartin, and Ruth Milkman, eds., *What Works for Workers? Public Policies and Innovative Local Strategies for Low-Wage Workers* (New York: Russell Sage Foundation, 2014).

24. Office of Public Affairs, "Just Employment Policy," Georgetown University, undated, http://publicaffairs.georgetown.edu, accessed January 17, 2016.

25. Clayton Sinyai, "Georgetown Models Catholic Social Teaching during Food Service Workers' Union Campaign," *America: The National Review*, April 10, 2011, http://america magazine.org, accessed January 17, 2016.

26. Lauren Weber, "Workers' Union Certified," *Hoya*, April 7, 2011, www.thehoya.com, accessed January 17, 2016.

27. For this history, see the Kalmanovitz Initiative report, "Just Employment in Action: Adjunct Unionization and Contract Negotiation at Georgetown University," July 8, 2015, http://lwp.georgetown.edu, accessed January 17, 2016.

28. Matt Gregory, "Epicurean Owner Denies Allegations of Abuse," *Hoya*, December 6, 2013, www.thehoya.com, accessed January 17, 2016.

29. On the Just Employment Policy Effort, see www.justemploymentpolicy.org. On Brandeis, see Andrew Nguyen, Julia Dougherty, and Tamara Lyssy, "Realign Employment Practices with the University Values," *Justice*, March 24, 2015, www.thejustice.org, accessed January 17, 2016.

30. David Weil, *The Fissured Workplace: Why Work Became So Bad for So Many and What Can Be Done to Improve It* (Cambridge, Mass.: Harvard University Press, 2014).

31. Joseph A. McCartin, "Bargaining for the Future: Rethinking Labor's Recent Past and Planning Strategically for Its Future," Kalmanovitz Initiative for Labor and the Working Poor, Washington, D.C., June 2014, https://georgetown.box.com/s/b4yvofm4ighzkqmu8zf9, accessed January 17, 2016.

32. For an example of how union demands can benefit the common good, see Mary Cathryn Ricker, "Teacher-Community Unionism: A Lesson from Saint Paul," *Dissent* 63.3 (summer 2015): 72–77.

33. For background on the Bargaining for the Common Good approach, see Joseph A. McCartin, "Public Sector Labor under Assault: How to Combat the Scapegoating of Organized Labor," *New Labor Forum* 22.3 (September 2013): 54–62.

34. In addition to Cohen, Lerner and Bhatti, other key planners for the "Bargaining for the Common Good" conference included Elissa McBride (AFSCME), Lynne Mingarelli (AFT), Amy Schur (ACCE), Tony Perlstein and Connie Razza (Center for Popular Democracy), Megan Sweeney (SEIU), and Dale Templeton (NEA).

35. On "Bargaining for the Common Good," see www.bargainingforthecommongood. org, accessed January 17, 2016.

36. On Fix LA, see http://fixla.org, accessed January 17, 2016.

CHAPTER 13

My Life as a Wonk

Colin Gordon

We should not labor under the illusion that there is a significant public audience for most of the work we do as historians. This is partly a consequence of our writing style. While exceptions abound, there can be little argument with the assessment, as Nicholas Kristof put it in 2014, that the academy has "fostered a culture that glorifies arcane unintelligibility while disdaining impact and audience."[1] This is partly a consequence of venue. Much of what we write—regardless of its quality or accessibility—is squirrelled away in scholarly monographs that are overpriced and under-promoted; in scholarly journals that cower behind site licenses or paywalls; or at the podiums of scholarly meetings where a successful session is one in which the audience outnumbers the panel. And this is partly a consequence of our system of professional rewards (employment, tenure) that is closely calibrated to the expectation that we write mostly for each other and mostly in venues in which only we are willing or able to participate.

This is a gloomy assessment, for which I offer no easy solutions or alternatives. One option, of course, is simply to take aim—systematically and self-consciously—at a different and larger audience by writing in plain and accessible prose, foregoing the theoretical flourishes and historiographical debater's points, and choosing venues that aren't indexed by JSTOR. Such options, of course, are multiplying in our digital age and include a deep library of journals that are born digital (*Salon, Slate, Logos*) or that combine a conventional print product with a robust online presence (*Dissent*, the *Atlantic, n+1, Jacobin*), and a wide array of well-curated group blogs (Crooked Timber, the Monkey Cage, LAWCHA's LaborOnline). My academic colleagues often roll their eyes at a world in which everyone blogs and no one reads, but I think that is a crude and inaccurate caricature. Good work finds an audience—through its initial venue, through content aggregators (*Huffington Post, Alternet, Truthout*) and through the promotional (and self-promotional) grapevine of social media. As a rule, serious web-based writing trades a much bigger audience for shorter shelf life.

Another option, well represented in the pages of this book, is to work much more closely with the communities about which we write—not just by collecting their stories but by collaborating on the focus and the direction of the research itself. Such work might be essentially archival (collecting oral histories, for example). It might be in response to a particular challenge or problem, such as the work of the Women's Committee of 100 for Welfare Justice in response to welfare reform in 1990s.[2] Or it might view organizing—the building of campus-community partnerships—as an end in itself.[3] These variations on public history, I am heartened to observe, are flourishing. But academic institutions and professional associations have been slow to recognize them and reluctant to reward them. Despite the stakes and intensity of such work, our prevailing conventions and standards discount its value as scholarship. It shows up on our professional resumes instead as service to the profession, as community outreach, or in the throw-away category of "non-peer reviewed" publications.

My own recent work sits at the intersection of these options. It is largely digital in form and format, a choice driven largely by a desire to take advantage of the tools (data visualization, video, geographic information system mapping) afforded by born-digital work. It is largely written for nonacademic audiences—the work is shorter, stripped of the usual scholarly apparatus (footnotes, historiography), and rarely peer reviewed. And it is unapologetically animated by the concerns of the present. History is the only social science that frets about the threat posed by "present-mindedness" to scholarly objectivity,[4] a concern I have always found overblown, misplaced, and deeply uninteresting. I am interested in the policy and political challenges we face today, and in the usefulness of history in illuminating their causes and consequences. We would, after all, never ask a sociologist to ignore the current state of the world, to engage in some sort of monastic retreat into the Current Population Survey in search of regressions unsullied by knowledge of the world around them.[5]

My scholarly interests and my choice of venue are, I am quite aware, luxuries afforded by two circumstances: First, I work in an area (modern U.S. political economy and policy) with obvious, direct, and tangible connections to the present. It is natural and productive—as an activist or scholar in this field—to work from the present backward. And second, I have tenure. As a full professor at a dismally funded public university, my choice of publishing venue has no impact (good or bad) on my career or compensation.

My recent work falls into a number of categories. The first of these is urban history, a continuation of the work I began with my 2008 monograph on the modern history of St. Louis.[6] The public history thrust of this was, in some respects, accidental. When the book came out, my publisher booked a number of events in and around St. Louis. Audiences were receptive but clearly wanted to place themselves—spatially and temporally—in the story. But the mapping I had done for the book, in which the city was colored by census units in order to illustrate key metrics (poverty, racial occupancy, fiscal capacity), often fell flat with local audiences. Few, after all, readily recognize the local geography of census units, let alone know what census tract they live in.[7] In this case, the audience for such a history was natural and receptive, but the presentation kept them at arm's length. The stale social science of these early maps was, like the historiographical or theoretical posturing that peppers much historical writing, an unnecessary and unfortunate obstacle.

Over the next few years, I developed an online version in which the data collected for the book were projected interactively (viewers can turn layers on and off and arrange them in virtually any combination) on a familiar Google Maps satellite image, and made available as downloadable files to those wanting to use them in their own online or desktop mapping applications.[8] The new accessibility of these data—in terms of its distribution on an open platform, its interactive presentation, and its visual familiarity—dramatically broadened and deepened the audience. And, more importantly, it made the work—the argument and its visual representation—much more relevant to those audiences.

In the year after the book was published, my presentations were largely in academic or professional settings where, as one does in such settings, I gamely made the case for its originality and contribution to scholarship. Since the development of the web-based companion, my presentations have been mostly to citizens' and policy groups—the Metropolitan St. Louis Equal Housing and Opportunity Council, the East-West Gateway Coordinating Council, the Transportation Engineering Association—for whom the work was merely useful. The overarching argument of *Mapping Decline*, that racial segregation in St. Louis was a deliberate and long-standing project of local realtors and planners, has helped in small ways to shift local conversations about schooling, housing, economic development, and transportation.[9] The death of Michael Brown in August 2014 gave this work a new and tragic currency; the work's form and format, in turn, made it much more accessible and nimble—easily adaptable to different venues and audiences interested in untangling the sorry history behind Ferguson.[10]

If the St. Louis project brought me from scholarship to policy advocacy, my work with the Iowa Policy Project ran in the other direction. As a graduate student in Madison, I was tangentially involved with the Center on Wisconsin Strategy (COWS), a think-and-do tank focused on state policy and affiliated with the Economic Policy Institute (EPI) and its organization for state partners, the Economic Analysis and Research Network (EARN).[11] When I moved to Iowa in 1994, after teaching for four years in Canada, I reconnected with this work. While my work at the time, both a book on the New Deal and another on health policy, dealt mostly with national policy, I was convinced of the growing importance of state-level challenges and solutions.[12] At the same time, the Iowa State Federation of Labor was looking to formalize and fund more ongoing state policy work, and was in conversation with my friends and colleagues Peter Fisher and David Osterberg regarding the details. Our pooled efforts yielded the Iowa Policy Project (IPP) and an affiliation with EARN, in 2001.

The Iowa Policy Project has published a wide range of work on labor, health, social, and environmental policies in Iowa. Our flagship publication, the annual *State of Working Iowa* report, surveys jobs, wages, and labor market conditions in Iowa—a project we complete in close collaboration with both EPI (which publishes its exhaustive *State of Working America* report every two years) and other state groups. IPP (in partnership with the Des Moines–based Iowa Child and Family Poverty Center) is also a member of the State Fiscal Analysis Institute, a state network of the Center on Budget and Policy Priorities (CBPP). Other research—ranging from water quality to tax credits—follows either issues before the statehouse or projects for which we can scare up funding.

Since 2001, I have worked for IPP as a senior research consultant. I have authored or coauthored all but one of the *State of Working Iowa* reports and also have done occasional work on economic development subsidies, health policy, and labor standards (including a 2012 report on wage theft in Iowa). This work relies little on my historical expertise (in the policy world, "history" usually means a data series that extends back to 1979), but extensively on a broader academic skill set. This is, in some respects, a happy confirmation of the spiel I routinely give to history majors: we are not so much teaching you to be an historian as we are striving to provide you the research, writing, and rhetorical skills to do a lot of other things.

My work with IPP pressed me to present basic research results to new and varied audiences—labor education classes, religious congregations, legislators, editorial boards—a task that shaped both my research and my teaching. And it brought with it a range of connections—to staff and scholars with other state groups (most notably COWS and Policy Matters Ohio), to national partners (EPI, CBPP, the National Employment Law Project, the Center for Economic and Policy Research, Good Jobs First)—and a range of opportunities for fruitful collaboration with smart people doing important work. Sometimes this involves contributing an historical perspective, as in work with colleagues at EPI on the long trajectory of union density and income inequality,[13] or work with In the Public Interest's Donald Cohen on the collapse of welfare capitalism in the United States.[14] But often it just involves more generic skills of analysis and synthesis. For its part, the annual EARN conference is focused, relevant, and even inspiring, an assessment rarely heard in the coatrooms at the annual conferences of the Organization of American Historians or the American Historical Association.

The common threads running through this work, as I slowly came to realize, were a commitment to an institutional analysis of economic problems and an effort to lean in against the view that we were all just marbles careening around on the surface of Thomas Friedman's flat world.[15] Big forces, including globalization and the pace of technological change, are shaping our lives. But our fate lies in the political response to those forces and in the political structure of the economy. The institutionalist view, in turn, is also necessarily historical—it is interested in public policies (or their absence), in the terms of political participation, and ultimately in power.[16]

This, in a sense, brought me full circle. While the work with IPP began as a purely political sideline, its larger logic pressed me to rethink and redirect my research—and to forge more meaningful connections between my political and scholarly efforts. Toward this end, a number of projects seem important and (I hope) useful. First, there is a pressing need to make the work of institutional economists more accessible to historians and to a wider public. Some do this very well on their own. Dean Baker at the Center for Economic and Policy Research is a model in this respect. His work is smart and accessible, he is a relentless watchdog of both the economics profession and economics reporting (through his *Beat the Press* blog), and he is an accomplished historian to boot.[17] But Baker, along with Brad Delong, Robert Reich, Jared Bernstein, Heather Boushey, Larry Mishel, and a scattering of others, are exceptions. As is typical in academic disciplines, most of the energy is expended convincing each other rather than in reaching a wider public. Second, there is an ongoing need to connect the work of institutional economists to a larger historical context—if only to tell a fuller (and longer) story. The fit, as I have suggested, is a natural one, but economists hesitate to go back farther than extracts from the Current Population Survey will take them, and historians hesitate to step much beyond the final crumbs on the archival trail. Such collaboration also promises to breathe new life into the work—the assembly of good, long-run data sets that bridge the divide between archival data and modern survey data—begun by the new economic historians. This work, represented well in the online Cambridge Historical Statistics of the United States and the historical datasets of the National Bureau of Economic Research, is more accessible than it has ever been but remains dramatically underused.[18]

Those goals, in turn, match up pretty well with the promise and potential of digital publishing, which can accommodate any length or format of presentation (from a blog post to a full-blown e-book) and incorporate tools (such as data visualization and mapping) that facilitate explanation. So this is where I put my time and energy. On a regular basis, I post short notes and data visualizations in a number of venues (including *Atlantic Cities* [now *CityLab*], EPI's *Working Economics* blog, the CEPR *Graphic Economics* series, and the *Dissent* blog) that either draw on recent work or strive to make complex data sets accessible and explicable.[19] This is accompanied by longer, often collaborative, work that tries to connect current economic problems and challenges to their historical background.[20]

All of this shorter work—blogging, data journalism, policy briefs—became the foundation for a major book-length, or at least book-like, project on the political origins of U.S. inequality. *Growing Apart*, first published by the Institute for Policy Studies in 2013, pulls together the best recent work in history and economics to build an institutional explanation for the growth of inequality in the United States in recent decades.[21] It surveys the dimensions of U.S. inequality (wages, incomes, wealth, demographics, etc.) across the last century and debunks some common explanations, such as those that focus on technological upheaval or globalization, for recent inequality trends. And then, in a series of chapters that combine historical background with interactive data visualizations, it zeroes in on the key policy drivers of U.S. inequality: the collapse of union density and basic labor standards, the ragged safety net offered by public and private welfare policies, the deregulation of finance, the shifting tax burden, the erosion of meaningful controls over executive pay, and a waning commitment to full employment.

Authored on the Scalar platform, *Growing Apart* is intended as a nimble product.[22] New content or references are added as new work becomes available, interactive data visualizations are updated in the background as new data are released, and readers can post comments or suggestions (or communicate their eye-rolling disdain) on the site. The work is meant to be synthetic, pulling together a wide range of work by others, but it does little archival work or data crunching of its own. It also aims to be accessible, and relevant—in the sense that it connects the recent past to the present, and sustains that connection even as the present advances.

*   *   *

In all honesty, it is hard to say what impact these efforts have had. Certainly the readership of my current work is much larger and much more varied than I could claim for the monographs and articles that punctuated the first half of my career as an historian. The policy work is a meaningful form of engagement, although the most we (at IPP or EARN) can claim is that we have lost ground more slowly as a result of our efforts. The engaged, digital scholarship in policy history is, I think (or hope), broadly useful—in part because it speaks directly to current political concerns; and in part because its essential elements (maps, data visualizations) are portable, and hence easy to download, share, paste, embed, or adapt.

More broadly, I think it is crucially important that academics simply make the effort to connect research to policy. This is a complex, and often frustrating, enterprise. But it is rendered less frustrating if we accept the different ways that connection can be made, the different ways in which our work or efforts might be useful. The research of Stephanie Luce and colleagues on the minimum wage, described in chapter 16 in this book, is exemplary in this respect. Such work might have a direct or *instrumental* impact, decisively making the case that a higher minimum wage—in a given city or state—is good public policy. More often, its impact is *strategic* (in the sense that it is politically useful or persuasive, a way of challenging the assumptions of opponents) or *conceptual* (in the sense that it helps build the case for "making work pay" labor market policies). And, in the politics of the minimum wage especially, making the case for the research *process* is as important as underscoring the findings. When the other side trots out its experts, with their dire predictions of slower growth and job loss, Luce and her colleagues rest their case on research design as much as they do on the results.[23] There can be little doubt that the arguments advanced here—that a higher minimum wage dampens poverty and inequality, that it is well targeted, and that its unintended consequences or costs are largely illusory—have changed both policy and public opinion.

The goal then, is simply to try to ensure that the work is useful in the larger conversation around our policy and political choices—to put one's shoulder to the wheel in whatever way seems most productive. The way to do that, in my experience, is to put aside the goal or pretense that one can make such a contribution *as an historian*, and to focus simply on the problems at hand. It might be that a pithy historical insight—a quotation from de Tocqueville or Debs, a cautionary reminder that we have been here before—will carry the day. But it is more likely that sustained civic participation and engagement—drawing simply on the time and resources and skills that come with most academic jobs—will make a lasting difference.[24]

Notes

1. Nicholas Kristof, "Professors, We Need You!," *New York Times*, February 15, 2014, www.nytimes.com, accessed September 5, 2015.

2. See Eileen Boris, "Scholarship and Activism: The Case of Welfare Justice," *Feminist Studies* 24.1 (spring 1998): 27–31.

3. Nancy MacLean, "Bringing the Organizing Tradition Home: Campus-Labor-Community Partnerships for Regional Power," *Labor Rising: The Past and Future of Working People in America*, edited by Daniel Katz and Richard A. Greenwald (New York: New Press, 2012), 65–80.

4. See Peter Novick, *That Noble Dream: The "Objectivity Question" and the American Historical Profession* (New York: Cambridge University Press, 1988).

5. Indeed, the American Sociological Association Code of Ethics makes clear the expectation that "when undertaking research," its members "strive to advance the science of sociology *and to serve the public good*" (emphasis added). ASA Code of Ethics, www.asanet.org, accessed September 5, 2015.

6. Colin Gordon, *Mapping Decline: St. Louis and the Fate of the American City* (Philadelphia: University of Pennsylvania Press, 2008).

7. See Colin Gordon, "Lost in Space, Or Confessions of an Accidental Geographer," *International Journal of History and Computing* 5.1 (2011): 1–22.

8. "Mapping Decline: St. Louis and the American City," Center for Geographic Analysis, http://worldmap.harvard.edu/maps/866, accessed September 5, 2015.

9. See Jerry Blair, "An Overview of the St. Louis Region," East-West Gateway Council of Governments, June 2009, www.ewgateway.org, accessed September 5, 2015; and Clarissa

Hayward, "Why It Takes More than Changing Beliefs to End Racial Inequality," *Urban Review STL*, June 2014, www.urbanreviewstl.com, accessed September 5, 2015.

10. See Colin Gordon, "The Making of Ferguson," *Dissent*, August 2014, www.dissent magazine.org, accessed September 5, 2015; "Segregation's Long Shadow," *Dissent*, September 2014, www.dissentmagazine.org, accessed September 5, 2015; "The Segregation Index," *Dissent*, winter 2015, www.dissentmagazine.org, accessed December 11, 2015; "How Racism Became Policy in Ferguson," *Dissent*, March 2015, www.dissentmagazine.org, accessed September 5, 2015; and "Border City Blues," *Dissent*, April 2015, www.dissentmagazine.org, accessed September 5, 2015.

11. The Economic Policy Institute (EPI) is a nonprofit, nonpartisan think tank created in 1986 to include the needs of low- and middle-income workers in economic policy discussions. EPI conducts research and analysis on the economic status of working America, highlighted by their signature biannual publication, *The State of Working America*. The Economic Analysis and Research Network (EARN) is a network of state-level research, policy, and advocacy organizations whose mission—at least in part—is to replicate and disseminate EPI's work at the state level.

12. See Joel Rogers and Richard Freeman, "The Promise of Progressive Federalism," in Joe Soss, Jacob Hacker, and Suzanne Mettler, eds., *Remaking America: Democracy and Public Policy in an Age of Inequality* (New York: Russell Sage Foundation, 2007), 205–27.

13. Ross Eisenberry and Colin Gordon, "As Unions Decline Inequality Rises," *Economic Policy Institute Economic Snapshot*, June 2012, www.epi.org, accessed September 5, 2015; and Colin Gordon, "Union Membership and the Income Share of the Top Ten Percent," *Working Economics*, October 2013, www.epi.org, accessed September 5, 2015.

14. Colin Gordon and Donald Cohen, "Do American Corporations Care What American Workers Earn?," *Dissent*, August 2012, www.dissentmagazine.org, accessed September 5, 2015.

15. I am referring of course to Thomas L. Friedman's *The World Is Flat: A Brief History of the Twenty-First Century* (New York: Farrar, Straus and Giroux, 2005).

16. See, for a concise summary view, John Schmitt, "Inequality as Policy: The United States Since 1979," CEPR, 2009.

17. Among his work is Dean Baker, *The United States since 1980* (New York: Cambridge University Press, 2007), the best general account of the last three decades in print.

18. Historical Statistics of the United States (HSUS) is available at http://hsus.cambridge .org; the discrete NBER datasets are available via the Federal Reserve Economic Data (FRED) portal maintained by the Federal Research Bank of St. Louis, http://research.stlouisfed.org/ fred2/.

19. This data journalism is collected and archived at www.telltalechart.org.

20. See, for example, Gordon and Cohen, "Do American Corporations Care What American Workers Earn?"; Ross Eisenberry and Colin Gordon, "As Unions Decline Inequality Rises," *Economic Policy Institute Economic Snapshot*, June 2012, www.epi.org, accessed September 5, 2015; John Schmitt and Colin Gordon, "What's So Bold about $9.00/Hour? Benchmarking the Minimum Wage," *Dissent*, March 2013, www.dissentmagazine.org, accessed September 5, 2015; and Colin Gordon, "The Irony and Limits of the Affordable Care Act," *Dissent*, October 2103, www.dissentmagazine.org, accessed September 5, 2015.

21. Colin Gordon, *Growing Apart: A Political History of American Inequality*, is hosted by IPS's Project on Inequality and the Common Good at www.inequality.org; it was also serialized at *Dissent* in spring 2014 as the ten-part series "Our Inequality."

22. According to its website, "Scalar is a free, open source authoring and publishing platform designed to make it easy for authors to write long-form, born-digital scholarship online. Scalar enables users to assemble media from multiple sources and to juxtapose them with their own writing in a variety of ways, with minimal technical expertise required." For a full background, and a showcase of Scalar projects, go to http://scalar.usc.edu/scalar, accessed September 5, 2015.

23. For this typology of "translational research," see Susan Maciolek, "Use of Research Evidence: Social Services Portfolio," William T. Grant Foundation, 2015; and National Research Council, *Using Science as Evidence in Public Policy*, National Academy of Sciences, 2012. For the decisive meta-analysis of the last generation of minimum wage research, see John Schmitt, "Why Does the Minimum Wage Have No Discernible Effect on Employment?," Center for Economic and Policy Research, 2013.

24. See Harry Boyte and Eric Fretz, "Civic Professionalism," *Journal of Higher Education Outreach and Engagement*, 14 (June 2010): 67–90.

CHAPTER 14

"The Soul Puts Together Its Pieces"

Lessons from the Casino Floor

Susan Chandler

> Our system is one of detachment: to keep silenced people from asking
> questions, to keep the judged from judging, to keep solitary people
> from joining together, and the soul from putting together its pieces.
> —Eduardo Galeano, *The Book of Embraces*

In 2006 Hattie Canty, widow and mother of ten, considered the road she had
traveled from rural Alabama poverty to maid work in a Mafia-run Las Vegas hotel
and eventually to the presidency of Las Vegas's sixty-thousand-member Culinary
Union: "I don't have a lot of pride. That I don't have. But guts, I got guts. And I
got what it takes to get certain things did. I'm just a southern country girl, one
who will not take no for an answer, one who [is] not going to be beat down by
the system. I guess that's what makes me a little different. I got what it takes to
overcome, what Reverend King was—I got that. And I cherish that. And I don't
forget it."[1]

Hattie Canty's story and those of dozens of women like her form the core of
Casino Women: Courage in Unexpected Places. A women-focused study and exploration in narrative, *Casino Women* traces the transformation of maids, cocktail
waitresses, laundry workers, and cooks as they came to realize through collective
action that they could challenge the gaming industry and change the world.

In this chapter, I examine *Casino Women* in light of the legacy of labor historians David Montgomery and Shelton Stromquist.[2] I also take this opportunity
to reflect on the relationship between my years of activism and my scholarship,
especially in the production of *Casino Women*.

* * *

To begin, a word on methodology. For over a decade, Jill Jones, my *Casino
Women* coauthor, and I talked with women who worked as maids, dealers, cocktail waitresses, food servers, janitors, keno runners, middle managers, and very
occasionally vice presidents in Las Vegas and Reno casinos. In two- to four-hour

interviews we asked about the women's backgrounds, their experience at work, and their opinions about the gaming industry and its relationship with workers, families, and the community. Focus groups of former casino workers, Latino leaders, educators, and of health and social service professionals who serve casino families supplemented the interviews. We also talked with dozens of key informants—demographers, economists, researchers, legislators, and community activists—and visited research centers, archives, libraries, corporate websites, federal courts, the Nevada legislature, union halls, demonstrations, bars, and coffee shops in Las Vegas and Reno, in our effort to assemble the context of the women's lives and become familiar with the industry that dominates Nevada.

At the heart of our inquiry was a close examination of the casino floor gained through hours of interviews with the women themselves. And because the women invariably talked at length about their health, bodies, children, families, and communities, the book that emerged from this comprehensive investigation took a broad perspective that extended far beyond the workplace.

The Context

Reno and Las Vegas are arguably the most gendered cities in the nation, and for years the enormous profitability of the gaming industry there has ridden on the backs of women assigned classic female occupations—making beds and serving food on the one hand and providing sexual allure on the other. Some feminists scorn this world, but to their loss. This is a world filled with women like Hattie Canty.

Las Vegas, with its array of lights in the night sky, is the only city you can see from space. Home to extensive international gaming operations—a trillion-dollar industry with legendary profit-making capabilities—Las Vegas for the last two decades has grown faster than any other major U.S. city. Over 50 million people annually visit Nevada, spending over six times more on gaming than is spent there on all other forms of sport and entertainment combined. Separated from the norm by neon, a Mafia history, and tens of thousands of acres of desert, Las Vegas and gambling feel like anomalies. In reality they are pure capitalism.

Corporate gaming is unquestionably a global industry, and in fact globalization was the initial focus of our study, which we designed—in the spirit of urban scholar Saskia Sassen—to use local processes to illuminate global realities.[3] Globalization drives the fabulously capital-rich tourist and entertainment industry in destinations like Las Vegas and Los Angeles, cities that embrace tourists and capital from all over the world and whose workforces epitomize the transmigration of labor. Patterns familiar to neoliberalism and globalization play out powerfully in Nevada, where a few corporate giants wield enormous influence in both the industry and by extension the whole state. "By [the gaming industry's] contributions to politicians," Sally Denton and Roger Morris write in *The Money and the Power*, "its tax revenue to reliant public treasuries, its hold over collateral enterprise, and not least its millions spent for ceaseless lobbying that leaves nothing to chance, the industry gains and wields unique influence throughout the nation and world. No political act is accomplished without their express approval."[4]

But of course not everything is controlled. Although Las Vegas is a global city, it is certainly an unusual one, for within it live sixty thousand union members and their families whose ability to fight together for their futures should never be underestimated. The story of Nevada's Culinary Union (Local 226, UNITE HERE) is arguably *the* grassroots organizing story of our time.[5] The collective action of Culinary Union activists has changed the lives of tens of thousands of working Nevadans significantly for the better. In Las Vegas, "the hottest union city in America," those changes include achieving wages on the Strip that enable a maid to buy a house; high-quality health coverage free to members and their families; the opportunity to acquire a better-paying job through free classes at the Culinary Training Academy; the opportunity to take a leave from work and participate in the union's powerful grassroots political machine; and, most important, dignity. These are enormous contributions that make Culinary Union families' lives quite different from those of hospitality workers generally.

The Narratives

The women, whose stories were extraordinarily diverse, claimed a range of different countries of origin, class backgrounds, sexual orientations, and religious affiliations; some had advanced degrees, others had grade school educations. They worked in many positions and were active both in and outside the union. Some lived in Reno, a mostly unorganized town where work conditions mirror those of many other hospitality workers. Others lived in Las Vegas, one of the country's great union towns, where the Culinary Union enjoys 95 percent density on the Strip. No single story represents the whole, but I share here portions of the narrative of "Alicia Bermudez" (a pseudonym), a Reno laundry worker, who describes with zest the "frictions of daily life," her growing activism, and her increasingly clear conception of class and economic power.

At the time we interviewed her in 2001, Alicia Bermudez had worked in the laundry of a high-end Reno casino for ten years and was earning $9.53 an hour. Her annual raises, like those of every Reno worker with whom we spoke, had been miniscule—"18 cents, 15 cents, the most high, 23 cents—and nobody can survive with that sum," Bermudez said emphatically. "I have a lot of fellow workers, and we really have a struggle with how we're going to spend our money. We have to count every cent."[6]

Working in a casino laundry, Bermudez said, is "like you work in a concentration camp." The work is heavy and "fast, fast, fast, like a machine." Supervisors hang over employees: "Always they're looking at you. Somebody go to the bathroom [and] spend like five or six minutes, and they're asking, 'Are you sick?' 'You should go see your doctor and bring us excuse, because we cannot tolerate to see you in the bathroom too many times.' Yes! We've been told that." Alicia's main concern, however, was with fire. The laundry was packed with dryers and ironers, and "when something catch here on fire," she said, "we're going to die like roast chicken."

Alicia was disgusted with management and especially with the famous corporation that had recently acquired her casino. "They're very tight," she said, "and very cheap. They don't care about employees like a human being. . . . They're treating us like donkeys, really. They don't care if [the employees] are sweating blood. They're happy with that. I'm very disappointed with them. And I'm very angry."

Injustice directed at new immigrant workers especially angered Bermudez. "I see my coworkers treated like nothing," she said, "and they don't talk back. Like now in my department, they just hire a lot of new Chinese people . . . and also some from India, from Mexico. The ones that can hardly say in English 'yes' or 'no.'" "I want to be treated the way you expect me to treat you," she went on. "I'm just a lousy employee here, but I'm human, you're human. I don't see the difference to treat us like nothing."

Alicia's concern for justice drew her to unions, which she had first encountered in Mexico. Growing up, she lived across the street from the headquarters of a large union, and on weekends she liked to sit on the curb and listen to the organizers. She learned, she said, "how unions protect workers' rights" and "how we can make more money being union." "The [corporations] want to abuse us," she continued, "because we're the minority. . . . They really like to make you feel like a little worm and just step on you. It's what I learned a long time ago. That's why I keep on fighting now."

After two failed union drives, the Culinary Union came to town, and many employees joined up. Culinary organizers came from across the United States, and Alicia was assigned "a good lady from California." The two women organized day and night, talking with employees about the union. "I wasn't expecting nothing," Alicia said. "Just having hope in my heart [that] one day I would have my contract, one day I want to win that union election."

Culinary Union organizing campaigns in Nevada are won carefully and systematically, one worker at a time, generally through off-hours home visits and lunch-break conversations. "Many nights, many days, I didn't have dinner," Alicia remembered. "I just have a cup of coffee and water. Just sit down around the cafeteria, finding this table, finding another table, until my forty minutes was over. And I did that for months, for years." Eventually, she said, "I enrolled those people in the union, yes. But I was fighting very hard for that. It's not easy. And to beat a big corporation, wasn't easy. Was very hard."

Alicia Bermudez's casino became the second of only two casinos in northern Nevada to go union. "Tears was coming from my eyes that night," she said, "I was very, very happy. It's like I have my hand full of gold—that's how I feel—because my salary is going up. I'm going to make more. I don't want to spend eighteen years and get ten-cent raise every year, or three cents."

Alicia Bermudez talked to her young daughter about everything that was going on with the union. Sometimes her daughter would say, "Why you do that, Mama? Because days you disappear." Taking her child in her arms, Bermudez replied: "I'm not disappeared. I disappear from the house, but I'm attending something very important. Maybe for you, because I don't know that you want to go to college. I don't want you to start like a cook over there making $5.50 or $5.25 or $6.25, how they pay the cooks now." "So I told her this is why I fighting," Alicia continued. "I can die tomorrow, but at least when I gone I'm going to be very happy because I see the people be protected by the union. They can have not the best salary, but they can have something decent at least."

Back-of-the-house workers like Alicia Bermudez—maids, laundry workers, porters, janitors, cooks, dishwashers—constitute the vast majority of casino and hotel workers, with maids alone accounting for between 25 and 30 percent of employees.[7] Nearly always female and, in Nevada, predominantly immigrant and Latina, these women serve as the base of gaming's enormous global empire, working long hours at low pay and in jobs characterized by hard labor, high rates of injury, and few if any ladders to advancement. Unseen and unheralded, back-of-the-house workers appear to labor without voice in a geography in which they are present but silent.

In our experience, however, back-of-the-house workers are neither silent nor invisible. We repeatedly encountered women like Alicia who speak out, form family-like ties with other workers, and defend each other. Critically, they build within the context of daily interactions a culture quite at odds with that of the casino and its drive to maximize profits. They often, like Alicia, possess a keen sense of both power and injustice as well as a sophisticated understanding of themselves as a group with interests utterly distinct from those of corporate management. Not satisfied with the rank to which they were assigned, back-of-the-house workers often embrace the improbable notion that they are more than arms that work and that together with their fellow workers they can actually change the world. They possess as well a sense of history and a vision for the future, like the one Alicia shared with her daughter. Somehow they find ways to educate themselves, whether sitting on a curb listening to labor organizers or absorbing lessons from union activists. It was a powerful process to witness, one in which the union and individual women together emerged as considerably more effective actors.

Themes

Three themes repeatedly asserted themselves in the women's narratives: transformation, collaboration, and the consequences of silence. The first theme to emerge was that of personal transformation. "I changed totally," a maid and Culinary

Union leader, said, summing up her experience as a Frontier Casino striker, "and . . . for the first time in many years I [felt] strong."[8] We heard this story of transformation again and again from the women activists we interviewed. How and why did they see change occur? How was it, for example, that an African American maid, Hattie Canty, despite being assigned a role at the bottom of the economy, joined with others to create the preeminent grassroots organizing union in the nation and in time became its president? Or that a white, Nevada-born, working-class woman and U.S. Navy veteran, Edna Harmon, moved from alcohol, tranquilizers, and card dealing to a lifelong connection with liberation theology and Maryknoll Missioners that led her both to Bolivia and to speaking at rallies of immigrants in Reno?

But the women's narratives unfold a story much larger than individual transformation. The collective actions of union activists significantly changed for the better the lives of tens of thousands of working Nevadans and their families. In Las Vegas, those changes included livable wages, comprehensive health coverage free for members and their families, free legal assistance (often used to regularize immigration status), job-upgrade classes at the Culinary Academy, and job security. Further, these changes were accomplished not by governors, legislators, agency leaders, or university personnel (including faculty), but rather, as one waitress said, "just workers organizing workers." How and why that was possible is a second theme the book explored.

But not all women took action. Many remained silent out of fear. Why that was—and the consequences of silence—forms the third theme that emerged from the women's stories. Casinos have an enormous impact on women workers, often for the worse. Dealers in particular reported being miserable at work but afraid to speak out—"one word and out you go," they said. They hated the noise, smoke, having to work holidays, and hated even more how casinos profited from greed and broken lives. But they felt stuck. Dealing cards, the women said, was hardly a transferable skill, and even if they went back to school, the jobs they might get would pay considerably less than they made dealing. Worst of all, they hated themselves for having stayed so long, as if by staying they had become all that they despised.

Relatively late in the process of writing the book, we became aware of the contrast between the two groups of women, one cohort at the bottom of the casino hierarchy that stood up against enormous odds, and the other set in more privileged positions that feared resistance or adopted corporate goals as their own. It was one of the most fascinating—and ultimately, most illuminating—of the book's findings.

We learned a great deal from the women who had taken action. It may be useful to sum up the factors at the heart of their activism and of the transformation they experienced. Why did some risk when others did not? Poverty and the lack of economic mobility were the first factors. The hard years; raises of ten cents a year; working two and even three jobs—all of these the women remembered acutely. And remembering their own experiences, they were consistently unwilling to turn away from suffering, another critical characteristic. They also were willing to see and feel beyond their own personal and family lives, to feel and do something about the pain of others. They opened themselves up to fellow workers from across the world and, in this way, countered the racism and xenophobia so prevalent in U.S. society and contemporary workplaces. Further, women who acted had close experience with power and an embodied consciousness that the interests of those in power were not their own. They had a robust suspicion of corporate power, including the knowledge that those in charge regularly speak one way and act another, and were outraged that profit generation in gaming corporations regularly trumped any concern for workers and families. In short, they had become class conscious.

The women also were willing to act collectively and militantly even when they were afraid. They found joy in struggling and laughing together, in "keeping on keeping on," and they knew that workers consigned to the bottom may yet have a role in history. "The compassion of the oppressed for the oppressed is indispensable," Bertolt Brecht writes. "It is the world's one hope."[9]

The book led us to ask if it is possible in a grossly unequal world to close ourselves and our families off from the suffering of others and enjoy our own modest or substantial resources. But it appears that life is not so simple, that we are in touch with our neighbors, and to ignore their suffering in some way fundamentally compromises our own well-being and certainly our ability to be authentic. For if we remain silent when another is abused, we become in some terrible way complicit in their abuse. Our relations with others take on a surface quality, and we are constrained from talking about what is real. Only in stepping forward can we be authentic and not alienated from ourselves, others, and our work. And it is only in being authentic, in acting, that we can find genuine connection with each other. The relation between acting and love was not difficult to find in the women's stories. It spilled out, an affirmation of the connections among us all that are so endangered in corporate-dominated worlds.

*   *   *

I have a favorite James Baldwin quotation: "People pay for what they do, and, still more, for what they have allowed themselves to become. And they pay for it very simply: by the lives they lead."[10] This quotation has particular relevance to scholars in labor studies who often come to academia from activism and who weigh life choices carefully: should I have become an academic? Am I making a contribution? How do I understand the relationship between my activism and scholarship?

I arrived at Oberlin College in 1961 a Young Republican, which was the political tradition of at least part of my Midwest family. There was a left side, too—my grandfather who homesteaded in Minnesota in the 1870s later became a member of the Industrial Workers of the World, but I did not learn about that until I reached my seventieth year. By the time I graduated in 1965, the civil rights movement, the emerging antiwar movement, the influence of African students on campus, and not incidentally my friendship with Ann Mullin (who later married the activist and labor historian Shelton Stromquist) were rapidly moving me left. In graduate school at the University of Wisconsin, I became part of the explosive activism of our generation, taking classes from Harvey Goldberg, William Appleman Williams, and others of that wonderful group of left professors. I vividly remember crowding into Goldberg's European history course along with six hundred other students, all of us hungry for analysis. But it was not principally the classroom that changed us. In 1967 I dropped out of school three credits short of a master's degree (I guessed we wouldn't need advanced degrees come the revolution) and became a full-time organizer for the Wisconsin Draft Resistance Union. We counseled draft resisters, played our part in the underground railroad to Canada, organized all over Wisconsin, traveled to demonstrations, and read, read, read—Marx, Lenin, and the many traditions of resistance in this country and internationally.[11]

I married Joe Chandler and through his old-left family—Russian Jewish immigrants on one side and Irish American workers on the other, many former Communist Party members—deepened my appreciation for the working class. So many organizing stories told, so many labor songs sung! In time we moved to Detroit, as part of a general effort in the New Left to integrate with the proletariat. That sounds foreign to contemporary ears, but it was a wonderful decision, critical to our development. Joe became a skilled tradesman at Chevrolet and I worked as a community organizer in anti–police brutality efforts, farmworker support, the U.S.-China Peoples Friendship Association, food co-ops, and, my favorite, the Detroit Inner City Youth Tour to China. We raised our family and were part of various New Left formations.

In Detroit we met Harry Haywood, then in his mid-seventies, who was a prominent African American theoretician in the Communist Party from 1928 to the early 1950s and later was affiliated with the Communist Party, Marxist-Leninist (CPML). Haywood had written *Negro Liberation* in 1948 and was a principal architect of the Black Belt Nation concept that emerged in 1928–32, the argument of which is that African Americans constitute an oppressed nation in the Black Belt South with full rights to self-determination. The party's focus on self-determination was, many believe, the basis of its strongest work on race. In the 1970s when we met him, Haywood was writing *Black Bolshevik*, his autobiography, and I became a stenographer, editor, typist, cook, and hauler of documents for him.[12] Most important, I went to the library. If, for example, Harry was writing about the Sharecroppers Union, I would find all the relevant books and archives and take them to Harry's little apartment, where we would talk for hours until he felt entirely reimmersed in his memories and the facts. It would be hard to overstate Haywood's impact on my thinking—there is no doubt that it inspired my interest in casino workers.

In 1981 we left Detroit—the auto industry was collapsing and perhaps we were exhausted from our years of organizing—and came to California, where in time I returned to graduate school and eventually earned a doctorate in social welfare, enabling me to find work in the School of Social Work at the University of Nevada, Reno.

I brought with me to academia a combination of rural Minnesota, the radicalism of my generation, and our family's experience of working-class Detroit. While I thrived in the classroom, in liberal faculty circles I felt distinctly Other and soon was at loggerheads with a particularly unethical administrator. Things got so bad that I finally concluded that the world was much larger than the unpleasant hall on which my office sat. That drove me first to a living-wage study for Nevada and then to *Casino Women*. (My advice to young faculty who hope to have an impact or find happiness is always to *scale* the high walls of academia and get out into the world.)

I was often torn during those first years, when Jill Jones and I worked on *Casino Women*. Every time we left an interview with a Culinary Union activist, I a) felt inspired and connected, as if a piece of my soul had been touched as it had not been since my old movement days, and b) wondered why in hell I was an academic and not an organizer. Still, I repeatedly chose to stay in academia, and now weigh *Casino Women*'s contributions as well as its limits. Who benefitted? Was anything changed?

There is no question that *I* benefitted from researching and writing *Casino Women*. Not so much financially—the book was published the very year that a moratorium on merit raises at the university was imposed, and my salary actually declined after its publication. I did earn $800 in royalties one year, but I hesitate to calculate the hourly wage over the ten years the book was in the making. Still, there were other gratifying personal gains—the opportunity to travel to conferences and meet scholar activists, invitations to speak, dinner once with UNITE HERE president John Wilhelm, and so on. Far more important were the friendships with casino women and a close knowledge of working-class Nevada, both of which continue to enrich my life today. These connections and insights developed from engagement with the women themselves and from our mutual commitment to social ideals. They speak to the necessity (and reward) of going beyond academic and scholarly pursuits.

As for contributions the book has made to a better world, I identify a few here. The greatest, I think, was putting into writing the lives, worldviews, and hard work of the casino women themselves. Far and away our most treasured book signing was at the Culinary Union hall in Las Vegas, where a long line of enthusiastic casino workers waited to buy the book and have it signed. At the beginning of our work together, Jill and I used to talk in good feminist fashion about "giving voice to the voiceless" and "making the invisible visible." That sounds paternalistic now. Very often the casino women, and especially the union activists, had larger voices and more wisdom, power, and organizing acumen than we assistant and associate professors could ever claim. In a very large sense, the women gave voice to us.

Another contribution is the space earned to talk about the Culinary Union and its work in a decidedly antiunion state. We gave dozens of talks locally—to religious and women's groups, libraries and retirement homes, bookstores, schools, and conferences—and everywhere saw the looks of disbelief change to interest and then to appreciation of casino workers and the Culinary Union. I enjoyed, too, shaking up the dominant ideology and perceptions about corporate gaming and casino owners like Steve Wynn and Sheldon Adelson, who in Nevada enjoy an entirely undeserved star status. Very few activists and no elected officials, Democrat or Republican, are willing to take gaming on, so we felt pleased to be speaking truth to power.

Probably the most personally meaningful contribution, though, came in relationship to my own working-class students who sometimes had worked in casinos themselves. First-generation Latino and Latina students often knew about casino life intimately, for it was their parents who came home exhausted from making beds, washing dishes, and holding down two jobs. "You wrote about my mother," a student would say with pride, knowing that it was his or her mother's hard labor that enabled him or her to be in a college classroom today.

In the end, these are modest contributions. Are they sufficient? I am not sure. I am glad though not to have disappeared into middle-class academic life and, in some fashion, to have kept the faith.

Casino Women ends on a similar theme. Leon Gieco, the Argentinian singer-songwriter who, like Bruce Springsteen, fills stadiums, writes "solo le pido a Dios"—

> The only thing I ask of God is that
> he not let me be indifferent to the suffering,
> and that when death, that dusty time, comes
> that I not be alone and empty, having not given my everything.

In Latin America, "Solo le Pido a Dios" is sung as a call for justice and against war. What is not apparent on the page but leaps out in performance is the anthem's joy, for behind the singular pronoun "I" is an implicit plural "we"—you and I and a thousand others together. In the end, that is what the casino women were saying. Don't sit alone declining to act. A committed life is so much more joyous than a life of self-protection and consumption, and connection with each other in struggle so much more rewarding than lives lived alone.

In closing, I would like to acknowledge David Montgomery and Shel and Ann Stromquist, who were and are never indifferent to the suffering.

Notes

The chapter epigraph is from Eduardo Galeano, *The Book of Embraces*, translated by Cedric Belfrage with Mark Schafer (New York: W. W. Norton, 1991).

1. Hattie Canty, interview with Jill Jones and the author, September 19, 2007, Las Vegas, Nev.

2. For a general discussion of Montgomery's work, see Shelton Stromquist, "David Montgomery: A Labor Historian's Legacies," *Journal of the Gilded Age and Progressive Era* 13.2 (2014): 256–76.

3. See Saskia Sassen, *Globalization and Its Discontents* (New York: New Press, 1998).

4. Sally Denton and Roger Morris, *The Money and the Power: The Making of Las Vegas and Its Hold on America, 1947–2000* (New York: Alfred A. Knopf, 2001), 8.

5. UNITE HERE is a labor union that merged two existing unions, UNITE (Union of Needletrades, Industrial, and Textile Employees) and HERE (Hotel Employees and Restaurant Employees International Union).

6. Alicia Bermudez (pseudonym), interview with Jill Jones and the author, February 26, 2001, Reno, Nev. All subsequent quotations from Alicia Bermudez are from this interview.

7. Annette Bernhardt, Laura Dresser, and Erin Hatton, "Moving Hotels to the High Road: Strategies that Help Workers and Firms Succeed," Center on Wisconsin Strategy (COWS), Madison, 2003, www.cows.org, accessed July 27, 2007.

8. Mirna Preciado and Geoconda Arguello Kline, interview with Jill Jones and the author, February 22, 2001, Las Vegas, Nev. The Frontier Strike (September 1991 to January 1998), which pitted 550 Frontier Casino workers against owner Margaret Elardi, was the longest strike in U.S. history. Its rallying cry, "One Day Longer," indicated union workers' determination to stay out one day longer than the Elardis. The strike solidified the Culinary Union's identity and strength, and for workers provided years of education in power and rights, grassroots organizing, and national and international solidarity.

9. Bertolt Brecht, "The World's One Hope," in *Against Forgetting: Twentieth-Century Poetry of Witness*, edited by Carolyn Forché (New York: W. W. Norton, 1993), 219.

10. James Baldwin, *No Name in the Street* (New York: Dial Press, 1972), 55.

11. Among the sources of information on intellectual life and political activism at the University of Wisconsin in the 1960s are the Harvey Goldberg Center for the Study of Contemporary History at the University of Wisconsin–Madison, http://goldberg.history.wisc.edu/; Paul Buhle, ed., *History and the New Left: Madison, Wisconsin, 1950–1970* (Philadelphia: Temple University Press, 1990); and David Maraniss, *They Marched into Sunlight: War and Peace, Vietnam and America, October 1967* (New York: Simon and Schuster, 2004).

12. Harry Haywood, *Black Bolshevik: Autobiography of an Afro-American Communist* (Chicago: Liberator Press, 1978).

CHAPTER 15

Disability and Labor Activism

The Pains and Joys of Coalitions

Kim E. Nielsen

The immediate and long-term impacts of work on the bodies and minds of those who labor are a core concern for labor and disability activists as well as for labor and disability historians. Wage and nonwage labor result in high rates of disability caused by physically and emotionally dangerous working conditions—whether due to workplace chemicals or toxins, equipment accidents, labor speed-ups, repetitive work injuries, or harassment by employers or other employees. Laborers and working-class activists have a long history of making safer working conditions a primary demand.

Disability activists have joined in this demand for safe working conditions but also wrestled with the long-standing reality that many people with disabilities don't have access to employment—much less safe employment. In 2013, 82.4 percent of people with disabilities were unemployed in the United States.[1] Ableism—in the form of segregated education, poor job training, low expectations, inaccessible transportation, employer disparagement, outright discrimination, and harassment by other employees—results in limited access to waged work opportunities for people with disabilities.[2] The resulting lack of wages significantly limits their political power, social capital, and basic well-being. For disabled people in marginalized communities, the ableism they encounter weaves together with classism, racism, or sexism (for example) to further complicate employment. Throughout the long history and development of the disability rights movement, activists have listed access to wage labor, and then safe working conditions, as primary demands.

Disability and labor activists, today as well as in the past, have much in common. They share the goal of securing fair wage employment for all people. They also share the goal of accessible, just, and quality health care. Both groups want to see safe workplaces created and maintained for all.

Despite these common goals, the two camps—disability activists and scholars on the one hand, and labor activists and scholars on the other—differ profoundly in their understanding of disability. Disability activists and scholars reject the categorization of disability as a *problem* to be eradicated. Labor activists and scholars, in contrast, often tie their calls for safer working conditions to the false assumption that disability constitutes a fearful, tragic, relationship-ending condition, an experience to be avoided at all costs. This difference in underlying assumptions creates an often-unacknowledged uneasiness in the alliances between disability and labor activists.[3]

Arguing that worker safety is necessary to avoid the *tragedy* of disability leaves little space—rhetorical or substantive—for activists comfortable with their disability identity and confident of their capacity for a full future. A disabled activist may be fully comfortable professionally, personally, and sexually as a wheelchair user, or may have found rich relationships in the neurodiversity community, or may revel in the insights blindness has enabled for her or him as poet and parent. Such activists embody the claim that disability is part of human diversity. Today we recognize that activism based on the assumption that women must become men in order to be happy and conquer their deficiencies, or that Asian Americans must become white in order to similarly do so, is corrosive and repugnant. Disabled activists experience much of work safety activism in a similar way.

How can disability and labor activists, who share so many goals, recognize and resist the exploitive (and often racist) nature of unsafe working conditions while avoiding the demonization of disability? How do we encourage safe working conditions while not dismissing certain bodies, and thus certain people and their futures, as undesirable? How do we begin to realize that such presumed undesirability is an ableist prejudice and grants permission for the denial of educational, employment, and civic rights? How can scholars, such as those in disability studies, help articulate new understandings that can ground more effective activist collaborations?

Scholarship and activism are the essential parts of this effort, for by unearthing the complex workings of ableism we are better able to dismantle it. Workplace safety and disability provide a way to think about this challenge. By better understanding the entwined ropes of racism, classism, sexism, and ableism, we create stronger activist coalitions. Coalitions give us strength; coalitions give us energy; and all of us benefit by rejecting ableist ideologies, language, and assumptions.[4]

Work Is Dangerous

As labor historians underscore, work is dangerous. The physical and emotional demands of both wage and nonwage labor sometimes result in death and frequently in disability. Railroad or factory accidents, the daily grind of farm labor or computer screen eye strain, and the handling of cleaning products, for example, can create physical disability. In offices, in locker rooms, and on the shop floor, speed-ups, harassment, and stress can either create or exacerbate the difficult consequences of psychiatric disabilities. Individual workers and labor unions have long fought to protect workers from the damages of laboring, and they have sought economic compensation (from employers as well as governmental agencies) or alternative employment as bodies changed due to accident, repeated stresses, or aging. Labor historians have also documented how employers and others have sought to avoid such responsibilities. For example, historian Sarah F. Rose documents this scholarship in "'Crippled' Hands: Disability in Labor and Working Class History."[5] Rose argues that experiences and issues of labor safety are central to labor history.

Workplace safety activism is an important part of labor history and an example of how disability history and labor history overlap. From the Progressive Era to the present, labor unions and social-welfare reformers have focused much attention on the dangers of work and the future lives of laborers who became disabled due to their employment. For example, in the late nineteenth century, public figures as disparate as President Benjamin Harrison and the American Federation of Labor leader Samuel Gompers agreed on the dangerous consequences of industrialization. Twenty-one years after Harrison warned in 1889 that railroad workers were subject "to a peril of life and limb as great as that of a soldier in time of war," Gompers asserted that "'compensation for the victims of injury' stood 'above all' other issues in terms of its legislative significance; no other issue was 'of half the importance.'"[6]

Although advocates of industrialization and mechanization argued that the miracles of technology led to safer working conditions, workers experienced the opposite. The dangers of industrialization and mechanization spread beyond the workplace to affect water and air quality, damaging not just workers' bodies but also their families, homes, and communities. In these circumstances, disabled union members have been important agents of change and inclusion in their unions, such as those who led democratization efforts among United Mine Workers members in the 1960s and 1970s. The Miners for Democracy, the Disabled Miners and Widows, and the Black Lung Association created a powerful coalition to remove corruption, establish just health care benefits for those whose bodies were damaged by coal mining, and rejuvenate the union. During a five-week strike in 1970, miners with mobility impairments resulting from mine cave-ins and those with lungs damaged by coal dust, along with their family members, joined non-disabled compatriots on the picket line.[7]

Activists have used the existence and threat of disability as a significant scare tactic to ignite labor activism, pursue worker safety legislation, and promote social-welfare programs.[8] The existence of disease clusters near industries spewing out chemical wastes, large-scale accidents and high accident rates, the health impacts of child labor, and the dramatic visual images that such incidents produce figure prominently in labor and working-class activism. Women poisoned by radium while working as dial painters, for example, highlighted their disfigurement to draw attention to their need for employer compensation in the early twentieth century.[9] César Chávez linked pesticide usage and a leukemia cluster to ignite United Farm Workers organizing.[10] Rhetoric and images that emphasize the tragedy of work-based disability have also been used to draw middle- and upper-class reformers into working-class activism. Examples include Lewis Hine's early-twentieth-century photographic portrayals of the damage done by child labor and the Women's Trade Union League attempts to connect working-class and elite women.

Trying to Get to Work

Activism among disabled people in the United States has always emphasized the necessity of stable employment and a living wage. In the nineteenth century, groups of disabled individuals began to organize around diagnostic identities, frequently also split by gender, religion, veteran status, or racial categories. Deaf people, blind people, disabled Civil War veterans, and wheelchair users, for example, organized to advance their own employment, housing, and social opportunities. In organizations such as the Society for the Welfare of the Jewish Deaf, which created the first labor board for deaf people in 1913, individuals shared employment information, lobbied for local as well as national legislative changes, provided mutual assistance, flirted with one another, worshipped, and created community. Some organizations were national, among them the National Association of the Deaf (1880), the National Fraternal Society for the Deaf (1901), the Disabled American Veterans (1920), and the National Federation of the Blind (1940). Regional organizations included the Grand Independent Order of Mutes of Georgia, created by black deaf Georgians in 1923.[11] These organizations and their members embraced self-advocacy. They rejected the dominant belief that disability rendered one unable to labor, rejected the presumption that disability was primarily a concern of social welfare and charity, and claimed agency to shape their own lives. Through their activism and organizations, disability activists sought the strengths that came with stable employment and a living wage.

Building on the lessons and strength that emerged from organized resistance, disability activism transformed significantly during World War II. For the first time, disabled people moved toward a unified identity as a disability community rather than as separate diagnostic communities in order to fight ableism and gain employment. An experienced labor organizer, Paul Strachan, founded the American Federation of the Physically Handicapped (AFPH), the first national cross-disability organization, and opened membership to all: "the blind, deaf, hard-of-hearing, those with cardiac conditions, those with tuberculosis, arthritics, epileptics, those with poliomyelitis, those with cerebral palsy, amputees, and diabetics."[12] Like union organizers who realized that cross-race, cross-gender labor organizations could marshal significant strength, Strachan and others sought to bring together all those who shared the experiences of the stigma of disability. They did so in ways that increasingly emphasized individual rights.

The newly united disability activists considered access to the training that leads to employment, access to employment, and access to safe workplaces vital elements of U.S. citizenship and rights. Disability, activists argued, was not a charity issue or a problem of individual bodies, but a rights issue. Charity demanded moral worthiness, presumed an inability to be productive, and assumed the *problem* of disability to be grounded in the individual. The *problems* of disability, activists now insisted, were actually problems of discrimination, segregation, and exclusion. Strachan railed against the "unreasonable, unjust prejudice against millions of Handicapped people" as they sought "the comforts, the feeling of security that comes from fair recognition of our rights, as citizens, and our needs, as Handicapped." The AFPH received much of its funding from labor unions, and considered workplace safety, labor discrimination, and public health major elements of its cause.[13] In later decades, disability activists with experience in the women's, racial, and student movements made similar rights claims—for education, for employment, and for physical access. Activists with Brooklyn College's Student Organization for Every Disability United for Progress (SOFEDUP), for example, organized to "bring down the walls of apathy, oppression, and discrimination."[14] Alongside labor, racial, and women's activists, disability activists claimed rights.

As a result of the wide spectrum of disability activism, much legislation pertaining to disability after World War II can be categorized as civil rights legislation rather than as charity or social welfare legislation. This includes the 1968 Architectural Barriers Act, the 1973 Rehabilitation Act, the 1975 Education of All Handicapped Children Act (later renamed the Individuals with Disabilities Education Act, IDEA), the 1984 Voting Accessibility Act, and the 1990 Americans with Disabilities Act. The goal of access to just and safe wage employment was part of nearly all of this legislation. As a Colorado activist testified in support of a state antidiscrimination bill in 1977, "People with handicaps don't all want rehabilitation. What they need is the opportunity to get their foot in the door and to be considered [for jobs]."[15]

Disability Pride and Disability Studies

The academic field of disability studies emerged from the disability pride movement of the twentieth century. Disability activists and scholars founded the field's first and primary scholarly organization, the Society for Disability Studies (SDS), in 1986. They purposefully and playfully chose this name in order to share an acronym with the now-defunct activist organization Students for a Democratic Society. Society for Disability Studies founders intended the name to imply scholarly rigor as well as fierce activism, reflecting the group's participatory democracy, radicalism, and direct action. Early SDS scholar-activists sought to foster scholarship imbedded in and resulting in activism, as well as activism grounded in scholarship.

Indeed, the basic premise of disability studies is activist. Our desire to dismantle ableism, to make more inclusive and accessible every aspect of society, is an explicitly activist impulse. The field argues that disability is not simply a biological condition of the individual body or mind. For example, people with disabilities disproportionately live in poverty, are unemployed, and have abysmally low rates of higher education. These are the results of specific social structures, including legal practices, industrialization and development policies, educational-access histories, tax structures, ideologies, and more. Just as the feminization of poverty is neither natural nor unavoidable, the high unemployment rates experienced by people with disabilities are neither natural nor unavoidable. Through history, sociology, economics, and other academic fields of scholarship, disability studies scholars are peeling away the many layers of ideology that have legitimated the isolation, poverty, discrimination, exclusion, and hostility experienced by many people with disabilities.[16] Disability is, as the field of disability studies posits, a life experience profoundly shaped by and inseparable from ideology, social institutions, and power hierarchies. Arguing that disability is not simply a biological condition may initially read as a placid claim, but it is instead a boldly radical claim that demands changes such as access to employment that is safe and that provides a living wage.

An additional premise of disability studies and disability activists is that, simply put, disability is not the end of the world. In fact, disability and illness are "part of what makes us human." As scholar and activist Alison Kafer has stated, the assumption that "disability is a fate worse than death or that disability prohibits a full life" is ableist. When disability is cast as an unending tragedy that eradicates an individual's future, we as a society are given permission to dismiss that individual's educational, employment, or civic rights. When we cast positive futures as those absent of disability, we assume a terrible future for all people with disabilities. Again in Kafer's words, assuming "that a 'good' future naturally and obviously depends upon the eradication of disability" is "colored by histories of ableism and disability oppression."[17] Laws, policies, and practices grounded in this erroneous assumption profoundly harm and limit not only people with disabilities, but all of us.

These claims are radical and discomforting. If unjust social conditions are constructed by human assumptions, actions, and institutions, then activists can transform social conditions by changing human perceptions, actions, and institutions. What is made can be undone. Activism matters.

Activist Matters

Losing one's sight or a limb due to inadequate safety precautions in the workplace is an outrage. Experiencing irreparable lung damage due to an employer's neglect of health and environmental protections is an outrage. Neither, however, inevitably results in a life of tragedy, unemployment, or all-encompassing misery. Nor does being born with a disability inevitably result in a tragic life. Presuming tragedy creates the social conditions that foster tragedy. Disability activists and scholars, then, teach us to be outraged by the denials of work or dismissals from work experienced by people with disabilities, who are presumed to be economically undeserving or irrelevant. Disability activists and scholars also cite the many cases when capital accumulation is valued over human lives, or when democratic governments fail to protect their citizens. The pervasive ableism in education, employment, social welfare, and popular culture is outrageous. Ableism demonizes disabled people, their bodies, and their futures as hopeless and undesirable, and then marks disabled people as incapable of exercising or ineligible for the rights of citizenship.

It is in the joint interests of disability and labor activists and scholars to create an accessible common ground that will enable us to rethink fundamental assumptions. When we dismiss disabled people as tragic and lacking any positive future, we grant permission for the denial of their educational, employment, and civic rights, just as the dismissal of working-class people as incapable of positive futures leads to the denial of rights and opportunities. Safe living and working conditions matter for all. Recognizing the exploitive nature of unsafe working conditions, while recognizing the ableism often present in worker safety activism, allows us to build activist coalitions of consequence.

The activist and scholarly challenge is thus to wrestle with the apparent conundrum of campaigning for worker safety to prevent disability while not presuming disability to be inherently tragic. This requires the rethinking of fundamental assumptions and the creation of scholarly and activist strategies that encompass rather than avoid such conundrums.

For labor historians and other scholars, this may involve the initial uncovering of the omnipresence and ordinariness of disability. It may include using disability analytically to better understand core labor history concepts, such as worker, capitalism, poverty, care labor, productivity, skilled work, and labor activism. One might consider, for example, how workers and unions used the language and concept of disability to demarcate good laborers from bad when they urged apprentices to "earn a competence." Labor historians have recognized that defining specific tasks and types of work as "skilled" or "unskilled" is not culturally neutral. These definitions are racialized and gendered. In intersecting ways, "skilled" and "unskilled" labor divisions also build on ableist notions of bodies and work capacity—they are, to coin a term, ableized.

For activists and scholars, confronting this conundrum might also include addressing disability segregation within places of employment, education, neighborhoods, and our social lives. Labor historians in concert with other scholars have revealed the policies that have explicitly created and then reinforced racial and gender segregation. Disability segregation is real, and its creation involved similar processes. Such segregation discourages and erodes effective coalitions for social justice and worker safety.

Most fundamentally, perhaps, rejecting the valuing of human bodies and minds based on their adherence to an idealized and often artificial standard of ability—a standard few of us can meet for even a small portion of our lives—can allow scholar-activists to begin demanding worker safety in a non-ableist framework. Today, with my forty-some-year-old body, with eyesight enabled by the prosthetics of eyeglasses, and with my female uterus, I have entered the workplace of academia. With such an embodiment, I would have been rejected as incapable of doing this work in earlier time periods. Whether we identify as disabled or not, all of us either have, currently do, or someday will fail to meet historically specific standards of ideal bodily and mental capacity. Despite this, and perhaps because of it, our safety and basic welfare are important.

Confronting racism and sexism leads scholar-activists in the right direction. It is time, and to the benefit of all of us, to continue in that pursuit by confronting ableism. Confronting ableism enables labor and disability activists to better build powerful coalitions around the shared goals of safe and just wage employment for all people. By confronting ableism we recognize not only our shared goals, but also the daily realities of our shared constituencies. These efforts are civic labors that matter.

Notes

For this relatively short essay, the list of those who provided invaluable guidance is quite long. Eric Fure-Slocum and Kristen Anderson were smart and patient editors. Additional thanks are due to Susan Burch, Jim Ferris, Chelsea Griffis, Catherine Kudlick, Michael Rembis, and Morgan Tuff.

1. U.S. Department of Labor, Bureau of Labor Statistics, "Persons with a Disability: Labor Force Characteristics Summary," 2013, accessed July 22, 2014, www.bls.gov.

2. *Ableism* is the discrimination or prejudice against people with disabilities.

3. Among others, Simi Linton theorizes the rejection of disability as a problem in her important *Claiming Disability: Knowledge and Identity* (New York: New York University Press, 1998).

4. This chapter is shaped by my continued consideration of Alison Kafer's tremendously smart *Feminist Queer Crip* (Bloomington: Indiana University Press, 2012).

5. Sarah F. Rose, "'Crippled' Hands: Disability in Labor and Working-Class History," *Labor: Studies in Working-Class History of the Americas* 2.1 (spring 2005): 27–54; Audra Jennings, "'The Greatest Numbers . . . Will Be Wage Earners': Organized Labor and Disability Activism, 1945–1953," *Labor: Studies in Working-Class History of the Americas* 4.4 (winter 2007): 35–52; Nancy M. Forestell, "'And I Feel Like I'm Dying from Mining for Gold': Disability, Gender, and the Mining Community, 1920–1950," *Labor: Studies in Working-Class History of the Americas* 3.3 (2007): 77–93; John Williams-Searle, "Cold Charity: Manhood, Brotherhood, and the Transformation of Disability," in *The New Disability History: American Perspectives*, edited by Paul K. Longmore and Lauri Umansky (New York: New York University Press, 2001), 157–86.

6. John Fabian Witt, *The Accidental Republic: Crippled Workingmen, Destitute Widows, and the Remaking of American Law* (Cambridge, Mass.: Harvard University Press, 2004), 24, 38.

7. Kim E. Nielsen, *A Disability History of the United States* (Boston: Beacon Press, 2012), 157–60; Barbara Ellen Smith, *Digging Our Graves: Coal Miners and the Struggle over Black Lung Disease* (Philadelphia: Temple University Press, 1987), 14; William Graebner, *Coal-Mining Safety* (Urbana-Champaign: University of Illinois Press, 1970), 56. For more on coal mining and the strikes of the 1970s, see Smith, *Digging Our Graves*; Paul F. Clark, *The Miners' Fight for Democracy: Arnold Miller and the Reform of the United Mine Workers* (Ithaca: New York State School of Industrial and Labor Relations, Cornell University, 1981); Robert L. Lewis, *Black Coal Miners in America: Race, Class, and Community Conflict, 1870–1980* (Louisville: University Press of Kentucky, 1987); Richard A. Brisbin, *A Strike Like No Other Strike: Law and Resistance during the Pittston Coal Strike of 1989–1990* (Baltimore, Md.: Johns Hopkins University Press, 2002); and Robyn Muncy, "Coal-Fired Reform: Social Citizenship, Dissident Miners, and the Great Society," *Journal of American History* 96.1 (2009): 72–98.

8. Rose, "'Crippled' Hands," 41–45.

9. Claudia Clark, *Radium Girls: Women and Industrial Health Reform, 1910–1935* (Chapel Hill: University of North Carolina Press, 1997).

10. Rose, "'Crippled' Hands," 43–44.

11. Sarah Abrevaya Stein, "Deaf American Jewish Culture in Historical Perspective," *American Jewish History* 95.3 (September 2009): 278–79. For other examples, see Susan Burch, *Signs of Resistance: American Deaf Cultural History, 1900 to 1942* (New York: New York University Press, 2002); Robert M. Buchanan, *Illusions of Equality: Deaf Americans in School and Factory, 1850–1950* (Washington, D.C.: Gallaudet University Press, 1999); David Gerber, "Blind and Enlightened: The Contested Origins of the Egalitarian Politics of the Blinded Veterans Association," in *The New Disability History: American Perspectives*, edited by Longmore and Umansky, 313–74; and Paul K. Longmore and David Goldberger, "The League of the Physically Handicapped and the Great Depression: A Case Study in the New Disability History," *Journal of American History* 87.3 (December 2000): 888–922.

12. Nielsen, *Disability History of the United States*, 150–53; Jennings, "'The Greatest Numbers . . . Will Be Wage Earners.'" This unity remains a struggle. Individuals with developmental, cognitive, and psychiatric disabilities are often excluded or devalued in disability activism and identity coalitions.

13. Paul Strachan quoted in Jennings, "'The Greatest Numbers . . . Will Be Wage Earners,'" 66.

14. Lindsey Patterson, "Points of Access: Rehabilitation Centers, Summer Camps, and Student Life in the Making of Disability Activism, 1960–1973," *Journal of Social History* 46.2 (winter 2012): 482.

15. Nielsen, *Disability History of the United States*, 167.

16. Historian Paul K. Longmore's personal account of experiencing and protesting work disincentives in federal disability-related welfare policies is an excellent introduction to this. Paul K. Longmore, *Why I Burned My Book and Other Essays on Disability* (Philadelphia: Temple University Press, 2003).

17. Kafer, *Feminist Queer Crip*, 2.

CHAPTER 16

Engaged Scholarship and
the Living-Wage Movement

Stephanie Luce

In the early 1990s, I was a sociology graduate student in Madison, Wisconsin, trying to complete a doctorate while engaged in local politics. When the Milwaukee chapter of the New Party launched a living-wage campaign in 1995, I became involved, knocking on doors and pushing for its passage. Having participated in many different issue campaigns in my life as a young activist, I had not yet bridged the gap between my political and academic interests. I had no inkling then that this issue was going to become the focus of my scholarly work.

After Wisconsin, I moved to Southern California and worked on a study with University of California–Riverside economist Robert Pollin, estimating the impact of a proposed living-wage ordinance in Los Angeles. The Los Angeles City Council passed the ordinance in 1997, giving a boost to the emerging movement. As campaigns spread across the country, Pollin began receiving requests for additional studies, but because we could not meet every request we decided to write a book explaining our methodology. This resulted in our book, *The Living Wage: Building a Fair Economy*. It also resulted in my decision to change my dissertation topic to one focused on the implementation and monitoring of the ordinances after passage. This dissertation eventually became *Fighting for a Living Wage*. As the political demand for living wages has only gotten louder, and the social need greater, I have now worked on living-wage campaigns in some form or another for twenty years.

In this chapter I discuss some of the rewards and challenges of that work, focusing on three key themes. First, I provide background on the minimum-wage and living-wage scholarship and campaigns, showing the ways in which theory and practice can intersect. I argue that academic work can be useful for campaigns, but that there are real challenges of working within a politicized context when you are expected to be "objective." Second, I explore some of the tensions that can arise between academics and activists over not only how to use research, but what questions should be examined and who should control both the research process and the outcomes. I argue that there is a crucial need for some form of detached criticism and evaluation of campaigns and movements, but both parties must be sensitive to the power differentials and politicized nature of the work. Finally, I discuss some of the issues that have arisen while I balanced activism with an academic career.

Theory and Practice: Debates and Campaigns

Since at least the days of Karl Marx, writers and activists have advocated for theory and practice to intersect. But this combination, whether defined as engaged scholarship or praxis, has provoked controversy. Critics on one side argue that academics lose their independence and objectivity by engaging in applied, activist research. On the other end, plenty of activists have dismissed academics' writing about movements as distracting and possibly a waste of time or a luxury that we cannot afford.

My perspective is that to make scholarship relevant to practice we must get our hands dirty and apply it, test it, and revise it. That requires theorizing about social movements, conducting research to test hypotheses and evaluate campaigns, and debating and revising theories of power, social change, and movement building. Sociologist Richard Flacks asserts that the bulk of research conducted by academics is of little use for those trying to improve the world. Instead, he argues, social scientists have an obligation to develop movement-relevant theories.[1] At the same time, activists must be open to critical evaluation of their own campaigns. For example, Myles Horton helped develop the Highlander Center, a school for activist education founded in Tennessee during the 1930s, because he believed activists must have space to learn the larger context of oppression and to reflect on their own life experiences and efforts to change. Horton believed that action had to immediately follow learning, in order to make them both relevant.[2] But going beyond critical pedagogy requires that what happens in classrooms and movements is later analyzed, assessed, and incorporated into theory. As David Croteau, William Hoynes, and Charlotte Ryan assert, "both activism and theory . . . are diminished by the failure to integrate the two."[3]

The connection between theory and practice in the living-wage movement, my own area of expertise, has not always been clear. The activists who launched the first living-wage campaign in Baltimore in 1994 did not choose the campaign because theory suggested it. Instead, it began with a problem. Pastors noticed that a lot of people coming into food pantries and shelters were employed but not earning enough to cover their basic expenses. Furthermore, some of these workers were employed in tourism and service-sector jobs that were part of development projects that the city had been promoting and building as a way to bring jobs to the city. Since city officials had asked for the communities' support to build these projects (such as Baltimore's Inner Harbor retail and entertainment zone), the pastors and community activists went back to those city officials to demand they find a way to raise wages for workers. After the Baltimore victory, activists around the country adopted the idea. As with Baltimore, this was not driven by a theory of social change or academic studies suggesting this as the most strategic use of resources, but by their own analysis that the idea was popular and winnable. The living-wage concept caught on quickly, spreading from Baltimore to Minneapolis, St. Paul, Milwaukee, Portland (Oregon), and elsewhere. The idea was popular with voters. But by the time a campaign was launched in Chicago, opponents began to mobilize, including the chambers of commerce and industry groups such as the Employment Policies Institute (EmPI). The EmPI commissioned an economic impact study by George Tolley of the University of Chicago and two colleagues. The study, presented to the Chicago City Council in 1996, found that a living-wage ordinance would cost the city $20 million a year, which would lead to a permanent tax increase and a loss of 1,300 jobs.[4] The city council decided not to consider the ordinance. (It was this study that prompted the Los Angeles campaign to look for additional research, hiring our team at Riverside.)

The Baltimore ordinance, and other early ordinances, applied to firms receiving city service contracts (often these were services that had once been performed by city employees but had more recently been contracted out to private firms for trash removal, janitorial services, parking meter collection, and so on). As the movement spread, activists expanded the ordinances to cover a range of categories of employment: direct city employees; firms receiving economic development subsidies; and firms operating on city-owned property (such as airports and ports). A few cities eventually adopted citywide minimum wages that covered all firms operating within city borders.[5]

Each living-wage campaign looked different; some lasted several years, whereas others were resolved fairly quickly. Some were led by labor union organizations like a labor council or Jobs with Justice, while others were spearheaded by community organizations such as the Association of Community Organizations for Reform Now (ACORN). Most were adopted by city councils, but a few went to the ballot. In any case, almost all included the formation of a labor-community coalition, a campaign to pressure the city council, and a battle of ideas and values. Below I describe three of the campaigns in which I was involved. Through my work on the economics of living-wage ordinances and related work on the dynamics of the campaigns and politics of enforcement, I have encountered numerous challenges, such as navigating the delicate balance of being simultaneously an activist and an academic. I have also had to find a way to maintain personal relationships with organizers that I write about, always working to build a space for constructive engagement where the research can be honest and critical about campaigns, and yet beneficial to the movement.

First, however, I discuss the context in which the movement emerged—a period in which the economics discipline was undergoing transformation, at least in regard to how economists understood the impact of minimum-wage laws. This work helped shape the direction of our living-wage research, serving as a useful barometer of the connection between research and social movements.

The Minimum-Wage Debates

The modern living-wage movement emerged just as a fierce debate about minimum wages raged. Neoclassical economics, the dominant strand of economic theory in the 1990s, denounced minimum-wage policies: if government mandates a wage floor, firms will be forced to pay wages above the marginal productivity of their lowest-paid workers and consequently will lay off workers. In other words, neoclassical economists said that a living wage would cause job loss. In addition, these economists predicted that a living-wage ordinance could lead to other negative consequences. Cities would raise taxes to cover the cost of higher service contracts, and small businesses would be unable to compete for costly city contracts. Firms would leave the city, or not come at all.[6] To those who had studied economics in college or those who were persuaded by neoclassical theory, this assertion made sense: wage increases resulted in decreased levels of employment. Economics textbooks asserted that this was the law of supply and demand. Policymakers and newspaper editorial staffs repeated the argument, continually stressing that living-wage ordinances would harm workers.

Yet around the same time that the early living-wage campaigns formed, a few economists were conducting "natural experiments" on this very question. Traditional experimental research is difficult to do in the social sciences, as it is nearly impossible to create a controlled environment and to isolate one treatment or policy from others. But economists David Card and Alan Krueger identified natural experiments available for analysis, such as when one state raised its minimum wage while neighboring states did not. Card and Krueger studied a number of these cases; one of the more famous studies examined the impact of a statewide minimum-wage increase in New Jersey in 1992. Card and Krueger surveyed 410 fast food restaurants along the New Jersey–Pennsylvania border. If neoclassical theory held, then fast food restaurants, highly dependent on cheap labor, would be among the first to lay off workers when their wages were raised while competitor restaurants just across the border did not have to raise wages. To their surprise, they found no evidence of job loss in New Jersey restaurants.[7]

What explained this outcome? Perhaps New Jersey restaurants could not function with fewer employees, so instead of laying off workers, they raised prices. Card and Krueger found that prices did indeed go up, but only by a small amount (on average, a hamburger went from $1 to $1.01). Other explanations focused on workplace behavior and workers' roles as consumers. By raising wages, firms experienced what are called "efficiency wage gains": workers who got the raise stuck around longer, reducing turnover; they gained skills and became more productive; they might even have been absent less as they worked harder to hold onto their jobs. Research suggests that employers do experience some savings through efficiency wage gains, though not likely enough to entirely compensate for the full wage increase. Another possibility is that workers with wage increases spend those higher wages in the community. That in turn creates increased demand for goods and services, generating more economic activity and a virtuous cycle. Keynesian economists call this the "multiplier effect." Card and Krueger did not claim to have a definitive answer for why they found no evidence of job loss, but they replicated their work in other localities and found the same results.[8]

Meanwhile a few scholars began conducting prospective studies for living-wage campaigns, attempting to predict what would happen should cities raise their wages. And a few years after the Baltimore ordinance was adopted, they started evaluating the impact. These were not easy cases of natural experiments, as most living-wage ordinances applied only to city service contracts and covered a small number of workers. Still, academics were able to conduct impact studies in a number of cities using firm and worker surveys, contract analysis, and examination of city budgets. These studies confirmed what Card and Krueger had found: no drop in employment, no significant increase in prices, and some reduction in turnover.[9]

Of course, none of this was happening in a vacuum. Conservative policymakers, writers, and organizations went on the offensive, challenging these findings. The EmPI, which is funded in part by the National Restaurant Association, provided economists David Neumark and William Wascher payroll records from seventy-one fast food restaurants. Neumark and Wascher found that the minimum wage led to employment loss in New Jersey, contrary to Card and Krueger's findings. Richard Berman, head of the EmPI, wrote a *Wall Street Journal* op-ed citing their study, stating that Card and Krueger's findings were "worse than flawed."[10] According to economist John Schmitt, "Berman's allegations kicked off a public op-ed and private whispering campaign to undermine the creditability of the study and the reputations of Card and Krueger."[11] Card and Krueger responded with a detailed explanation of their methodology. This, and all the public attention, pushed Neumark and Wascher to revisit their work. They conducted their own survey, reran their numbers, and found no statistical difference in employment growth in New Jersey and Pennsylvania in their own survey sample. However, they maintained that using the combined samples from their own work and those collected by the EmPI showed a negative impact from the minimum wage.[12]

The battle over minimum and living-wage studies continued into the early 2000s. Despite backtracking somewhat on the minimum-wage studies, David Neumark continued to publish studies asserting that both minimum-wage laws and living-wage ordinances were more harmful than helpful. Using the Bureau of Labor Statistics' Current Population Survey (CPS) data to analyze the impact of living-wage ordinances, he found that, while they reduced poverty in cities, they did result in some job loss. Economists Mark Brenner, Jeannette Wicks-Lim, and Robert Pollin challenged his methodology, asserting that there was no way to properly analyze the impact of living-wage ordinances with CPS data, since living-wage ordinances cover relatively few workers in every city and the CPS sample size is not large enough, nor drawn correctly, to represent those covered workers.[13]

Over the next decade, from the early 2000s to the present, new studies of minimum-wage laws, using advanced methodologies and statistical techniques, confirmed Card and Krueger's original findings and their challenge to neoclassical interpretations. Even the mainstream of the economics field has shifted its thinking. While no consensus on the actual dynamics at play exists yet, an increasing number of economists agree that raises in the minimum wage do not lead to job loss and that any potential negative impacts are outweighed by the positives.[14] In early 2014, over six hundred economists, including seven Nobel Prize laureates, signed a letter calling on Congress to raise the federal minimum wage to $10.10 per hour, stating that the weight of evidence shows a minimum-wage increase would not hurt employment and, in fact, could act as a stimulus for job creation.[15]

This shift in the field of economics, however, has only recently and rather unevenly translated to policy. Most policy makers continue to assert that raising wages results in job loss and possibly inflation (a claim that not even the anti-minimum-wage economists make), and minimum-wage and living-wage opponents have taken a hard stance. In 2012, New York City mayor Michael Bloomberg compared a living-wage ordinance to a Soviet planned economy and asserted that it would drive employers out of the city.[16] The next year, the EmPI's Michael Saltsman wrote a *Forbes Magazine* op-ed headlined "The Record Is Clear: Minimum Wage Hikes Destroy Jobs."[17] This striking disjuncture between the academic research and public commentary gets at the heart of some of the difficult questions about engaged scholarship. It highlights the ways in which knowledge is political and politicized, and it raises questions about objectivity, facts, and methodology. Engaged scholars should see it as an obligation to try to reduce this divide. The following three cases of living-wage campaigns explore these issues and tensions in more detail.

Los Angeles: Finding a Place in a Movement

When the Los Angeles Alliance for a New Economy (LAANE) launched its living-wage campaign in 1996, it had a plan to take the concept born in Baltimore and expand it beyond only service contractors.[18] LAANE, the research "think and do tank" founded by the Hotel Employees and Restaurant Employees (HERE) union, also realized that adopting an ordinance was just one tool. Workers ultimately needed to belong to unions to win the broader workplace changes. The living wage could increase the hourly wage, but it could neither guarantee minimum hours of work nor protect against layoffs or unfair treatment.

LAANE approached economist Robert Pollin, then at the University of California–Riverside, to conduct an impact study of the Los Angeles proposal. This project, as I noted earlier, opened the door to my decades of living-wage research. Pollin agreed to conduct the study for the campaign, but he insisted on total independence and the freedom to publish the results, even if he found the living wage to have negative consequences, including a loss of jobs. LAANE's director, Madeline Janis, readily agreed to his request. In her view, the study was stronger if it was written by an objective academic. The LA proposal was ambitious: the living wage would apply not only to service contracts, but also to subcontractors, concessionaries on city-owned properties (such as the airport), and recipients of large economic development subsidies. The ordinance would mandate that firms pay a wage of $7.25 per hour with health benefits, or $8.50 without such benefits—all at a time when the federal minimum wage was $4.25 per hour.

We concluded that while the absolute value of the LA proposal was significant— up to $68 million—the ordinance would be a relatively small expense for most of the one thousand firms affected. In fact, the cost of the wage increase would amount to only 1.5 percent of the average firm's operating costs. We found that the costs of the ordinance were relatively low and that the benefits, applying to over 7,600 workers, were significant. Furthermore, we predicted that the ordinance would not result in job loss or higher taxes, as affected firms had other means of passing on or absorbing the wage increases. First, the firms would recoup some of the costs through savings resulting from lower turnover and absenteeism, as well as higher productivity from workers staying on the job longer. Second, firms and municipalities could absorb some of the wage increases by paying less in contract overhead or salaries for management.[19]

As Janis had predicted, the study found little negative impact but significant positive impact for the affected workers. But she also had a vision of a campaign in which research was only one component. She described the campaign like a wheel with many spokes: one spoke was the religious partners, engaged in making a moral and ethical case for the living wage. Another spoke was small-business owners who organized for the living wage because they felt it could make things fairer and better for small businesses. Another spoke was the worker organizing. Research was just one more spoke in a multifaceted campaign.

This vision highlighted that research or facts alone would not win the day, but that academic skills and expertise could aid the larger process. Janis recognized that policy campaigns are not just about who has the best idea, or about who has the most solid data to support their claims. Social scientists may be tempted to believe that the facts should speak for themselves, but this is rarely or never the case. A few city council members may have been swayed by our report—and indeed, the ordinance was adopted in 1997—but it is unlikely that many of them even read it. Instead, they were more likely swayed by pressure from constituents, personal testimony of city workers, or even visits from clergy. But by having the report and being able to counter the opposition's claims, the living-wage campaign was on more solid ground. The success in LA gave a boost to the emerging movement.

New Orleans: What about the Facts?

The important but often constrained role of "facts" in living-wage campaigns became even clearer in our next major effort, this one in the Deep South. In 1996, activists in New Orleans had begun to collect signatures to qualify a ballot initiative that would establish a citywide minimum wage at one dollar above the federal minimum wage. Not all municipalities have the authority to set their own wages: it depends on whether the state has "home-rule" laws. New Orleans did have that right, but after the ballot measure qualified by collecting fifty thousand signatures, opponents of a local minimum wage—particularly the hotel and restaurant lobbyists—pressured the Louisiana legislature to overturn "home rule" and block the city's authority to set its own wage. Living-wage proponents, led by ACORN, took the case to the courts.

My colleagues at the University of Massachusetts–Amherst and I decided to conduct a study of the potential economic impact of the minimum wage. Opponents argued that the higher wage would cause economic harm to the city and state, and therefore the state had a vested interest in blocking the wage. We launched a survey of New Orleans businesses to assess their employment levels, wages, and business expenses, in order to estimate the potential impact.[20] Our survey of 444 firms found that a one-dollar increase would have little impact on the average business. We estimated that the total costs, including the mandated increase and associated ripple-effect wage increases within the firm, would amount to less than 1 percent of total operating costs. For a few firms, the costs would be larger, particularly those service industries that relied heavily on low-wage labor, such as eating and drinking establishments and hotels. The average increase would be approximately 2 percent. But even if this cost was passed on entirely to consumers in the form of higher prices, the impact would be minimal. We compiled an extensive report, examining every possible impact of the proposal, and estimated that approximately 47,000 workers would benefit from the raise.[21]

The courts allowed the measure to go on the city ballot in February 2002, and the measure won, with 63 percent voting in favor. Employers went back to the courts in an effort to block the law from being implemented. We were brought in once again to testify that the law would not cause economic harm to the state. The first judge refused to block implementation, but then the case went to the state supreme court. We presented our extensive report. The opposition presented a surprisingly simple case. They did not present their own data, and they barely challenged ours. Opponents did not even bring in any business owners to testify that they would be hurt by the higher wage. It seemed like an easy victory for living-wage advocates, but the court quickly ruled against them, blocking implementation of the law stating that only the state, and not New Orleans or any other city, had the authority to set a minimum wage.[22]

The experience showed even more starkly that policy is not necessarily set according to the best research. We employed over a dozen people to conduct a detailed survey over several months and put in hundreds of hours of work to produce a report and then testimony. We had double and triple checked our calculations, expecting the opposition to search for any possible mistake. Yet in the end, the opposing lawyers paid little attention, and the Louisiana Supreme Court justices did not engage with the research in their decision. The court ruled: "Because we find La. R.S. 23:642, prohibiting local governmental subdivisions from establishing a minimum wage rate which a private employer would be required to pay employees, is a legitimate exercise of the state's police power, we conclude the City's minimum wage law, which sets a minimum wage rate private employers are required to pay their employees, abridges the police power of the state. Therefore, we find the minimum wage law invalid."[23] While we will never know for certain, it seems that heavy pressure from powerful employers and their lobbyists had more influence on the decision than any data.

Still, while the research was not the deciding factor in the outcome, I would argue that the results helped bolster the campaign. Advocates could use the findings to make a stronger case for their position, countering claims made by opponents that the ordinance would do more harm than good. Despite the loss, advocates continued their efforts to pass ordinances around the country.

New York: Going Backward?

New York adopted living-wage ordinances applying to city contractors in 1996 and home-care workers in 2002. But in 2010, a coalition formed to pass the Fair Wages for New Yorkers Act, designed to require that firms receiving economic development assistance pay their employees no less than $10 per hour. Although Michael Bloomberg was the mayor who signed the 2002 ordinance into law, he strongly opposed the new effort, arguing that the measure would kill jobs and drive away business. Perhaps to delay a vote, the mayor's Economic Development Corporation (EDC) commissioned a study on the potential impact of the ordinance. By this point, numerous economists had conducted impact studies of living-wage ordinances around the country, moving beyond prospective studies that attempted to estimate potential impact to post-implementation studies. Yet the EDC chose to commission a $1 million contract to the conservative consulting group Charles Rivers Associates, which brought on board the notorious living- and minimum-wage opponent David Neumark. This was shocking; to my knowledge, no living-wage study had cost anywhere close to that amount. The study seemed a deliberate stall tactic as well as borderline graft. This was particularly true when the report was initially released and it became clear that the authors had not even studied the correct proposal. Nor did they bother to contact city officials from other cities that had similar laws already in place or include analyses of these experiences in the report.[24]

By the time of this campaign in 2010, the living-wage movement was more than fifteen years old. For the most part, the movement had been expanding and growing: new campaigns tested the boundaries by covering new categories of workers, such as going from only city contracts to including airports and then geographic zones and entire cities. Ordinances also pushed the required wage levels upward, going from the poverty line for a family of three, to the poverty line for a family of four, and in some cases, up to 110 or 120 percent of the poverty line. While the New York Fair Wages Act attempted to expand coverage to economic development projects, it was discouraging to see a proposed wage level of only $10. At that time, many living-wage ordinances, in place for more than 10 years, had been increasing annually and were up to around $13 or $14 an hour. Washington State had a statewide minimum of $8.55 per hour, and San Francisco had its own citywide minimum of $9.79 per hour. For New York City to be so hotly debating $10 an hour, in one of the highest cost-of-living cities in the country, was disheartening. Nonetheless, the opposition fiercely objected to the very modest proposal.[25]

For the Fair Wages Act to be passed, City Council Speaker Christine Quinn needed to move the proposal to a vote. Quinn, a Democrat known for several progressive positions, had her sights on running for mayor in 2013, after Bloomberg left office.[26] She played it cautiously, to avoid upsetting the business community, and let the proposal languish for over a year in 2010 and 2011.

Although I did not conduct research on the proposal, on several occasions I was invited to submit testimony based on prior research in support of the act. Once again, the business community mobilized to fight the bill. And the movement appeared to be going backward in New York City. In other cities, living-wage opponents initially had opposed the ordinances by claiming they would cause massive job loss and hardship. Over the years, as more and more cities adopted ordinances and as evidence of the dire predictions failed to materialize, opponents began to make more nuanced arguments. They argued that, while employment might not drop, employers would begin to shift hiring strategies, seeking more educated, white workers, instead of workers with less education or people of color (what economists call "labor-labor substitution"). Their argument was that the ordinances would hurt the most vulnerable workers—those the laws were attempting to assist. Opponents also argued that the higher wage requirement would make it harder for minority and women business owners to compete for city contracts. These were more complex critiques made when the extreme negative outcomes previously predicted did not appear to hold in the first hundred or so cities that passed living-wage laws.

Yet in New York, the rhetoric appeared to go back in time. The *New York Post* published an article titled "Death by Living Wage," which began, "What, exactly, do Manhattan Borough President Scott Stringer, city Comptroller John Liu, Bronx BP Ruben Diaz and 28 City Council members have against poor, young immigrants and blacks?" The author claimed that "mountains of research" showed that the law would at best result in workers "stealing" city subsidy money from their bosses, and at worst it would kill jobs altogether.[27] This was in 2010, long after the Card and Krueger studies, and after the tide had already turned in the field of economics.

Similarly, chamber of commerce representatives testified that the proposal would kill jobs. The president of the Manhattan Chamber stated, "In city after city wherever wage mandates have been tried, the very people who are supposed to be at benefit are hurt the most."[28] One chamber testifier insisted that the council should disregard the many references to research and studies that they likely would hear since all that matters is "the truth," which this speaker defined simply with the unsubstantiated maxim that "living wage laws kill jobs."[29]

Finally, the emergence of Occupy Wall Street on the scene in September 2011 exerted increased pressure on the city council to address inequality. Quinn scheduled hearings to begin in November 2011. In the end, living-wage advocates agreed to a weaker form of the proposal that would cover only the developers receiving subsidies, but not the tenants in those developments. For example, the developer of a mall would be required to pay direct employees a living wage, but the retail shops and fast food outlets inside the mall would not be covered.

Challenges for Engaged Scholarship and Activism

These cases highlight key tensions for engaged scholarship and activism, evident in the living-wage work but likely present in other arenas, as well. There is no doubt that the research has played an important role in this movement. Advocates need a legitimate and fact-based response to the claims of job loss and economic hardship. Serious activists also wanted to investigate the objections to see if they held merit. After all, if the living wage did result in job loss, or if it meant the most vulnerable workers would lose their jobs to more privileged workers, activists would want to know and respond accordingly. Research allowed the movement to understand potential pitfalls, such as how raising wages could result in reduced government assistance for some workers or how implementation and enforcement could be improved.[30] At the same time, the role of research was far less prominent than some scholars might expect. Many campaigns were fought on the grounds of ideology, political lobbying, and even deceptive tactics, more so than on data. The "best idea"—the most economically sound proposal, or the most solid research—is not necessarily what wins.

Still, even when the research itself does not determine the campaign outcome, it can still play a valuable role in organizing. Bolstered with data, activists can solidify their coalitions and assuage concerns that living-wage ordinances may in fact have unintended consequences. Furthermore, the research can help coalition members educate themselves so they are more confident talking to their elected officials or to the press. This kind of applied research, done in service of a campaign, is often useful and affords academics and activists the opportunity to work together.

As social scientists, we are trained to gather data and use the best methods possible to analyze and interpret. But in the political world, "data" are not seen as objective. The politics of the researchers come into play as well. For example, while living-wage scholars attempted to maintain their objectivity, the campaigns sometimes made the researchers into campaign targets. The EmPI's booklet, *Living Wage Policy: The Basics*, contained sections investigating researchers who had done pro-living-wage research, such as "Who is Robert Pollin?" and "Who is David Reynolds?" that highlighted the progressive affiliations each held. For their part, living-wage advocates attempted to find researchers who appeared to have the most credibility: university academics are more credible than union researchers and peer-reviewed journal studies are more credible than trade books. My PhD is in sociology, but on more than one occasion advocates asked if they could list me as an economist when I was testifying before city councils.

Despite this, I have been surprised that I haven't been challenged more often. In my two decades of doing this work, I have yet to have opponents attempt to discredit me based on my own long history of political activism. Even more surprisingly, I have yet to have an opponent challenge the heart of the work. I am certain there must be errors in our work, as it involves hundreds of calculations and multiple datasets. However, to this day, not one person has questioned a number or formula in any of the reports, which makes me wonder whether the opposition even reads the studies, instead focusing on ideological arguments.

My colleagues and I have worked hard to maintain objectivity in relation to the data and results. We have asked outside readers to review the work; we have double and triple checked calculations. I remind myself of the early advice of my advisor, who challenged me to find the weaknesses in the campaigns, if they exist. On the other hand, I am honest about the reality that I am not neutral about the topic. I believe that wages are too low in this country and that our economy could be structured in more just and effective ways.

Because I have spent time as a political activist, I understand that in campaigns I am asked to play the role of expert, discuss the economic impact of ordinances, and provide scholarly advice on how best to implement the laws. My role is not central, and it is not to give an impassioned ideological argument. I have been able to accept this role and see it for what it is. That may be difficult for many researchers who have been trained to believe the data should speak for itself.

It is much more difficult for me to remain neutral when I read op-eds or listen to testimony that blatantly disregards the research. Even the economists who find a negative impact from minimum-wage hikes no longer claim it results in mass job loss or inflation. But policy makers and pundits continue to assert these fictions as fact. I find it challenging to engage with the press or politicians who insist on simplifying and reject nuance. As a researcher, I know that these issues are complex, so I want to acknowledge the assumptions I use in my data analysis and note potential caveats. Most reporters, however, are rarely interested in this level of specificity.

Relations with Activists

So far I have focused primarily on the tensions that arise in the context of dueling academic studies and tensions that arise in the campaigns. But my many years as a living-wage researcher have also raised minor internal tensions for me, including how to handle my relationships with activists. Initially, we were contracted to conduct impact studies by people we did not know. Although I was politically sympathetic to the living-wage concept, I had never met anyone at LAANE when we started our study of the Los Angeles ordinance. Over the years, I have come to know many living-wage supporters and activists well, and a few have become close friends. For the most part, this has not created tension around the economic-impact work. But I also have studied and written about the dynamics of the campaigns and the organizations behind them. At times I had serious critiques of the ways in which campaigns were run or the ways that organizations functioned in coalition. This is trickier. If I write a negative assessment of a particular organization, I might find it difficult to get access in the future. But I cannot allow myself to write anything that I do not agree with. At times I have dealt with this by advising the activists ahead of time that I was going to publish something that was critical. At other times, I chose not to write about the topic or campaign altogether, or spoke off the record to other researchers or journalists.

I have written about some limitations of the living-wage movement. Many campaigns are run on behalf of low-wage workers and do not involve workers themselves. I see this as problematic. The movement, I would argue, should be about building worker power in the long run, and not just passing a quick policy fix to raise wages. If workers do not even know about the laws or lack confidence to speak up for their rights, it is unlikely the laws will be enforced. In fact, in my dissertation research, I found that only a small number of cities had active and broad enforcement of the laws. In some cases, cities refused to implement the laws altogether. In many, the city took minimal steps to implement the ordinance but failed to check whether employers were complying.

In addition, the movement has at times suffered from "least common denominator" politics. Since the idea of a living wage is so popular, building a broad coalition for a campaign is easy. But that means coalitions might not agree on much else beyond living wages. Some people support living wages as a way to boost the economy and save capitalism from destructive business cycles. Others support living wages because they want to build alternative economic models. This means that while living-wage coalitions are easy to form, they can also easily fall apart. And, by sticking only to the least common denominator, you miss a chance to build deeper and more radical movements.

Another limitation of the living-wage movement can be found in target wages that are not high enough to truly cover workers' basic necessities. Before the "Fight for $15" movement, most target wages were pegged only to the federal poverty line, and most experts agree that the poverty line is out of date and too low. Furthermore, many low-wage workers struggle to get a full forty hours of work per week. This means they would need an even higher hourly wage to make a true annual living income.

These and other limitations are not necessarily a surprise to living-wage activists, many of whom recognize the constraints of their campaigns. But engaged scholars must find ways to analyze campaigns and share results in ways that help move toward the ultimate goal. While researchers must learn to accept their limited role in a campaign, they should not assume this means a passive, unilateral relationship, in which the research exists only to serve the campaign. Ideally, the relationship is bilateral. This would mean that researchers have open access to the internal workings of the organizations and campaigns in order to fully evaluate and analyze, looking for weaknesses that might prevent the organization from achieving its goals or building a larger movement. Unfortunately, that is not always easy. In some activist circles, there is a degree of anti-intellectualism—born in some cases out of frustration with irrelevant theory, but in others from a view that there is no time for debate or analysis.[31]

A serious scholar and activist must be honest about the limitations of movements or campaigns. Not everything needs to be published, but we must create space for researchers or analysts to provide constructive criticism. This means that researchers must be able and willing to be honest and forthcoming about weaknesses or problems with campaigns or proposed legislation. For example, if we found that living-wage ordinances did, in fact, have unintended negative consequences, it would be vital to share that information with activists and policymakers. Yet, in some circles, movement organizations want to control the information that is released, fearing it will hurt their cause or perhaps damage their opportunities to raise money from funders. Some organizers fear airing any internal tensions or weaknesses, knowing that opponents are ready to use any problems for their own gains. For example, I have worked with organizations or institutions that support living wages as city policy but do not pay their own staff a living wage. I also have seen activists exaggerate their victories, putting an overly positive spin on the size or depth of their coalition or the scope of the policy they passed. These are the kinds of dynamics that could undermine the work in the long run.

Balancing Activism and an Academic Career

A second internal tension relates to how to balance life as an activist with a career in academia. This has at least two dimensions. First, as activists we make ourselves vulnerable to political attacks. I have been fortunate to be on the faculty in labor studies departments that encourage applied research and activism. Labor studies is a vulnerable field, however, in many universities, under attack from administrators and state legislators. When a colleague and I were among the faculty up for tenure and "mini-tenure," respectively, our provost refused to sign off on our cases, even though we both had strong publication records and highly favorable reviews from outside readers and all levels of university committees.[32] The provost signed all the cases except ours. Luckily, we had a faculty union that filed grievances on our behalf, and our cases were settled immediately. But the provost noted that she did not think the university should give tenure in labor studies.

At that time, I managed to keep my job and progress in the university system, but I knew that I was vulnerable because of my activism. Although a few senior faculty members advised me early on to be careful about attending rallies on campus or being too visible in political work, I decided that postponing my activism until tenure was unacceptable. I could not give up political work just to keep my job. Instead, I decided to be forthright and visible, yet work extra hard to excel in my publishing, teaching, and service work.

At the same time, I have gained tremendously from engaged research. I am certain the quality of my own research would have been weaker if I had not continued to stay active in political work while writing about it. I gained many insights from organizers and campaign strategists, and I learned firsthand how individual campaigns can help build a broader movement. Unfortunately, much of the academic work currently produced is written for academics, not activists.[33] I wanted my work to be relevant to movements and organizers working to change the world. To do that, I had to stay active in movements myself. This helps me ask the right questions and keeps me focused on the audience I want both to reach and to engage. This means I seek to write articles and books that activists can read and learn from. I also want to write for other academics, but they are a secondary audience.

Second, by choosing to be active in movements and carrying out applied research for campaigns, I have been less productive in producing peer-reviewed research. This is particularly true since I received tenure. I have prioritized writing applied research reports over submitting articles to journals, and I primarily attend activist meetings and conferences rather than academic ones. There is no easy way around this choice; the hours in the day are limited. For most people, making activist work and scholarship a priority means less time to do traditional scholarly work.

Conclusion

Engaged scholarship is deeply rewarding but filled with tensions and challenges. My history with the living-wage movement has taught me that the research, no matter how important, is only one part of a larger campaign. The best study will not necessarily prevail. The work itself may only serve a limited purpose—helping campaigners respond to critics. Beyond that, I have seen clearly that the research exists inside a politicized environment. Ultimately, victory may depend on a judge or city council or voters, and research may seem irrelevant. The New York City case shows clearly that, no matter how solid the research, it can be trumped by ideological arguments and often no amount of reasoned dialogue prevails. Furthermore, I have learned that analyzing, critiquing, and writing about activists and organizations can be difficult, as it can jeopardize personal relationships, political relationships, and future access to sources. But engaged scholars cannot shy away from this difficult work. Of course, not all critique has to be put into a peer-reviewed journal article. It may be that this kind of critical research is best shared in other forums, such as white papers or popular publications sympathetic to social-justice movements. But scholars have an obligation to find ways to engage in constructive critique with the campaigns they study. This will also almost certainly help make for better scholarship, as a critical engagement with social movements, when done with an open mind and willingness to rethink assumptions, will yield the best insights.

At the same time, living-wage and minimum-wage research has played a valuable role in the movement. Over the course of the past twenty years, the economics discipline has witnessed a remarkable shift. In the early 1990s, David Card and Alan Krueger's work came as a surprise and prompted critiques asserting that it must be wrong. Over time, as the number of studies on wage floors increased and the methodologies became more sophisticated, and as evidence mounted that living wages had no discernible negative impacts, the number of economists advocating for higher wage floors has increased. The U.S. Department of Labor website now posts a "Minimum Wage Mythbusters" page, citing numerous studies that find no negative impacts of wage increases.[34] Research was utilized in most of the hundreds of living-wage and minimum-wage campaigns, the vast majority of which were victorious. It is impossible to know how the movement would have unfolded without the research, but given the constant stream of anti-living-wage arguments coming from the chambers of commerce and other business lobbyists, it is hard to imagine that politicians would have had the audacity to pass so many wage ordinances. Academics often do not get such an opportunity to influence public policy and social movements, particularly policy that can have such an immediate impact on the well-being of millions of workers.[35]

While it may be difficult to know the relevance or effect of research in each campaign, this is also true for almost any aspect of organizing. Without controlled experiments we do not know if a rally or postcard campaign had an impact. We cannot distill whether coalition building or leadership development was worth the time. Ironically, it would take solid research to evaluate these efforts. But as with any component of an organizing effort, we should evaluate the impact of research not just on the short-term direct outcomes, such as a City Council vote, but also on the long-term evolution of activist commitment, public discourse, and movement building.

Notes

Dan Clawson, Penny Lewis, Carolina Bank Muñoz, and Rachel Sherman all provided helpful comments on earlier drafts of this chapter.

1. Richard Flacks, "Knowledge for What? Thoughts on the State of Social Movement Studies," in *Rethinking Social Movements: Structure, Culture, and Emotion*, edited by Jeff Goodwin and James M. Jasper (Lanham, Md.: Rowman and Littlefield, 2004), 135–54.

2. Jon N. Hale, "Early Pedagogical Influences on the Mississippi Freedom Schools: Myles Horton and Critical Education in the Deep South," *American Education History Journal* 34 (2007): 315–30.

3. David Croteau, William Hoynes, and Charlotte Ryan, *Rhyming Hope and History: Activists, Academics, and Social Movement Scholarship* (Minneapolis: University of Minnesota Press, 2005).

4. George Tolley, Peter Bernstein, and Michael Lesage, *Economic Analysis of a Living Wage Ordinance* (Washington, D.C.: Employment Policies Institute, 1999).

5. Among the few cities adopting universal citywide minimum wages were San Francisco, California; Santa Fe, New Mexico; and Washington, D.C.

6. For examples of anti-living-wage arguments and op-eds, see Stephanie Luce, *Fighting for a Living Wage* (Ithaca, N.Y.: Cornell University Press, 2004).

7. David Card and Alan B. Krueger, "Minimum Wages and Employment: A Case Study of the Fast-Food Industry in New Jersey and Pennsylvania," *American Economic Review* 84 (1994): 772–93; David Card and Alan B. Krueger, *Myth and Measurement: The New Economics of the Minimum Wage* (Princeton, N.J.: Princeton University Press, 2004).

8. Card and Krueger, *Myth and Measurement*.

9. See, for example, Mark D. Brenner, "The Economic Impact of the Boston Living Wage Ordinance," *Industrial Relations* 44 (2005): 59–83; Mark D. Brenner and Stephanie Luce, *Living Wage Laws in Practice: The Boston, New Haven and Hartford Experiences* (Amherst, Mass.: Political Economy Research Institute, 2005), http://livingwagesonoma.org, accessed January 7, 2016; Andrew J. Elmore, *Living Wage Laws and Communities: Smarter Economic Development, Lower than Expected Costs* (New York: Brennan Center for Justice, 2003); David Fairris, "The Impact of Living Wages on Employers: A Control Group Analysis of the Los Angeles Ordinance," *Industrial Relations* 44 (2005): 84–105; Candace Howes, "Living Wages and Retention of Homecare Workers in San Francisco," *Industrial Relations* 44 (2005): 139–63; and Michael Reich, Peter Hall, and Ken Jacobs, "Living Wage Policies at the San Francisco Airport: Impacts on Workers and Businesses," *Industrial Relations* 44 (2005): 106–38.

10. Richard Berman, "Dog Bites Man: Minimum Wage Hikes Still Hurt," *Wall Street Journal*, March 29, 1995.

11. John Schmitt, "Cooked to Order," *American Prospect*, December 19, 2001, http://prospect.org, accessed January 7, 2016.

12. For more on this debate and dueling studies, see Schmitt, "Cooked to Order"; and Jeff Chapman, *Employment and the Minimum Wage—Evidence from Recent State Labor Market Trends* (Washington, D.C.: Economic Policy Institute, 2004).

13. Mark Brenner, Jeannette Wicks-Lim, and Robert Pollin, "Measuring the Impact of Living Wage Laws: A Critical Appraisal of David Neumark's How Living Wage Laws Affect Low Wage Workers and Low-Income Families," Working Paper No. 43, Political Economy Research Institute, Amherst, Mass., 2002.

14. Of course, there is likely a wage at which significant job loss would occur. How high the current minimum wage could go before reaching that "tipping point" is not clear. A number of recent studies suggest that the economy could absorb a $15 per hour minimum wage with little negative impact, but this is still prospective research, and we will not know for several years what the actual impact of the $15 wage will be.

15. "Over 600 Economists Sign Letter in Support of $10.10 Minimum Wage," Economic Policy Institute, January 14, 2014, www.epi.org/minimum-wage-statement, accessed January 7, 2016. Congress last passed an increase in 2007. That increase was phased in over three years, with the last raise, to $7.25 per hour, in 2009. If the minimum wage had kept pace with inflation since it reached its peak in 1968, it would be $9.54 today. If it had kept pace with average worker productivity, it would be close to $18.42 per hour today. Nicholas Buffie and Dean Baker, "An $18.42 Minimum Wage?," *CEPR Blog*, July 23, 2015, www.cepr.net, accessed August 2, 2015.

16. Sam Levin, "Mayor Bloomberg Compares Living Wage Bill to Communism, Says He'll Sue," *Village Voice*, April 13, 2012, www.villagevoice.com, accessed January 7, 2016.

17. Michael Saltsman, "The Record Is Clear: Minimum Wage Hikes Destroy Jobs," *Forbes*, April 17, 2013, www.forbes.com, accessed January 7, 2016.

18. At the time, LAANE was called the Tourism Industry Development Council. The name was changed in the late 1990s.

19. Robert Pollin and Stephanie Luce, *The Living Wage: Building a Fair Economy* (Ithaca, N.Y.: Cornell University Press, 1998).

20. See chapter 4 in Robert Pollin, Mark Brenner, Jeanette Wicks-Lim, and Stephanie Luce, *A Measure of Fairness: The Economics of Living Wages and Minimum Wages in the United States* (Ithaca, N.Y.: Cornell University Press, 2008), 49–69.

21. Pollin et al., *Measure of Fairness*.

22. Wade Rathke, *Citizen Wealth: Winning the Campaign to Save Working Families* (San Francisco: Berrett-Koehler, 2009).

23. Louisiana Supreme Court, news release 64, *New Orleans Campaign for a Living Wage, Jean Matthews and Philomenia Johnson v. City of New Orleans, Marc Morial, Mayor, the Council of the City of New Orleans and the State of Louisiana*, 02-CA-0991, September 4, 2002, 13, www.lasc.org, accessed January 7, 2016.

24. Paul Sonn of National Employment Law Project, interview with the author, May 5, 2011.

25. The Greater New York Chamber of Commerce testified against the proposal at all hearings, and the Employment Policies Institute sent staff from Washington, D.C., to testify against it, as well.

26. On the conclusion of Christine Quinn's 2013 run for mayor, see Michael M. Grynbaum, "Quinn, Humor Intact, Endorses an Old Rival," *New York Times*, September 17, 2013.

27. Adam Brodsky, "Death by Living Wage," *New York Post*, November 12, 2010.

28. CBS News, "City Council to Debate Living Wage Legislation in NYC," May 12, 2011.

29. Author's notes from the Manhattan City Council hearing, November 22, 2011.

30. Our research found that some workers did lose some government assistance as a result of the wage increase, but on average, still experienced a net increase in income. For more on implementation, see Luce, *Fighting for a Living Wage*.

31. Liza Featherstone, Doug Henwood, and Christian Parenti, "'Action Will Be Taken': Left Anti-Intellectualism and Its Discontents," *Radical Society* 29.1 (April 2002): 25–30.

32. Mini-tenure is when an assistant professor is reviewed after three years to determine whether the employment contract will be renewed for another three years. Some universities call this a third-year review.

33. See Douglas Bevington and Chris Dixon, "Movement-Relevant Theory: Rethinking Social Movement Scholarship and Activism," *Social Movement Studies* 4 (2005): 185–208.

34. See "Minimum Wage Mythbusters," U.S. Department of Labor, www.dol.gov/minwage/mythbuster.htm, accessed January 7, 2016.

35. It is difficult to determine how many workers have benefitted directly or indirectly from living-wage ordinances. But since living-wage activists have also worked to raise city, state, and the federal minimum wage, we can assume that at least tens of millions have benefitted in some form. Since the living-wage movement started in 1994, there have been two increases to the federal minimum wage. The Economic Policy Institute estimates that 16.7 million workers would directly benefit from increasing the federal minimum wage from $7.25 to $10.10 per hour. Another 11.1 million would benefit indirectly. See David Cooper, "Raising the Federal Minimum Wage to $10.10 Would Lift Wages for Millions and Provide a Modest Economic Boost," EPI Briefing Paper 371, Economic Policy Institute, Washington, D.C., 2013.

Carry It On!

Creative Research and Social Action

David Montgomery

David Montgomery (d. 2011) spoke during the summer 2011 Working-Class Worlds Conference in Iowa City, Iowa, which inspired this volume. The conference, organized to honor the work of Shelton Stromquist, brought together many of Montgomery's former students, especially from his time at the University of Pittsburgh, as well as numerous colleagues in the field of labor history. His address, "Creative Research and Social Action: Shel and His Generation," was delivered during an evening picnic in City Park.¹

Before the main address, John McKerley and Cecelia Bucki offered introductory remarks that underscored Montgomery's indelible imprint on the field of labor history, while also recalling his work as a machinist and union activist before he

David Montgomery addressing a gathering of labor historians and activists in Iowa City, Iowa, July 8, 2011. Photo credit: Anna Fure-Slocum.

entered academia. Perhaps more than any other labor historian of his generation, he exemplified the possibility of combining high scholarly standards, excellence as a teacher and mentor, and a commitment to working-class empowerment and the democratic transformation of U.S. society.[2]

Montgomery began his talk by reflecting on the conference and responding, only partly in jest, to the rumor that he "kept his tools sharp" to allow him to fall back on his old trade as a machinist should his ongoing activism get him ejected from the university.

*   *   *

I keep my tools sharp, but I need a little more than that today because the world keeps changing on us. When I left the machine shop, basically the same tools—the same lathes, the same milling machines—were there that one would have encountered in 1910. Today everything is tape controlled, everything is numerically operated. I don't know anything about that. So I had to behave myself in the academic world and make sure I didn't get tossed out into a world that was changing too fast for me at that time.

This has been a wonderful day for me. It's been a wonderful day, being around such a great group of people from every age and walk of life and having them all here for the same purpose—to say we love Shel. Right? I had the great good fortune to meet him many years ago after he had already come out of a career of activism and scholarship at Yale and in the Mississippi Freedom Summer. I'm a latecomer to his development here.

Shel came to Pittsburgh at a time when an absolutely marvelous group of people gathered.[3] And it wasn't only in Pittsburgh. In Pittsburgh, in Binghamton, in Rochester, in Berkeley, in New York, there were new clusters of people wanting to study the history of workers. And they were coming to that history for two reasons.

The first is that this was a time of enormous upheaval among young people in schools and colleges around the country. This was a time of an absolutely ruthless, bloody, and pointless war in Vietnam. The question of bringing that war to a halt was crucial. This also was a time when all of America was being shaken by the civil rights struggles. Even Pittsburghers, as soon as I went there, were getting on the buses and going to Birmingham to take part in that activity.

Second, this was a time when people raised questions about the kind of society that we had inherited. Gunnar Myrdal wrote an important book, *Rich Lands and Poor*, in the 1950s.[4] You should all read it; it's only about a hundred pages long. But it's a perfect summation of the dominant ideology of the 1950s. In it he says that everybody knows you have to have economic planning. That everybody knows that embedded liberalism is the way society works. And everybody knows that the basic history of our times has been correctly interpreted by the consensus school; there are no great divisions in the United States. Oh, there was a little something called slavery at one time. But aside from that, we all move along the same path.

And that was the message of modernization theory. Even Pittsburgh was heavily dominated by modernization theory, the new Whig history. Everything moves in the same direction. No matter where you are, it's going to end up the same way. We are modern, not antimodern. Think of how much that phrase is still used in the news, talking about the rest of the world and where we are today.

There was a revolt against this style of history. There was a revolt against a very bureaucratically encrusted academic life that students went through in the rapidly growing universities of that time. And so the country was ablaze with student discontent and student activities. But many of those discontented students were very suspicious of the labor movement. They saw it as an essentially conservative force standing in our way at that time. Until, I would say, that earthshaking event—the post office workers strike in New York in 1970.[5] Suddenly, here was something that swelled up from the grassroots, went right through the law, forgot all the existing rules and regulations that had been created, and brought many students who had been very skeptical of the working class out on the picket lines for the first time in their lives. Quite a number of the people who came to Pitt had been through that experience.

So when I came back from two years working in England, here waiting for me was one of the greatest bunches of students anybody could ever hope to come across. Shel Stromquist was one of them, Peter Rachleff was one of them, Cecelia Bucki was one of them, and Jim Barrett was one of them.[6] They're all over the place at this gathering. And they all quickly came together around certain basic principles. The first was that the time had come to concentrate our historical work on ordinary people, on the workers—white, black, yellow, whatever nationality, wherever they might be at the time. Also of crucial importance, well spelled out this morning at the conference, was a focus on community; in the railroad studies especially, you see the crucial role of community. One book coming out of this approach was Shel's book on railroad workers, in which he located those workers in the communities where they lived, in the jobs where they lived, in the character of those jobs.[7] Another book I have to mention because only half of it ever got published is Peter Rachleff's book on Richmond, which showed how a city in the South became a union stronghold in the aftermath of the Civil War. Two parallel union movements developed, one among the white workers and one among the black workers, but actually associating with each other and collaborating. He studied the people in that community and on their jobs, asking what kind of struggles they engaged in and what kinds of goals they set for themselves.[8]

Much of this study was influenced by new thinking in Europe. England had an enormous influence. And if there was ever a book that everybody knew, it was Thompson's *The Making of the English Working Class*.[9] To learn that it's not assigned in some graduate labor history courses anymore! Oh, this is a shock to me. It's a long book, that's true. But this was the book that, more than any other, contributed to the rethinking of the working class. Thompson had to break with the old, dogmatic, Third International Marxist notion that the history of workers was one of gathering together on the job and being oppressed and then learning there was a vanguard who could show them the way out of the oppression. Everything was a study of leadership. The role of the workers was simply to suffer, until they were mobilized and were led out into struggle. Thompson's book was a study in which the initiatives and the thinking of working men and women themselves played the central role. And class was not just a statistical category. What was Thompson's famous phrase? Class is the friction when some people in society rub up against others, day by day. A sense of who is in what class comes out of that daily encounter on the job and in the home.[10]

This sense then really invigorated many of the students at Pitt and led to several very important beliefs. One was that history is a collective project. This was not a place where we wanted to see who is the great shining star. Oh, we love to have shining stars around! This was a place where all of us gathered together and singled out tasks to underscore and build on each other. So each student could count on the help, the assistance, and the collaboration of the others within that class. You Iowans may think this is a rather familiar notion. This was the dominant sense there as well.

It was a sense that we had to study working men and women themselves. And working men and women, we quickly realized, especially in the United States, were coming from the four corners of the earth, this massive movement of immigrants. The one study the students had to read in every class was an essay by Frank Thistlethwaite on migration from Europe to the Americas, the movement of fifty-five million people. They would complain: "Here we go again; you take another class with Montgomery and you've got to read Thistlethwaite—the first thing you do."[11] But this movement of people made a new kind of working-class life here, within the United States itself. The great struggles that took place from the Civil War and Reconstruction onward expressed the different ways in which different races and different nationalities of workers formed themselves together to make their contribution to the working-class movement.

And finally, these students sensed that in teaching and writing history, it was crucial to be close to today's labor movement. All of that Pittsburgh gang found itself active in the labor movement, both in the Pittsburgh area and the great struggles that were then developing in the country. Since that time, look what has happened. Shel, Jim, Peter, Cecelia went out. And here's an entirely new generation. In fact, it's been so long that that generation is now out teaching a next generation. They are carrying on the word of what to do, but carrying on in new circumstances and often, therefore, facing new problems.

New circumstances beginning, I think, with what has often been called the Great U-Turn of the 1970s. Suddenly, corporate leaders realized that in the United States (also in England where I was for two years before that) the living standards of working people were creeping upward. And this was hurting profits. So, what to do? What to do, then, was institute first of all incomes policies. And every country set up regulations—contract regulations—limiting what raises could be won. Richard Nixon used the power of the state more heavily than any other president we had ever had in his attempts to control what was coming out of labor negotiations. But soon it was clear that that was not enough. I urge you all to read a book that I suspect very few of you have. Do any of you remember William Simon, the secretary of the treasury under Nixon and Ford? The secretary of the treasury wrote a book called *A Time for Truth* that discussed why, when New York City overspent its budget and almost went bankrupt, the U.S. Treasury refused to come up with money.[12] The *Daily News* had that famous headline: "FORD TO CITY: DROP DEAD."[13] And here was the first signal of this new policy: excessive spending is our problem, we have to revitalize the private sector of the economy. This sense of privatization, cutting down the budgets, cutting down taxes on the rich (which have gone down steadily ever since the 1970s in this country) became the crucial theme. This was joined with a theme that Barry Goldwater proclaimed, but in recent years has become almost a gospel, the theme that the only person that really matters in this world is me. That the beauty of life is to be a hog, with both feet in the trough, if at all possible. This notion of not taking care of others when they should be taking care of themselves. Ayn Rand advanced this theme, as well.[14] The more personally devoted you are to yourself, and your wealth, and your initiative, then the better it will be for the whole of society. And therefore we've got to get rid of all of this wasteful expenditure today. Everything is considered a wasteful expenditure except, of course, for massive military budgets, as it becomes our self-assigned project to control the entire globe in these times.

This reversal has had the profound effect that we've been talking about again and again and again today. First of all, with one industry shutting down after another, until the country becomes full of ghost towns. Second, with firms basically getting into the business of buying up other firms, rather than manufacturing things, and sending as much as possible to other parts of the world to do. This results in what a U.N. study came up with not long ago—at the end of the 1990s, 78 percent of the workers in manufacturing in the world were outside of the domain of the old industrial countries. Europe and North America were becoming the minority segment for manufacturing as firms were moving their undertakings all around the globe. Third, that migration has come back on a scale that even Frank Thistlethwaite couldn't imagine. The latest U.N. figure is that there are about 210 million immigrants in the world today, coming mostly not to the United States (although a lot are) and mostly not to Europe. The Arab world is a major destination; both the Arab world and Southeast Asia especially are drawing this new migration of people.[15]

So we've got to take a lot of these old subjects and think of them in brand-new ways, because the categories that worked for thinking about the old industrial core of the world back in the 1960s and 1970s will probably not work today. But what we are trying to do is to discover, interpret, and teach what it is that working people have contributed to this society and are contributing elsewhere around the world today. To revitalize and redefine that whole sense of internationalism—which for somebody like Shel is almost second nature, realizing that the whole world is really his oyster here.[16] And to do so in a way that keeps us committed to our neighbors, to our fellow working people, and to others around the world in working-class struggles. These become the lessons of the past, of that 1960s generation, that we must now translate into new terms. Translating for today, as the message of that old song went, "carry it on!"[17]

Notes

1. The editors are grateful to the late Martel Montgomery, as well as Edward Montgomery and Claude Montgomery, for permission to publish this version of the address. Eric Fure-Slocum transcribed, edited, and annotated the address.

2. On David Montgomery's contribution to labor history and its practice, see James R. Barrett, "Remembering David Montgomery (1926–2011) and His Impact of Working-Class History," *Labour/Le Travail* 70 (fall 2012): 203–23; Shelton Stromquist, "David Montgomery: A Labor Historian's Legacies," *Journal of the Gilded Age and Progressive Era* 13.2 (April 2014): 256–76; and Stromquist's chapter 1 in this book.

3. Montgomery taught history at the University of Pittsburgh from 1963 to 1979, after receiving his doctorate from the University of Minnesota in 1962. Stromquist began his graduate work at the University of Pittsburgh in 1971.

4. Gunnar Myrdal, *Rich Lands and Poor: The Road to World Prosperity* (New York: Harper and Row, 1957).

5. On this wildcat action that began in New York and spread nationally, see Aaron Brenner, "Striking against the State: The Postal Wildcat of 1970," *Labor's Heritage* 7.4 (June 1996): 4–27.

6. These members of the Pittsburgh cohort, among others, were present at the Working-Class Worlds conference.

7. Shelton Stromquist, *A Generation of Boomers: The Pattern of Railroad Labor Conflict in Nineteenth-Century America* (Urbana: University of Illinois Press, 1987).

8. Peter Rachleff, *Black Labor in Richmond, 1865–1890* (Philadelphia: Temple University Press, 1984); and Peter Jay Rachleff, "Black, White, and Gray: Working-Class Activism in Richmond, Virginia, 1865–1900" (Ph.D. diss., University of Pittsburgh, 1981).

9. E. P. Thompson, *The Making of the English Working Class* (New York: Pantheon Books, 1963).

10. On class as the *"friction of interests,"* see Thompson's 1965 "The Peculiarities of the English," reprinted in E. P Thompson, *The Poverty of Theory and Other Essays* (New York: Monthly Review Press, 1978), 295.

11. Frank Thistlethwaite, "Migration from Europe Overseas in the Nineteenth and Twentieth Centuries," XIe Congrès International des Sciences Historiques, *Rapports* (Uppsala, 1960), 5:32–60. The essay also is reprinted in Rudolph J. Vecoli and Suzanne M. Sinke, eds., *A Century of European Migrations, 1830–1930* (Urbana: University of Illinois Press, 1991), 17–49.

12. William E. Simon, *A Time for Truth* (New York: Reader's Digest Press, 1978). Simon Served as U.S. secretary of the treasury (1974–77) under Presidents Richard Nixon and Gerald Ford.

13. *New York Daily News*, 30 October 1975. On Simon, Ford, and New York's fiscal crisis, see Joshua B. Freeman, *Working-Class New York: Life and Labor since World War II* (New York: New Press, 2000), 256–87.

14. See Kim Phillips-Fein, *Invisible Hands: The Making of the Conservative Movement from the New Deal to Reagan* (New York: W. W. Norton, 2009); and Jennifer Burns, *Goddess of the Market: Ayn Rand and the American Right* (New York: Oxford University Press, 2009).

15. See, for instance, Department of Social and Economic Affairs, *World Economic and Social Survey 2010: Retooling Global Development* (New York: United Nations, 2010); Department of Social and Economic Affairs, Population Division, *International Migration Report 2009: A Global Assessment* (New York: United Nations, 2011); and the issue on "Migrant Workers and the Middle East," *International Labor and Working-Class History* 79 (spring 2011).

16. See Shelton Stromquist, "Reclaiming Political Space: Workers, Municipal Socialism and the Reconstruction of Local Democracy in Transnational Perspective," in *Workers across the Americas: The Transnational Turn in Labor History*, edited by Leon Fink (New York: Oxford University Press, 2011), 303–28.

17. "Carry It On" (1964), written by folksinger Gil Turner, became a civil rights standard.

CONTRIBUTORS

KRISTEN ANDERSON is associate professor of history at Webster University. Her publications include "German Americans, African Americans, and the Republican Party in St. Louis, 1865–1872," *Journal of American Ethnic History* 28 (2008).

DANIEL E. ATKINSON is an independent scholar and an ethnomusicologist focusing on Afro-American vernacular expression. He is the author of "Angola Is America" (PhD diss., University of Washington, 2011).

JAMES R. BARRETT is professor emeritus of history and African American studies at the University of Illinois at Urbana-Champaign. His publications include *The Irish Way: Becoming American in the Multi-Ethnic City* (2012).

SUSAN ROTH BREITZER teaches at Campbell University. Her publications include "Race, Immigration, and Contested Americanness: Black Nativism and the American Labor Movement, 1880–1930," *Race/Ethnicity: Multidisciplinary Global Context* 4.2 (2011).

SUSAN CHANDLER is associate professor emeritus of social work at the University of Nevada, Reno. Her book *Casino Women: Courage in Unexpected Places* (2011, coauthored with Jill B. Jones) won the 2012 Oral History Association National Book Award.

SAM DAVIES is professor of history in the School of Humanities and Social Sciences, Liverpool John Moores University. His publications include *Dock Workers: International Explorations in Comparative Labour History, 1790–1970* (2000).

DENNIS DESLIPPE is associate professor of American studies and of women's and gender studies at Franklin & Marshall College. His publications include *Protesting Affirmative Action: The Struggle over Equality after the Civil Rights Revolution* (2012).

ERIC FURE-SLOCUM is associate professor of history and American studies at St. Olaf College. His publications include *Contesting the Postwar City: Working-Class and Growth Politics in 1940s Milwaukee* (2013).

COLIN GORDON is professor of history at the University of Iowa. His publications include *The Politics of Health Care in Modern America* (2008) and *Mapping*

Decline: St. Louis and the Fate of the American City (2008). He is a senior research consultant with the Iowa Policy Project.

MICHAEL INNIS-JIMÉNEZ is associate professor of American studies at the University of Alabama. His publications include *Steel Barrio: The Great Mexican Migration to South Chicago, 1915–1940* (2013). He is a project scholar for the Levine Museum of the New South's Latino New South project.

STEPHANIE LUCE is professor of labor studies at the Joseph S. Murphy Institute for Worker Education, and professor of sociology at the Grad Center, City University of New York. Her publications include *Labor Movements: Global Perspectives* (2014) and *Fighting for a Living Wage* (2004).

JOSEPH A. MCCARTIN is professor of history and director of the Kalmanovitz Initiative for Labor and the Working Poor at Georgetown University. His publications include *Collision Course: Ronald Reagan, the Air Traffic Controllers, and the Strike that Changed America* (2011).

JOHN W. MCKERLEY is the oral historian for the Iowa Labor History Oral Project at the University of Iowa Labor Center. His publications include, as coeditor, *Foot Soldiers for Democracy: The Men, Women, and Children of the Birmingham Civil Rights Movement* (University of Illinois Press, 2009).

MATTHEW M. METTLER is an independent scholar. His publications include "A Workers' Cold War in the Quad Cities: The Fate of Labor Militancy in the Farm Equipment Industry, 1949–1955," *Annals of Iowa* 68 (2009).

STEPHEN MEYER is emeritus professor of history at the University of Wisconsin–Milwaukee. His publications include *Stalin over Wisconsin: The Making and Unmaking of Militant Unionism, 1900–1950* (1992) and *Manhood on the Line: Working Class Masculinities in the American Heartland* (University of Illinois Press, 2016).

DAVID MONTGOMERY (d. 2011) was the Farnam Professor of History at Yale University. His many publications include *The Fall of the House of Labor: The Workplace, the State, and American Labor Activism, 1865–1925* (1989).

KIM E. NIELSEN is professor of disability studies and history at the University of Toledo. Her publications include *A Disability History of the United States* (2012).

PETER RACHLEFF is professor emeritus of history at Macalester College and founding co-executive director of East Side Freedom Library (http://EastSide FreedomLibrary.org). His publications include "'Rebellion to Tyrants, Democracy for Workers': The Madison Uprising, Collective Bargaining, and the Future of the Labor Movement," *South Atlantic Quarterly* 111 (winter 2012).

RALPH SCHARNAU has retired from a fifty-year history teaching career in public and private higher education institutions. His publications include "From Pioneer

Days to the Dawn of Industrial Relations: The Emergence of the Working Class in Dubuque, 1833–1855," *Annals of Iowa* 70 (summer 2011).

JENNIFER SHERER is director of the University of Iowa Labor Center. Her publications include (as coauthor) "Labor Education and Leadership Development for Union Women: Assessing the Past, Building for the Future," *Labor Studies Journal* 41 (March 2016), and "Wage Theft in Iowa" (2012).

SHELTON STROMQUIST is professor emeritus of history at the University of Iowa. His book publications include *Reinventing "the People": The Progressive Movement, the Class Problem, and the Origin of Modern Liberalism* (University of Illinois Press, 2006). He is completing "The City and Social Democracy: The Municipal Origins of Labor Politics in Comparative Perspective, 1890–1925."

EMILY E. LB. TWAROG is assistant professor for the School of Labor and Employment Relations at University of Illinois at Urbana-Champaign. Her publications include (as coauthor) "Labor Education and Leadership Development for Union Women: Assessing the Past, Building for the Future," *Labor Studies Journal* 41 (March 2016).

JOHN WILLIAMS-SEARLE is an independent scholar. He is currently working on a history of the running boom. His publications include "Cold Charity: Manhood, Brotherhood, and the Transformation of Disability, 1870–1900," in *The New Disability History: American Perspectives*, edited by Paul Longmore and Lauri Umansky (2001).

INDEX

ableism, 237–44
academic freedom, 11
academic isolationism, 1
Achebe, Chinua, 62–63
Adams, Henry C., 13
Addams, Jane, 15
Adelson, Sheldon, 235
AFL-CIO: Alabama immigrant worker advocacy, 90; Bargaining for the Future project, 210–11; Dubuque Federation of Labor, 45–46, 48; Graduate Employees Organization (GEO) and, 117; Iowa Federation of Labor, 110, 162–63, 219–20; Iowa Labor History Oral Project and, 162–64, 166–68; Kalmanovitz Initiative and, 203–6; as labor history feeder, 115; labor movement unity and, 200–201; labor statistics, 50–51; summer training program, 198; women in leadership roles, 181, 185
air traffic controller union, 66, 202–3, 206
Alabama Appleseed, 90
Alabama HB 56 immigrant labor law, 39–40, 85–92
Alianza Nacional de Campesinas, 208
Alinsky, Saul, 194
Allen-Bradley, 149
Allis-Chalmers, 68
Almeida, Tico, 198
Alternet, 217
alt-labor organizations, 180, 188n16
Amalgamated Bank, 204
ameliorative labor reform, 15–16
American Association of University Professors (AAUP), 42–44, 46, 48, 67, 117–18, 124, 145, 152
American Economic Association (AEA), 12
American Federation of Labor (AFL), 13, 14
American Federation of State, County, and Municipal Employees (AFSCME), 45, 70, 73, 129–30, 134, 177, 183, 212
American Federation of Teachers (AFT), 44, 48, 53n30, 117–18, 148, 152, 212

American Federation of the Physically Handicapped (AFPH), 240–41
American Historical Association, 220
American History Teachers' Collaborative, 116
American Legislative Exchange Council (ALEC), 82–83
Americans for Prosperity, 70–71, 82–83
Andiappan, P., 184
Angelou, Maya, 62
Angola Prison (Louisiana State Penitentiary at Angola), 38, 54–62, 64n17
anti-intellectualism, 1–2, 259
anti-sweatshop movement, 198–99
Aquinas College, 151
Aramark, 210
Aranda-Yanoc, Edgar, 209
As Goes Janesville, 79–80
Associated Society of Locomotive Engineers and Firemen (ASLEF), 100
Association of Californians for Community Empowerment (ACCE), 212
Association of Community Organizations for Reform Now (ACORN), 197, 248, 253
Atkinson, Daniel, 38
Atlantic, 217
auto industry, 233–34

Bacon, David, 137
Baker, Dean, 221
Baldwin, James, 232
Baldwin, Tammy, 69
Bankson, Virgil, 159–60, 162, 169
bank teller unionization, 129–30
Barber, William, II, 208
Bargaining for the Common Good project, 212
Bargaining for the Future project, 210–11
Baron, Ava, 27
Barrett, James R., 109, 111, 267–68
Barrett, Tom, 70–71, 80, 82
Bayard, Marc, 208

THE WORKING CLASS IN AMERICAN HISTORY

On the Line: Essays in the History of Auto Work
    Edited by Nelson Lichtenstein and Stephen Meyer III
Labor's Flaming Youth: Telephone Operators and
    Worker Militancy, 1878–1923   *Stephen H. Norwood*
Another Civil War: Labor, Capital, and the State in the
    Anthracite Regions of Pennsylvania, 1840–68   *Grace Palladino*
Coal, Class, and Color: Blacks in Southern
    West Virginia, 1915–32   *Joe William Trotter Jr.*
For Democracy, Workers, and God: Labor Song-Poems
    and Labor Protest, 1865–95   *Clark D. Halker*
Dishing It Out: Waitresses and Their Unions
    in the Twentieth Century   *Dorothy Sue Cobble*
The Spirit of 1848: German Immigrants, Labor Conflict,
    and the Coming of the Civil War   *Bruce Levine*
Working Women of Collar City: Gender, Class,
    and Community in Troy, New York, 1864–86   *Carole Turbin*
Southern Labor and Black Civil Rights: Organizing
    Memphis Workers   *Michael K. Honey*
Radicals of the Worst Sort: Laboring Women in
    Lawrence, Massachusetts, 1860–1912   *Ardis Cameron*
Producers, Proletarians, and Politicians: Workers and Party Politics
    in Evansville and New Albany, Indiana, 1850–87   *Lawrence M. Lipin*
The New Left and Labor in the 1960s   *Peter B. Levy*
The Making of Western Labor Radicalism: Denver's Organized
    Workers, 1878–1905   *David Brundage*
In Search of the Working Class: Essays in American Labor History
    and Political Culture   *Leon Fink*
Lawyers against Labor: From Individual Rights
    to Corporate Liberalism   *Daniel R. Ernst*
"We Are All Leaders": The Alternative Unionism
    of the Early 1930s   *Edited by Staughton Lynd*
The Female Economy: The Millinery and Dressmaking
    Trades, 1860–1930   *Wendy Gamber*
"Negro and White, Unite and Fight!": A Social History
    of Industrial Unionism in Meatpacking, 1930–90   *Roger Horowitz*
Power at Odds: The 1922 National Railroad
    Shopmen's Strike   *Colin J. Davis*
The Common Ground of Womanhood: Class, Gender,
    and Working Girls' Clubs, 1884–1928   *Priscilla Murolo*
Marching Together: Women of the Brotherhood
    of Sleeping Car Porters   *Melinda Chateauvert*
Down on the Killing Floor: Black and White Workers
    in Chicago's Packinghouses, 1904–54   *Rick Halpern*
Labor and Urban Politics: Class Conflict and the Origins
    of Modern Liberalism in Chicago, 1864–97   *Richard Schneirov*
All That Glitters: Class, Conflict, and Community
    in Cripple Creek   *Elizabeth Jameson*
Waterfront Workers: New Perspectives on Race
    and Class   *Edited by Calvin Winslow*

Labor Histories: Class, Politics, and the Working-Class Experience
   Edited by Eric Arnesen, Julie Greene, and Bruce Laurie
The Pullman Strike and the Crisis of the 1890s: Essays on Labor and Politics
   Edited by Richard Schneirov, Shelton Stromquist, and Nick Salvatore
AlabamaNorth: African-American Migrants, Community,
   and Working-Class Activism in Cleveland, 1914–45   *Kimberley L. Phillips*
Imagining Internationalism in American and
   British Labor, 1939–49   *Victor Silverman*
William Z. Foster and the Tragedy of American Radicalism
   James R. Barrett
Colliers across the Sea: A Comparative Study of Class Formation
   in Scotland and the American Midwest, 1830–1924   *John H. M. Laslett*
"Rights, Not Roses": Unions and the Rise of Working-Class
   Feminism, 1945–80   *Dennis A. Deslippe*
Testing the New Deal: The General Textile Strike of 1934
   in the American South   *Janet Irons*
Hard Work: The Making of Labor History   *Melvyn Dubofsky*
Southern Workers and the Search for Community:
   Spartanburg County, South Carolina   *G. C. Waldrep III*
We Shall Be All: A History of the Industrial Workers of the World
   (abridged edition)   *Melvyn Dubofsky, ed. Joseph A. McCartin*
Race, Class, and Power in the Alabama Coalfields, 1908–21   *Brian Kelly*
Duquesne and the Rise of Steel Unionism   *James D. Rose*
Anaconda: Labor, Community, and Culture
   in Montana's Smelter City   *Laurie Mercier*
Bridgeport's Socialist New Deal, 1915–36   *Cecelia Bucki*
Indispensable Outcasts: Hobo Workers and Community
   in the American Midwest, 1880–1930   *Frank Tobias Higbie*
After the Strike: A Century of Labor Struggle at Pullman
   Susan Eleanor Hirsch
Corruption and Reform in the Teamsters Union   *David Witwer*
Waterfront Revolts: New York and London Dockworkers,
   1946–61   *Colin J. Davis*
Black Workers' Struggle for Equality in Birmingham
   Horace Huntley and David Montgomery
The Tribe of Black Ulysses: African American Men
   in the Industrial South   *William P. Jones*
City of Clerks: Office and Sales Workers in Philadelphia,
   1870–1920   *Jerome P. Bjelopera*
Reinventing "The People": The Progressive Movement, the Class Problem,
   and the Origins of Modern Liberalism   *Shelton Stromquist*
Radical Unionism in the Midwest, 1900–1950   *Rosemary Feurer*
Gendering Labor History   *Alice Kessler-Harris*
James P. Cannon and the Origins of the American Revolutionary
   Left, 1890–1928   *Bryan D. Palmer*
Glass Towns: Industry, Labor, and Political Economy
   in Appalachia, 1890–1930s   *Ken Fones-Wolf*
Workers and the Wild: Conservation, Consumerism,
   and Labor in Oregon, 1910–30   *Lawrence M. Lipin*

The University of Illinois Press
is a founding member of the
Association of American University Presses.

———————————————————————————

University of Illinois Press
1325 South Oak Street
Champaign, IL 61820-6903
www.press.uillinois.edu